French Vocabulary

by

CHRISTOPHER KENDRIS, Ph.D.

Formerly Assistant Professor
Department of French and Spanish
State University of New York at Albany

Diplômé, Faculté des Lettres, Université de Paris et Institut de Phonétique, Paris (en Sorbonne)

Certificat, Ecole Pédagogique de l'Alliance Française de Paris

BARRON'S

New York • London • Toronto • Sydney

To my family with love

All inquiries should be addressed to:
Barron's Educational Series, Inc.
250 Wireless Boulevard
Hauppauge, New York 11788

Library of Congress Catalog Card No. 90-42767

International Standard Book No. 0-8120-4496-7

Library of Congress Cataloging-in-Publication Data

Kendris, Christopher.
French vocabulary / by Christopher Kendris.
p. cm.
Includes index.
ISBN 0-8120-4496-7
1. French language—Vocabulary. 2. French language—Conversation and phrase books—English. I. Title.
PC2445.K38 1990
448.3'421—dc20 90-42767
CIP

PRINTED IN THE UNITED STATES OF AMERICA
0123 5500 987654321

CONTENTS

HOW TO USE THIS BOOK

This book is one of a new series of handy vocabulary reference guides. It is designed for students, business people, and others who want to "brush up" their knowledge of French vocabulary in any given subject area. Whether you are just beginning your study of French or have had some French and want to review, this book is for you. Previous knowledge of French vocabulary has not been taken for granted in these pages.

OVERALL DESIGN

The French vocabulary in this pocket reference book is arranged by topics. Subtopics contain several themes related in thought to the main topic. Under a subtopic you can find many commonly used basic words, phrases, and expressions useful in everyday situations. These are valuable not only for students and teachers but also for the general public; for example, travelers in France and other French-speaking countries and regions, persons in the world of business, banking, science and technology, politics, the fine arts, telecommunications, mathematics, the natural sciences, and many others.

The first thing to do is browse through the table of contents. You will find topics of special interest to you because of the wide range of topics. For example, the second chapter is of interest to everyone because it is about people: members of a family, relatives, friends, descriptions of people, personalities, social traits, moods, general human characteristics, basic personal information, parts of the human body, bodily processes and movements, sensory perception, and looking after one's health. If any given topic is of particular interest to you, turn to the page where it begins. I am certain that the section you select will provide you with many interesting and useful basic words, phrases, and expressions.

FEATURES

English words are listed on the left side of the page. French equivalents appear in the middle of the page. Next to the French, you will find abbreviations that indicate gender or part of speech. On the right side of the page you are given sound transcriptions to help you pronounce the French words effectively for communication. The pronounciation guide in the beginning pages of the book introduces you to a simple system of sound transcriptions that I devised.

I sincerely hope that this book will be of some help to you in expanding your knowledge and power of French vocabulary.

Christopher Kendris
B.S., M.S., M.A., Ph.D.

FRENCH PRONUNCIATION GUIDE

The purpose of this guide is to help you pronounce French words as correctly as possible so you can communicate effectively. It is not intended to perfect your pronunciation of French; that is accomplished by imitating correct spoken French .

In French there are several spellings for the same sound; for example, the following spellings are all pronounced *ay*, as in the English word *say*.

et (j')ai (parl)é (av)ez (all)er (l)es

The system of transcription of French sounds used here is English letters in italics. As soon as you catch on to this system, you will find it *ee-zee*. At first, you will have to refer to the list repeatedly until it is fixed in your mind. The sounds are arranged alphabetically in a list in transcription form. This is the easiest way for you to find quickly the transcription as you read the English letters next to the French words.

Consonant sounds are approximately the same in French and English. Any variations in the pronunciation of some French consonants are found in the sound transcriptions. When speaking French, stress is evenly distributed on the vowels but you must raise your voice slightly on the last transcription sound when more than one is in a group; for example, in pronouncing **s'il vous plaît** (please), raise your voice slightly on *pleh* in *seel-voo-pleh*.

There are only four nasal vowel sounds in French. They are expressed in the following catchy phrase, which means a good white wine.

un	**bon**	**vin**	**blanc**
UH	*bOH*	*vEH*	*blAH*

A nasal vowel is indicated by two italicized capital letters. How do you nasalize a vowel in French? Instead of letting your breath (air) out of your mouth, you must push it up your nose so that it does not come out of your mouth.

Remember that the two italicized capital letters are nasal vowels. They do not indicate any stress or raising of your voice in pronunciation.

The hyphens in the transcription sounds do not indicate a division of words into syllables. They indicate a separation of the different sounds so you can find them easily in the alphabetical list of italicized transcription letters. Whenever the final consonant of a French word is pronounced and linked, as in a liaison, with the first vowel or silent **h** of the word that follows, this is indicated in the sound transcriptions; for example, normally, **vous** is pronounced *voo*, but in **vous avez** it is pronounced *voo-zavay*.

Transcription letters	Pronounced approximately as in the English word	Pronounced approximately as in the French word	Sound transcription
a	at	la	*la*
ah	ah!	pas	*pah*
ay	say	ai	*ay*
e	the	le	*le*
ee	see	ici	*ee-see*
eh	egg	mère	*mehr*
ew	few	lu	*lew*
ew-ee	you eat	huit	*ew-eet*
ny	canyon	montagne	*mOH-ta-ny*
o	also	hôtel	*o-tehl*
oh	oh!	chose	*sh-oh-z*
oo	too	ou	*oo*
or	or	porte	*port*
sh	ship	chose	*sh-oh-z*
ss	kiss	cesse	*seh-ss*
u	bun	bonne	*bun*
uh	pudding	peux	*puh*
ur	purr	heure	*ur*
y	yes	joyeux	*zh-wah-yuh*
yay	yea	payer	*pay-yay*
z	zero	zéro	*zay-roh*
zh	measure	je	*zhe*
	NASAL VOWELS		
UH	sung	un	*UH*
OH	song	bon	*bOH*
EH	sang	vin	*vEH*
AH	yonder	blanc	*blAH*

ABBREVIATIONS

adj adjective
adv adverb
conj conjunction
f feminine
fam familiar form
indef indefinite
m masculine
n noun
pl plural
pol polite form
prep preposition
pron pronoun
s singular
v verb

BASIC INFORMATION

1. ARITHMETIC

a. CARDINAL NUMBERS

zero	zéro	*zay-ro*
one	un	*UH*
	une	*ewn*
two	deux	*duh*
three	trois	*trwah*
four	quatre	*katr*
five	cinq	*sEHk*
six	six	*seess*
seven	sept	*seht*
eight	huit	*ew-eet*
nine	neuf	*nuf*
ten	dix	*dees*
eleven	onze	*OH-z*
twelve	douze	*dooz*
thirteen	treize	*trehz*
fourteen	quatorze	*ka-torz*
fifteen	quinze	*kEHz*
sixteen	seize	*sehz*
seventeen	dix-sept	*dee-seht*
eighteen	dix-huit	*dee-zew-eet*
nineteen	dix-neuf	*deez-nuf*
twenty	vingt	*vEH*
twenty-one	vingt et un	*vEH tay UH*
twenty-two	vingt-deux	*vEH-duh*
twenty-three	vingt-trois	*vEH-trwah*
twenty-four	vingt-quatre	*vEH-katr*
twenty-five	vingt-cinq	*vEH-sEHk*
twenty-six	vingt-six	*vEH-seess*
twenty-seven	vingt-sept	*vEH-seht*
twenty-eight	vingt-huit	*vEH-tew-eet*
twenty-nine	vingt-neuf	*vEH-nuf*
thirty	trente	*trAHt*
thirty-one	trente et un	*trAHt-ay-UH*
thirty two	trente-deux	*trAHt-duh*
thirty-three	trente-trois	*trAHt-trwah*
. . .		
forty	quarante	*ka-rAHt*
forty-one	quarante et un	*ka-rAHt-ay-UH*
forty-two	quarante-deux	*ka-rAHt-dUH*
forty-three	quarante-trois	*ka-rAHt-trwah*

. . .		
fifty	cinquante	*sEH-kAHt*
fifty-one	cinquante et un	*sEH-kAHt-ay-UH*
fifty-two	cinquante-deux	*sEH-kAHt-duh*
fifty-three	cinquante-trois	*sEH-kAHt-trwah*
. . .		
sixty	soixante	*swa-sAHt*
. . .		
seventy	soixante-dix	*swa-sAHt-dees*
. . .		
eighty	quatre-vingts	*katr-vEH*
eighty-one	quatre-vingt-un	*katr-vEH-UH*
. . .		
ninety	quatre-vingt-dix	*katr-vEH-dees*
ninety-one	quatre-vingt-onze	*katr-vEH-OH-z*
. . .		
one hundred	cent	*sAH*
one hundred and one	cent un	*sAH-UH*
one hundred and two	cent deux	*sAH-duh*
. . .		
two hundred	deux cents	*duh-sAH*
two hundred and one	deux cent un	*duh-sAH-UH*
. . .		
three hundred	trois cents	*trwah-sAH*
. . .		
one thousand	mille	*meel*
one thousand and one	mille un	*meel-UH*
. . .		
two thousand	deux mille	*duh meel*
two thousand and one	deux mille un	*duh meel UH*
. . .		
three thousand	trois mille	*trwah meel*
. . .		
four thousand	quatre mille	*katr meel*
. . .		
one hundred thousand	cent mille	*sAH meel*
. . .		
two hundred thousand	deux cent mille	*duh sAH meel*
. . .		
one million	un million	*UH meel-yOH*
one million and one	un million un	*UH meel-yOH UH*
one million and two	un million deux	*UH meel-yOH duh*
. . .		
two million	deux millions	*duh meel-yOH*

. . .		
three million	trois millions	*trwah meel-yOH*
. . .		
one hundred million	cent millions	*sAH meel-yOH*
. . .		
one billion	un milliard	*UH meel-yar*
. . .		
two billion	deux milliards	*duh meel-yar*

b. ORDINAL NUMBERS

first	premier (*adj/m*)	*prem-yay*
	première (*adj/f*)	*prem-yehr*
second	second	*se-gOH*
	seconde	*se-gOH-d (if the 2nd of 2)*
	deuxième	*duhz-yehm (if the 2nd of more than 2)*
third	troisième	*trwahz-yehm*
fourth	quatrième	*katr-yehm*
fifth	cinquième	*sEHk-yehm*
sixth	sixième	*seez-yehm*
seventh	septième	*seht-yehm*
eighth	huitième	*ew-eet-yehm*
ninth	neuvième	*nuhv-yehm*
tenth	dixième	*deez-yehm*
eleventh	onzième	*OHz-yehm*
twelfth	douzième	*dooz-yehm*
thirteenth	treizième	*trehz-yehm*
. . .		
twenty-third	vingt-troisième	*vEH-trwahz-yehm*
thirty-third	trente-troisième	*trAHt-trwahz-yehm*
forty-third	quarante-troisième	*ka-rAHt-trwahz-yehm*
. . .		
hundredth	centième	*sAHt-yehm*
. . .		
thousandth	millième	*meel-yehm*
. . .		
millionth	millionième	*meel-yun-yehm*
. . .		
billionth	milliardième	*meel-yard-yehm*

c. FRACTIONS

a (one) half	un demi	*UH dmee*
a (one) third	un tiers	*UH tyehr*
a (one) fourth	un quart	*UH kar*
a (one) fifth	un cinquième	*UH sEHk-yehm*

APPROXIMATE AMOUNTS

about ten	une dizaine	*ewn dee-zehn*
about fifteen	une quinzaine	*ewn kEH-zehn*
about twenty	une vingtaine	*ewn vEH-tehn*
about thirty	une trentaine	*ewn trAH-tehn*
about forty	une quarantaine	*ewn karAH-tehn*
about fifty	une cinquantaine	*ewn sEH-kAH-tehn*
about sixty	une soixantaine	*ewn swa-sAH-tehn*
about a hundred	une centaine	*ewn sAH-tehn*
about a thousand	un millier	*UH meel-yay*

d. TYPES OF NUMBERS

number	nombre (*m*)	*nOH-bre*
	numéro (*m*)	*new-may-ro*
• **number**	numéroter (*v*)	*new-may-rut-ay*
• **numeral**	numéral (*m*)	*new-may-ral*
• **numerical**	numérique (*adj*)	*new-may-reek*
Arabic	arabe (*adj*)	*arab*
cardinal	cardinal (*adj*)	*kar-dee-nal*
complex	complexe (*adj*)	*kOH-plehks*
digit	chiffre (*m*)	*sheefre*
even	pair (*adj*)	*pehr*
fraction	fraction (*f*)	*fraks-yOH*
• **fractional**	fractionnel (*adj*)	*fraks-yun-ehl*
imaginary	imaginaire (*adj*)	*ee-ma-zh-ee-nehr*
integer	nombre entier (*m*)	*nOH-bre AHt-yay*
irrational	irrationnel (*adj*)	*ee-ras-yun-ehl*
natural	naturel (*adj*)	*na-tewr-ehl*
negative	négatif (*adj*)	*nay-ga-teef*
odd	impair (*adj*)	*EH-pehr*
ordinal	ordinal (*adj*)	*ur-dee-nal*
positive	positif (*adj*)	*pu-see-teef*
prime	nombre premier (*m*)	*nOH-bre prem-yay*
rational	rationnel (*adj*)	*ras-yun-ehl*

real	réel (*adj*)	*ray-ehl*
reciprocal	réciproque (*adj*)	*ray-see-pruk*
Roman	romain (*adj*)	*rum-EH*

e. BASIC OPERATIONS

arithmetical operations	opérations fondamentales (*f,pl*)	*up-ay-ras-yOH fOH-da-mAH-tal*
add (on)	ajouter (*v*)	*azh-oo-tay*
• **addition**	addition (*f*)	*a-dee-sy-OH*
• **plus**	plus	*plewss*
	et	*ay*
• **two plus two equals four**	deux et deux font quatre	*duh ay duh fOH katr*
subtract	soustraire (*v*)	*soos-trehr*
• **subtraction**	soustraction (*f*)	*soos-trak-sy-OH*
• **minus**	moins	*mwEH*
• **three minus two equals one**	trois moins deux font un	*trwah mwEH duh fOH UH*
multiply	multiplier (*v*)	*mewl-tee-ply-ay*
• **multiplication**	multiplication (*f*)	*mewl-tee-plee-kas-yOH*
• **multiplication table**	table de multiplication (*f*)	*tabl de mewl-tee-plee-kas-yOH*
• **multiplied by**	multiplié par	*mewl-tee-ply-ay-par*
• **three times two equals six**	trois fois deux font six	*trwah fwa duh fOH seess*
divide	diviser (*v*)	*dee-vee-zay*
• **divided by**	divisé par	*dee-vee-zay par*
• **division**	division (*f*)	*dee-vee-zyOH*
• **six divided by three equals two**	six divisés par trois font deux	*seess dee-vee-zay par trwah fOH duh*
raise to a power	élever (*v*) à une puissance	*ayl-vay a ewn pew-ee-sAH-ss*
• **to the power of**	à la puissance de	*a la pew ee-sAH-ss de*
• **squared**	au carré	*oh ka ray*
• **cubed**	au cube	*oh kewb*
• **to the fourth power**	à la quatrième puissance	*a la katr-yehm pew-ee-sAH-ss*
• **to the nth power**	à la puissance n	*a la pew-ee-sAH-ss ehn*
• **two squared equals four**	deux au carré égalent quatre	*duh oh ka-ray ay-gal katr*
extract a root	extraire (*v*) la racine	*eks-trehr la ra-seen*
• **square root**	racine au carré	*ra-seen oh ka-ray*
• **cube root**	racine cubique	*ra-seen kew-beek*
• **nth root**	à la racine n	*a la ra-seen ehn*
• **(the) square root of nine is three**	la racine au carré de neuf est trois	*la ra-seen oh ka-ray de nuf eh trwah*

ratio	proportion (*f*)	*pru-por-syOH*
• **twelve is to four as nine is to three**	douze est à quatre comme neuf est à trois	*dooz eh ta katr kum nuf eh ta trwah*

FOCUS: Arithmetical Operations

Addition—Addition

$2 + 3 = 5$	two plus three equals five	deux et trois font cinq

Subtraction—Soustraction

$9 - 3 = 6$	nine minus three equals six	neuf moins trois font six

Multiplication—Multiplication

$4 \times 2 = 8$	four times two equals eight	quatre fois deux font huit
$4 \cdot 2 = 8$	four multiplied by two equals eight	quatre multipliés par deux égalent huit

Division—Division

$10 \div 2 = 5$	ten divided by two equals five	dix divisés par deux font cinq

Raising to a power—Elévation à une puissance

$3^2 = 9$	three squared (or to the second power) equals nine	trois au carré égalent neuf
$2^3 = 8$	two cubed (or to the third power) equals eight	deux au cube égalent huit
$2^4 = 16$	two to the fourth power equals sixteen	deux à la quatrième égalent seize
x^n	x to the ninth power	x à la puissance n

Extraction of root—Extraction d'une racine

$\sqrt[2]{4} = 2$	the square root of four is two	la racine carrée de quatre est deux
$\sqrt[2]{27} = 3$	the cube root of twenty-seven is three	la racine cubique de vingt-sept est trois
$\sqrt[n]{x}$	the nth root of x	la racine n de x

Ratio—Proportion

$12:4 = 9:3$	twelve is to four as nine is to three	douze est à quatre comme neuf est à trois

f. ADDITIONAL MATHEMATICAL CONCEPTS

algebra	algèbre (*f*)	*al-zh-ehbr*
• **algebraic**	algébrique (*adj*)	*al-zh-ay-breek*
arithmetic	arithmétique (*f*)	*a-reet-may-teek*
• **arithmetical**	arithmétique (*adj*)	*a-reet-may-teek*
average	moyenne (*f*)	*mwa-yehn*
calculate	calculer (*v*)	*kal-kew-lay*
• **calculation**	calcul (*m*)	*kal-kewl*
constant	constante (*f*)	*kOH-stAHt*
count	compter (*v*)	*kOH-tay*
• **countable**	comptable (*adj*)	*kOH-tabl*
decimal	décimal (*adj*)	*day-see-mal*
difference	différence (*f*)	*dee fay-rAH-ss*
equality	égalité (*f*)	*ay-ga-lee-tay*
• **equals**	est égal à	*eh tay-gal a*
• **does not equal**	n'est pas égal à	*neh pa-zay-gal a*
• **is equivalent to**	est équivalent à	*eh tay-kee-val-AH a*
• **is greater than**	est supérieur à	*eh sew-pay-ry-ur a*
• **is less than**	est inférieur à	*eh tEH-fay-ry-ur a*
• **is similar to**	est pareil à	*eh pa-ray a*
equation	équation (*f*)	*ay-kwas-yOH*
factor	facteur (*m*)	*fak-tur*
• **factor**	mettre en facteurs (*v*)	*meht-re AH fak-tur*
• **factorization**	factorielle (*f*)	*fak-tu-ry-ehl*
function	fonction (*f*)	*fOH-ks-yOH*
logarithm	logarithme (*m*)	*lug-a-reet-me*
logarithmic	logarithmique (*adj*)	*lug-a-reet-meek*
multiple	multiple (*m*)	*mewl-teepl*
percent	pour cent	*poor sAH*
• **percentage**	pourcentage (*m*)	*poor-sAH-tazh*
problem	problème (*m*)	*prub-lehm*
• **problem to solve**	problème à résoudre	*prub-lehm a ray-zoo-dr*
product	produit (*m*)	*prud-ew-ee*
quotient	quotient (*m*)	*kuss-yAH*
set	ensemble (*m*)	*AH-sAH-bl*
solution	solution (*f*)	*sul-ew-syOH*
• **solve**	résoudre (*v*)	*ray-zoo-dr*
statistics	statistique (*f*)	*sta-tees-teek*
• **statistical**	statistique (*adj*)	*sta-tees-teek*
sum	somme (*f*)	*sum*
• **sum up**	sommer (*v*)	*sum-ay*
symbol	symbole (*m*)	*sEH-bul*
variable	variable (*f*)	*var-ya-bl*

2. *GEOMETRY*

a. FIGURES

plane figures	figures planes (*f*)	*feeg-ewr plan*
triangle	triangle (*m*)	*tree-yAH-gl*
• **acute-angled**	acutangle (*adj*)	*akew-tAH-gl*
• **equilateral**	équilatéral (*adj*)	*ay-kew-ee-la-tay-ral*
• **isosceles**	isocèle (*adj*)	*ee-zu-sehl*
• **obtuse-angled**	obtusangle (*adj*)	*up-tew-zAH-gl*
• **right-angled**	rectangle (*adj*)	*rehk-tAH-gl*
• **scalene**	scalène (*adj*)	*ska-lehn*
four-sided figures	figures à quatre côtés	*feeg-ewr a katr ko-tay*
• **parallelogram**	parallélogramme (*m*)	*para-lay-lu-gram*
• **rectangle**	rectangle (*m*)	*rehk-tAH-gl*
• **rhombus**	rhombe (*m*)	*rOH-b*
• **square**	carré (*m*)	*ka-ray*
• **trapezium**	trapèze (*m*)	*tra-pehz*
n-sided figures	figures à côtés n	*fee-gewr a ko-tay ehn*
• **pentagon**	pentagone (*m*)	*pAH-ta-gun*
• **hexagon**	hexagone (*m*)	*ehg-za-gun*
• **heptagon**	heptagone (*m*)	*ehp-ta-gun*
• **octagon**	octogone (*m*)	*uk-tug-un*
• **decagon**	décagone (*m*)	*day-ka-gun*
circle	cercle (*m*)	*sehr-kl*
• **center**	centre (*m*)	*sAH-tr*
• **circumference**	circonférence (*f*)	*seer-kOH-fay-rAH-ss*
• **diameter**	diamètre (*m*)	*dya-meh-tr*
• **radius**	rayon (*m*)	*reh-yOH*
• **tangent**	tangente (*f*)	*tAH-zh-AHt*
solid figures	figures solides (*f*, *pl*)	*feeg-ewr sul-eed*
prism	prisme (*m*)	*preesm*
• **right prism**	prisme droit	*preesm drwa*
cube	cube (*m*)	*kewb*
pyramid	pyramide (*f*)	*pee-ra-meed*
polyhedron	polyèdre (*m*)	*pul-yehdr*
• **tetrahedron**	tétraèdre (*m*)	*tay-tra-ehdr*
• **octahedron**	octaèdre (*m*)	*uk-ta-ehdr*
cylinder	cylindre (*m*)	*see-lEH-dr*
cone	cône (*m*)	*kOHn*
sphere	sphère (*f*)	*sfehr*

FOCUS: Geometrical Figures

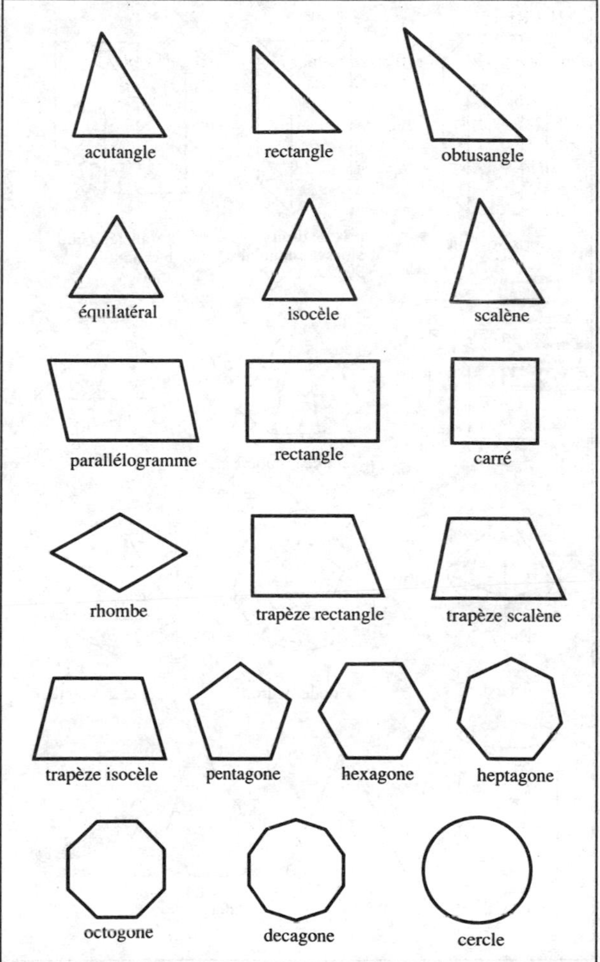

FOCUS: Geometrical Solids

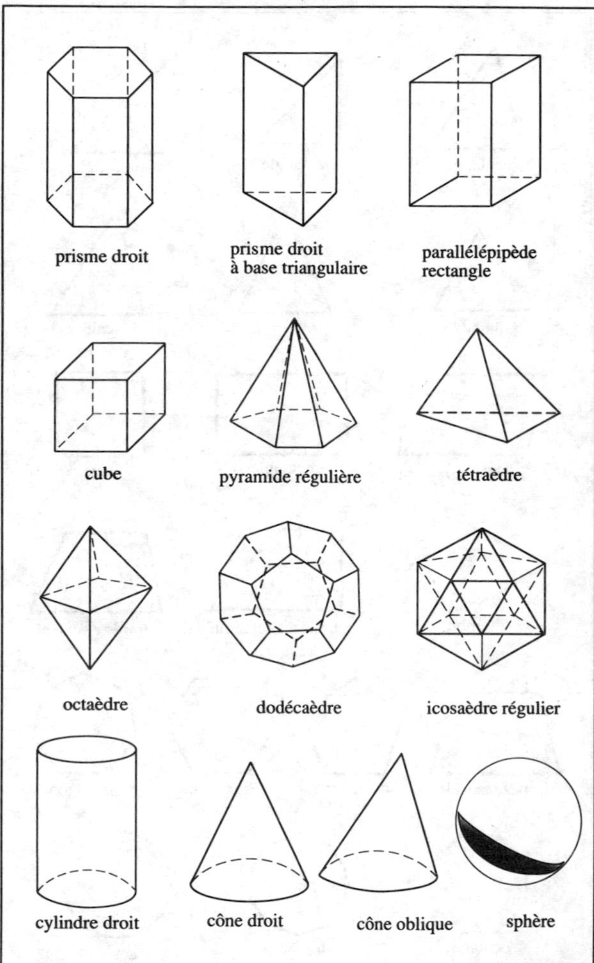

FOCUS: Angles

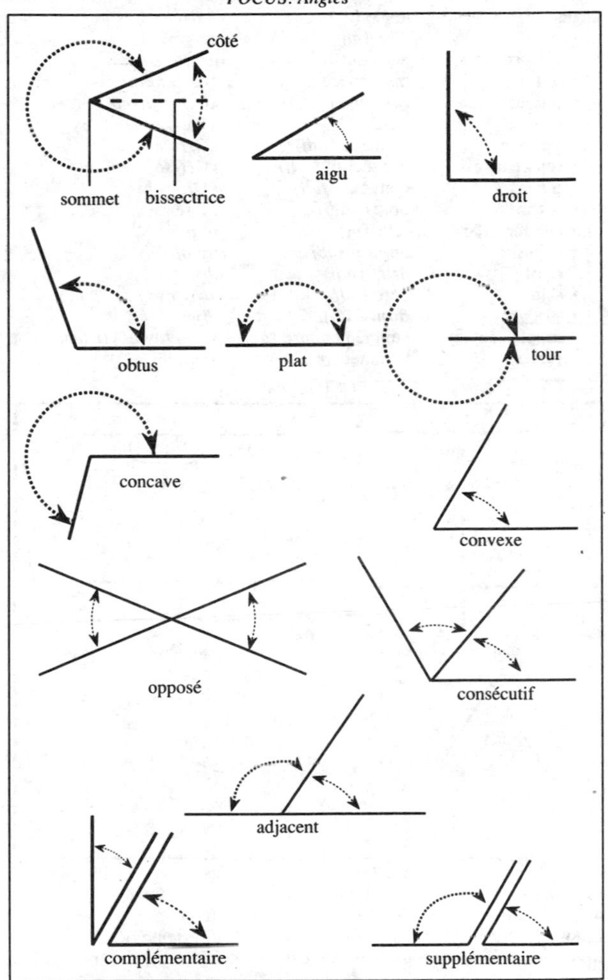

b. CONCEPTS

angle	angle (*m*)	*AH-gl*
• **acute**	aigu (*adj*)	*ay-gew*
• **adjacent**	adjacent (*adj*)	*ad-zha-sAH*
• **bisector**	bissectrice (*f*)	*bee-sehk-treess*
• **complementary**	complémentaire (*adj*)	*kOH-play-mAH-tehr*
• **concave**	concave (*adj*)	*kOH-kav*
• **consecutive**	consécutif (*adj*)	*kOH-say-kew-teef*
• **convex**	convexe (*adj*)	*kOH-vehks*
• **obtuse**	obtus (*adj*)	*up-tew*
• **one turn (360°)**	tour (*m*)	*toor*
• **opposite**	opposé (*adj*)	*up-oh-zay*
• **right**	droit (*adj*)	*drwa*
• **side**	côté (*adj*)	*koh-tay*
• **straight**	droit (*adj*)	*drwa*
• **supplementary**	supplémentaire (*adj*)	*sew-play-mAH-tehr*
• **vertex**	sommet (*m*)	*sum-eh*

FOCUS: Lines

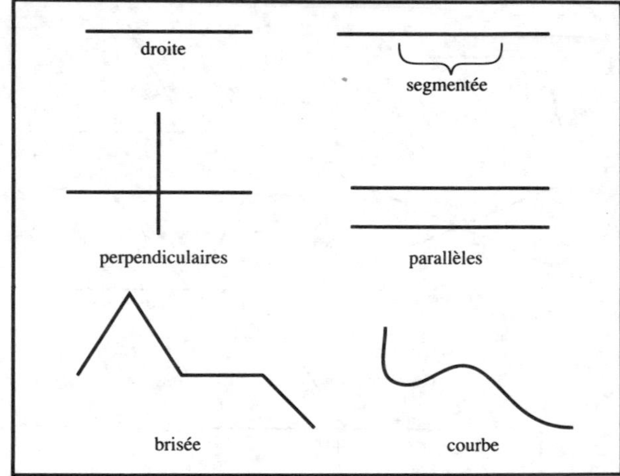

axis	axe (*m*)	*aks*
coordinate	coordonnée (*f*)	*ku-or-dun-ay*
degree	degré (*m*)	*de-gray*
draw	dessiner (*v*)	*day-see-nay*
drawing instruments	instruments de dessin	*EH-strew-mAH de day-sEH*

• **compass**	compas (*m*)	*kOH-pa*
• **eraser**	gomme (*f*)	*gum*
• **pen**	stylo (*m*)	*steel-o*
• **pencil**	crayon (*m*)	*kreh-yOH*
• **protractor**	goniomètre (*m*)	*gun-yu-mehtr*
• **ruler**	règle (*f*)	*rehgl*
• **template**	gabarit (*m*)	*ga-ba-ree*
geometry	géométrie (*f*)	*zhay-u-may-tree*
• **geometrical**	géométrique (*adj*)	*zhay-u-may-treek*
line	ligne (*f*)	*lee-ny*
• **broken**	brisée (*adj*)	*bree-zay*
• **curved**	courbe (*adj*)	*koorb*
• **parallel**	parallèle (*adj*)	*pa-ra-lehl*
• **perpendicular**	perpendiculaire (*adj*)	*pehr-pAH-dee-kew-lehr*
• **segment**	segmentée (*adj*)	*sehg-mAH-tay*
• **straight**	droite (*adj*)	*drwat*
point	point (*m*)	*pwEH*
space	espace (*m*)	*ehs-pas*
trigonometry	trigonométrie (*f*)	*tree-gun-u-may-tree*
• **trigonometric**	trigonométrique (*adj*)	*tree-gun-u-may-treek*
• **cosecant**	cosécante (*f*)	*kus-ay-kAHt*
• **cosine**	cosinus (*m*)	*kus-ee-newss*
• **cotangent**	cotangente (*f*)	*kut-AH-zhAHt*
• **secant**	sécante (*f*)	*say-kAHt*
• **sine**	sinus (*m*)	*see-news*
• **tangent**	tangente (*f*)	*tAH-zhAHt*
vector	vecteur (*m*)	*vehk-tur*

3. QUANTITY AND SPACE

a. WEIGHTS AND MEASURES

area	surface (*f*)	*sewr-fas*
	superficie (*f*)	*sew-pehr-fee-see*
• **hectare**	hectare (*m*)	*ehk-tar*
• **square centimeter**	centimètre carré	*sAH-tee-mehtr ka-ray*
• **square kilometer**	kilomètre carré	*kee-lu-mehtr ka-ray*
• **square meter**	mètre carré	*mehtr ka-ray*
• **square millimeter**	millimètre carré	*meel-ee-mehtr ka-ray*
length	longueur (*f*)	*lOH-gur*
• **centimeter**	centimètre (*m*)	*sAH-tee-mehtr*
• **kilometer**	kilomètre (*m*)	*keel-u-mehtr*
• **meter**	mètre (*m*)	*mehtr*
• **millimeter**	millimètre (*m*)	*meel-ee-mehtr*
speed	vélocité (*f*)	*vay-luss-ee-tay*
• **per hour**	à l'heure	*a-lur*

• **per minute**	à la minute	*a-la-meen-ewt*
• **per second**	à la seconde	*a-la-se-gOHd*
volume	volume (*m*)	*vul-ewm*
• **cubic centimeter**	centimètre cubique	*sAH-tee-mehtr kew-beek*
• **cubic kilometer**	kilomètre cubique	*keel-u-mehtr kew-beek*
• **cubic meter**	mètre cubique	*mehtr kew-beek*
• **cubic millimeter**	millimètre cubique	*meel-ee-mehtr kew-beek*
• **liter**	litre (*m*)	*leetr*
• **quart**	quart de gallon	*kar de gal-OH*
weight	poids (*m*)	*pwah*
• **gram**	gramme (*m*)	*gram*
• **hectogram**	hectogramme (*m*)	*ehk-tu-gram*
• **kilogram**	kilogramme (*m*)	*keel-u-gram*

b. WEIGHING AND MEASURING

dense	dense (*adj*)	*dAH-s*
• **density**	densité (*f*)	*dAH-see-tay*
dimension	dimension (*f*)	*dee-mAH-sy-OH*
extension	extension (*f*)	*ehks-tAH-sy-OH*
heavy	lourd (*adj, m*)	*loor*
	lourde (*f*)	*loord*
light	léger (*adj, m*)	*lay-zhay*
	légère (*f*)	*lay-zh-ehr*
long	long (*adj, m*)	*lOH*
	longue (*f*)	*lOH-g*
mass	masse (*f*)	*mas*
maximum	maximum (*m*)	*maks-ee-mum*
measure	mesurer (*v*)	*me-zewr-ay*
measuring tape	mètre à ruban	*mehtr a rew-bAH*
medium	moyenne (*f*)	*mwa-y-ehn*
	moyen (*adj, m*)	*mwa-yEH*
minimum	minimum (*m*)	*mee-nee-mum*
narrow	étroit (*adj, m*)	*ay-trwa*
	étroite (*f*)	*ay-trwat*
short (thing)	court (*adj, m*)	*koor*
	courte (*f*)	*koort*
size	mesure (*f*)	*me-zewr*
	taille (*f*)	*ta-y*
tall	haut (*adj, m*)	*oh*
	haute (*f*)	*oh-t*
	grand (*m*)	*grAH*
	grande (*f*)	*grAH-d*
thick	épais (*adj, m*)	*ay-peh*
	épaisse (*f*)	*ay-pehs*
thin	maigre (*adj*)	*meh-gr*
weigh	peser (*v*)	*pe-zay*
wide	large (*adj*)	*larzh*
• **width**	largeur (*f*)	*lar-zh-ur*

c. CONCEPTS OF QUANTITY

English	French	Pronunciation
a lot, much	beaucoup (*adv*)	*bo-koo*
	une grande quantité	*ewn grAH-d kAH-tee-tay*
all, everything	tout (*adj*)	*too*
	toute chose	*toot sh-oh-z*
• **everyone**	tout le monde	*tool mOH-d*
almost, nearly	presque (*adv*)	*prehs-ke*
approximately	à peu près (*adv*)	*a puh preh*
	environ	*AH-vee-rOH*
as much as	tant que	*tAH ke*
	autant que	*oh-tAH ke*
big, large	grand (*adj, m*)	*grAH*
	grande (*f*)	*grAH-d*
	gros (*adj, m*)	*gro*
	grosse (*f*)	*gros*
• **become big**	grandir (*v*)	*grAH-deer*
	agrandir (*v*)	*a-grAH-deer*
	grossir (*v*)	*gro-seer*
both	les deux	*lay duh*
	tous (*m*) les deux	*too lay duh*
	toutes (*f*) les deux	*toot lay duh*
capacity	capacité (*f*)	*ka-pa-see-tay*
decrease	diminution (*f*)	*dee-mee-newss-yOH*
• **decrease**	diminuer (*v*)	*dee-mee-new-ay*
double	double (*adj*)	*doobl*
empty	vide (*adj*)	*veed*
• **empty**	vider (*v*)	*vee-day*
enough	assez (*adv*)	*a-say*
	suffisant (*adj*)	*sew-fee-zAH*
• **be enough**	suffire (*v*)	*sew-feer*
	être assez (*v*)	*eh-tre a-say*
entire	entier (*adj*)	*AH-ty-ay*
	entière	*AH-ty-ehr*
every, each	chaque (*adj*)	*shak*
fill	remplir (*v*)	*rAH-pleer*
• **full**	plein (*adj*)	*plEH*
	pleine	*plehn*
grow	croître (*v*)	*krwa-tr*
• **growth**	croissance (*f*)	*krwa-sAH-s*
half	demi (*m*)	*de-mee*
	demie (*f*)	*de-mee*
how much	combien (*adv*)	*kOH-byEH*
increase	augmentation (*f*)	*ug-mAH-ta-syOH*
• **increase**	augmenter (*v*)	*ug-mAH-tay*
less	moins (*adv*)	*mwEH*
little (*size*)	petit (*adj, m*)	*ptee*

	petite (*f*)	*pteet*
• **a little**	peu (*adv*)	*puh*
more	plus (*adv*)	*plew, plewss*
no one	personne (*pro*)	*pehr-sun*
nothing	rien (*adv/pro*)	*ryEH*
	nul (*adj/pro, m*)	*newl*
	nulle (*f*)	*newl*
pair	paire (*f*)	*pehr*
part	part (*f*)	*par*
	partie (*f*)	*par-tee*
piece	pièce (*f*)	*pyehs*
portion	morceau (*m*)	*mor-so*
	portion (*f*)	*porsyOH*
quantity	quantité (*f*)	*kAH-tee-tay*
several	plusieurs (*adj/adv*)	*plew-zy-ur*
small	petit (*adj, m*)	*ptee*
	petite (*f*)	*pteet*
• **become small**	rendre plus petit	*rAH-dr plew ptee*
	rapetisser (*v*)	*rap-tee-say*
some	quelque(*s*) (*adj*)	*kehl-ke*
• **some of it, them**	en (*pro*)	*AH*
• **I have some of it/them.**	J'en ai.	*zh-AH nay*
suffice	suffire (*v*)	*sew-feer*
• **sufficient**	suffisant (*adj*)	*sew-fee-zAH*
too much	trop (*adv*)	*troh*
triple	triple (*adj*)	*tree-pl*

d. CONCEPTS OF LOCATION

above	au-dessus (*adv*)	*ohd-sew*
	en haut	*AH oh*
across	à travers (*prep*)	*a-tra-vehr*
ahead, forward	avant (*adv*)	*a-vAH*
among	parmi (*prep*)	*parmee (among more than two)*
away	au loin (*adv*)	*oh-lwEH*
back, backward	en arrière (*adv*)	*AH-na-ree-ehr*
beside, next to	à côté (de) (*prep*)	*a-ko-tay (de)*
between	entre (*prep*)	*AH-tre (between only two)*
beyond	au-delà (de) (*adv/prep*)	*ohd-la (de)*
bottom	fond (*m*)	*fOH*
• **at the bottom**	au fond	*oh-fOH*
compass	boussole (*f*)	*boo-sul*
direction	direction (*f*)	*dee-rehk-syOH*
distance	distance (*f*)	*dee-stAH-s*

down	bas (*adv*)	*bah*
	en bas	*AH-bah*
east	est (*m*)	*ehst*
• eastern	oriental (*adj*)	*or-yAH-tal*
• to the east	à l'est	*a-lehst*
edge	bord (*m*)	*bor*
far	loin (*adv*)	*lwEH*
	lointain (*adj*)	*lwEH-tEH*
fast	vite (*adj/adv*)	*veet*
	rapide	*ra-peed*
from	de (*prep*)	*de*
here	ici (*adv*)	*ee-see*
horizontal	horizontal (*adj*)	*or-ee-zOH-tal*
in	dans (*prep*)	*dAH*
• inside	dedans (*adv*)	*de-dAH*
in front of	devant (*adv/prep*)	*dvAH*
in the middle	au centre	*oh-sAHtr*
	au milieu	*oh-meel-yuh*
left	gauche (*adj*)	*gohsh*
• to the left	à gauche	*a-gohsh*
level	niveau (*m*)	*nee-voh*
near	près (de) (*adv*)	*preh (de)*
north	nord (*m*)	*nor*
• northern	septentrional (*adj*)	*sehp-tAH-tree-yun-al*
• to the north	au nord	*oh-nor*
nowhere	nulle part (*adv*)	*newl-par*
on	sur (*prep*)	*sewr*
outside	dehors (*adv*)	*de-or*
place	endroit (*m*)	*AH-drwa*
	lieu (*m*)	*lyuh*
position	position (*f*)	*pu-zee-syOH*
right	droit (*adj, m*)	*drwa*
	droite (*f*)	*drwat*
• to the right	à droite	*a-drwat*
somewhere	quelque part	*kehl-ke par*
south	sud (*m*)	*sewd*
• southern	méridional (*adj*)	*may-ree-dy-un-al*
• to the south	au sud	*oh-sewd*
there	là (*adv*)	*la*
through	par (*prep*)	*par*
	à travers	*a-tra-vehr*
to, at	à (*prep*)	*a*
• to, at someone's place	chez (*prep*)	*shay*
top	sommet (*m*)	*sum-eh*
• at the top	au sommet	*oh-sum-eh*
	en haut	*AH-oh*
toward	vers (*prep*)	*vehr*

under	sous (*prep*)	*soo*
up	haut (*adv*)	*oh*
	en haut	*AH-oh*
vertical	vertical (*adj*)	*vehr-tee-kal*
west	ouest (*m*)	*west*
• **western**	occidental (*adj*)	*uk-see-dAH-tal*
• **to the west**	à l'ouest	*al-west*
where	où (*adv*)	*oo*

FOCUS: Compass Points

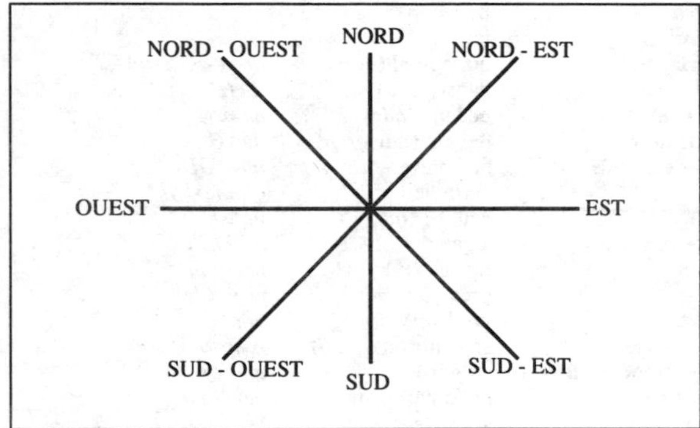

e. MOVEMENT

arrive	arriver (*v*)	*a-ree-vay*
come	venir (*v*)	*vneer*
drive	conduire (*v*)	*kOH-dew-eer*
enter	entrer (*v*)	*AH-tray*
fall	tomber (*v*)	*tOH-bay*
follow	suivre (*v*)	*sew-eevr*
get up, rise	se lever (*v*)	*se-levay*
go	aller (*v*)	*alay*
• **go away**	s'en aller (*v*)	*sAH-nalay*
• **go down, descend**	descendre (*v*)	*day-sAH-dr*
• **go on foot**	aller à pied (*v*)	*alay a pyay*
• **go out, exit**	sortir (*v*)	*sor-teer*
• **go up, climb**	monter (*v*)	*mOH-tay*
leave, depart	partir (*v*)	*par-teer*
lie down	se coucher (*v*)	*se-koo-shay*
lift	lever (*v*)	*le-vay*
motion	motion (*f*)	*mo-syOH*

move	bouger (*v*)	*boo-zhay*
	remuer (*v*)	*re-mew-ay*
• **move oneself**	se déplacer (*v*)	*se-day-pla-say*
	bouger (*v*)	*boo-zhay*
• **movement**	mouvement (*m*)	*moov-mAH*
pass by	passer (*v*)	*pa-say*
pull	tirer (*v*)	*tee-ray*
put	mettre (*v*)	*meht-re*
	placer (*v*)	*pla-say*
• **put down**	poser (*v*)	*po-zay*
quickly	vite (*adv*)	*veet*
return	retourner (*v*)	*re-toor-nay*
run	courir (*v*)	*koo-reer*
send	envoyer (*v*)	*AH-vwa-yay*
sit down	s'asseoir (*v*)	*sa-swar*
slow	lent (*adj, m*)	*lAH*
	lente (*f*)	*lAHt*
• **slowly**	lentement (*adv*)	*lAHt-mAH*
stop	arrêter (*v*)	*a-reht-ay*
• **stop oneself**	s'arrêter (*v*)	*sa-reht-ay*
turn	tourner (*v*)	*toor-nay*
walk	marcher (*v*)	*marsh-ay*
	aller (*v*) à pied	*alay a pyay*
• **walk**	promenade (*f*)	*prum-nad*
• **take a walk**	faire (*v*) une promenade	*fehr ewn prum-nad*

4. TIME

a. GENERAL EXPRESSIONS OF TIME

afternoon	après-midi (*m*)	*apreh-mee-dee*
• **in the afternoon**	dans l'après-midi	*dAH lap-reh mee-dee*
	de l'après-midi	*de lap-reh-mee-dee*
• **this afternoon**	cet après-midi	*seht-apreh-mee-dee*
• **tomorrow afternoon**	demain après-midi	*de-mEH apreh-mee-dee*
dawn	aube (*f*)	*ohb*
day	jour (*m*)	*zh-oor*
• **all day**	toute la journée	*toot la zh-oor-nay*
evening	soir (*m*)	*swar*
• **in the evening**	dans le soir	*dAHl-swar*
	du soir	*dew swar*
• **this evening**	ce soir	*se-swar*
• **tomorrow evening**	demain soir	*de-mEH swar*
midnight	minuit (*m*)	*mee-new-ee*
• **at midnight**	à minuit	*a-mee-new-ee*

morning	matin (*m*)	*ma-tEH*
• **in the morning**	dans le matin	*daHl-ma-tEH*
	du matin	*dew-ma-tEH*
• **this morning**	ce matin	*se-ma-tEH*
• **tomorrow morning**	demain matin	*de-mEH ma-tEH*
night	nuit (*f*)	*new-ee*
• **at night**	de nuit	*de-new-ee*
	dans la nuit	*dAH-la-new-ee*
• **last night**	cette nuit	*seht-new-ee (actual night)*
	hier soir	*yehr swar (actual evening)*
• **this night**	cette nuit	*seht new-ee*
• **tomorrow night**	demain pendant la nuit	*de-mEH pAH-dAH la new-ee (actual night)*
	demain soir	*de-mEH swar (actual evening)*
noon	midi (*m*)	*mee-dee*
• **at noon**	à midi	*a-mee-dee*
sunrise	lever (*m*) du soleil	*le-vay dew sul-ay*
sunset	coucher (*m*) du soleil	*koo-shay dew sul-ay*
time (*in general*)	temps (*m*)	*tAH*
• **time (hour)**	heure (*f*)	*ur*
• **time (as in *every time*)**	fois (*f*)	*fwa*

Time flies! = Le temps fuit! *le tAH few-ee*
at the present time = à l'heure actuelle *a-lur ak-tew ehl*
Once upon a time . . . = Il était une fois *eel ay-teh tewn fwa*
to be on time = être à l'heure *eh-tre a-lur*

today	aujourd'hui (*adv*)	*oh-zhoor-dew-ee*
tomorrow	demain (*adv*)	*de-mEH*
• **day after tomorrow**	lendemain (*adv*)	*lAHd-mEH*
tonight	cette nuit	*seht new-ee (actual night)*
	ce soir	*se swar (evening)*
yesterday	hier (*adv*)	*yehr*
• **day before yesterday**	avant-hier (*adv*)	*avAH-tyehr*
• **yesterday afternoon**	hier après-midi	*yehr apreh-mee-dee*
• **yesterday morning**	hier matin	*yehr ma-tEH*

b. TELLING TIME

What time is it?	Quelle heure est-il?	*kehl ur eh-teel*
• **It's 1:00.**	Il est une heure.	*eel eh-tewn ur*
• **It's 2:00.**	Il est deux heures.	*eel eh duh-zur*
• **It's 3:00.**	Il est trois heures.	*eel eh trwa-zur*
• **It's exactly 3:00.**	Il est trois heures précises.	*eel eh trwa-zur pray-seez*
• **It's 3:00 on the dot.**	Il est trois heures juste.	*eel eh trwa-zur zh-ewst*
	Il est trois heures pile.	*eel eh trwa-zur peel*
• **It's 1:10.**	Il est une heure dix.	*eel eh tewn ur dees*
• **It's 4:25.**	Il est quatre heures vingt-cinq.	*eel eh katr ur vEH-sEHk*
• **It's 3:15.**	Il est trois heures et quart.	*eel eh trwa-zur ay kar*
• **It's 3:30.**	Il est trois heures et demie.	*eel eh trwa-zur ayd-mee*
• **It's 2:45.**	Il est trois heures moins un quart.	*eel eh trwa-zur mwEH-zUH kar*
	Il est deux heures quarante-cinq.	*eel eh duh-zur ka-rAHt sEHk*
• **It's 5:50.**	Il est six heures moins dix.	*eel eh see-zur mwEH dees*

> The 24-hour clock is used throughout France.

• **It's 5:00 AM.**	Il est cinq heures.	*eel eh sEH-kur*
• **It's 5:00 PM.**	Il est dix-sept heures.	*eel eh dee-seht ur*
• **It's 10:00 AM.**	Il est dix heures.	*eel eh dee-zur*
• **It's 10:00 PM.**	Il est vingt-deux heures.	*eel eh vEH-duh zur*
At what time?	À quelle heure?	*a kehl ur*
• **At 1:00.**	À une heure.	*a ewn ur*
• **At 2:00.**	À deux heures.	*a duh-zur*
• **At 3:00.**	À trois heures.	*a trwa-zur*

c. UNITS OF TIME

century	siècle (*m*)	*see-ehkl*
day	jour (*m*)	*zhoor*
• **daily**	quotidien (*adj*)	*kut-ee-dy-EH*
	quotidiennement (*adv*)	*kut-ee-dy-ehn-mAH*

decade	décennie (*f*)	*day-sehn-ee*
hour	heure (*f*)	*ur*
• **hourly**	à l'heure	*a-lur*
instant	instant (*m*)	*EH-stAH*
minute	minute (*f*)	*meen-ewt*
moment	moment (*m*)	*mum-AH*
month	mois (*m*)	*mwa*
• **monthly**	mensuellement (*adv*)	*mAH-sew-ehl-mAH*
	mensuel (*adj*)	*mAH-sew-ehl*
second	seconde (*f*)	*se-gOHd*
week	semaine (*f*)	*smehn*
• **weekly**	hebdomadaire (*adj*)	*ehb-dum-ad-ehr*
	hebdomadairement (*adv*)	*ehb-dum-ad-ehr-mAH*
year	an (*m*)	*AH*
	année (*f*)	*a-nay*
• **yearly, annually**	annuel, annuelle (*adj*)	*a-new-ehl*
	annuellement (*adv*)	*a-new-ehl-mAH*

d. TIMEPIECES

alarm clock	réveille-matin (*m*)	*ray-veh-y mat-EH*
clock	horloge (*f*)	*or-lu-zh*
dial	cadran (*m*)	*ka-drAH*
grandfather clock	horloge à pendule (*f*)	*or-lu-zh a pAH-dewl*
	horloge normande (*f*)	*or-lu-zh nor-mAHd*
hand (of a clock)	aiguille (*f*)	*ayg-ew-ee-y*
watch	montre (*f*)	*mOH-tre*
• **The watch is fast.**	La montre avance.	*la mOH-tre avAH-s*
• **The watch is slow.**	La montre retarde.	*la mOH-tre re-tard*
watchband	bracelet (*m*) d'une montre	*bras-leh dewn mOH-tre*
watch battery	pile d'une montre	*peel dewn mOH-tre*
wind	remonter (*v*)	*re-mOH-tay*
wristwatch	bracelet-montre (*m*)	*bras-leh mOH-tre*

e. CONCEPTS OF TIME

after	après (*adv*)	*apreh*
again	encore une fois (*adv*)	*AH-kor ewn fwa*

	de nouveau (*adv*)	*de-noo-voh*
ago	il y a (*adv*)	*eel-yah*
almost never	presque jamais (*adv*)	*prehs-ke zh-a-meh*
already	déjà (*adv*)	*day-zh-a*
always	toujours (*adv*)	*too-zh-oor*
anterior	antérieur(e) (*adj*)	*AH-tay-ree-ur*
as soon as	dès que (*conj*)	*deh-ke*
	aussitôt que (*conj*)	*o-see-toh-ke*
at the same time	en même temps	*AH-mehm-tAH*
	à la fois	*a-la-fwa*
be about to, be on the point/verge of	être sur le point de	*eh-tre sewr le pwEH de*
be on time	être à l'heure	*eh-tre a-lur*
become	devenir (*v*)	*devneer*
before	avant (*adv*)	*avAH*
	auparavant (*adv*)	*o-par-avAH*
begin	commencer (*v*)	*kum-AH-say*
• **beginning**	commencement (*m*)	*kum-AH-smAH*
brief	bref, brève (*adj, m, f*)	*brehf, brehv*
• **briefly**	en bref	*AH brehf*
	brièvement (*adv*)	*bree-ehv-mAH*
change	changer (*v*)	*shAH-zh-ay*
continue	continuer (*v*)	*kOH-teen-ew-ay*
• **continually**	continuellement (*adv*)	*kOH-teen-ew-ehl-mAH*
during	pendant (*prep*)	*pAH-dAH*
early	tôt (*adv*)	*toh*
	de bonne heure (*adv*)	*de-bun-ur*
• **be early**	être tôt (*v*)	*eh-tre-toh*
	être de bonne heure (*v*)	*eh-tre de-bun-ur*
end, finish	finir (*v*)	*fee-neer*
• **end**	fin (*f*)	*fEH*
frequent	fréquent(e) (*adj, m, f*)	*fray-kAH(t)*
• **frequently**	fréquemment (*adv*)	*fray-kam-AH*
future	futur (*m*)	*few-tewr*
	avenir (*m*)	*avneer*
happen, occur	se produire (*v*)	*se-pro-dew-eer*
in an hour's time	dans une heure	*dAH-zewn-ur*
• **in two minutes' time**	dans deux minutes	*dAH duh meen-ewt*
in the meanwhile	dans l'intervalle	*dAH-lEH-tehr-val*
in time	à temps	*a-tAH*
just now	à l'instant	*a-lEH-stAH*
last	durer (*v*)	*dewr-ay*

• last a long time	durer longtemps (*v*)	*dew-rayl-OH-t-AH*
• last a short time	durer peu de temps (*v*)	*dewr-ay puh de tAH*
last	dernier (*adj, m*)	*dehrn-yay*
	dernière (*f*)	*dehrn-yehr*
	passé(e) (*adj*)	*pah-say*
• last month	le mois dernier (passé)	*le mwa dehrn-yay (pah-say)*
• last year	l'an dernier (*m*)	*lAH dehrn-yay*
	l'année dernière (*f*)	*la-nay dehrn-yehr*
late	tard	*tar*
	en retard (*adv*)	*AH re-tar*
• be late	être tard (en retard)	*eh-tre tar (AH-re-tar)*

Better late than never! Mieux vaut tard que jamais! *myuh voh tar ke zh-a-meh*

long-term	à long terme	*a-lOH-tehrm*
look forward to	s'attendre à (*v*)	*sat-AH-dre-a*
never	jamais (*adv*)	*zh-a-meh*
• almost never	presque jamais (*adv*)	*prehs-ke zh-a-meh*
now	maintenant (*adv*)	*mEHt-nAH*
	à présent (*adv*)	*a pray-zAH*
• for now	pour maintenant	*poor mEHt-nAH*
• from now on	dès maintenant	*deh mEHt-nAH*
	désormais (*adv*)	*day-zor-meh*
nowadays	de nos jours	*de noh zh-oor*
occasionally	de temps en temps (*adv*)	*de-tAH-zAH-tAH*
often	souvent (*adv*)	*soovAH*
once	une fois	*ewn fwa*
• once in a while	de temps à autre	*de tAH za oh-tre*
• once upon a time	il était une fois	*eel ay-teh tewn fwa*
only	seulement (*adv*)	*sulmAH*
past	passé (*m*)	*pah-say*
posterior	postérieur(e) (*adj*)	*pus-tay-ree-ur*
present	présent (*m*)	*prayz-AH*
	présent(e) (*adj, m, f*)	*prayz-AH(t)*
	actuel(le) (*adj, m, f*)	*ak-tew-ehl*
• presently	actuellement (*adv*)	*ak-tew-ehlm-AH*
previous	précédent(e) (*adj, m, f*)	*pray-sayd-AH(t)*
• previously	précédemment (*adv*)	*pray-say-dam-AH*
rare	rare (*adj*)	*rahr*

• rarely	rarement (*adv*)	*rahrm-AH*
recent	récent(e) (*adj, m, f*)	*rayss-AH(t)*
• recently	récemment (*adv*)	*ray-sam-AH*
regular	régulier (*adj, m*)	*ray-gewl-yay*
	régulière (*f*)	*ray-gewl-yehr*
• regularly	régulièrement (*adv*)	*ray-gewl-yehrm-AH*
right away	tout de suite (*adv*)	*tood-sweet*
short-term	à court terme	*a-koor-tehrm*
simultaneous	simultané(e) (*adj, m, f*)	*seem-ewl-ta-nay*
• simultaneously	simultanément (*adv*)	*seem-ewl-ta-naym-AH*
since, for	depuis (*prep*)	*de-pew-ee*
• since Monday	depuis lundi	*de-pew-ee-lUH-dee*
• since yesterday	depuis hier	*de-pew-ee-yehr*
• for three days	depuis trois jours	*de-pew-ee trwa zhoor*
slow	lent(e) (*adj, m, f*)	*l-AH-(t)*
• slowly	lentement (*adv*)	*l-AH-tem-AH*
soon	bientôt (*adv*)	*by-EH toh*
• as soon as	dès que (*conj*)	*deh-ke*
	aussitôt que	*o-see-toh-ke*
• sooner or later	tôt ou tard (*adv*)	*toh oo tar*
spend (*time*)	passer (*v*)	*pah-say*
spend (*money*)	dépenser (*v*)	*daypAH-say*
sporadic	sporadique (*adj*)	*spu-ra-deek*
• sporadically	sporadiquement (*adv*)	*spu-ra-deek-m-AH*
still	encore (*adv*)	*AH-kor*
	toujours	*too-zhoor*
take place	avoir lieu	*avwar lee-yuh*
temporary	temporaire (*adj*)	*tAH-pu-rehr*
• temporarily	temporairement (*adv*)	*tAH-pu-rehrm-AH*
then	lors	*lor*
	alors (*adv*)	*a-lor*
timetable, schedule	horaire (*m*)	*u-rehr*
to this day	jusqu'à ce jour (*adv*)	*zh-ews-ka-se-zhoor*
until	jusque(s) (*prep*)	*zh-ews-ke*
usually	usuellement (*adv*)	*ew-zew-ehlm-AH*
wait (for)	attendre (*v*)	*at-AH-dre*
when	quand (*adv*)	*k-AH*
while	pendant que (*conj*)	*p-AH-d-AH-ke*
within (*a certain time*)	en (*prep*)	*AH*
yet	encore (*adv*)	*AH-kor*

5. *DAYS, MONTHS, AND SEASONS*

a. DAYS OF THE WEEK

day of the week	jour (*m*) de la semaine	*zhoord-la-smehn*
• **Monday**	lundi (*m*)	*lUH-dee*
• **Tuesday**	mardi (*m*)	*mar-dee*
• **Wednesday**	mercredi (*m*)	*mehr-kre-dee*
• **Thursday**	jeudi (*m*)	*zhuh-dee*
• **Friday**	vendredi (*m*)	*vAH-dre-dee*
• **Saturday**	samedi (*m*)	*sam-dee*
• **Sunday**	dimanche (*m*)	*dee-mAH-sh*
• **on Mondays**	le lundi	*le-l-UH-dee*
• **on Saturdays**	le samedi	*le-sam-dee*
• **on Sundays**	le dimanche	*le-dee-mAH-sh*
holiday	un jour férié	*UH zhoor fay-ree-ay*
weekend	la fin de semaine	*laf-EH-de-smehn*
What day is it?	Quel jour est-ce?	*kehl zhoor eh-ss*
workday	un jour de travail	*UH zhoor-de-tra-va-y*

b. MONTHS OF THE YEAR

month of the year	mois (*m*) de l'année	*mwad-la-nay*
• **January**	janvier (*m*)	*zh-AH-vee-ay*
• **February**	février (*m*)	*fay-vree-ay*
• **March**	mars (*m*)	*marss*
• **April**	avril (*m*)	*avreel*
• **May**	mai (*m*)	*meh*
• **June**	juin (*m*)	*zh-ew-EH*
• **July**	juillet (*m*)	*zh-ew-ee-yay*
• **August**	août (*m*)	*oo (oot)*
• **September**	septembre (*m*)	*sehpt-AH-bre*
• **October**	octobre (*m*)	*uktubre*
• **November**	novembre (*m*)	*nuv-AH-bre*
• **December**	décembre (*m*)	*dayss-AH-bre*
calendar	calendrier (*m*)	*kal-AH-dree-yay*
leap year	une année bissextile	*ewn anay bee-sehks-teel*
monthly	mensuellement (*adv*)	*m-AH-sew-ehlm-AH*
school year	année scolaire	*anay skul-ehr*
What month are we in?	Quel mois sommes-nous?	*kehl mwa sum noo*
What month is it?	Quel mois est-ce?	*kehl mwa eh-ss*

c. SEASONS

season	**saison (*f*)**	***sehz-OH***
• **spring**	**printemps (*m*)**	***preEH-tAH***
• **summer**	**été (*m*)**	***ay-tay***
• **fall**	**automne (*m*)**	***utun***
• **winter**	**hiver (*m*)**	***eev-ehr***
equinox	**équinoxe (*m*)**	***ay-kee-nuks***
moon	**lune (*f*)**	***lewn***
solstice	**solstice (*m*)**	***sulsteess***
sun	**soleil (*m*)**	***sul-ay***

FOCUS: The Seasons

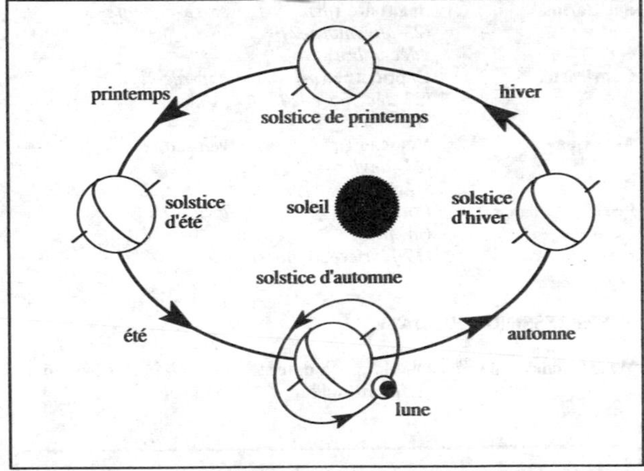

d. THE ZODIAC

horoscope	**horoscope (*m*)**	***u-rus-kup***
zodiac	**zodiaque (*m*)**	***zud-yak***
• **signs of the zodiac**	**signes du zodiaque**	***see-ny dew zud-yak***
Aries	**Bélier (*m*)** ***(21 mars–20 avril)***	***bayl-yay***
Taurus	**Taureau (*m*)** ***(21 avril–21 mai)***	***toro***

Gemini	Gémeaux (*m, pl*) (*22 mai–21 juin*)	*zhay-mo*
Cancer	Cancer (*m*) (*22 juin–22 juillet*)	*kAH-sehr*
Leo	Lion (*m*) (*23 juillet–23 août*)	*ly-OH*
Virgo	Vierge (*f*) (*24 août–23 septembre*)	*vy-erzh*
Libra	Balance (*f*) (*24 septembre–23 octobre*)	*bal-AH-ss*
Scorpio	Scorpion (*m*) (*24 octobre–22 novembre*)	*skor-pyOH*
Sagittarius	Sagittaire (*m*) (*23 novembre–21 décembre*)	*sa-zh-ee-tehr*
Capricorn	Capricorne (*m*) (*22 décembre–20 janvier*)	*kap-ree-kurn*
Aquarius	Verseau (*m*) (*21 janvier–18 février*)	*vehr-so*
Pisces	Poissons (*m, pl*) (*19 février–20 mars*)	*pwas-OH*

e. EXPRESSING THE DATE

What's today's date?	Quelle est la date aujourd'hui?	*kehl eh la dat oh-zhoor-dew-ee*

> Use the ordinal *premier* for the first of each month, and cardinal numbers for the other days.

• **It's October first.**	C'est le premier octobre.	*seh le prem-yay uktubre*
• **It's January second.**	C'est le deux janvier.	*seh le duh zh-Ah-vee-ay*
• **It's May third.**	C'est le trois mai.	*seh le trwa meh*
What year is it?	Quelle année est-ce?	*kehl anay eh-ss*
• **It's 1991.**	C'est 1991.	*seh 1991*

When were you born?	Quand êtes-vous né? (*m, pol*)	*kAH eht-voo nay*
	Quand êtes-vous née (*f, pol*)	*kAH eht-voo nay*
	Quand es-tu né (*m, fam*)	*kAH eh-tew nay*
	Quand es-tu née (*f, fam*)	*kAH eh-tew nay*
• I was born in 19 . . .	Je suis né (*m*)/née (*f*) en 19 . . .	*zhe sew-ee nay AH 19*

f. IMPORTANT DATES

the New Year	le Nouvel An	*le noo-vehl AH*
New Year's Day	le Jour de l'An	*le zhoor del AH*
New Year's Eve	la Veille du Nouvel An	*la veh-y dew noo-vehl AH*
Assumption (August 15, National French holiday)	Assomption (*f*)	*as-OH-psy-OH*
Easter	Pâques (*f, pl*)	*pahk*
Christmas	Noël (*m*)	*nuh-ehl*

6. *TALKING ABOUT THE WEATHER*

a. GENERAL WEATHER VOCABULARY

air	air (*m*)	*ehr*
atmosphere	atmosphère (*f*)	*at-muss-fehr*
• atmospheric conditions	conditions atmosphériques (*f, pl*)	*kOH-dee-sy-OH at-muss-fay-reek*
awful	mauvais (*adj*)	*muv-eh*
• be awful (weather)	faire (*v*) un temps mauvais	*fehr UH tAH muv-eh*
beautiful	beau (*dj*)	*bo*
• be beautiful (weather)	faire (*v*) beau temps	*fehr bo tAH*
clear	clair (*adj*)	*klehr*
• The sky is clear.	Le ciel est clair.	*le syehl eh klehr*
climate	climat (*m*)	*klee-ma*
• continental	continental(e) (*adj*)	*kOH-teen-AH-tal*
• dry	sec (*adj, m*)	*sehk*
	sèche (*f*)	*seh-sh*
• humid	humide (*adj*)	*ew-meed*

• **Mediterranean**	méditerranéen (*adj, m*)	*may-dee-tehr-anay-EH*
	méditerranéenne (*f*)	*may-dee-tehr-anay-ehn*
• **tropical**	tropical(e) (*adj, m, f*)	*trup-ee-kal*
cloud	nuage (*m*)	*new-azh*
• **cloudy**	nuageux (*adj, m*)	*new-azh-uh*
	nuageuse (*f*)	*new-azh-uhz*

to be in the clouds (to have one's head in the clouds) = être dans les nuages *eh-tre dAH lay new-azh*

cold	froid (*m*)	*frwa*
• **be cold (weather)**	faire froid	*fehr frwa*
cool	frais (*adj*)	*freh*
• **be cool (weather)**	faire frais	*fehr freh*
dark	sombre (*adj*)	*sOH-bre*
• **It's dark today.**	Il fait sombre aujourd'hui.	*eel feh sOH-bre oh-zhoor-dew-ee*
drop (e.g., of rain)	goutte (*f*)	*goot*
fog	brouillard (*m*)	*broo-yar*
• **foggy**	brumeux (*adj*)	*brewm-uh*
freeze	geler (*v*)	*zhe-lay*
• **frozen**	gelé(e) (*adj, m, f*)	*zhe-lay*
hail	grêle (*f*)	*grehl*
• **hail**	grêler (v)	*gray-lay*
How's the weather?	Quel temps fait-il?	*kehl tAH feh-teel*
• **It's a bit hot (cold, etc.).**	Il fait un peu chaud. Il fait un peu froid.	*eel feh UH puh sho* *eel feh UH puh frwa*
• **It's awful.**	Il fait un temps affreux.	*eel feh UH tAH af-ruh*
• **It's beautiful.**	Il fait beau temps.	*eel feh bo tAH*
• **It's cloudy.**	Il fait un temps couvert.	*eel feh UH tAH koo-vehr*
• **It's cold.**	Il fait froid.	*eel feh frwa*
• **It's cool.**	Il fait frais.	*eel feh freh*
• **It's foul (weather).**	Il fait un temps pourri.	*eel feh UH tAH poo-ree*
• **It's hot.**	Il fait chaud.	*eel feh sho*
• **It's humid.**	Il fait humide.	*eel feh ew-meed*
• **It's mild.**	Il fait doux.	*eel feh doo*
• **It's muggy.**	Il fait un temps lourd.	*eel feh UH tAH loor*

• **It's pleasant.**	Il fait un temps agréable.	*eel feh UH tAH a-gray-ahble*
• **It's raining.**	Il pleut.	*eel pluh*

> **It's raining buckets.** = Il pleut à seaux. *eel pluh a so*

• **It's snowing.**	Il neige.	*eel neh-zh*
• **It's sunny.**	Il fait (du) soleil.	*eel feh (dew) sul-ay*
• **It's thundering.**	Il tonne.	*eel tun*
• **It's very cold.**	Il fait très froid.	*eel feh treh frwa*
• **It's very hot.**	Il fait très chaud.	*eel feh treh sho*
• **It's windy.**	Il fait du vent.	*eel feh dew vAH*
• **There's lightning.**	Il fait des éclairs.	*eel feh day zay-klehr*
humid, damp	humide (*adj*)	*ew-meed*
• **be humid**	faire humide	*fehr ew-meed*
• **humidity**	humidité (*f*)	*ew-mee-dee-tay*
hurricane	ouragan (*m*)	*oor-ag-AH*
ice	glace (*f*)	*glass*
light	lumière (*f*)	*lew-myehr*
lightning	éclair (*m*)	*ay-klehr*
• **flash/bolt of lightning**	faire (*v*) des éclairs	*fehr day zay-klehr*
	un coup d'éclair	*UH koo day-klehr*
mild	doux (*adj, m*)	*doo*
	douce (*f*)	*doos*
• **be mild**	faire doux	*fehr doo*
moon	lune (*f*)	*lewn*
mugginess	lourdeur (*f*)	*loord-ur*
• **muggy**	lourd (*adj, m*)	*loor*
	lourde (*f*)	*loord*
• **be muggy**	faire un temps lourd	*fehr UH tAH loor*
rain	pluie (*f*)	*plew-ee*
• **rain**	pleuvoir (*v*)	*pluh-vwar*
• **It's rainy.**	Il fait un temps pluvieux.	*eel feh UH tAH plewv-yuh*
sea	mer (*f*)	*mehr*
shadow, shade	ombre (*f*)	*OH-bre*
sky	ciel (*m*)	*syehl*
snow	neige (*f*)	*neh-zh*
• **snow**	neiger (*v*)	*nay-zh-ay*
star	étoile (*f*)	*ay-twal*
storm	tempête (*f*)	*tAH-peht*
sun	soleil (*m*)	*sul-ay*
thunder, clap of thunder	tonnerre (*m*)	*tun-ehr*

• **thunder**	faire un bruit de tonnerre	*fehr UH brew-ee de tun-ehr*
tornado	tornade (*f*)	*tur-nad*
weather	temps (*m*)	*tAH*
• **The weather is beautiful.**	Il fait beau temps.	*eel feh bo tAH*

The weather is rotten. = Il fait un temps pourri. *eel feh UH tAH poo-ree*

wind	vent (*m*)	*vAH*
• **be windy**	faire (*v*) du vent	*fehr dew vAH*

b. REACTING TO THE WEATHER

be cold	avoir (*v*) froid	*avwar frwa*
• **I am cold.**	J'ai froid.	*zh-ay frwa*
be hot	avoir (*v*) chaud	*avwar sho*
• **I am hot.**	J'ai chaud.	*zh-ay sho*
have chills	être (*v*) frileux (frileuse)	*eh-tre free-luh (free-luhz)*
I can't stand the cold.	Je ne supporte pas le froid.	*zhen sew-port pahl frwa*
I can't stand the heat.	Je ne supporte pas la chaleur.	*zhen sew-port pah la sha-lur*
I love the cold.	J'aime le froid.	*zh-ehm le frwa*
I love the heat.	J'aime la chaleur.	*zh-ehm la sha-lur*
perspire	transpirer (*v*)	*trAH-spee-ray*
warm up	se chauffer (*v*)	*se-sho-fay*

c. WEATHER-MEASURING INSTRUMENTS AND ACTIVITIES

barometer	baromètre (*m*)	*ba-rum-eht-re*
• **barometric pressure**	pression (*f*) barométrique	*prehs-yOH ba-rum-ay-treek*
Celsius	Celsius	*sehl-see-ews*
Centigrade	centigrade (*adj*)	*sAH-tee-grad*
degree	degré (*m*)	*de-gray*
Fahrenheit	Fahrenheit	*fa-rehn-a-eet*
mercury	mercure (*m*)	*mehr-kewr*
minus	moins (*adv*)	*mwEH*
plus	plus (*adv*)	*plew(s)*

temperature	température (*f*)	*tAH-pay-ra-tewr*
• **high**	élevée (*adj*)	*ayl-vay*
• **low**	basse (*adj*)	*bahs*
• **maximum**	maximum (*adj*)	*mak-see-mum*
• **minimum**	minimum (*adj*)	*mee-nee-mum*
thermometer	thermomètre (*m*)	*tehrm-u-meht-re*
• **boiling point**	point (*m*) d'ébullition	*pwEH day-bewl-ee-syOH*
• **melting point**	point (*m*) de fusion	*pwEH de few-zyOH*
thermostat	thermostat (*m*)	*tehr-mus-ta*
weather forecast	prévision (*f*) scientifique du temps	*pray-veez-yOH syAH-tee-feek dew tAH*
weather report, bulletin	bulletin (*m*) météorologique	*bewltEH may-tay-u-ru-lu-zh-eek*
zero	zéro (*m*)	*zay-ro*
• **above zero**	dessus zéro	*de-sew zay-ro*
• **below zero**	dessous zéro	*de-soo zay-ro*

7. COLORS

a. BASIC COLORS

What color is it?	De quelle couleur est-ce?	*de kehl koo-lur eh-ss*
It's . . .	C'est . . .	*seh*
• **black**	noir	*nwar*
• **blue**	bleu	*bluh*
• **dark blue**	bleu foncé	*bluh fOH-say*
• **light blue**	bleu clair	*bluh klehr*
• **brown**	brun	*brUH*
• **gold**	or de couleur	*or-de-koo-lur*
• **gray**	gris	*gree*
• **green**	vert	*vehr*
• **orange**	orangé	*or-AH-zh-ay*
• **pink**	rose	*rohz*
• **purple**	pourpre	*poor-pre*
• **red**	rouge	*roozh*
• **silver**	argenté	*ar-zh-AH-tay*
• **white**	blanc	*blAH*
• **yellow**	jaune	*zh-ohn*

to see life "in the pink" = voir la vie en rose *vwar la vee AH rohz*
to be green with fear = être vert de peur *eh-tre vehr de pur*
to become red with anger = devenir rouge de colère *devneer roozh de kul-ehr*
to force an uneasy smile = sourire jaune *soo-reer zh-ohn*
Mrs. Durand is a bluestocking (*i.e., learned, bookish woman*). = Madame Durand est un bas-bleu *ma-dahm dewr-AH eht UH bah-bluh*

b. DESCRIBING COLORS

bright	éclatant	*ay-klat-AH*
dark	sombre	*sOH-bre*
dull	terne	*tehrn*
light	clair	*klehr*
lively	vif	*veef*
opaque	opaque	*up-ak*
pale	pâle	*pahl*
pure	pur	*pewr*
transparent	transparent	*tr-AH-spar-AH*
vibrant	vibrant	*veebr-AH*

c. ADDITIONAL VOCABULARY: COLORS

color	couleur (*f*)	*koo-lur*
• **color**	colorer (*v*)	*kul-u-ray*
• **colored**	coloré(e) (*adj, m, f*)	*kul-u-ray*
• **coloring**	colorant (*m*)	*kul-ur-AH*
• **food coloring**	colorant alimentaire	*kul-ur-AH aleem-AH tehr*
crayon	crayon (*m*) de couleur	*kreh-y-OH de koo-lur*
felt pen	crayon feutre (*m*)	*kreh-y-OH fuh-tre*
paint	peindre (*v*)	*pEH-dre*
painter	peintre (*m*)	*pEH-tre*
	femme peintre (*f*)	*fam pEH-tre*
pen	stylo (*m*)	*stee-lo*
tint	teinte (*f*)	*tEHt*
• **tint**	teindre (*v*)	*tEH-dre*

8. BASIC GRAMMAR

a. GRAMMATICAL TERMS

adjective	adjectif (*m*)	*ad-zh-ehk-teef*
• **demonstrative**	démonstratif (*adj*)	*daym-OH-stra-teef*
• **descriptive**	descriptif (*adj*)	*dehs-kreep-teef*
• **indefinite**	indéfini (*adj*)	*EH-day-fee-nee*
• **interrogative**	interrogatif (*adj*)	*EH-teh-rug-a-teef*
• **possessive**	possessif (*adj*)	*puss-ay-seef*
adverb	adverbe (*m*)	*ad-vehrb*
alphabet	alphabet (*m*)	*al-fa-beh*
• **accent**	accent (*m*)	*aks-AH*
• **consonant**	consonne (*f*)	*kOH-sun*
• **letter**	lettre (*f*)	*leht-re*
• **phonetics**	phonétique (*f*)	*fun-ay-teek*
• **pronunciation**	prononciation (*f*)	*prun-OH-syah-sy-OH*
• **vowel**	voyelle (*f*)	*vwa-yehl*
article	article (*m*)	*ar-teekle*
• **definite**	défini (*adj*)	*day-fee-nee*
• **indefinite**	indéfini (*adj*)	*EH-day-fee-nee*
clause	proposition (*f*)	*pru-poh-zee-syOH*
• **main**	principale (*adj*)	*prEH-see-pal*
• **relative**	relative (*adj*)	*re-la-teev*
• **subordinate**	subordonnée (*adj*)	*sew-bur-dun-ay*
comparison	comparaison (*f*)	*kOH-par-ayz-OH*
conjunction	conjonction (*f*)	*kOH-zh-OH-ksyOH*
discourse	discours (*m*)	*dees-koor*
• **direct**	direct (*adj*)	*deer-ehkt*
• **indirect**	indirect (*adj*)	*EH-deer-ehkt*
gender	genre (*m*)	*zh-AH-re*
• **masculine**	masculin (*m*)	*mas-kewl-EH*
• **feminine**	féminin (*m*)	*fay-meen-EH*
grammar	grammaire (*f*)	*gram-ehr*
interrogative	interrogatif (*m*)	*EH-teh-rug-a-teef*
mood	mode (*m*)	*mud*
• **conditional**	conditionnel (*adj*)	*kOH-dee-sy-un-ehl*
• **imperative**	impératif (*adj*)	*EH-pay-ra-teef*
• **indicative**	indicatif (*adj*)	*EH-dee-ka-teef*
• **subjunctive**	subjonctif (*adj*)	*sewb-zh-OH-kteef*
noun	nom (*m*)	*nOH*
number	nombre (*m*)	*nOH-bre*
• **plural**	pluriel (*adj*)	*plew-ry-ehl*
• **singular**	singulier (*adj*)	*sEH-gewl-yay*
object	complément d'objet (*m*)	*kOH-playm-AH dub-zh-eh*
• **direct**	direct (*adj*)	*deer-ehkt*
• **indirect**	indirect (*adj*)	*EH-deer-ehkt*

participle	participe (*m*)	*par-tee-seep*
• **past**	passé (*adj*)	*pah-say*
• **present**	présent (*adj*)	*prayz-AH*
partitive	partitif (*m*)	*par-tee-teef*
person	personne (*f*)	*pehr-sun*
• **first**	première (*adj*)	*prem-yehr*
• **second**	deuxième (*adj*)	*duhz-yehm*
• **third**	troisième (*adj*)	*trwahz-yehm*
predicate	attribut (*m*)	*a-tree-bew*
preposition	préposition (*f*)	*pray-poh-zee-sy-OH*
pronoun	pronom (*m*)	*pro-nOH*
• **demonstrative**	démonstratif (*adj*)	*daym-OH-stra-teef*
• **interrogative**	interrogatif (*adj*)	*EH-teh-rug-a-teef*
• **object**	complément d'objet (*m*)	*kOH-playm-AH dub-zh-eh*
• **personal**	personnel (*adj*)	*pehr-sun-ehl*
• **possessive**	possessif (*adj*)	*puss-ay-seef*
• **reflexive**	personnel réfléchi (*adj*)	*pehr-sun ehl ray-flay-shee*
• **relative**	relatif (*adj*)	*re-la-teef*
• **subject**	sujet (*m*)	*sew-zh-eh*
sentence	phrase (*f*)	*frahz*
• **declarative**	déclarative (*adj.*)	*day-klar-a-teev*
• **interrogative**	interrogative (*adj*)	*EH-teh-rug-a-teev*
subject	sujet (*m*)	*sew-zh-eh*
tense	temps (*m*)	*tAH*
• **future**	futur (*m*)	*few-tewr*
• **imperfect**	imparfait (*m*)	*EH-par-feh*
• **past**	passé composé (*m*)	*pah-say kOH-poh-zay*
• **past absolute**	passé simple (*m*)	*pah-say sEH-ple*
• **perfect**	parfait (*m*)	*par-feh*
• **pluperfect**	plus-que-parfait (*m*)	*plews-ke-par-feh*
• **present**	présent (*m*)	*prayz-AH*
verb	verbe (*m*)	*vehrb*
• **active**	active (*adj*)	*ak-teev*
• **conjugation**	conjugaison (*f*)	*kOH-zh-ew-gehz-OH*
• **gerund**	gérondif (*m*)	*zh-ayr-OH-deef*
• **infinitive**	infinitif (*m*)	*EH-fee-nee-teef*
• **intransitive**	intransitif (*adj*)	*EH-tr-AH-see-teef*
• **irregular**	irrégulier (*adj*)	*eer-ray-gewl-yay*
• **modal**	modal (*adj*)	*mud-al*
• **passive**	passive (*adj*)	*pah-seev*
• **reflexive**	pronominal (*adj*)	*pru-num-ee-nal*
• **regular**	régulier (*adj*)	*ray-gewl-yay*
• **transitive**	transitif (*adj*)	*tr-AH-see-teef*

b. DEFINITE ARTICLES

the	le (*m, s*)	*le*
	la (*f, s*)	*la*
	l' (*m/f, s*)	*l*
	les (*m/f, pl*)	*lay*

FOCUS: The Definite Article System

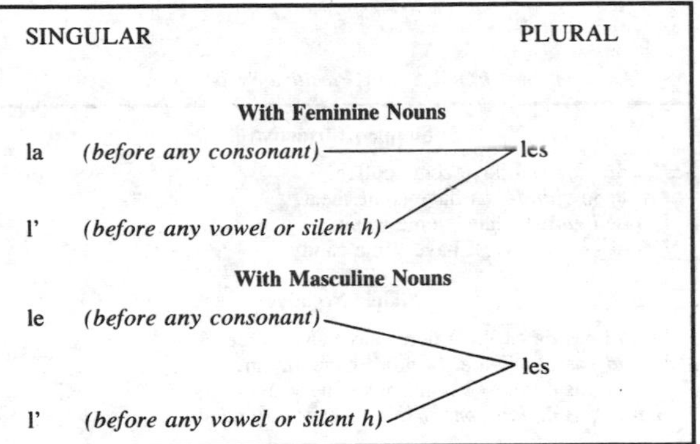

c. INDEFINITE ARTICLES

a, an	un (*m, s*)	*UH*
	une (*f, s*)	*ewn*

FOCUS: The Indefinite Article System

WITH FEMININE NOUNS		WITH MASCULINE NOUNS	
une	*(before any consonant)*	un	*(before any consonant)*
une	*(before any vowel or silent h)*	un	*(before any vowel or silent h)*

d. THE PARTITIVE

some (any)	du (*m, s*)	*dew*
	de l' (*m, s*)	*del*
	de la (*f, s*)	*de la*
	de l' (*f, s*)	*del*
	des (*m/f, pl*)	*day*

FOCUS: The Partitive System

Simple Affirmative

J'ai **du** *café*. / I have some coffee.
J'ai **de la** *viande*. / I have some meat.
J'ai **de** *l'eau*. / I have some water.
J'ai **des** *bonbons*. / I have some candy.

Simple Negative

Je **n'***ai* **pas de** *café*. / I don't have any coffee.
Je **n'***ai* **pas de** *viande*. / I don't have any meat.
Je **n'***ai* **pas d'***eau*. / I don't have any water.
Je **n'***ai* **pas de** *bonbons*. / I don't have any candy.

With an Adjective

J'ai **de jolis** *chapeaux*. / I have some pretty hats.
J'ai **de jolies** *robes*. / I have some pretty dresses.

e. DEMONSTRATIVE ADJECTIVES

this, that	ce (*m, s*)	*se*
	cet (*m, s*)	*seht*
	cette (*f, s*)	*seht*
these, those	ces (*m/f, pl*)	*say*

FOCUS: The Demonstrative Adjective System

Ce garçon est beau. / This boy is handsome.
Cet arbre est beau. / This tree is beautiful.
Cette femme est belle. / This woman is beautiful.
Ces hommes sont beaux. / These men are handsome.
Ces livres sont beaux. / These books are beautiful.
Ces dames sont belles. / These ladies are beautiful.

If you wish to make a contrast between "this" and "that" or "these" and "those," add *-ci* (this, these) or *-là* (that, those) to the noun with a hyphen.

Ce garçon-ci est plus fort que ce garçon-là. / This boy is stronger than that boy.

The form *cet* is used in front of a masculine singular noun or adjective beginning with a vowel or silent *h: cet arbre, cet homme.*
If there is more than one noun, a demonstrative adjective must be used in front of each noun: *cette dame et ce monsieur.*

f. POSSESSIVE ADJECTIVES

my	mon (*m, s*)	*mOH*
	ma (*f, s*)	*ma*
	mes (*m/f, pl*)	*may*
your *(pol)*	votre (*m/f, s*)	*vutr*
	vos (*m/f, pl*)	*vo*
your *(fam)*	ton (*m, s*)	*tOH*
	ta (*f, s*)	*ta*
	tes (*m,/f*), (*pl*)	*tay*
his, her	son (*m, s*)	*sOH*
	sa (*f, s*)	*sa*
	ses (*m/f, pl*)	*say*
our	notre (*m/f*, (*s*)	*nutr*
	nos (*m/f, pl*)	*no*
their	leur (*m/f, s*)	*lur*
	leurs (*m/f, pl*)	*lur*

FOCUS: The Possessive Adjective System

MASCULINE	
Singular	**Plural**
mon livre/my book	*mes livres*/my books
ton stylo/your pen	*tes stylos*/your pens
son ballon/ his (her, its) balloon	*ses ballons*/ his (her, its) balloons
notre parapluie/our umbrella	*nos parapluies*/our umbrellas
votre sandwich/your sandwich	*vos sandwichs*/your sandwiches
leur gâteau/their cake	*leurs gâteaux*/their cakes
FEMININE	
Singular	**Plural**
ma robe/my dress	*mes robes*/my dresses
ta jaquette/your jacket	*tes jaquettes*/your jackets
sa balle/his (her, its) ball	*ses balles*/his (her, its) balls
notre maison/our house	*nos maisons*/our houses
votre voiture/your car	*vos voitures*/your cars
leur soeur/their sister	*leurs soeurs*/their sisters

g. PREPOSITIONS

among	parmi	*par-mee*
at	à	*a*
between	entre	*AH-tre*
for	pour	*poor*
from	de	*de*
in	dans	*dAH*
of	de	*de*
on	sur	*sewr*
to	à	*a*
with	avec	*av-ehk*

FOCUS: Prepositional Contractions

Preposition		Article		Contraction
à *a*	+	le *le*	=	au *oh*
	+	les *lay*	=	aux *oh*
de *de*	+	le *le*	=	du *dew*
	+	les *lay*	=	des *day*

h. SUBJECT PRONOUNS

I	je	*zhe*
you	tu (*s, fam*)	*tew*
you	vous (*s, pol*)	*voo*
he, it	il	*eel*
she, it	elle	*ehl*
one	on (*indef*)	*OH*
we	nous	*noo*
you	vous (*pl*)	*voo*
they	ils (*m*)	*eel*
	elles (*f*)	*ehl*

i. DIRECT OBJECT PRONOUNS

me	me	*me*
you	te (*s, fam*)	*te*
you	vous (*s, pol*)	*voo*
him	le	*le*
her	la	*la*
it	le (*m*)	*le*
	la (*f*)	*la*
us	nous	*noo*
you	vous (*pl*)	*voo*
them	les	*lay*

FOCUS: Direct Object Pronouns

Person	Singular	Plural
1st	*me* (*m'*)/me	*nous*/us
2d	*te*(*t'*)/you (familiar)	*vous*/you (singular polite or plural)
3d	*le* (*l'*)/him, it *la* (*l'*)/her, it (person or thing)	*les*/them (persons or things)

j. INDIRECT OBJECT PRONOUNS

to me	me	*me*
to you	te (*s, fam*)	*te*
	vous (*s, pol*)	*voo*
to him/to her	lui	*lew-ee*
to us	nous	*noo*
to you	vous (*pl*)	*voo*
to them	leur	*lur*

FOCUS: Indirect Object Pronouns

Person	Singular		Plural	
1st	*me (m')*	to me	*nous*	to us
2d	*te(t')*	to you (familiar)	*vous*	to you (singular polite or plural)
3d	*lui*	to him, to her	*leur*	to them

k. REFLEXIVE PRONOUNS (ALL BEFORE VERBS)

myself	me	*me*
yourself	te (*s, fam*)	*te*
yourself	vous (*s, pol*)	*voo*
himself/herself/ oneself	se	*se*
ourselves	nous	*noo*
yourselves	vous	*voo*
themselves	se	*se*

FOCUS: Reflexive Pronouns

Person	Singular	Plural
1st	*je me lave*	*nous nous lavons*
2d	*tu te laves*	*vous vous lavez*
3rd	*il se lave* *elle se lave* *on se lave*	*ils se lavent* *elles se lavent*

l. DISJUNCTIVE PRONOUNS

FOCUS: Disjunctive Pronouns (as objects of prepositions)

Person	Singular		Plural	
1st	*moi*	me, I	*nous*	us, we
2nd	*toi*	you (familiar)	*vous*	you (formal singular or plural)
3rd	*soi* *lui* *elle*	oneself him, he her, she	*eux* *elles*	them, they (m.) them, they (f.)

m. DEMONSTRATIVE PRONOUNS

FOCUS: Demonstrative Pronouns

	Singular	Plural
Masculine	*celui*/the one	*ceux*/the ones
Feminine	*celle*/the one	*celles*/the ones

n. POSSESSIVE PRONOUNS

FOCUS: Possessive Pronouns

MASCULINE			
Singular		**Plural**	
le mien	mine	*les miens*	mine
le tien	yours (familiar)	*les tiens*	yours (familiar)
le sien	his, hers, its	*les siens*	his, hers, its
le nôtre	ours	*les nôtres*	ours
le vôtre	yours	*les vôtres*	yours
le leur	theirs	*les leurs*	theirs
FEMININE			
Singular		**Plural**	
la mienne	mine	*les miennes*	mine
la tienne	yours (familiar)	*les tiennes*	yours (familiar)
la sienne	his, hers, its	*les siennes*	his, hers, its
la nôtre	ours	*les nôtres*	ours
la vôtre	yours	*les vôtres*	yours
la leur	theirs	*les leurs*	theirs

FOCUS: Word Order of Pronouns in Four Types of Sentences

Declarative Sentence with a Verb in a Simple Tense (e.g., present)

$$\textbf{SUBJECT} \rightarrow \textbf{ne (n')} + \left\{\begin{matrix} \textit{me (m')} \\ \textit{te (t')} \\ \textit{se (s')} \\ \textit{nous} \\ \textit{vous} \end{matrix}\right\} \text{OR} \left\{\begin{matrix} \textit{le} \\ \textit{la} \\ \textit{l'} \\ \textit{les} \end{matrix}\right\} \textit{AND/OR} \left\{\begin{matrix} \textit{lui} \\ \textit{leur} \end{matrix}\right\}$$

$$\text{OR } \textit{y} + \textit{en} + \textbf{VERB} \rightarrow \textit{pas}$$

Declarative Sentence with a Verb in a Compound Tense (e.g., passé composé)

$$\textbf{SUBJECT} \rightarrow \textbf{\textit{ne (n')}} + \left\{\begin{matrix} \textit{me (m')} \\ \textit{te (t')} \\ \textit{se (s')} \\ \textit{nous} \\ \textit{vous} \end{matrix}\right\} \text{ OR } \left\{\begin{matrix} \textit{le} \\ \textit{la} \\ \textit{l'} \\ \textit{les} \end{matrix}\right\} \text{ AND/OR } \left\{\begin{matrix} \textit{lui} \\ \textit{leur} \end{matrix}\right\}$$

$$\text{OR } \textit{y} + \textit{en} + \underset{\substack{\text{(auxiliary verb} \\ \textit{avoir} \text{ or } \textit{être} \text{ in} \\ \text{a simple tense)}}}{\textbf{VERB}} \rightarrow \textbf{\textit{pas}} + \text{past participle}$$

Affirmative Imperative Sentence

$$\textbf{VERB} + \left\{\begin{matrix} \textit{le} \\ \textit{la} \\ \textit{l'} \\ \textit{les} \end{matrix}\right\} \text{ OR } \left\{\begin{matrix} \textit{moi (m')} \\ \textit{toi (t')} \\ \textit{nous} \\ \textit{vous} \end{matrix}\right\} \text{ AND/OR } \left\{\begin{matrix} \textit{lui} \\ \textit{leur} \end{matrix}\right\} \text{ OR } \textit{y} + \textit{en}$$

Negative Imperative Sentence

$$\textbf{Ne (N')} + \left\{\begin{matrix} \textit{me (m')} \\ \textit{te (t')} \\ \textit{nous} \\ \textit{vous} \end{matrix}\right\} \text{ OR } \left\{\begin{matrix} \textit{le} \\ \textit{la} \\ \textit{l'} \\ \textit{les} \end{matrix}\right\} \text{ OR } \left\{\begin{matrix} \textit{lui} \\ \textit{leur} \end{matrix}\right\} \text{ OR } \textit{y} + \textit{en} + \textbf{VERB} \rightarrow \textbf{\textit{pas}}$$

o. OTHER PRONOUNS

everyone	tout le monde (*m*)	*tool mOHd*
everything	tout (*m*)	*too*
	toute (*f*)	*toot*

no one	personne (*indef*)	*pehr-sun*
one (*in general*)	on (*indef*)	*OH*
others	autrui (*indef*)	*oh-trew-ee*
some, of it, of them	en (*before or after a verb*)	*AH*
some (*people*)	des gens	*day zh-AH*
someone	quelqu'un (*m*)	*kehlk-UH*
	quelqu'une (*f*)	*kehlk-ewn*
something	quelque chose	*kehlke sh-oh-z*

p. CONJUNCTIONS

although	bien que	*byEH-ke*
	quoique	*kwa-ke*
and	et	*ay*
as (since)	comme	*kum*
as if	comme si	*kum-see*
as soon as	dès que	*deh-ke*
	aussitôt que	*oh-see-toh-ke*
because	parce que	*pars-ke*
but	mais	*meh*
even though	même si	*mehm-see*
however	pourtant	*poor-tAH*
if	si	*see*
in order that, so that	afin que	*afEH-ke*
	pour que	*poor-ke*
or	ou	*oo*
provided that	pourvu que	*poor-vew-ke*
since	depuis que	*de-pew-ee-ke*
therefore, consequently	donc	*dOHk*
unless	à moins que	*a-mwEH-ke*
until	jusqu'à ce que	*zh-ews-kas-ke*
when	quand	*kAH*
while, whereas	tandis que	*tAH-dee-ke*

9. REQUESTING INFORMATION

answer	réponse (*f*)	*rayp-OH-s*
• **answer**	répondre (*v*)	*rayp-OH-dre*
ask (for)	demander (*v*)	*dem-AH-day*
• **make a request**	faire une demande	*fehr ewn dem-AH-de*
Can you tell me . . . ?	Pourriez-vous me dire . . .? (*pol*)	*poor-ee-ay voom deer*
	Peux-tu me dire . . . ? (*fam*)	*puh-tewm deer*

How?	Comment?	*kum-AH*
How come?	Mais comment?	*meh kum-AH*
How much?	Combien?	*kOH-byEH*
I don't understand	Je ne comprends pas.	*zhen kOH-pr-AH pah*
So?	Et alors?	*ay al-or*
What?	Comment?	*kum-AH*
	Pardon?	*pard-OH*
What do you call this (that) in French?	Comment appelle-t-on ceci (cela) en français?	*kum-AH a-pehl-tOH se-see(sla) AH frAH seh*
What does it mean?	Que veut dire cela?	*ke-vuh-deer-sla*
	Que signifie cela?	*ke-see-ny-ee-fee-sla*
When?	Quand?	*kAH*
Where?	Où?	*oo*
Which (one)?	Lequel? (*m*)	*le-kehl*
	Laquelle? (*f*)	*la-kehl*
Who?	Qui?	*kee*
Why?	Pourquoi?	*poor-kwa*

PEOPLE

10. FAMILY AND FRIENDS

a. FAMILY MEMBERS

aunt	tante (*f*)	*tAHt*
brother	frère (*m*)	*frehr*
• **brother-in-law**	beau-frère (*m*)	*boh-frehr*
cousin	cousin (*m*)	*koo-zEH*
	cousine (*f*)	*koo-zeen*
dad	papa (*m*)	*pa-pa*
daughter	fille (*f*)	*fee-y*
• **daughter-in-law**	belle-fille (*f*)	*behl-fee-y*
family	famille (*f*)	*fa-mee-y*
• **family relationship**	parenté (*f*)	*pa-rAH-tay*
father	père (*m*)	*pehr*
• **father-in-law**	beau-père (*m*)	*boh-pehr*
grandchildren	petits-enfants (*m, f, pl*)	*ptee-zAH-fAH*
grandfather	grand-père (*m*)	*grAH-pehr*
grandmother	grand-mère (*f*)	*grAH-mehr*
husband	mari (*m*)	*ma-ree*
mom	maman (*f*)	*ma-mAH*
mother	mère (*f*)	*mehr*
• **mother-in-law**	belle-mère (*f*)	*behl-mehr*
nephew	neveu (*m*)	*ne-vuh*
niece	nièce (*f*)	*nee-ehss*
parents	parents (*m, pl*)	*pa-rAH*
relatives	proches parents (*m, pl*)	*prush parAH*
sister	sœur (*f*)	*sur*
• **sister-in-law**	belle-sœur (*f*)	*behl-sur*
son	fils (*m*)	*fee-ss*
• **son-in-law**	gendre (*m*)	*zh-AH-dre*
twin	jumeau (*m*)	*zh-ew-moh*
	jumelle (*f*)	*zh-ew-mehl*
uncle	oncle (*m*)	*OH-kle*
wife	femme (*f*)	*fam*
	épouse (*f*)	*ay-pooz*

b. FRIENDS

acquaintance	connaissance (*f*)	*kun-eh-sAH-ss*

boyfriend	ami (*m*)	*a-mee*
	petit ami (m)	*ptee-a-mee*
chum	copain (*m*)	*kup-EH*
	copine (*f*)	*kup-een*
colleague, work associate	collègue (*m, f*)	*kul-ehg*
enemy	ennemi(e) (*m, f*)	*ehn-mee*
fiancé	fiancé (*m*)	*fee-AH-say*
fiancée	fiancée (*f*)	*fee-AH-say*
friend	ami(e) (*m, f*)	*a-mee*
• **become friends**	devenir (*v*) amis	*de-vneer-a-mee*
	faire (*v*) l'amitié	*fehr la-mee-tee-ay*
• **between friends**	entre amis	*AH-tre a-mee*
• **break off a friendship**	rompre (*v*) une amitié	*rOHm-pre ewn a-mee-tee-ay*
• **close friend**	ami(e) intime (*m, f*)	*a-mee EH-teem*
• **dear friend**	cher (chère) ami(e) (*m, f*)	*sh-ehr a-mee*
• **family friend**	ami(e) (*m, f*) de famille	*a-meed fa-mee-y*
• **friendship**	amitié (*f*)	*a-mee-tee-ay*
girlfriend	amie (*f*)	*a-mee*
	petite amie (*f*)	*ptee-ta-mee*
lover	amant (*m*)	*a-mAH*
	amante (*f*)	*a-mAH-t*
• **love affair**	affaire (*f*) d'amour	*a-fehr da-moor*

11. DESCRIBING PEOPLE

a. GENDER AND APPEARANCE

attractive	attractif (*adj, m*)	*a-trak-teef*
	attractive (*f*)	*a-trak-teev*
beautiful, handsome	beau (*adj, m*)	*boh*
	bel (*adj, m*)	*behl*
	belle (*f*)	*behl*
• **beauty**	beauté (*f*)	*boh-tay*
big	grand (*adj, m*)	*grAH*
	grande (*f*)	*grAHd*
• **bigness**	grandeur (*f*)	*grAH-dur*
• **become big**	grandir (*v*)	*grAH-deer*
blond	blond (*m*)	*blOH*
• **blonde**	blonde (*f*)	*blOHd*
body	corps (*m*)	*ku-r*
• **bodily physique**	physique (*m*)	*fee-zeek*
boy	garçon (*m*)	*gar-sOH*
clean	propre (*adj*)	*pru-pre*

curly-haired	cheveux bouclés	*shvuh boo-klay*
dark-haired	cheveux bruns	*shvuh brUH*
dirty	sale (*adj*)	*sal*
elegance	élégance (*f*)	*ay-lay-gAH-ss*
• **elegant**	élégant (*adj, m*)	*ay-lay-gAH*
	élégante (*f*)	*ay-lay-gAH-t*
• **elegantly**	élégamment (*adv*)	*ay-lay-ga-mAH*
• **inelegant**	inélégant (*adj, m*)	*ee-nay-lay-gAH*
	inélégante (*f*)	*ee-nay-lay-gAH-t*
fat	gros (*adj, m*)	*groh*
	grosse (*f*)	*groh-ss*
• **become fat**	grossir (*v*)	*groh-seer*
• **obesity**	obésité (*f*)	*u-bay-zee-tay*
female	femelle (*f*)	*fe-mehl*
• **feminine**	féminin (*adj, m*)	*fay-mee-nEH*
	féminine (*f*)	*fay-mee-neen*
gentleman	monsieur (*m*)	*me-sy-uh*
girl	jeune fille (*f*)	*zh-uhn fee-y*
health	santé (*f*)	*sAH-tay*
• **healthy**	sain (*adj, m*)	*sEH*
	saine (*f*)	*sehn*
	en bonne santé	*AH bun sAH-tay*
height	taille (*f*)	*tah-y*
	stature (*f*)	*sta-tewr*
• **How tall are you?**	Quelle taille avez-vous?	*kehl tah-y avay-voo*
• **I am . . . tall.**	J'ai la taille . . .	*zh-ay la tah-y*
• **medium (average) height**	la taille moyenne	*la tah-y mwa-y-ehn*
• **short**	petit (*adj, m*)	*ptee*
	petite (*f*)	*pteet*
• **tall**	grand (*adj, m*)	*grAH*
	grande (*f*)	*grAHd*
lady	dame	*dahm*
• **young lady**	demoiselle	*de-mwah-zehl*
large	grand (*adj, m*)	*grAH*
	grande (*f*)	*grAHd*
male	mâle	*mahl*
• **masculine**	masculin	*mas-kew-lEH*
• **virile**	viril(e) (*m, f*)	*vee-reel*
man	homme	*um*
• **young man**	jeune homme	*zh-un um*
physique (appearance)	aspect physique	*as-peh fee-zeek*
red-haired	roux (*adj, m*)	*roo*
	rousse (*f*)	*roos*
sex	sexe (*m*)	*sehks*
sick	malade (*adj*)	*ma-lahd*

• sickness	maladie (*f*)	*ma-lah-dee*
• become sick	tomber (*v*) malade	*tOH-bay ma-lahd*
small, little	petit (*adj, m*)	*ptee*
	petite (*f*)	*pteet*
strength	force (*f*)	*forss*
• strong	fort (*adj, m*)	*for*
	forte (*f*)	*fort*
ugly	laid (*adj, m*)	*leh*
	laide (*f*)	*lehd*
• ugliness	laideur (*f*)	*lehd-ur*
weak	faible (*adj*)	*feh-ble*
• weakness	faiblesse (*f*)	*feh-bless*
• become weak	s'affaiblir (*v*)	*sa-feh-bleer*
weight	poids (*m*)	*pwah*
• heavy	lourd (*adj, m*)	*loor*
	lourde (*f*)	*loord*
• How much do you weigh?	Combien pesez-vous?	*kOH-byEH pe-zay voo*
• I weigh . . .	Je pèse . . .	*zhe pehz*
• light	léger (*adj, m*)	*lay-zh-ay*
	légère (*f*)	*lay-zh-ehr*
• skinny, thin	maigre (*adj*)	*meh-gre*
• slim, slender	svelte	*svehlt*
	mince	*mEH-ss*
• weigh oneself	se peser (*refl v*)	*se pe-zay*
• become thin	maigrir (*v*)	*meh-greer*
• gain weight	prendre (*v*) du poids	*prAH-dre dew pwah*
• lose weight	perdre (*v*) du poids	*pehr-dre dew pwah*
woman	femme	*fam*

b. CONCEPTS OF AGE

adolescence	adolescence (*f*)	*a-du-leh-sAH-ss*
• adolescent, teenager	adolescent (*m*)	*a-du-leh-sAH*
	adolescente (*f*)	*a-du-leh-sAH-t*
adult	adulte (*m, f*)	*a-dewlt*
age	âge (*m*)	*ah-zh*
baby, child	bébé	*bay-bay*
	enfant (*m, f*)	*AH-fAH*
• children	enfants	*AH-fAH*
boy	garçon	*gar-sOH*
elderly person	une personne âgée	*ewn pehr-sun ah-zh-ay*
• have white hair	avoir les cheveux blancs	*a-vwahr lay shvuh blAH*
girl	(jeune) fille	*(zh-un) fee-y*
grow up	grandir (*v*)	*grAH-deer*

old	vieux (*m*)	*vyuh*
	vieil (*m*)	*vy-eh-y*
	vieille (*f*)	*vy-eh-y*
• **old age**	vieillesse (*f*)	*vyeh-yehss*
• **older**	plus vieux	*plew vyuh*
• **older brother**	frère aîné	*frehr eh-nay*
• **older sister**	sœur aînée	*s-ur eh-nay*
• **How old are you?**	Quel âge avez-vous (*pol*)?	*kehl ah-zh a-vay voo*
	Quel âge as-tu (*fam*)?	*kehl ah-zh a tew*
• **I am . . . old.**	J'ai . . . ans	*zh-ay AH*
• **two-year-old**	de deux ans	*de duh zAH*
• **three-year-old**	de trois ans	*de trwah zAH*
• **become old**	vieillir (*v*)	*vyeh-yeer*
young	jeune (*adj*)	*zh-un*
• **younger**	plus jeune	*plew zh-un*
• **younger brother**	frère cadet	*frehr ka-deh*
• **younger sister**	sœur cadette	*s-ur ka-deht*
• **youth**	jeunesse (*f*)	*zh-un-ehss*
• **youthful**	juvénile (*adj*)	*zh-ew-vay-neel*

c. MARRIAGE AND THE HUMAN LIFE CYCLE

anniversary	anniversaire (*m*)	*a-nee-vehr-sehr*
• **diamond anniversary**	noces (*f, pl*) de diamant	*nuss de dya-mAH*
• **golden anniversary**	noces d'or	*nuss dur*
• **silver anniversary**	noces d'argent	*nuss dar-zh-AH*
bachelor, unmarried	célibataire	*say-lee-ba-tehr*
birth	naissance (*f*)	*neh-sAH-ss*
• **birthday**	anniversaire (*m*)	*a-nee-vehr-sehr*
• **celebrate one's birthday**	fêter (*v*) l'anniversaire	*feh-tay la-nee-vehr-sehr*
• **Happy birthday!**	Bon anniversaire!	*bun-a-nee-vehr-sehr*
• **be born**	naître (*v*)	*neh-tre*
• **I was born on . . .**	Je suis né(e) le . . .	*zhe sew-ee nay le*
bride	mariée (*f*)	*ma-ree-ay*
death	mort (*f*)	*mor*
• **die**	mourir (*v*)	*moo-reer*
divorce	divorce (*m*)	*dee-vorss*
• **divorce**	divorcer (*v*)	*dee-vor-say*
• **divorced**	divorcé (*adj*)	*dee-vor-say*

engagement	fiançailles (*f, pl*)	*fee-AH-sa-y*
• become engaged	se fiancer (*refl v*)	*se fee-AH-say*
• engaged	fiancé (*adj*)	*fee-AH-say*
fiancé	fiancé	*fee-AH-say*
fiancée	fiancée	*fee-AH-say*
get used to	s'habituer (*v*)	*sa-bee-tew-ay*
gift	cadeau (*m*)	*ka-doh*
• give a gift	donner (*v*) un cadeau	*dun-ay UH ka-doh*
go to school	aller (*v*) à l'école	*alay a lay-kul*
groom (bridegroom)	marié (*m*)	*ma-ree-ay*
heredity	hérédité (*f*)	*ay-ray-dee-tay*
• inherit	hériter (*v*)	*ay-ree-tay*
honeymoon	lune (*f*) de miel	*lewn de mee-ehl*
husband	époux	*ay-poo*
	mari	*ma-ree*
kiss	baiser (*m*)	*beh-zay*
• kiss	embrasser (*v*)	*AH-bra-say*
life	vie (*f*)	*vee*
• live	vivre (*v*)	*vee-vre*
love	amour (*m*)	*a-moor*
• love	aimer (*v*)	*ay-may*
• fall in love	tomber (*v*) amoureux	*tOH-bay a-moo-ruh*
• in love	amoureux (*adj*)	*a-moo-ruh*
marital status	état civil	*ay-ta see-veel*
marriage, matrimony	mariage (*m*)	*ma-ree-ah-zh*
• married	marié(e) (*n, adj, m, f*)	*ma-ree-ay*
• marry (someone)	épouser (*v*)	*ay-poo-zay*
	se marier (*v*) avec	*se-ma-ree-ay avehk*
• unmarried	célibataire	*say-lee-ba-tehr*
• newlyweds	nouveaux-mariés (*n, m, pl*)	*noo-voh ma-ree-ay*
pregnancy	grossesse (*f*)	*groh-seh-ss*
• be pregnant	être (*v*) enceinte	*eh-tre AH-sEHt*
• give birth	accoucher (*v*)	*a-koo-shay*
• have a baby	avoir (*v*) un enfant	*avwar UH nAH-fAH*
raise (someone)	élever (*v*)	*ayl-vay*
reception	réception (*f*)	*ray-sehp-syOH*
separation	séparation (*f*)	*say-pa-ra-syOH*
• separate	se séparer (*v*)	*se say-pa-ray*
• separated	séparé (*adj*)	*say-pa-ray*
spouse	époux (*m*)	*ay-poo*
	épouse (*f*)	*ay-pooz*
wedding	mariage (*m*)	*ma-ree-ah-zh*
	noce (*f*)	*nuss*

• wedding invitation	faire-part de mariage (*m*)	*fehr par de ma-ree-ah-zh*
• wedding ring	anneau (*m*) d'alliance	*a-noh da-lee-AH-ss*
widow	veuve	*vuv*
widower	veuf	*vuf*
wife	femme	*fam*
	épouse	*ay-pooz*

d. RELIGION AND RACE

For nationalities see Section 30.

agnostic	agnostique (*adj/m, f*)	*ag-nus-teek*
archbishop	archevêque	*arsh-vehk*
atheism	athéisme (*m*)	*a-tay-ee-sm*
• atheist	athée (*m, f*)	*a-tay*
baptism	baptême (*m*)	*ba-tehm*
belief	crédence (*f*)	*kray-dAH-ss*
	croyance (*f*)	*krwah-yAH-ss*
• believe	croire (*v*)	*krwar*
• believe in	croire (*v*) en	*krwahr AH*
• believer	croyant (*m*)	*krwa-yAH*
	croyante (*f*)	*krwa-yAHt*
bishop	évêque	*ay-vehk*
Buddhism	Bouddhisme (*m*)	*boo-dees-me*
• Buddhist	Bouddhiste (*m, f*)	*boo-deest*
catechism	catéchisme (*m*)	*ka-tay-shee-sme*
Catholic	Catholique (*adj*)	*ka-tul-eek*
• Catholicism	Catholicisme (*m*)	*ka-tul-ee-sees-me*
Christian	Chrétien (*m*)	*kray-tee-yEH*
	Chrétienne (*f*)	*kray-tee-yehn*
• Christianity	Christianisme (*m*)	*krees-tee-a-nee-sme*
church	église (*f*)	*ay-gleez*
confirmation	confirmation (*f*)	*kOH-feer-ma-syOH*
faith	foi (*f*)	*fwa*
• faithful	fidèle (*adj*)	*fee-dehl*
God	Dieu	*dyuh*
Hebrew, Jewish	Hébreu	*ay-bruh*
	juif (*m*)	*zh-ew-eef*
	juive (*f*)	*zh-ew-eev*
human	humain (*m*)	*ew-mEH*
	humaine (*f*)	*ew-mehn*

• **human being**	être humain (*m*)	*eh-tre ew-mEH*
• **humanity**	humanité (*f*)	*ew-ma-nee-tay*
Hindu	Hindou (*n/adj, m*)	*EH-doo*
	Hindoue (*n/adj, f*)	*EH-doo*
Islamic	Islamique (*adj*)	*ee-sla-meek*
layperson	laïc, laïque (*adj, m, f*)	*la-eek*
• **laity**	laïcité (*f*)	*la-ee-see-tay*
Mass	Messe (*f*)	*mehss*
minister	ministre (*m*)	*mee-nee-stre*
monk	moine	*mwahn*
mosque	mosquée (*f*)	*mus-kay*
Muslim	Musulman (*m*)	*mew-zewl-mAH*
	Musulmane (*f*)	*mew-zewl-mahn*
myth	mythe (*m*)	*meet*
nun	religieuse	*re-lee-zh-yuhz*
oriental	oriental(e) (*m, f*)	*or-yAH-tal*
Orthodox	Orthodoxe	*or-tud-uks*
pagan	païen (*n/adj, m*)	*pa-yEH*
	païenne (*n, adj, f*)	*pa-yehn*
people	gens (*m & f, pl*)	*zh-AH*
person	personne (*f*)	*pehr-sun*
pray	prier (*v*)	*pree-yay*
• **prayer**	prière (*f*)	*pree-yehr*
priest	prêtre (*m*)	*preh-tre*
Protestant	Protestant (*m*)	*pru-tehs-tAH*
	Protestante (*f*)	*pru-tehs-tAHt*
• **Protestantism**	Protestantisme (*m*)	*pru-tehs-tAH-tees-me*
rabbi	rabbin	*ra-bEH*
race	race (*f*)	*rass*
religion	religion (*f*)	*re-lee-zh-yOH*
• **religious**	pieux (*adj, m*)	*pyuh*
	pieuse (*f*)	*pyuhz*
rite	rite (*m*)	*reet*
soul	âme (*f*)	*ahm*
spirit	esprit (*m*)	*ehs-pree*
• **spiritual**	spirituel(le) (*adj, m, f*)	*spee-ree-tew-ehl*
synagogue	synagogue (*f*)	*see-na-gug*
temple	temple (*m*)	*tAH-ple*
western	occidental(e) (*adj, m, f*)	*uks-ee-dAH-tal*

e. CHARACTERISTICS AND SOCIAL TRAITS

active	actif (*adj, m*)	*ak-teef*
	active (*f*)	*ak-teev*

• activity	activité (*f*)	*ak-tee-vee-tay*
adapt	adapter (*v*)	*a-dap-tay*
• adaptable	adaptable (*adj*)	*a-dap-ta-bl*
affection	affection (*f*)	*a-fehk-syOH*
• affectionate	affectueux (*adj, m*)	*a-fehk-tew-uh*
	affectueuse (*f*)	*a-fehk-tew-uhz*
aggressive	agressif (*adj, m*)	*a-greh-seef*
	agressive (*f*)	*a-greh-seev*
• aggressiveness	agressivité (*f*)	*a-greh-see-vee-tay*
altruism	altruisme (*m*)	*al-trew-ee-sm*
• altruistic, altruist	altruiste (*m/f*)	*al-trew-eest*
ambition	ambition (*f*)	*AH-bee-syOH*
• ambitious	ambitieux (*adj, m*)	*AH-bee-syuh*
	ambitieuse (*f*)	*AH-bee-syuhz*
anger	colère (*f*)	*kul-ehr*
• angry	en colère	*AH kul-ehr*
	fâché(e) (*adj*)	*fah-shay*
• become angry	se fâcher (*v*)	*se fah-shay*
anxious	anxieux (*adj, m*)	*AH-ksyuh*
	anxieuse (*f*)	*AH-ksyuhz*
• anxiousness	anxiété (*f*)	*AH-ksee-ay-tay*
arrogant	arrogant (*adj, m*)	*a-rug-AH*
	arrogante (*f*)	*a-rug-AHt*
art	art (*m*)	*ar*
artistic, talented	artistique (*adj*)	*ar-tees-teek*
astute	astucieux (*adj, m*)	*a-stew-syuh*
	astucieuse (*f*)	*a-stew-syuhz*
• astuteness	astuce (*f*)	*a-stewss*
attractive	attrayant (*adj, m*)	*a-treh-yAH*
	attrayante (*f*)	*a-treh-yAHt*
avarice, greed	avarice (*f*)	*a-va-rees*
• avaricious, greedy	avare (*adj, n*)	*a-var*
bad, mean	méchant (*adj, m*)	*may-shAH*
	méchante (*f*)	*may-shAHt*
• meanness	méchanceté (*f*)	*may-shAH-stay*
brash, bold	effronté(e) (*adj*)	*ay-frOH-tay*
brilliant	brillant(e) (*adj*)	*bree-yAH(t)*
calm	calme (*adj*)	*kalm*
• calmness	calme (*m*)	*kalm*
character	caractère (*m*)	*ka-rak-tehr*
• characteristic	caractéristique (*adj, n, f*)	*ka-rak-tay-rees-teek*
• characterize	caractériser (*v*)	*ka-rak-tay-ree-zay*
conformist	conformiste (*m, f*)	*kOH-furm-eest*
• nonconformist	non-conformiste (*m, f*)	*nOH-kOH-furm-eest*

conscience	conscience (*f*)	*kOH-syAH-ss*
• **conscientious**	consciencieux (*adj, m*)	*kOH-syAH-syuh*
	consciencieuse (*f*)	*kOH-syAH-syuhz*
conservative	conservateur (*adj, m*)	*kOH-sehr-va-tur*
	conservatrice (*f*)	*kOH-sehr-va-treess*
courage	courage (*m*)	*koo-ra-zh*
• **courageous**	courageux (*adj, m*)	*koo-ra-zh-uh*
	courageuse (*f*)	*koo-ra-zh-uhz*
courteous	courtois (*adj, m*)	*koor-twa*
	courtoise (*f*)	*koor-twaz*
• **courtesy**	courtoisie (*f*)	*koor-twa-zee*
• **discourteous**	discourtois (*adj, m*)	*dees-koor-twa*
	discourtoise (*f*)	*dees-koor-twaz*
crazy, mad	fou (*adj, m*)	*foo*
	fol (*adj, m*)	*ful*
	folle (*f*)	*ful*
• **madness**	folie (*f*)	*ful-ee*
creative	créatif (*adj, m*)	*kray-a-teef*
	créative (*f*)	*kray-a-teev*
critical	critique (*adj*)	*kree-teek*
cry	pleurer (*v*)	*plur-ay*
• **crying**	en larmes	*AH larm*
cultured	cultivé(e) (*adj, m, f*)	*kewl-tee-vay*
curiosity	curiosité (*f*)	*kew-ryo-zee-tay*
• **curious**	curieux (*adj, m*)	*kew-ry-uh*
	curieuse (*f*)	*kew-ry-uhz*
delicate	délicat(e) (*adj, m, f*)	*day-lee-ka(t)*
diligence	diligence (*f*)	*dee-lee-zh-AH-s*
• **diligent, hard-working**	diligent(e) (*adj, m, f*)	*dee-lee-zh-AH(t)*
diplomatic	diplomatique (*adj*)	*dee-plu-ma-teek*
dishonest	malhonnête (*adj*)	*mal-un-eht*
• **dishonesty**	malhonnêteté (*f*)	*mal-un-eht-tay*
dynamic	dynamique (*adj*)	*dee-na-meek*
eccentric	excentrique (*adj*)	*ehk-sAH-treek*
egoism	égoïsme (*m*)	*ay-gu-ees-me*
• **egoist, egoistic**	égoïste (*adj*)	*ay-gu-eest*
eloquence	éloquence (*f*)	*ay-luk-AH-s*
• **eloquent**	éloquent(e) (*adj, m, f*)	*ay-luk-AH(t)*
energetic	énergique (*adj*)	*ay-nehr-zh-eek*
• **energy**	énergie (*f*)	*ay-nehr-zh-ee*
envious	envieux (*adj, m*)	*AH-vyuh*
	envieuse (*f*)	*AH-vyuhz*
• **envy**	envie (*f*)	*AH-vee*
faithful	fidèle (*adj*)	*fee-dehl*

fascinate	fasciner (*v*)	*fa-see-nay*
• **fascinating**	fascinant(e) (*adj, m, f*)	*fa-see nAH(t)*
• **fascination, attractiveness**	fascination (*f*)	*fa-see-nah-syOH*
fool, clown	bouffon (*m*)	*boo-fOH*
	clown (*m*)	*kloon*
• **foolish, silly**	bête (*adj*)	*beht*
	sot (*adj, m*)	*soh*
	sotte (*f*)	*sut*
friendly	amical(e) (*adj, m, f*)	*a-mee-kal*
funny	drôle (*adj*)	*drohl*
	comique (*adj*)	*kum-eek*
	marrant(e) (*adj, m, f*)	*marAH(t)*
fussy	méticuleux (*adj, m*)	*may-tee-kew-luh*
	méticuleuse (*f*)	*may-tee-kew-luhz*
generosity	générosité (*f*)	*zh-ay-nay-roh-zee-tay*
• **generous**	généreux (*adj, m*)	*zh-ay-nay-ruh*
	généreuse (*f*)	*zh-ay-nay-ruhz*
gentle	gentil(le) (*adj, m, f*)	*zhAHtee (y)*
good, kind	bon (*adj, m*)	*bOH*
	bonne (*f*)	*bun*
• **goodness, kindness**	bonté (*f*)	*bOH-tay*
good (*at something*)	habile (*adj*)	*a-beel*
graceful	gracieux (*adj, m*)	*gra-syuh*
	gracieuse (*f*)	*gra-syuhz*
habit	habitude (*f*)	*a-bee-tewd*
happiness	bonheur (*m*)	*bun-ur*
	contentement (*m*)	*kOH-tAHt-mAH*
	félicité (*f*)	*fay-lee-see-tay*
• **happy**	heureux (*adj, m*)	*ur-uh*
	heureuse (*f*)	*ur-uhz*
	content(e) (*adj, m, f*)	*kOH-tAH(t)*
	fortuné(e) (*adj, m, f*)	*for-tew-nay*
hate	haine (*f*)	*ehn*
• **hate**	haïr (*v*)	*a-eer*
• **hateful**	détestable (*adj*)	*day-tehs-tabl*
honest	honnête (*adj*)	*un-eht*
• **honesty**	honnêteté (*f*)	*un-eht-tay*
humanitarian	humanitaire (*adj*)	*ew-ma-nee-tehr*
humble	humble (*adj*)	*UH-bl*
• **humility**	humilité (*f*)	*ew-mee-lee-tay*
humor	humour (*m*)	*ew-moor*
• **sense of humor**	sens (*m*) de l'humour	*sAHs de lew-moor*

idealism	idéalisme (*m*)	*ee-day-a-leesm*
• **idealist, idealistic**	idéaliste (*m*)	*ee-day-a-leest*
imagination	imagination (*f*)	*ee-ma-zh-ee-na-syOH*
• **imaginative**	imaginatif (*adj, m*)	*ee-ma-zh-ee-na-teef*
	imaginative (*f*)	*ee-ma-zh-ee-na-teev*
impudence	impudence (*f*)	*EH-pew-dAH-ss*
• **impudent**	impudent(e) (*adj, m, f*)	*EH-pew-dAH(t)*
impulse	impulsion (*f*)	*EH-pewl-syOH*
• **impulsive**	impulsif (*adj, m*)	*EH-pewl-seef*
	impulsive (*f*)	*EH-pewl-seev*
indecisive	indécis(e) (*adj, m, f*)	*EH-day-see(z)*
independent	indépendant(e) (*adj, m, f*)	*EH-day-pAH-dAH(t)*
individualist	individualiste (*adj*)	*EH-dee-vee-dew-al-eest*
ingenious, clever	ingénieux (*adj, m*)	*EH-zhay-nyuh*
	ingénieuse (*f*)	*EH-zhay-nyuhz*
• **ingenuity, cleverness**	ingénuité (*f*)	*EH-zhay-new-ee-tay*
ingenuous, naive	ingénu(e) (*adj, m, f*)	*EH-zhay-new*
	naïf (*adj, m*)	*na-eef*
	naïve (*f*)	*na-eev*
innocence	innocence (*f*)	*ee-nu-sAH-ss*
• **innocent**	innocent(e) (*adj, m, f*)	*ee-nu-sAH(t)*
insolence	insolence(*f*)	*EH-sul-AH-ss*
• **insolent**	insolent(e) (*adj, m, f*)	*EH-sul-AH(t)*
intelligence	intelligence (*f*)	*EH-tay-lee-zh-AH-s*
• **intelligent**	intelligent(e) (*adj, m, f*)	*EH-tay-lee-zh-AH(t)*
irascible	irascible (*adj*)	*ee-ra-see-bl*
irony	ironie (*f*)	*ee-run-ee*
• **ironical**	ironique (*adj*)	*ee-run-eek*
irritable	irritable (*adj*)	*ee-ree-tabl*
jealous	jaloux (*adj, m*)	*zh-a-loo*
	jalouse (*f*)	*zh-a-looz*
laugh	rire (*v*)	*reer*
• **laughter**	rire (*m*)	*reer*
laziness	paresse (*f*)	*pa-reh-s*
• **lazy**	paresseux (*adj, m*)	*pa-reh-suh*
	paresseuse (*f*)	*pa-reh-suhz*
liberal	libéral(e) (*adj, m, f*)	*lee-bay-ral*
lively	vif (*adj, m*)	*veef*
	vive (*f*)	*veev*
	vivace (*adj*)	*vee-vas*

love	amour (*m*)	*a-moor*
• **love**	aimer (*v*)	*ay-may*
• **lovable**	adorable (*adj*)	*a-du-ra-bl*
malicious	malicieux (*adj, m*)	*ma-lee-syuh*
	malicieuse (*f*)	*ma-lee-syuhz*
mischievous	capricieux (*adj, m*)	*ka-pree-syuh*
	capricieuse (*f*)	*ka-pree-syuhz*
mood	humeur (*f*)	*ew-mur*
• **be in a bad mood**	être de mauvaise humeur	*eh-tre de mu-vehz ew-mur*
• **be in a good mood**	être de bonne humeur	*eh-tre de bun ew-mur*
neat	ordonné(e) (*adj, m, f*)	*or-dun-nay*
nice	sympathique (*adj*)	*sEH-pa-teek*
not nice, odious	antipathique (*adj*)	*AH-tee-pa-teek*
obstinate	obstiné(e) (*adj, m, f*)	*up-stee-nay*
optimism	optimisme (*m*)	*up-tee-mee-sm*
• **optimist, optimistic**	optimiste (*m/f*)	*up-tee-meest*
original	original(e) (*adj, m, f*)	*o-ree-zh-ee-nal*
patience	patience (*f*)	*pa-sy-AH-s*
• **patient**	patient (e) (*adj, m, f*)	*pa-sy-AH(t)*
• **impatient**	impatient(e) (*adj, m, f*)	*EH-pa-sy-AH(t)*
perfection	perfection (*f*)	*pehr-fehk-syOH*
• **perfectionist**	perfectionniste (*m/f*)	*pehr-fehk-sy-un-eest*
personality	personnalité (*f*)	*pehr-sun-a-lee-tay*
pessimism	pessimisme (*m*)	*pay-see-mee-sm*
• **pessimist, pessimistic**	pessimiste (*m/f*)	*pay-see-meest*
picky	tatillon (*adj, m*)	*ta-tee-yOH*
	tatillonne (*f*)	*ta-tee-yun*
pleasant, likeable	aimable (*adj*)	*ay-ma-ble*
	sympathique (*adj*)	*sEH-pa-teek*
• **like**	aimer (*v*) bien	*ay-may byEH*
poor	pauvre (*adj*)	*poh-vr*
possessive	possessif (*adj, m*)	*pus-ay-seef*
	possessive (*f*)	*pus-ay-seev*
presumptuous	présomptueux (*adj, m*)	*pray-zOH-ptew-uh*
	présomptueuse (*f*)	*pray-zOH-ptew-uhz*
pretentious	prétentieux (*adj, m*)	*pray-tAH-syuh*
	prétentieuse (*f*)	*pray-tAH-syuhz*

proud	fier, fière (*adj, m, f*)	*fyehr*
prudent	prudent (*adj, m*)	*prew-dAH*
	prudente (*f*)	*prew-dAHt*
rebellious	rebelle(e) (*adj, m, f*)	*re-behl*
refined	raffiné(e) (*adj, m, f*)	*ra-fee-nay*
reserved	réservé(e) (*adj, m, f*)	*ray-zehr-vay*
restless	agité(e) (*adj, m, f*)	*a-zh-ee-tay*
rich	riche (*adj/m/f*)	*reesh*
romantic	romantique (*adj*)	*rum-AH-teek*
rough	brut, brute (*adj, m, f*)	*brewt*
rude	rude (*adj*)	*rewd*
	grossier (*adj, m*)	*groh-sy-ay*
	grossière (*f*)	*groh-sy-ehr*
sad	triste (*adj*)	*treest*
• **sadness**	tristesse (*f*)	*tree-stehs*
sarcasm	sarcasme (*m*)	*sar-kasm*
• **sarcastic**	sarcastique (*adj*)	*sar-kas-teek*
seduction	séduction (*f*)	*say-dewk-syOH*
• **seductive**	séduisant(e) (*adj, m, f*)	*say-dew-ee-zAH(t)*
self-sufficient	indépendant(e) (*adj, m, f*)	*EH-day-pAH-dAH(t)*
sensitive	sensible (*adj*)	*sAH-seebl*
sentimental	sentimental(e) (*adj, m, f*)	*sAH-tee-mAH-tal*
serious	sérieux (*adj, m*)	*say-ryuh*
	sérieuse (*f*)	*say-ryuhz*
shrewd	rusé(e) (*adj, m, f*)	*rew-zay*
• **shrewdness**	ruse (*f*)	*rewz*
shy	timide (*adj*)	*tee-meed*
simple	simple (*adj*)	*sEH-pl*
sincere	sincère (*adj*)	*sEH-sehr*
• **sincerity**	sincérité (*f*)	*sEH-say-ree-tay*
sloppy, disorganized	désorganisé(e) (*adj, m, f*)	*day-zor-ga-nee-zay*
smart	intelligent(e) (*adj, m, f*)	*EH-tay-lee-zh-AH(t)*
smile	sourire (*m*)	*soo-reer*
• **smile**	sourire (*v*)	*soo-reer*
snobbish	hautain (*adj, m*)	*oh-tEH*
	hautaine (*f*)	*oh-tehn*
	snob (*adj*)	*snub*
stingy	pingre (*adj*)	*pEH-gre*
	avare (*adj*)	*a-var*
strong	fort (*adj, m*)	*for*
	forte (*f*)	*fort*

stubborn	têtu(e) (*adj*)	*teht-ew*
stupid	stupide (*adj*)	*stew-peed*
superstitious	superstitieux (*adj, m*)	*sew-pehr-stee-syuh*
	superstitieuse (*f*)	*sew-pehr-stee-syuhz*
sweet	doux (*adj, m*)	*doo*
	douce (*f*)	*dooss*
traditional	traditionnel(le) (*adj, m, f*)	*tra-dee-sy-un-ehl*
troublemaker	provocateur (*m*)	*pru-vuk-a-tur*
	provocatrice (*f*)	*pru-vuk-a-treess*
vain	vaniteux (*adj, m*)	*va-nee-tuh*
	vaniteuse (*f*)	*va-nee-tuhz*
versatile	versatile (*adj*)	*vehr-sa-teel*
vulnerable	vulnérable (*adj*)	*vewl-nay-rabl*
weak	faible (*adj*)	*fehbl*
well-mannered	bien élevé(e) (*adj, m, f*)	*byEH ayl-vay*
willingly	volontiers (*adv*)	*vul-OH-tyay*
wisdom	sagesse (*f*)	*sa-zh-ess*
• **wise**	sage (*adj*)	*sa-zh*

f. BASIC PERSONAL INFORMATION

For jobs and professions see Section 38.

address	adresse (*f*)	*a-drehss*
• **avenue**	avenue (*f*)	*av-new*
• **street**	rue (*f*)	*rew*
• **square**	square (*m*)	*skwar*
	place (*f*)	*plass*
• **live somewhere**	demeurer (*v*)	*de-mur-ay*
• **Where do you live?**	Où demeurez-vous (*pol*)?	*oo de-mur-ay voo*
	Où demeures-tu (*fam*)?	*oo de-mur tew*
• **I live on . . . Street.**	Je demeure rue . . .	*zhe de-mur rew*
• **house number**	numéro de la maison	*new-may-roh de la may-zOH*
be from	être de	*eh-tre de*
• **city, town**	ville (*f*)	*veel*
• **country**	pays (*m*)	*pay-ee*
• **state**	état (*m*)	*ay-ta*
• **village**	village (*m*)	*vee-lazh*

career	carrière (*f*)	*ka-ryehr*
date of birth	date (*f*) de naissance	*dat de neh-sAH-ss*
education	éducation (*f*)	*ay-dew-ka-syOH*
• **go to school**	aller (*v*) à l'école	*a-lay a lay-kul*
• **finish school**	finir (*v*) l'école	*fee-neer lay-kul*
• **university degree**	licence (*f*)	*lee-sAH-ss*
	doctorat (*m*)	*duk-tu-ra*
• **diploma**	diplôme (*m*)	*deep-lohm*
• **graduate**	obtenir un diplôme	*up-te-neer UH deep-lohm*
• **graduate (*from university*)**	recevoir sa licence	*res-vwar sa lee-sAH-ss*
	recevoir son doctorat	*res-vwar sOH duk-tu-ra*
employment	emploi (*m*)	*AH-plwa*
• **employer**	employeur (*m*)	*AH-plwa-yur*
	employeuse (*f*)	*AH-plwa-yuhz*
• **employee**	employé(e) (*m, f*)	*AH-plwa-yay*
identification	identification (*f*)	*ee-dAH-tee-fee-ka-syOH*
job	travail (*m*)	*tra-va-y*
name	nom (*m*)	*nOH*
• **first name**	prénom (*m*)	*pray-nOH*
• **family name, surname**	nom (*m*) de famille	*nOH de fa-meey*
• **be called**	s'appeler (*v*)	*sap-lay*
• **How do you spell your name?**	Comment s'écrit ton nom (*fam*)?	*kum-AH say-kree tOH nOH*
	Comment s'écrit votre nom (*pol*)?	*kum-AH say-kree vutre nOH*
• **Print your name.**	Ecrire (*v*) en lettres majuscules	*ay-kreer AH lehtr ma-zh-ew-skewl*
• **What's your name?**	Quel est ton nom (*fam*)?	*kehl eh tOH nOH*
	Quel est votre nom (*pol*)?	*kehl eh vutre nOH*
• **My name is . . .**	Mon nom est . . .	*mOH nOH eh*
• **sign**	signer (*v*)	*see-ny-ay*
• **signature**	signature (*f*)	*see-ny-a-tewr*
nationality	nationalité (*f*)	*na-syun-a-lee-tay*
place of birth	lieu (*m*) de naissance	*lyuh de neh-sAH-ss*
place of employment	lieu d'emploi	*lyuh dAH-plwa*
profession	profession (*f*)	*pruf-ehs-yOH*
• **professional**	professionnel (*m*)	*pru-fehs-yun-ehl*
	professionnelle (*f*)	*pru-fehs-yun-ehl*
residence	domicile (*m*)	*dum-ee-seel*
telephone number	numéro (*m*) de téléphone	*new-may-ro de tay-lay-fun*

title	titre (*m*)	*teetr*
• **Dr.**	docteur (*m*)	*duktur*
	un docteur femme	*un duktur fam*
• **Miss, Ms.**	mademoiselle	*mad-mwa-zehl*
• **Mr.**	monsieur	*me-sy-uh*
• **Mrs., Ms.**	madame	*ma-dam*
• **Prof.**	professeur (*m*)	*pruf-ehs-ur*
	un professeur femme	*UH pruf-ehs-ur fam*
work	travail (*m*)	*tra-va-y*
• **work**	travailler (*v*)	*tra-va-yay*
• **line of work**	genre de travail	*zh-AH-r de tra-va-y*

12. THE BODY

FOCUS: Parts of the Body

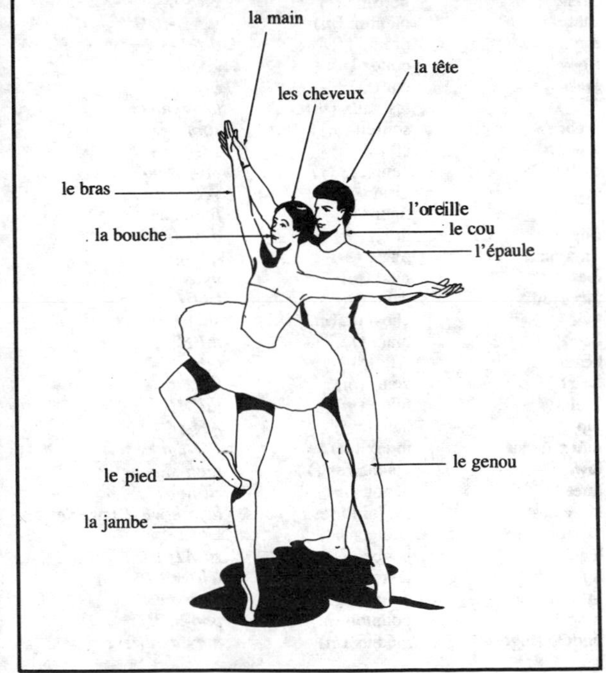

a. PARTS OF THE BODY

See also Section 40.

ankle	cheville (*f*)	*sh-e-vee-y*
arm	bras (*m*)	*bra*
beard	barbe (*f*)	*barb*
blood	sang (*m*)	*sAH*
body	corps (*m*)	*kor*
bone	os (*m*)	*us*
	les os (*pl*)	*lay zoh*
brain	cerveau (*m*)	*sehr-vo*
breast	sein (*m*)	*sEH*
cheek	joue (*f*)	*zh-oo*
chest	poitrine (*f*)	*pwa-treen*
chin	menton (*m*)	*mAH-tOH*
ear	oreille (*f*)	*u-reh-y*
elbow	coude (*m*)	*kood*
eye	œil (*m*)	*u-y*
	les yeux (*pl*)	*lay zyuh*
eyebrow	sourcil (*m*)	*soor-see*
eyelash	cil (*m*)	*seel*
eyelid	paupière (*f*)	*po-py-ehr*
face	visage (*m*)	*vee-za-zh*
	figure (*f*)	*fee-gewr*
finger	doigt (*m*)	*dwa*
fingernail	ongle (*m*)	*OH-gl*
foot	pied (*m*)	*pyay*
forehead	front (*m*)	*frOH*
hair	cheveux (*m, pl*)	*shvuh*
hand	main (*f*)	*mEH*
head	tête (*f*)	*teht*
heart	cœur (*m*)	*kur*
heel	talon (*m*)	*talOH*
hip	hanche (*f*)	*AH-sh*
index finger	index (*m*)	*EH-dehks*
jaw	mâchoire (*f*)	*mah-sh-war*
knee	genou (*m*)	*zh-noo*
knuckles	les jointures (*f*) des doigts	*lay zh-wEH-tewr day dwa*
leg	jambe (*f*)	*zh-AH-b*
lip	lèvre (*f*)	*leh-vr*
little finger	petit doigt (*m*)	*ptee dwa*
lung	poumon (*m*)	*poo-mOH*
middle finger	médius (*m*)	*may-dy-ewss*

moustache	moustache (*f*)	*moos-tash*
mouth	bouche (*f*)	*boosh*
muscle	muscle (*m*)	*mews-kl*
neck	cou (*m*)	*koo*
nose	nez (*m*)	*nay*
nostril	narine (*f*)	*na-reen*
penis	pénis (*m*)	*pay-nees*
ring finger	annulaire (*m*)	*a-new-lehr*
shoulder	épaule (*f*)	*ay-pohl*
skin	peau (*f*)	*poh*
stomach	estomac (*m*)	*ehs-tum-a*
thigh	cuisse (*f*)	*kew-ees*
throat	gorge (*f*)	*gor-zh*
thumb	pouce (*m*)	*poos*
toe	orteil (*m*)	*or-teh-y*
tongue	langue (*f*)	*lAH-g*
tooth	dent (*f*)	*dAH*
vagina	vagin (*m*)	*va-zh-EH*
waist	taille (*f*)	*tah-y*
wrist	poignet (*m*)	*pwa-ny-eh*

to be at the tip of one's tongue = être sur le bout de la langue *eh-tre sewr le boo de la lAH-g*
to pay through the nose; to pay an arm and a leg = payer un œil *pay-yay UH nu-y*
He (She) is a pain in the neck! = C'est un casse-pieds! *seh tUH kahs-pyay*
Knucklehead! = Tête de nœud! *teht de nuh*

b. PHYSICAL STATES AND ACTIVITIES

be cold	avoir (*v*) froid	*avwar frwa*
be hot	avoir (*v*) chaud	*avwar sho*
be tired	être (*v*) fatigué(e)	*eh-tre fa-tee-gay*
breathe	respirer (*v*)	*rehs-pee-ray*
drink	boire (*v*)	*bwar*
eat	manger (*v*)	*mAH-zh-ay*

fall asleep	s'endormir (*v*)	*sAH-dor-meer*
feel bad	se sentir (*v*) mal	*se sAH-teer mal*
	avoir (*v*) mal	*avwar mal*
feel well	se sentir (*v*) bien	*se sAH-teer byEH*
	aller (*v*) bien	*a-lay byEH*
get up	se lever (*v*)	*se le-vay*
go to bed	se coucher (*v*)	*se koo-shay*
hunger	faim (*f*)	*fEH*
• be hungry	avoir (*v*) faim	*avwar fEH*
relax	se relaxer (*v*)	*se re-laks-ay*
rest	se reposer (*v*)	*se re-po-zay*
run	courir (*v*)	*koo-reer*
sleep	dormir (*v*)	*durm-eer*
• be sleepy	avoir (*v*) sommeil	*avwar sum-ay*
thirst	soif (*f*)	*swaf*
• be thirsty	avoir (*v*) soif	*avwar swaf*
wake up	se réveiller (*v*)	*se ray-vay-yay*
walk	marcher (*v*)	*marshay*
	aller (*v*) à pied	*alay a pyay*

c. SENSORY PERCEPTION

blind person	aveugle (*m/f*)	*a-vuh-gl*
• blindness	cécité (*f*)	*say-see-tay*
deaf person	sourd (*m*)	*soor*
	sourde (*f*)	*soord*
• deafness	surdité (*f*)	*sewr-dee-tay*
flavor	saveur (*f*)	*sa-vur*
• taste	goûter (*v*)	*goo-tay*
hear	entendre (*v*)	*AH-tAH-dr*
• hearing	ouïe (*f*)	*wee*
listen (to)	écouter (*v*)	*ay-koo-tay*
look	regarder (*v*)	*re-gar-day*
mute person	muet (*m*)	*mew-eh*
	muette (*f*)	*mew-eht*
noise	bruit (*m*)	*brew-ee*
• noisy	bruyant(e) (*adj, m, f*)	*brew-yAH(t)*
perceive	percevoir (*v*)	*pehr-se-vwar*
	apercevoir (*v*)	*a-pehr-se-vwar*
• perception	perception (*f*)	*pehr-sehp-syOH*
see	voir (*v*)	*vwar*
• sight	vision (*f*)	*vee-zyOH*
	vue (*f*)	*vew*
sense	sens (*m*)	*sAH-s*
• sense, feel	sentir (*v*)	*sAH-teer*

smell	odeur (*f*)	*ud-ur*
	senteur (*f*)	*sAHt-ur*
• smell	sentir (*v*)	*sAH-teer*
sound	son (*m*)	*sOH*
touch	toucher (*m*)	*too-shay*
• touch	toucher (*v*)	*too-shay*

d. PERSONAL CARE

barber	coiffeur (*m*)	*kwa-fur*
• barber shop	salon (*m*) de coiffure pour hommes	*salOH de kwa-fewr poor um*
beautician	esthéticien (*m*)	*ehs-tay-tee-syEH*
	esthéticienne (*f*)	*ehs-tay-tee-syehn*
brush	brosse (*f*)	*bruss*
• brush	se brosser (*v*)	*se bruss-ay*
clean	propre (*adj*)	*prup-re*
• clean oneself	se débarbouiller (*v*)	*se day-bar-boo-yay*
comb	peigne (*m*)	*peh-ny*
• comb	se peigner (*v*)	*se peh-ny-ay*
curls	boucles (*f*) de cheveux	*book-le de shvuh*
	cheveux (*m, pl*) frisés	*shvuh free-zay*
• curler	bigoudi (*m*)	*bee-goo-dee*
cut one's hair	se faire couper (*v*) les cheveux	*se fehr koo-pay lay sh-vuh*
dirty	sale (*adj*)	*sal*
dry oneself	se sécher (*v*)	*se say-shay*
grooming	laque (*f*) pour les cheveux	*lak poor lay shvuh*
hair spray	spray (*m*)	*spreh*
hairdresser	coiffeur (*m*)	*kwa-fur*
	coiffeuse (*f*)	*kwa-fuhz*
hygiene	hygiène (*f*)	*ee-zh-y-ehn*
• hygienic	hygiénique (*adj*)	*ee-zh-y-ay-neek*
makeup	fard (*m*)	*far*
	maquillage (*m*)	*mak-ee-y-ah-zh*
• put on makeup	se farder (*v*)	*se far-day*
	se maquiller (*v*)	*se mak-ee-yay*
manicure	soins (*m, pl*) esthétiques des mains	*swEH ehs-tay-teek day mEH*
mascara	mascara (*m*)	*mas-ka-ra*
massage	massage (*m*)	*ma-sazh*

nail polish	vernis (*m*) à ongles	*vehr-nee a OH-gl*
perfume	parfum (*m*)	*par-fUH*
• **put on perfume**	se parfumer (*v*)	*se par-few-may*
permanent (wave)	permanente (*f*)	*pehr-ma-nAH-t*
razor	rasoir (*m*)	*rahz-war*
• **electric razor**	rasoir électrique (*m*)	*rahz-war ay-lehk-treek*
• **razor blade**	lame (*f*)	*lam*
scissors	ciseaux (*m*)	*see-zoh*
shampoo	shampooing (*m*)	*sh-AH-pwEH*
shave (*oneself*)	(se) raser (*v*)	*(se) rah-zay*
soap	savon (*m*)	*sa-vOH*
toothbrush	brosse (*f*) à dents	*bruss a dAH*
toothpaste	pâte dentifrice (*f*)	*paht dAH-tee-frees*
towel, handcloth	serviette de toilette (*f*)	*sehr-vee-y-eht de twa-leht*
wash oneself	se laver (*v*)	*se la-vay*
• **wash one's hair**	se laver les cheveux	*se la-vay lay shvuh*

THE PHYSICAL, PLANT, AND ANIMAL WORLDS

13. THE PHYSICAL WORLD

For Signs of the Zodiac, see Section 5.

a. THE UNIVERSE

astronomy	astronomie (*f*)	*as-trun-um-ee*
comet	comète (*f*)	*kum-eht*
cosmos	cosmos (*m*)	*kus-mohs*
eclipse	éclipse (*f*)	*ay-kleeps*
• **lunar eclipse**	éclipse lunaire	*ay-kleeps lew-nehr*
• **solar eclipse**	éclipse solaire	*ay-kleeps sul-ehr*
galaxy	galaxie (*f*)	*ga-lak-see*
gravitation	gravitation (*f*)	*gra-vee-tahs-yOH*
• **gravity**	gravité (*f*)	*gra-vee-tay*
light	lumière (*f*)	*lewm-yehr*
• **infrared light**	lumière infrarouge	*lewm-yehr EH-fra-roozh*
• **light year**	année (*f*) lumière	*a-nay lewm-yehr*
• **ultraviolet light**	lumière ultraviolette	*lewm-yehr ewl-tra-vy-uh-leht*

to come to light = mettre en lumière *meht-re AH lewm-yehr*
to shed light on = tirer quelque chose au clair *tee-ray kehlke sh-oh-z oh klehr*

meteor	météore (*m*)	*may-tay-or*
moon	lune (*f*)	*lewn*
• **full moon**	pleine lune	*plehn lewn*
• **moonbeam, ray**	rayon (*m*) de lune	*ray-yOHd lewn*
• **new moon**	nouvelle lune	*noo-vehl lewn*

honeymoon = une lune de miel *ewn lewn de mee-ehl*
to be absent-minded = être dans la lune *eh-tre dAH la lewn*

orbit	orbite (*f*)	*or-beet*
• **orbit**	mettre (*v*) en orbite	*mehtr AH nor-beet*
	placer (*v*) sur orbite	*pla-say sewr or-beet*
	être (*v*) en orbite	*eh-tre AH nor-beet*

planet	planète (*f*)	*plan-eht*
• **Earth**	Terre (*f*)	*tehr*
• **Jupiter**	Jupiter (*m*)	*zh-ew-pee-tehr*
• **Mars**	Mars (*m*)	*mars*
• **Mercury**	Mercure (*m*)	*mehr-kewr*
• **Neptune**	Neptune (*m*)	*nehp-tewn*
• **Pluto**	Pluton (*m*)	*plewt-OH*
• **Saturn**	Saturne (*m*)	*sa-tewrn*
• **Uranus**	Uranus (*m*)	*ewr-an-ewss*
• **Venus**	Vénus (*f*)	*vay-newss*
satellite	satellite (*m*)	*sa-tehl-eet*
space	espace (*m*)	*ehs-pas*
• **three-dimensional space**	espace tridimensionnel	*ehs-pas tree-deem-AH-sy-un-ehl*
star	étoile (*f*)	*ay-twal*
sun	soleil (*m*)	*sul-ay*
• **sunlight**	lumière solaire	*lewm-yehr sul-ehr*
• **sunray**	rayon (*m*) de soleil	*ray-yOHd sul-ay*
• **solar system**	système (*m*) solaire	*sees-tehm sul-ehr*
universe	univers (*m*)	*ew-nee-vehr*
world	monde (*m*)	*mOHd*

b. THE ENVIRONMENT

See also Section 44.

archipelago	archipel (*m*)	*arsh-ee-pehl*
atmosphere	atmosphère (*f*)	*at-muss-fehr*
• **atmospheric**	atmosphérique (*adj*)	*at-muss-fay-reek*
basin	bassin (*m*)	*bas-EH*
bay	baie (*f*)	*beh*
beach	plage (*f*)	*pla-zh*
channel	canal (*m*)	*ka-nal*
cloud	nuage (*m*)	*new-azh*
	nuée (*f*)	*new-ay*
coast	côte (*f*)	*koht*
desert	désert (*m*)	*dayz-ehr*
earthquake	tremblement (*m*) de terre	*trAH-ble-mAH de tehr*
environment	environnement (*m*)	*AH-veer-un-mAH*
farmland	terrain (*m*) agricole	*tehr-EH a-gree-kul*
field	champ (*m*)	*shAH*
forest	forêt (*f*)	*for-eh*

grass	herbe (*f*)	*ehrb*
gulf	golfe (*m*)	*gulf*
hill	colline (*f*)	*kul-een*
	coteau (*m*)	*kut-o*
ice	glace (*f*)	*glas*
island	île (*f*)	*eel*
lake	lac (*m*)	*lak*
land	terre (*f*)	*tehr*
	terrain (*m*)	*tehr-EH*
landscape	paysage (*m*)	*pay-eez-azh*
layer	couche (*f*)	*koosh*
mountain	montagne (*f*)	*mOH-ta-ny*
• **mountain chain**	chaîne (*f*) de montagnes	*sh-ehn de mOH-ta-ny*
• **mountainous**	montagneux (*adj, m*)	*mOH-ta-ny-uh*
	montagneuse (*f*)	*mOH-ta-ny-uhz*
• **peak**	sommet (*m*)	*sum-eh*
nature	nature (*f*)	*na-tewr*
• **natural**	nature(le) (*adj, m, f*)	*na-tewr-ehl*
ocean	océan (*m*)	*us-ay-AH*
• **Antarctic**	Antarctique (*adj*)	*AH-tark-teek*
• **Arctic**	Arctique (*adj*)	*ark-teek*
• **Atlantic**	Atlantique (*adj*)	*atl-AH-teek*
• **Pacific**	Pacifique (*adj*)	*pa-see-feek*
peninsula	péninsule (*f*)	*payn-EH-sewl*
	presqu'île (*f*)	*prehs-keel*
plain	plaine (*f*)	*plehn*
river	fleuve (*m*)	*fl-uhv*
• **flow**	couler (*v*)	*koo-lay*
rock	roche (*f*)	*rush*
	rocher (*m*)	*rush-ay*
sand	sable (*m*)	*sah-bl*
sea	mer (*f*)	*mehr*
sky	ciel (*m*)	*see-ehl*
stone	pierre (*f*)	*py-ehr*
tide	marée (*f*)	*mar-ay*
valley	vallée (*f*)	*val-ay*
	val (*m*)	*val*
vegetation	végétation (*f*)	*vay-zh-ay-tas-yOH*
volcano	volcan (*m*)	*vulk-AH*
• **eruption**	éruption (*f*)	*ay-rewps-yOH*
• **lava**	lave (*f*)	*lav*
wave	onde (*f*)	*OHd*
	vague (*f*)	*vag*
	flot (*m*)	*floh*
woods	bois (*m, s/pl*)	*bwah*

c. MATTER AND THE ENVIRONMENT

See also Section 42.

acid	acide (*m*)	*a-seed*
air	air (*m*)	*ehr*
ammonia	ammoniaque (*f*)	*am-un-yak*
atom	atome (*m*)	*a-tohm*
• **charge**	charge (*f*)	*shar-zhe*
• **electron**	électron (*m*)	*ay-lehk-tr-OH*
• **neutron**	neutron (*m*)	*nuh-tr-OH*
• **nucleus**	noyau (*m*)	*nwa-yoh*
	nucléole (*m*)	*newk-lay-ul*
• **proton**	proton (*m*)	*prut-OH*
bronze	bronze (*m*)	*br-OH-z*
carbon (*element*)	carbone (*m*)	*kar-bun*
chemical	chimique (*adj*)	*shee-meek*
• **chemistry**	chimie (*f*)	*shee-mee*
chlorine	chlore (*m*)	*klor*
coal	charbon (*m*)	*sharb-OH*
• **coal mine**	mine (*f*) de houille	*meen de oo-y*
• **coal mining**	houille (*f*)	*oo-y*
compound	composé (*m*)	*kOH-po-zay*
copper	cuivre (*m*)	*kew-eevr*
cotton	coton (*m*)	*kut-OH*
electrical	électrique (*adj*)	*ay-lehk-treek*
• **electricity**	électricité (*f*)	*ay-lehk-tree-see-tay*
element	élément (*m*)	*ay-laym-AH*
energy	énergie (*f*)	*ay-nehr-zh-ee*
• **fossil**	fossile (*m*)	*fus-eel*
• **nuclear energy**	énergie nucléaire	*ay-nehr-zh-ee new-klay-ehr*
• **radioactive waste**	déchets (*m, pl*) radioactifs	*day-sh-eh rad-yu-ak-teef*
• **solar energy**	énergie solaire	*ay-nehr-zh-ee sul-ehr*
fiber	fibre (*f*)	*fee-br*
fire	feu (*m*)	*fuh*
fuel	carburant (*m*)	*kar-bewr-AH*
fuel	combustible (*m*)	*kOH-bews-teebl*
• **fossil fuel**	combustibles (*m, pl*) fossiles	*kOH-bews-teebl fu-seel*
gas	gaz (*m*)	*gahz*
• **car gas**	essence (*f*)	*ays-AH-s*
• **natural gas**	gaz naturel	*gahz na-tewr-ehl*
gold	or (*m*)	*or*

heat	chaleur (*f*)	*sha-lur*
hydrogen	hydrogène (*m*)	*eed-ru-zh-ehn*
industrial	industriel (le) (*adj, m, f*)	*EH-dews-tree-ehl*
• **industry**	industrie (*f*)	*EH-dews-tree*
iodine	iode (*m*)	*yud*
iron	fer (*m*)	*fehr*
laboratory	laboratoire (*m*)	*la-bor-a-twar*
lead	plomb (*m*)	*plOH*
leather	cuir (*m*)	*kew-eer*
liquid	liquide (*m*)	*lee-keed*
material	matériel (*m*)	*ma-tayr-y-ehl*
matter	matière (*f*)	*mat-yehr*
mercury	mercure (*m*)	*mehr-kewr*
metal	métal (*m*)	*may-tal*
methane	méthane (*m*)	*may tahn*
microscope	microscope (*m*)	*meek-ru-skup*
mineral	minéral (*m*)	*mee-nay-ral*
molecule	molécule (*f*)	*mul-ay-kewl*
• **model**	modèle (*m*)	*mud-ehl*
• **molecular formula**	formule (*f*) moléculaire	*for-mewl mul-ay-kew-lehr*
• **structure**	structure (*f*)	*strewk-tewr*
natural resources	ressources (*f, pl*) naturelles	*re-soorss na-tewr-ehl*
nitrogen	azote (*m*)	*a-zut*
	nitrogène (*m*)	*neet-ru-zh-ehn*
oil	huile (*f*)	*ew-eel*
organic	organique (*adj*)	*or-gan-eek*
• **inorganic**	inorganique (*adj*)	*een-or-gan-eek*
oxygen	oxygène (*m*)	*uks-ee-zh-ehn*
particle	particule (*f*)	*par-tee-kewl*
petroleum	pétrole (*m*)	*pay-trul*
physical	physique (*adj*)	*fee-zeek*
• **physics**	physique (*f*)	*fee-zeek*
plastic	plastique (*m*)	*plas-teek*
platinum	platine (*m*)	*pla-teen*
pollution	pollution (*f*)	*pul-ews-yOH*
salt	sel (*m*)	*sehl*
silk	soie (*f*)	*swa*
silver	argent (*m*)	*ar-zh-AH*
smoke	fumée (*f*)	*fewm-ay*
sodium	sodium (*m*)	*sud-yum*
solid	solide (*m*)	*sul-eed*
steel	acier (*m*)	*as-yay*
• **stainless steel**	acier inoxydable	*as-yay een-uks-eed-abl*
stuff	étoffe (*f*)	*ay-tuf*
	tissu (*m*)	*tees-ew*

substance	substance (*f*)	*sewp-st-AH-s*
sulphur	soufre (*m*)	*soof-re*
	sulfure (*m*)	*sewl-fewr*
• **sulphuric acid**	acide (*m*) sulfurique	*a-seed sewl-fewr-eek*
textile	textile (*m*)	*tehk-steel*
vapor	vapeur (*f*)	*va-pur*
water	eau (*f*)	*oh*
wool	laine (*f*)	*lehn*

d. CHARACTERISTICS OF MATTER

artificial	artificiel (*adj*)	*ar-tee-fee-sy-ehl*
authentic	authentique (*adj*)	*ut-AH-teek*
elastic	élastique (*adj*)	*ay-las-teek*
fake	faux (*adj*)	*foh*
hard	dur (*adj*)	*dewr*
heavy	lourd (*adj*)	*loor*
light	léger (*adj*)	*lay-zh-ay*
malleable	malléable (*adj*)	*mal-ay-abl*
opaque	opaque (*adj*)	*up-ak*
pure	pur (*adj*)	*pewr*
resistant	résistant (*adj*)	*ray-zeest-AH*
robust	robuste (*adj*)	*rub-ewst*
rough	rude (*adj*)	*rewd*
smooth	lisse (*adj*)	*lees*
soft	mou (*adj*)	*moo*
	doux (*adj*)	*doo*
	mœlleux (*adj*)	*mwal-uh*
soluble	soluble (*adj*)	*sul-ew-bl*
stable	stable (*adj*)	*sta-bl*
strong	fort (*adj*)	*for*
synthetic	synthétique (*adj*)	*sEH-tay-teek*
transparent	transparent (*adj*)	*tr-AH-spar-AH*
weak	faible (*adj*)	*feh-bl*

e. GEOGRAPHY

For names of countries, cities, etc. see Section 30.

Antarctic Circle	Pôle (*m*) antarctique	*pohl AH-tark-teek*
	Cercle (*m*) antarctique	*sehr-kle AH-tark-teek*
Arctic Circle	Pôle (*m*) arctique	*pohl ark-teek*
	Cercle (*m*) arctique	*sehr-kle ark-teek*
area	superficie (*f*)	*sewp-ehr-fee-see*
	surface (*f*)	*sewr-fas*

border	frontière (*f*)	*frOH-ty-ehr*
• **border**	borner (*v*)	*bor-nay*
	toucher (*v*)	*too-shay*
city	ville (*f*)	*veel*
• **capital**	capitale (*f*)	*ka-pee-tal*
continent	continent (*m*)	*kOH-teen-AH*
• **continental**	continental(e) (*adj, m, f*)	*kOH-teen-AH-tal*
country	pays (*m*)	*pay-ee*

From what country are you? = De quel pays êtes-vous? *de kehl pay-ee eht-voo*

equator	équateur (*m*)	*ay-kwa-tur*
geographical	géographique (*adj*)	*zh-ay-u-gra-feek*
• **geography**	géographie (*f*)	*zh-ay-u-gra-fee*
globe	globe (*m*)	*glub*
hemisphere	hémisphère (*m*)	*ay-mees-fehr*
• **hemispheric**	hémisphérique (*adj*)	*ay-mees-fay-reek*
latitude	latitude (*f*)	*la-tee-tewd*
longitude	longitude (*f*)	*lOH-zh-ee-tewd*
locate	localiser (*v*)	*luk-al-ee-zay*
	situer (*v*)	*see-tew-ay*
• **location**	localité (*f*)	*luk-al-ee-tay*
• **be located**	se trouver (*v*)	*se-troo-vay*
map	carte (*f*)	*kart*
meridian	méridien (*m*)	*may-reed-y-EH*
• **prime meridian**	méridien origine	*may-reed-y-EH or-ee-zh-een*
nation	nation (*f*)	*nahs-y-OH*
• **national**	national(e) (*adj, m, f*)	*nahs-yun-al*
pole	pôle (*m*)	*pohl*
• **North Pole**	Pôle Nord	*pohl nor*
• **South Pole**	Pôle Sud	*pohl sewd*
province	province (*f*)	*pruv-EH-s*
region	région (*f*)	*ray-zh-y-OH*
state	état (*m*)	*ay-ta*
territory	territoire (*m*)	*tehr-eet-war*
tropic	tropique (*m*)	*trup-eek*
• **Tropic of Cancer**	Tropique du Cancer	*trup-eek dew kAH-sehr*
• **Tropic of Capricorn**	Tropique du Capricorne	*trup-eek dew ka-pree-korn*
• **tropical**	tropique (*adj*)	*trup-eek*
zenith	zénith (*m*)	*zay-neet*
zone	zone (*f*)	*zohn*

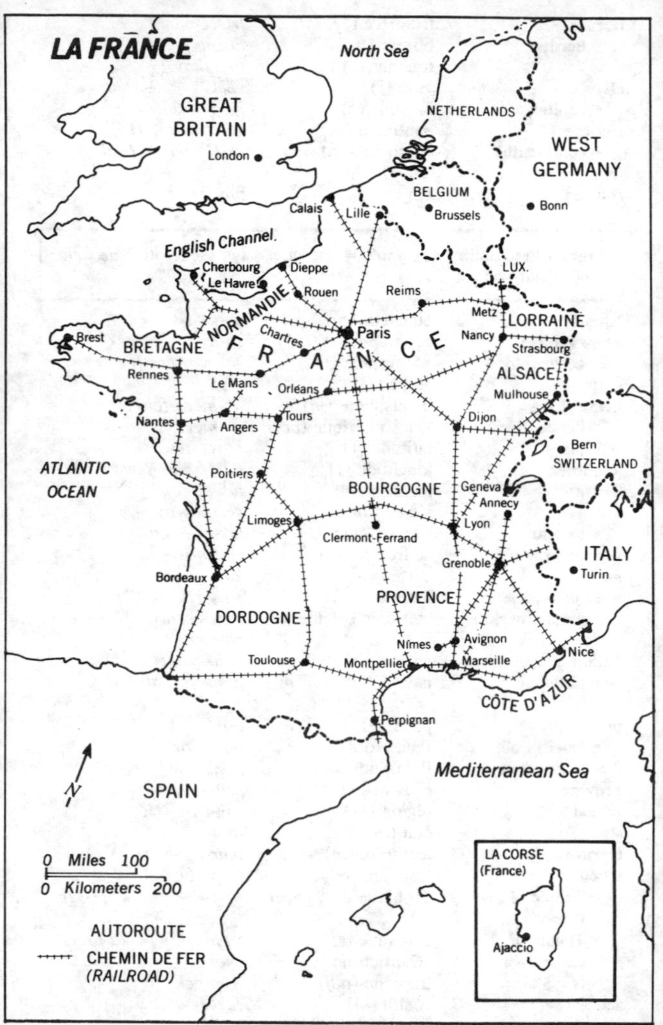
LA FRANCE
North Sea
GREAT BRITAIN
London
NETHERLANDS
WEST GERMANY
BELGIUM
Brussels
Bonn
Calais
Lille
English Channel
LUX.
Cherbourg
Dieppe
Le Havre
Rouen
Reims
NORMANDIE
Metz
LORRAINE
Brest
Chartres
Paris
Nancy
BRETAGNE
F R A N C E
Strasbourg
Rennes
ALSACE
Le Mans
Orléans
Mulhouse
Nantes
Tours
Dijon
Angers
Bern
SWITZERLAND
ATLANTIC OCEAN
Poitiers
BOURGOGNE
Geneva
Annecy
Limoges
Lyon
Clermont-Ferrand
Grenoble
ITALY
Bordeaux
Turin
PROVENCE
DORDOGNE
Nîmes
Avignon
Toulouse
Montpellier
Marseille
Nice
CÔTE D'AZUR
Perpignan
Mediterranean Sea
N
SPAIN
0 Miles 100
0 Kilometers 200
AUTOROUTE
CHEMIN DE FER (RAILROAD)
LA CORSE (France)
Ajaccio

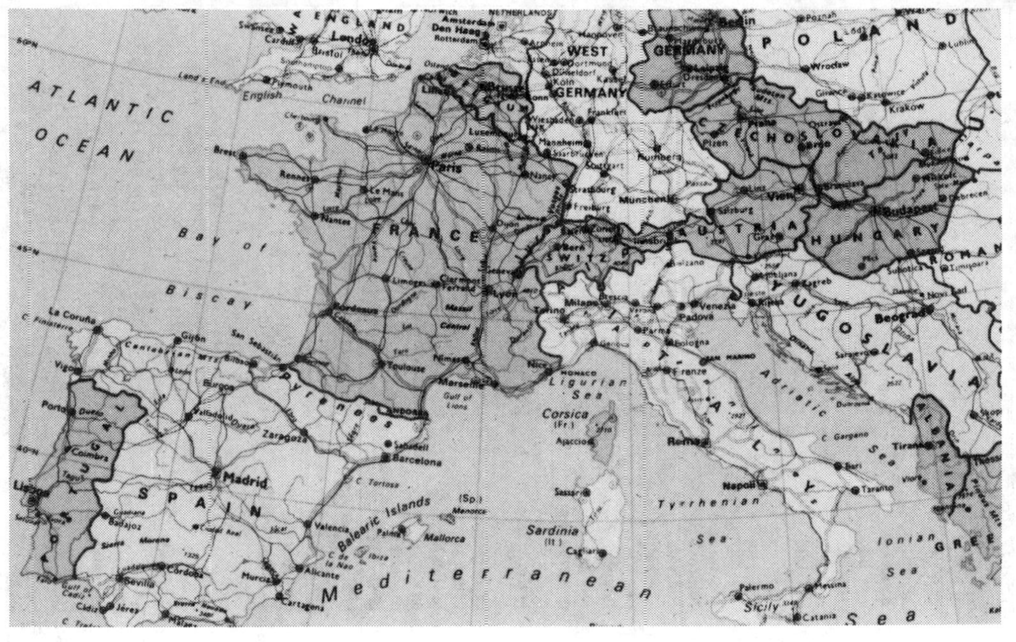
ATLANTIC OCEAN
ENGLAND
London
Bristol
Plymouth
Land's End
English Channel
Amsterdam
Den Haag
Rotterdam
NETHERLANDS
WEST GERMANY
GERMANY
Berlin
POLAND
Wroclaw
Krakow
CZECHOSLOVAKIA
Praha
Plzen
Brno
Wien
AUSTRIA
Salzburg
Graz
Budapest
HUNGARY
ROMANIA
Frankfurt
Mannheim
Stuttgart
Nurnberg
Munchen
Strasbourg
SWITZ
Bern
Paris
Brest
Rennes
Le Mans
Nantes
FRANCE
Bay of Biscay
Limoges
Bordeaux
Clermont Ferrand
Lyon
Massif Central
Toulouse
Marseille
Gulf of Lions
Nice
Monaco
Pyrenees
La Coruña
C. Finisterre
Gijón
San Sebastian
Bilbao
Burgos
Vigo
Porto
Coimbra
Lisboa
Valladolid
Zaragoza
Barcelona
Sabadell
C. Tortosa
Madrid
SPAIN
Badajoz
Valencia
Alicante
Murcia
Cartagena
Córdoba
Sevilla
Cádiz
Jerez
Gulf of Cádiz
Balearic Islands
(Sp.)
Menorca
Mallorca
Palma
Ibiza
C. de la Nao
Mediterranean Sea
Corsica
(Fr.)
Ajaccio
Sardinia
(It.)
Sassari
Cagliari
Ligurian Sea
Torino
Milano
Brescia
Venezia
Padova
Parma
Bologna
Genova
Firenze
ITALY
Roma
Napoli
Bari
Taranto
C. Gargano
Palermo
Messina
Catania
Sicily
Tyrrhenian Sea
Adriatic Sea
Ionian Sea
YUGOSLAVIA
Ljubljana
Zagreb
Rijeka
Sarajevo
Beograd
Novi Sad
Subotica
Debrecen
ALBANIA
Tirana
Vlorë
GREECE

14. PLANTS

a. GENERAL VOCABULARY

agriculture	agriculture (*f*)	*a-gree-kewl-tewr*
bloom	fleurir (*v*)	*flur-eer*
botanical	botanique (*adj*)	*but-a-neek*
• botany	botanique (*f*)	*but-a-neek*
branch	branche (*f*)	*brAHsh*
bud	bourgeon (*m*)	*boor-zh-OH*
• bud	bourgeonner (*v*)	*boor-zh-un-ay*
bulb	bulbe (*m*)	*bewlb*
cell	cellule (*f*)	*sehl-ewl*
• membrane	membrane (*f*)	*mAH-bran*
• nucleus	nucléole (*m*)	*newk-lay-ul*
chlorophyll	chlorophylle (*f*)	*klu-ru-feel*
cultivate	cultiver (*v*)	*kewl-tee-vay*
• cultivation	culture (*f*)	*kewl-tewr*
dig	creuser (*v*)	*kruh-zay*
flower	fleurir (*v*)	*flur-eer*
foliage	feuillage (*m*)	*fuh-ya-zh*
gather, reap	récolter (*v*)	*ray-kul-tay*
	cueillir (*v*)	*kuh-yeer*
grain, wheat	froment (*m*)	*frum-AH*
	blé (*m*)	*blay*
greenhouse	serre (*f*)	*sehr*
hedge	haie (*f*)	*eh*
horticulture	horticulture (*f*)	*or-tee-kewl-tewr*
leaf	feuille (*f*)	*fuh-y*
organism	organisme (*m*)	*or-gan-ee-sm*
photosynthesis	photosynthèse (*f*)	*fu-tus-EH-tehz*
plant	plante (*f*)	*pl-AH-t*
• plant	planter (*v*)	*pl-AH-tay*
pollen	pollen (*m*)	*pul-AH*
reproduce	reproduire (*v*)	*re-prud-ew-eer*
• reproduction	reproduction (*f*)	*re-prud-ewks-y-OH*
ripe	mûr(e) (*adj, m, f*)	*mewr*
root	racine (*f*)	*ra-seen*
rotten	pourri(e) (*adj, m, f*)	*poor-ee*
seed	semence (*f*)	*sem-AH-s*
• seed	semer (*v*)	*se-may*
species	espèce (*f*)	*ehs-pehs*
stem	tige (*f*)	*tee-zh*
transplant	transplantation (*f*)	*tr-AH-spl-AH-tahs-y-OH*
• transplant	transplanter (*v*)	*tr-AH-spl-AH-tay*
trunk	tronc (*m*)	*tr-OH*
water	arroser (*v*)	*a-ro-zay*

b. FLOWERS

carnation	œillet (*m*)	*uh-yeh*
cyclamen	cyclamen (*m*)	*seek-la-men*
dahlia	dahlia (*m*)	*dal-ya*
daisy	marguerite (*f*)	*mar-ge-reet*
flower	fleur (*f*)	*flur*
• **bouquet of flowers**	botte (*f*) de fleurs	*but de flur*
• **flower bed**	parterre (*m*) de fleurs	*par-tehr de flur*
• **wildflower**	fleur sauvage	*flur so-va-zh*
• **wilted flower**	fleur (*f*) fanée	*flur fan-ay*
geranium	géranium (*m*)	*zh-ay-ra-ny-um*
gladiolus	glaïeul (*m*)	*gla-yul*
lily	lis/lys (*m*)	*lees*
orchid	orchidée (*f*)	*or-kee-day*
petal	pétale (*m*)	*pay-tal*
petunia	pétunia (*m*)	*pay-tewn-ya*
(to) pick flowers	cueillir (*v*) des fleurs	*kuh-yeer day flur*
poppy	pavot (*m*)	*pa-vo*
	coquelicot (*m*)	*kuk-lee-ko*
rose	rose (*f*)	*rohz*
thorn	épine (*f*)	*ay-peen*
tulip	tulipe (*f*)	*tew-leep*
violet	violette (*f*)	*vyu-leht*

c. TREES

beech tree	hêtre (*m*)	*eh-tr*
chestnut tree	châtaignier (*m*)	*sha-tay-ny-ay*
cypress tree	cyprès (*m*)	*see-preh*
fir tree	sapin (*m*)	*sap-EH*
fruit tree	fruitier (*m*)	*frew-eet-yay*
• **apple tree**	pommier (*m*)	*pum-yay*
• **cherry tree**	cerisier (*m*)	*se-reez-yay*
• **fig tree**	figuier (*m*)	*feeg-yay*
• **lemon tree**	citronnier (*m*)	*see-trun-yay*
• **olive tree**	olivier (*m*)	*ul-eev-yay*
• **orange tree**	oranger (*m*)	*or-AH-zh-ay*
• **peach tree**	pêcher (*m*)	*pay-shay*
• **pear tree**	poirier (*m*)	*pwa-ree-yay*
• **walnut tree**	noyer (*m*)	*nwa-yay*
maple tree	érable (*m*)	*ay-ra-ble*
oak tree	chêne (*m*)	*sh-ehn*
palm tree	palmier (*m*)	*palm-yay*

pine tree	pin (*m*)	*pEH*
poplar tree	peuplier (*m*)	*puh-plee-yay*
tree	arbre (*m*)	*ar-br*

d. FRUITS

apple	pomme (*f*)	*pum*
apricot	abricot (*m*)	*a-bree-ko*
banana	banane (*f*)	*ba-nan*
cherry	cerise (*f*)	*sreez*
chestnut	marron (*m*)	*mar-OH*
	châtaigne (*f*)	*sha-teh-ny*
citrus	agrumes (*m, pl*)	*ag-rewm*
• **citric**	citrique (*adj*)	*see-treek*
date	datte (*f*)	*dat*
fig	figue (*f*)	*feeg*
fruit	fruit (*m*)	*frew-ee*
grapefruit	pamplemousse (*m/f*)	*pAH-ple-mooss*
grapes	raisin (*m*)	*rehz-EH*
lemon	citron (*m*)	*seetr-OH*
mandarin orange	mandarine (*f*)	*mAH-da-reen*
melon	melon (*m*)	*mel-OH*
olive	olive (*f*)	*ul-eev*
orange	orange (*f*)	*or-AH-zh*
peach	pêche (*f*)	*peh-sh*
pear	poire (*f*)	*pwar*
pineapple	ananas (*m*)	*a-na-nas*
plum	prune (*f*)	*prewn*
prune	pruneau (*m*)	*prew-no*
raisin	raisin (*m*) sec	*rehz-EH sehk*
raspberry	framboise (*f*)	*fr-AH-bwaz*
strawberry	fraise (*f*)	*frehz*
walnut	noix (*f*)	*nawh*
watermelon	pastèque (*f*)	*pas-tehk*

e. VEGETABLES AND HERBS

artichoke	artichaut (*m*)	*ar-tee-sh-o*
asparagus	asperge (*f*)	*as-pehr-zh*
basil	basilic (*m*)	*ba-zee-leek*
bean	haricot (*m*)	*aree-ko*
	fèves (*f*) de haricot	*fehv de aree-ko*
beet	betterave (*f*)	*beht-rav*
broccoli	brocoli (*m*)	*bruk-u-lee*
cabbage	chou (*m*)	*shoo*
carrot	carotte (*f*)	*ka-rut*
cauliflower	chou-fleur (*m*) (*pl*, choux-fleurs)	*shoo-flur*

celery	céleri (*m*)	*sehl-ree*
corn	maïs (*m*)	*ma-ees*
cucumber	concombre (*m*)	*kOH-kOH-br*
eggplant	aubergine (*f*)	*o-behr-zh-een*
fennel	fenouil (*m*)	*fe-noo-y*
garden	jardin (*m*)	*zh-ard-EH*
• **vegetable garden**	potager (*m*)	*pu-ta-zh-ay*
garlic	ail (*m*)	*ah-y*
grass	herbe (*f*)	*ehrb*
green pepper	piment (*m*)	*peem-AH*
lentil	lentille (*f*)	*l-AH-tee-y*
lettuce	laitue (*f*)	*lay-tew*
lima bean	fève (*f*)	*fehv*
mint	menthe (*f*)	*m-AH-t*
mushroom	champignon (*m*)	*sh-AH-pee-ny-OH*
onion	oignon (*m*)	*u-ny-OH*
parsley	persil (*m*)	*pehr-see*
pea	(petits) pois (*m*)	*(ptee) pwa*
potato	pomme (*f*) de terre	*pum de tehr*
pumpkin	courge (*f*)	*koor-zh*
	citrouille (*f*)	*see-troo-y*
radish	radis (*m*)	*ra-dee*
rosemary	romarin (*m*)	*rum-ar-EH*
spinach	épinard (*m*)	*ay-pee-nar*
string bean	haricot vert (*m*)	*aree-ko vehr*
tomato	tomate (*f*)	*tum-at*
vegetable	légume (*m*)	*layg-ewm*
zucchini	courgette (*f*)	*koor-zh-eht*

15. THE ANIMAL WORLD

a. ANIMALS

animal	animal (*m*)	*a-nee-mal*
bat	chauve-souris (*f*)	*sh-ohv-soo-ree*
	pipistrelle (*f*)	*pee-pee-strehl*
bear	ours (*m*)	*oors*
beast	bête (*f*)	*beht*
buffalo	buffle (*m*)	*bew-fl*
bull	taureau (*m*)	*tor-o*
camel	chameau (*m*)	*sha-mo*
cat	chat (*m*)	*sha*
	chatte (*f*)	*shat*
• **meow**	miauler (*v*)	*mee-yo-lay*
cow	vache (*f*)	*vash*
deer	cerf (*m*)	*sehr*

dog	chien (*m*)	*sh-y-EH*
	chienne (*f*)	*sh-y-ehn*
• bark	aboyer (*v*)	*a-bwa-yay*
donkey	âne (*m*)	*ahn*
elephant	éléphant (*m*)	*ay-layf-AH*
farm	ferme (*f*)	*fehrm*
• barn	grange (*f*)	*gr-AH-zh*
• farmer	fermier (*m*)	*fehrm-yay*
	fermière (*f*)	*fehrm-yehr*
• fence	clôture (f)	*klo-tewr*
	barrière (*f*)	*bar-yehr*
fox	renard (*m*)	*re-nar*
giraffe	girafe (*f*)	*zh-ee-raf*
goat	chèvre (*f*)	*sh-ehvre*
hare	lièvre (*m*)	*lee-ehvre*
hippopotamus	hippopotame (*m*)	*ee-pu-pu-tam*
horse	cheval (*m*)	*shval*
• neigh	hennir (*v*)	*ehn-eer*
human	humain (*adj, m*)	*ew-mEH*
	humaine (*adj, f*)	*ew-mehn*
human being	être (*m*)	*eh-tr*
	être (*m*) humain	*eh-tr ew-mEH*
hunter	chasseur (*m*)	*sha-sur*
	chasseuse (*f*)	*sha-suhz*
• hunting	chasse (*f*)	*shass*
hyena	hyène (*f*)	*yehn*
lamb	agneau (*m*)	*a-ny-o*
leopard	léopard (*m*)	*lay-up-ar*
lion	lion (*m*)	*lee-y-OH*
• roar	rugir (*v*)	*rew-zh-eer*
mammal	mammifère (*m*)	*ma-mee-fehr*
mole	taupe (*f*)	*tohp*
monkey	singe (*m*)	*sEH-zh*
mouse	souris (*f*)	*soo-ree*
mule	mulet (*m*)	*mew-leh*
ox	bœuf (*m*)	*buhf*
	bœufs (*pl*)	*buh*
paw	patte (*f*)	*pat*
pet	animal favori (domestiqué) (*m*)	*a-nee-mal fa-vor-ee (dum-ehs-tee-kay)*
pig	cochon (*m*)	*ku-sh-OH*
pony	poney (*m*)	*pun-eh*
primate	primate (*m*)	*pree-mat*
rabbit	lapin (*m*)	*lap-EH*
rat	rat (*m*)	*ra*
rhinoceros	rhinocéros (*m*)	*reen-u-say-rus*
sheep	mouton (*m*)	*moot-OH*
• bleat	bêler (*v*)	*bay-lay*

to stand in line, to line up, queue up = faire la queue *fehr la kuh*

tail	queue (*f*)	*kuh*
tiger	tigre (*m*)	*teeg-re*
vertebrate	vertébré(e) (*adj, m, f*)	*vehr-tay-bray*
• **invertebrate**	invertébré(e) (*adj, m, f*)	*EH-vehr-tay-bray*
wild animal	animal sauvage (*m*)	*a-nee-mal so-va-zh*
wolf	loup (*m*)	*loo*
• **howl**	hurler (*v*)	*ewr-lay*
zebra	zèbre (*m*)	*zeh-bre*
zoo	zoo (*m*)	*zoo*
	jardin zoologique (*m*)	*zh-ard-EH zu-ul-uzh-eek*
• **zoological**	zoologique (*adj*)	*zu-ul-uzh-eek*
• **zoology**	zoologie (*f*)	*zu-ul-uzh-ee*

FOCUS: Some Common Animals

b. BIRDS AND FOWL

albatross	albatros (*m*)	*al-ba-tros*
beak	bec (*m*)	*behk*
bird	oiseau (*m*)	*wa-zoh*
blackbird	merle (*m*)	*mehrl*
chick	poussin (*m*)	*poos-EH*
chicken	poule (*f*)	*pool*
	poulet (*m*)	*pool-eh*
dove	colombe (*f*)	*kul-OH-b*
duck	canard (*m*)	*kan-ar*
eagle	aigle (*m*)	*ehg-l*
feather	plume (*f*)	*plewm*
goose	oie (*f*)	*wa*
hen	poule (*f*)	*pool*
nightingale	rossignol (*m*)	*rus-ee-ny-ul*
ostrich	autruche (*f*)	*oh-trew-sh*
owl	hibou (*m*)	*ee-boo*
parakeet	perruche (*f*)	*pay-rew-sh*
parrot	perroquet (*m*)	*pehr-uk-eh*
pelican	pélican (*m*)	*pay-leek-AH*
penguin	pingouin (*m*)	*pEH-gwEH*
pigeon	pigeon (*m*)	*pee-zh-OH*

> **to be the fool in an affair** = être le pigeon dans une affaire *eh-tr le pee-zh-OH d-AH zewn a-fehr*

rooster	coq (*m*)	*kuk*
seagull	mouette (*f*)	*mweht*
sparrow	moineau (*m*)	*mwa-no*
	piaf (*m*)	*pyaf*
stork	cigogne (*f*)	*see-gu-ny*
swallow	hirondelle (*f*)	*eer-OH-dehl*
swan	cygne (*m*)	*see-ny*
turkey	dindon (*m*)	*dEH-dOH*
wing	aile (*f*)	*ehl*

c. FISH, REPTILES, AMPHIBIANS, AND MARINE ANIMALS

catfish	poisson-chat (*m*)	*pwas-OH-sha*
codfish	morue (*f*)	*mor-ew*
crocodile	crocodile (*m*)	*kru-ku-deel*
dolphin	dauphin (*m*)	*dof-EH*
eel	anguille (*f*)	*AH-gee-y*
fish	poisson (*m*)	*pwas-OH*
• **fin**	nageoire (*f*)	*na-zh-war*
• **fish**	pêcher (*v*)	*pay-shay*
	aller (*v*) à la pêche	*a-lay a la peh-sh*

• **fishbone**	arête (*f*)	*ar-eht*
• **fisherman**	pêcheur (*m*)	*peh-sh-ur*
	pêcheuse (*f*)	*peh-sh-uhz*
• **fishing**	pêche (*f*)	*peh-sh*
• **fishing rod**	canne (*f*) à pêche	*kan a peh-sh*
• **hook**	hameçon (*m*)	*ams-OH*
frog	grenouille (*f*)	*gre-noo-y*
goldfish	poisson rouge (*m*)	*pwas-OH roo-zh*
octopus	pieuvre (*f*)	*pee-yuv-re*
	poulpe (*m*)	*poolp*
reptile	reptile (*m*)	*rehp-teel*
salamander	salamandre (*f*)	*sa-la-mAH-dr*
sardine	sardine (*f*)	*sar-deen*
seal	phoque (*m*)	*fuk*
snake	serpent (*m*)	*sehrp-AH*
sole fish	sole (*f*)	*sul*
swordfish	espadon (*m*)	*ehs-pad-OH*
toad	crapaud (*m*)	*kra-po*
trout	truite (*f*)	*trew-eet*
tuna	thon (*m*)	*tOH*
turtle	tortue (*f*)	*tor-tew*
whale	baleine (*f*)	*bal-ehn*

d. INSECTS AND OTHER INVERTEDRATES

ant	fourmi (*f*)	*foor-mee*
bed bug	punaise (*f*)	*pew-nehz*
bee	abeille (*f*)	*a-beh-y*
butterfly	papillon (*m*)	*pa-pee-y-OH*
caterpillar	chenille (*f*)	*she-nee-y*
cockroach	blatte (*f*)	*blat*
	cafard (*m*)	*ka-far*
flea	puce (*f*)	*pewss*
fly	mouche (*f*)	*moosh*
insect	insecte (*m*)	*EH-sehkt*
louse	pou (*m*) (*pl*, poux)	*poo*
maggot	asticot (*m*)	*as-tee-ko*
metamorphosis	métamorphose (*f*)	*may-ta-mor-foz*
mosquito	moustique (*m*)	*moos-teek*
moth	phalène (*f*)	*fal-ehn*
organism	organisme (*m*)	*organ-ees-me*
scorpion	scorpion (*m*)	*skor-py-OH*
silkworm	ver (*m*) à soie	*vehr a swa*
spider	araignée (*f*)	*ar-ay-ny-ay*
termite	termite (*m*)	*tehr-meet*
tick	tique (*f*)	*teek*
wasp	guêpe (*f*)	*gehp*
worm	ver (*m*)	*vehr*

COMMUNICATING, FEELING, AND THINKING

16. BASIC SOCIAL EXPRESSIONS

a. GREETINGS AND FAREWELLS

Farewell!	Adieu!	*ad-yuh*
Good afternoon!	Bonjour!	*bOH-zhoor*
Good evening!	Bonsoir!	*bOH-swar*
Good morning!	Bonjour!	*bOH-zhoor*
Good night!	Bonsoir!	*bOH-swar*
	Bonne nuit! (*when going to bed*)	*bun new-ee*
Good-bye!	Au revoir!	*or-vwar*
greet	saluer (*v*)	*sal-ew-ay*
• **greeting**	salut (*m*)	*sal-ew*
	salutation (*f*)	*sal-ew-tas-y-OH*
Hello!	Bonjour! (*during daytime*)	*bOH-zhoor*
	Bonsoir! (*during evening hours*)	*bOH-swar*
Hi!	Salut!	*sal-ew*
How are you?	Comment allez-vous? (*pol*)	*kum-AH tal-ay voo*
	Comment vas-tu? (*fam*)	*kum-AH va-tew*
How's it going?	Comment ça va?	*kum-AH sa-va*
	Ça va?	*sa-va*
• **Bad(ly)**	Mal!	*mal*
• **Fine!**	Bien!	*byEH*
• **Not bad!**	Pas mal!	*pah mal*
• **Quite well!**	Très bien!	*treh byEH*
• **So, so!**	Comme-ci, comme-ça!	*kum-see kum-sa*
• **Very well!**	Très bien	*treh byEH*
	Ça tape!	*sa tap*
Please give my regards/greetings to . . .	Mon bon souvenir à . . .	*mOH bOH soov-neer a*
See you!	Salut!	*sal-ew*
• **See you later!**	À tout à l'heure!	*a-too-ta-lur*
• **See you soon!**	À bientôt!	*a-byEH-toh*
• **See you Sunday!**	À dimanche!	*a-deem-AH-sh*

shake hands	serrer (*v*) la main à quelqu'un	*sehr-ay lam-EH a kehlk-UH*
	donner (*v*) la main à quelqu'un	*dun-ay lam-EH a kehlk-UH*
• handshake	poignée de main (*f*)	*pwa-ny-ayd-mEH*

b. FORMS OF ADDRESS AND INTRODUCTIONS

A pleasure!	C'est un plaisir!	*seht-UH-play-zeer*
• The pleasure is mine!	C'est mon plaisir!	*sehm-OH-play-zeer*
acquaintance	connaissance (*f*)	*kun-eh-sAH-s*
Allow me to introduce myself.	Permettez-moi de me présenter.	*pehrm-eht-ay-mwa dem prayz AH-tay*
Allow me to introduce you to . . .	Permettez-moi de vous présenter à . . .	*pehrm-eht-ay-mwa de voo prayz-AH-tay a*
be seated	s'asseoir (*v*)	*sas-war*
• be seated, please.	Asseyez-vous, s'il vous plaît. (*pol*)	*ass-ay-yay-voo, seel-voo-pleh*
	Assieds-toi, s'il te plaît. (*fam*)	*ass-yay-twa seel-te-pleh*
be on a first-name basis	tutoyer (*v*)	*tew-twa-yay*
be on a formal basis	vouvoyer (*v*)	*voo-vwa-yay*
calling card	carte (*f*) de visite	*kart de vee-zeet*
Come in!	Entrez! (*pol*)	*AH-tray*
	Entre! (*fam*)	*AH-tre*
• enter (into)	entrer (*v*) (dans)	*AH-tray (dAH)*
Delighted!	Heureux! (*m*)	*ur-uh*
	Heureuse! (*f*)	*ur-uhz*
Happy to make your acquaintance!	Heureux(-euse) de faire votre connaissance! (*pol*)	*ur-uh(-uhz) de fehr vut-re kun-eh-sAH-s*
	Heureux(-euse) de faire ta connaissance! (*fam*)	*ur-uh(-uhz) de fehr ta kun-eh-sAH-s*
introduce someone	présenter (*v*) quelqu'un	*prayz-AH-tay kehl-kUH*
• introduction	présentation (*f*)	*prayz-AH-tas-y-OH*
know someone	connaître quelqu'un	*kun-eht-re kehl-kUH*
Let me introduce you to . . .	Je vous présente à . . . (*pol*)	*zhe-voo-prayz-AH-t a*
	Je te présente à . . . (*fam*)	*zh-te-prayz-AH-t a*

meet, run into someone	rencontrer (*v*)	*rAH-kOH-tray*
	pour la première fois (*for the first time*)	*poor la prem-yehr fwa*
title	titre (*m*)	*tee-tre*
• **Dr. (*M.D. degree*)**	docteur (*m*)	*duk-tur*
	docteur femme (*f*)	*duk-tur fahm*
• **Dr. (*Ph.D. degree*)**	docteur (*m*)	*duk-tur*
	doctoresse (*f*)	*duk-tur-ehs*
• **Miss, Ms.**	mademoiselle	*mad-mwa-zehl*
• **Mr.**	monsieur	*me-sy-uh*
• **Mrs.**	madame	*ma-dahm*
What's your name?	Comment vous appelez-vous? (*pol*)	*kum-AH voo-zap-lay-voo*
	Comment t'appelles-tu? (*fam*)	*kum-AH tap-ehl-tew*
• **My name is . . .**	Je m'appelle . . .	*zhem-ap-ehl*
• **I'm . . .**	Je suis . . .	*zhe-swee*

c. COURTESY

Best wishes!	Meilleurs vœux!	*meh-y-ur vuh*
Bless you! (*after a sneeze*)	Dieu vous (te) bénisse!	*dyuh voo (te) bay-neess*
	À vos souhaits! (*pol*)	*a-vo-sw-eh*
	À tes souhaits! (*fam*)	*a-tay-sw-eh*
Cheers!	À votre santé!	*a vut-re sAH-tay*
	À la vôtre!	*a-la-voh-tre*
Congratulations!	Félicitations!	*fay-lee-see-tas-y-OH*
Don't mention it!	De rien!	*der-yEH*
	Il n'y a pas de quoi!	*eel-ny-a-pahd-kwa*
Enjoy your meal!	Bon appétit!	*bun-apay-tee*
Excuse me!	Excusez-moi! (*pol*)	*ehks-kew-zay-mwa*
	Excuse-moi! (*fam*)	*ehks-kewz-mwa*
	Pardonnez-moi! (*pol*)	*par-dun-ay-mwa*
	Pardonne-moi! (*fam*)	*par-dun-mwa*
Good luck!	Bonne chance!	*bun-sh-AH-s*
Happy New Year!	Bonne et heureuse année!	*bun ay ur-uhz a-nay*
Have a good holiday!	Bonnes vacances!	*bun vak-AH-s*
Have a good time!	Amusez-vous bien! (*pol*)	*a-mew-zay-voo byEH*
	Amuse-toi bien! (*fam*)	*a-mewz-twa byEH*

Have a good trip!	Bon voyage!	*bOH vwa-ya-zh*
Have a happy birthday!	Bon anniversaire!	*bun a-nee-vehr-sehr*
Many thanks!	Merci mille fois!	*mehr-see meel fwa*
	Merci infiniment!	*mehr-see EH-fee-neem-AH*
May I come in?	Puis-je entrer?	*pew-ee-zh AH-tray*
May I help you?	Vous désirez?	*voo day-zee-ray*
	Puis-je vous aider?	*pew-ee-zh voo-zay-day*
Merry Christmas!	Joyeux Noël!	*zh-wa-yuh nu-ehl*
No!	Non!	*nOH*
OK!	D'accord!	*dak-or*
	Entendu!	*AH-t-AH-dew*
Please!	S'il vous plaît! (*pol*)	*seel-voo-pleh*
	S'il te plaît (*fam*)	*seel-te-pleh*
Thank you!	Merci!	*mehr-see*
Yes!	Oui!	*wee*
You're welcome!	Je vous en prie! (*pol*)	*zhe vooz-AH-pree*
	Je t'en prie! (*fam*)	*zh-tAH-pree*

17. SPEAKING AND TALKING

a. SPEECH ACTIVITIES AND TYPES

advice	conseil (*m*)	*k-OH-say*
• **advise**	conseiller (*v*)	*k-OH-say-yay*
allude	faire (*v*) allusion	*fehr al-ewz-y-OH*
analogy	analogie (*f*)	*a-na-luzh-ee*
announce	annoncer (*v*)	*an-OH-say*
• **announcement**	annonce (*f*)	*an-OH-s*
answer	réponse (*f*)	*rayp-OH-s*
• **answer**	répondre (*v*)	*rayp-OH-dre*
argue	disputer (*v*)	*dees-pew-tay*
	arguer (de)	*ar-gew-ay (de)*
• **argument**	dispute (*f*)	*dees-pewt*
	argument (*m*)	*ar-gewm-AH*
articulate	articuler (*v*)	*ar-tee-kew-lay*
ask	demander (*v*)	*dem-AH-day*
beg to do (*something*)	prier (*v*) de faire quelque chose	*pree-yayd fehr kehlke sh-oh-z*
call	appeler (*v*)	*aplay*
change subject	changer (*v*) de sujet	*sh-AH-zh-ayd sew-zh-eh*
chat	causer (*v*)	*ko-zay*
communicate	communiquer (*v*)	*kum-ewn-ee-kay*
• **communication**	communication (*f*)	*kum-ewn-ee-kas-y-OH*
compare	comparer (*v*)	*k-OH-pa-ray*
• **comparison**	comparaison (*f*)	*k-OH-par-ehz-OH*

conclude	conclure (*v*)	*k-OH-klewr*
• conclusion	conclusion (*f*)	*k-OH-klewz-y-OH*
congratulate	féliciter (*v*)	*fay-lee-see-tay*
conversation	conversation (*f*)	*k-OH-vehr-sas-y-OH*
debate	débat (*m*)	*day-ba*
• debate	débattre (*v*)	*day-bat-re*
declare	déclarer (*v*)	*day-klar-ay*
deny	nier (*v*)	*nee-yay*
describe	décrire (*v*)	*day-kreer*
• description	description (*f*)	*dehs-kreeps-y-OH*
dictate	dicter (*v*)	*deek-tay*
digress	faire (*v*) une digression	*fehr ewn deeg-rays-y-OH*
discuss	discuter (*v*)	*dees-kew-tay*
• discussion	discussion (*f*)	*dees-kews-y-OH*
emphasis	emphase (*f*)	*AH-fahz*
• emphasize	accentuer (*v*)	*aks-AH-tew-ay*
excuse	excuse (*f*)	*ehks-kewz*
• excuse oneself	s'excuser (*v*)	*sehks-kew-zay*
explain	expliquer (*v*)	*ehks-plee-kay*
• explanation	explication (*f*)	*ehks-plee-kahs-y-OH*
express	exprimer (*v*)	*ehks-pree-may*
• express oneself	s'exprimer (*v*)	*sehks-pree-may*
• expression	expression (*f*)	*ehks-prehs-y-OH*
figure of speech	figure (*f*) de rhétorique	*feeg-ewr de ray-tor-eek*
• allegory	allégorie (*f*)	*al-ay-gor-ee*
• literal	litéral(e) (*adj, m, f*)	*lee-tay-ral*
• metaphor	métaphore (*f*)	*may-ta-for*
• symbol	symbole (*m*)	*s-EH-bul*
gossip	potin (*m*)	*put-EH*
• gossip	potiner (*v*)	*put-een-ay*
hesitation	hésitation (*f*)	*ay-zee-tahs-y-OH*
• hesitate	hésiter (*v*)	*ay-zee-tay*
identify	identifier (*v*)	*eed-AH-teef-yay*
indicate, point out	indiquer (*v*)	*EH-dee-kay*
• indication	indication (*f*)	*EH-dee-kahs-y-OH*
inform	informer (*v*)	*EH-form-ay*
	faire savoir (*v*)	*fehr savwar*
interrupt	interrompre (*v*)	*EH-tayr-OH-pre*
• interruption	interruption (*f*)	*EH-tayr-ewps-y-OH*
invite	inviter (*v*)	*EH-vee-tay*
jest	plaisanter (*v*)	*plehz-AH-tay*
joke	plaisanterie (*f*)	*plehz-AH-tree*
• tell a joke	raconter (*v*) une plaisanterie	*rak-OH-tay ewn plehz-AH-tree*
keep quiet	se taire (*v*)	*se-tehr*
lecture	conférence (*f*)	*kOH-fayr-AH-s*

• **lecture**	donner (*v*) une conférence	*dun-ay ewn kOH-fayr-AH-s*
lie	mensonge (*m*)	*m-AH-s-OH-zh*
• **lie**	mentir (*v*)	*m-AH-teer*
• **liar**	menteur (*m*)	*m-AH-tur*
	menteuse (*f*)	*mAH-tuhz*
listen to	écouter (*v*)	*ay-koo-tay*
malign, speak badly	diffamer (*v*)	*deef-a-may*
mean	signifier (*v*)	*see-ny-eef-yay*
	vouloir dire (*v*)	*vool-war deer*
• **meaning**	signification (*f*)	*see-ny-ee-fee-kas-y-OH*
	sens (*m*)	*sAHs*
mention	mentionner (*v*)	*mAH-sy-un-ay*
mumble	grommeler (*v*)	*grum-lay*
murmur	murmurer (*v*)	*mewr-mew-ray*
nag	grogner (*v*)	*gru-ny-ay*
offend	offenser (*v*)	*uf-AH-say*
oral	oral(e) (*adj, m, f*)	*or-al*
• **orally**	oralement (*adv*)	*or-alm-AH*
order	ordre (*m*)	*or-dre*
• **order**	ordonner (*v*)	*or-dun-ay*
outspokenly	franchement (*adv*)	*frAH-sh-mAH*
	carrément (*adv*)	*kar-ay-mAH*
praise	louer (*v*)	*lway*
pray	prier (*v*)	*pree-yay*
• **prayer**	prière (*f*)	*pree-yehr*
preach	prêcher (*v*)	*pray-shay*
• **sermon**	sermon (*m*)	*sehrm-OH*
promise	promesse (*f*)	*prum-ehs*
• **promise**	promettre (*v*)	*prum-eh-tre*
pronounce	prononcer (*v*)	*prun-OH-say*
• **pronunciation**	prononciation (*f*)	*prun-OH-see-yas-yOH*
propose	proposer (*v*)	*prup-OH-zay*
recommend	recommander (*v*)	*re-kum-AH-day*
relate	raconter (*v*)	*rak-OH-tay*
repeat	répéter (*v*)	*ray-pay-tay*
• **repetition**	répétition (*f*)	*ray-pay-tees-y-OH*
report	compte rendu (*m*)	*kOHt-rAH-dew*
• **report**	faire (*v*) un compte rendu	*fehr UH kOHt-rAH-dew*
	faire (*v*) un rapport sur	*fehr UH ra-por sewr*
reproach	reprocher (*v*)	*re-prush-ay*
request	demande (*f*)	*dem-AH-d*
• **request**	demander (*v*)	*dem-AH-day*
rhetoric	rhétorique (*f*)	*ray-tor-eek*
• **rhetorical**	rhétorique (*adj*)	*ray-tor-eek*

• **rhetorical question**	demande (*f*) rhétorique	*dem-AH-d ray-tor-eek*
rumor	bruit (*m*)	*brew-ee*
• **Rumor has it that . . .**	Le bruit court que . . .	*le brew-ee koor ke*
say, tell	dire (*v*)	*deer*
shout, yell	cri (*m*)	*kree*
• **shout, yell**	crier (*v*)	*kree-yay*
shut up	se taire (*v*)	*se-tehr*
• **Shut up!**	Taisez-vous!	*teh-zay-voo*
silence	silence (*m*)	*seel-AHs*
• **silent**	silencieux(-euse) (*adj, m, f*)	*seel-AHs-yuh(-yuhz)*
speak, talk	parler (*v*)	*par-lay*
• **speech, talk**	discours (*m*)	*dees-koor*
state	affirmer (*v*)	*a-feerm-ay*
• **statement**	affirmation (*f*)	*a-feerm-as-y-OH*
story	conte (*m*)	*kOHt*
	histoire (*f*)	*ees-twar*
• **tell (*a story*)**	conter (*v*)	*kOH-tay*
	raconter (*v*) une histoire	*rakOH-tay ewn ees-twar*
suggest	suggérer (*v*)	*sewg-zh-ay-ray*
summarize	résumer (*v*)	*ray-zewm-ay*
• **summary**	sommaire (*m*)	*sum-ehr*
	résumé (*m*)	*ray-zewm-ay*
swear *(e.g., in court)*	jurer (*v*)	*zh-ew-ray*
• ***(e.g., profanity)***	dire (*v*) des jurons	*deer day zh-ewr-OH*
thank	remercier (*v*)	*re-mehr-see-yay*
threat	menace (*f*)	*me-nas*
• **threaten**	menacer (*v*)	*me-nas-ay*
toast	toast (*m*)	*tost*
• **toast**	porter (*v*) un toast	*por-tay UH tost*
translate	traduire (*v*)	*trad-ew-eer*
• **translation**	traduction (*f*)	*trad-ewks-yOH*
vocabulary	vocabulaire (*m*)	*vu-ka-bew-lehr*
warn	avertir (*v*)	*a-vehr-teer*
	prévenir (*v*)	*pray-vneer*
• **warning**	avis (*m*)	*a-vee*
	prévenance (*f*)	*pray-vn-AH-s*
whisper	chuchoter (*v*)	*shew-shut-ay*
word	mot (*m*) (*written*)	*mOH*
	parole (*f*) (*spoken*)	*pa-rul*
yawn	bâillement (*m*)	*bah-y-mAH*
• **yawn**	bâiller (*v*)	*bah-yay*

b. USEFUL EXPRESSIONS

Actually	effectivement (*adv*)	*ay-fehk-teev-mAH*
As a matter of fact	au fait	*oh-feht*
Briefly	en bref	*AH-brehf*
By the way	à propos	*a-pro-po*
Go ahead!	Allez-y! (*pol*)	*a-lay-zee*
	Vas-y! (*fam*)	*va-zee*
How do you say . . . in French?	Comment dit-on . . . en français?	*kum-AH deet-OH . . . AH frAH-seh*
I don't understand!	Je ne comprends pas!	*zhen-kOH-prAH-pah*
I'm sure that	Je suis sûr(e) (*m, f*) que	*zhe swee sewr ke . . .*
Isn't it so?	N'est-ce pas?	*nehs-pas*
It seems that	Il semble que	*eel sAH-bl ke*
It's necessary that	Il faut que	*eel foh ke*
	Il est nécessaire que	*eel eh nay-say-sehr ke*
It's not true!	Ce n'est pas vrai!	*se-neh-pah vreh*
It's obvious that	Il est évident que	*eel eh tay-veed-AH ke*
It's true!	C'est vrai!	*seh vreh*
Listen	Écoutez (*pol*)	*ay-koo-tay*
	Écoute (*fam*)	*ay-koot*
Now	Maintenant	*mEHt-nAH*
To sum up	En somme	*AH sum*
What was I saying?	Qu'est-ce que je disais?	*kehs-ke zhe dee-zeh*
Who knows?	Qui sait?	*kee seh*

FOCUS: Some Common Gestures

> In common speech situations, French people gesticulate quite noticeably. They also tend to touch each other much more upon greeting each other.

Are you crazy?	Êtes-vous (*pol*) fou (*m*)/folle (*f*)?	*eht-voo foo (ful)*
	Es-tu (*fam*) fou (*m*)/ folle (*f*)?	*eh-tew foo (ful)*
	Êtes-vous (*pol*) loufoque (*m/f*)?	*eht-voo loo-fuk*
	Es-tu (*fam*) loufoque (*m/f*)?	*eh-tew loo-fuk*

English	French	Pronunciation
Come here! 	Venez (*pol*) ici! Viens (*fam*) ici!	*vnay-zee-see* *vy-EH-zee-see*
Hello (*pol*)! 	Bonjour! (*during daytime*) Bonsoir! (*during evening hours*) (see also 16a)	*bOH-zhoor* *bOH-swar*
Hi (*fam*)! 	Salut!	*sal-ew*
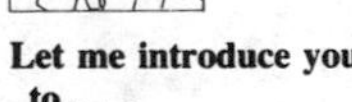 **Let me introduce you to . . .** 	Je vous (*pol*) présente à . . . Je te (*fam*) présente à . . .	*zhe voo prayz-AH-t a . . .* *zh-te prayz-AH-t a . . .*
No way! 	Pas de moyen! Pas possible!	*pahd-mwa-yEH* *pah pus-eebl*
Uhm . . . good! 	C'est très bon! C'est si bon!	*seh treh bOH* *seh see bOH*

18. THE TELEPHONE

a. TELEPHONES AND ACCCESSORIES

answering machine	répondeur téléphonique enregistreur (*m*)	*rayp-OH-dur tay-lay-fun-eek AH-re-zh-ees-trur*
	téléphone-répondeur (*m*)	*tay-lay-fun rayp-OH-dur*
cable	câble (*m*) téléphonique	*kah-bl tay-lay-fun-eek*
fax machine	transmetteur (*m*) FAX	*tr-AH-s-meht-ur fahks*
intercom	interphone (*m*)	*EH-tehr-fun*
receiver (*handset*)	combiné (*m*)	*kOH-bee-nay*
• **earphone**	écouteur (*m*)	*ay-koot-ur*
telecommunication	télécommunication (*f*)	*tay-lay-kum-ew-nee-kas-yOH*
• **telecommunications satellite**	satellite (*m*) de télécommunications	*sat-eh-leet de tay-lay-kum-ew-nee-kas-yOH*
telephone	téléphone (*m*)	*tay-lay-fun*
• **outlet (*phone*)**	prise (*f*)	*preez*
• **pay phone**	téléphone (*m*) public	*tay-lay-fun pew-bleek*
• **phone book**	annuaire (*m*) du téléphone	*a-new-ehr dew tay-lay-fun*
	bottin (*m*)	*but-EH*
• **phone booth**	cabine (*f*) téléphonique	*ka-been tay-lay-fun-eek*
• **plug**	fiche (*f*) téléphonique	*feesh tay-lay-fun-eek*
• **portable phone**	téléphone (*m*) portatif	*tay-lay-fun por-ta-teef*
• **telephone set**	appareil (*m*) téléphonique	*a-pa-ray tay-lay-fun-eek*
• **telephone**	téléphoner (*v*)	*tay-lay-fun-ay*
telephone credit card	télécarte (*f*)	*tay-lay-kart*
telex machine	transmetteur (*m*) TELEX	*tr-AH-s-meht-ur tay-lehks*
token	jeton (*m*)	*zh-tOH*
• **slot (*for tokens*)**	fente (*f*)	*fAHt*
yellow pages	pages (*f*, *pl*) jaunes	*pazh zh-ohn*

b. USING THE TELEPHONE

answer	répondre (*v*)	*rayp-OH-dre*
• **pick up (the phone)**	décrocher (*v*)	*day-krush-ay*

area code	code (*m*) régional	*kud ray-zh-un-al*
collect call	téléphoner en P.C.V.	*tay-lay-fun-ay AH pay-say-vay*
dial	composer le numéro	*kOH-poh-zayl new-may-roh*
• **direct dialing**	téléphoner en direct	*tay-lay-fun-ay AH dee-rehkt*
fax	FAX	*fahks*
hang up	accrocher (*v*)	*ak-rush-ay*
information	renseignement (*m*)	*rAH-seh-ny-mAH*
long-distance call	appel à l'extérieur	*ap-ehl al ehks-tay-ree-ur*
make a call	faire (*v*) un appel téléphonique	*fehr UH nap-ehl tay-lay-fun-eek*
• **Hello!**	Allô!	*a-loh*
• **Is . . . in?**	Est-ce que . . . est là?	*ehs-ke eh la*
• **This is . . .**	Ici . . .	*ee-see*
• **Who's speaking?**	Qui parle?	*kee parl*
• **Wrong number!**	Mauvais numéro!	*muv-eh new-may-roh*
message	message (*m*)	*may-sa-zh*
operator	téléphoniste (*m/f*)	*tay-lay-fun-eest*
• **switchboard operator**	standardiste (*m/f*)	*stAH-dard-eest*
phone	téléphoner (*v*)	*tay-lay-fun-ay*
phone bill	facture (*f*)	*fak-tewr*
phone call	appel (*m*) téléphonique	*ap-ehl tay-lay-fun-eek*
phone line	ligne (*f*) téléphonique	*lee-ny tay-lay-fun-eek*
• **busy (line)**	occupée (*adj*)	*uk-ew-pay*
• **free (line)**	libre (*adj*)	*lee-bre*
phone number	numéro (*m*) de téléphone	*new-may-rohd tay-lay-fun*
ring ***(phone)***	sonner (*v*)	*sun-ay*
telex	télex (*m*)	*tay-lehks*

19. LETTER WRITING

a. FORMAL SALUTATIONS/CLOSINGS

Dear Sir	Monsieur	*me-sy-uh*
Dear Madam	Madame	*ma-dahm*
To whom it may concern	À qui de droit	*a-kee de drwa*
Yours truly	salutations distinguées	*sa-lew-tas-yOH deest-EH-gay*

With cordial greetings	Sentiments cordiaux	*sAH-teem-AH kord-y-oh*
Please accept	Veuillez accepter	*vuh-yay ak-sehp-tay*
	Veuillez agréer	*vuh-yay a-gray-ay*

b. FAMILIAR SALUTATIONS/CLOSINGS

Dear	Cher (*adj/m*); (*pl*, chers)	*sh-ehr*
	Chère (*f*); (*pl*, chères)	*sh-ehr*
Yours	Bien à toi	*byEH a twa*
Greetings	Sincères salutations	*sEH-sehr sa-lew-tas-yOH*
Affectionately	Affectueusement (*adv*)	*a-fehk-tew-uhz-mAH*
Give my regards to	Un bon souvenir à	*UH bOH soo-vneer a*
A kiss	baiser (*m*)	*bay-zay*
A hug	embrassement (*m*)	*AH-bras-mAH*

c. PARTS OF A LETTER/PUNCTUATION

body	contenu (*m*)	*kOH-te-new*
	corps (*m*)	*kor*
closing	formule (*f*) finale	*for-mewl fee-nal*
	salutation (*f*) finale	*sa-lew-tas-yOH fee-nal*
date	date (*f*)	*dat*
heading	l'en-tête (*f*)	*lAH-teht*
	vedette (*f*)	*ve-deht*
place	lieu (*m*)	*ly-uh*
punctuation	ponctuation (*f*)	*pOHk-tew-as-yOH*
• **accent**	accent (*m*)	*aks-AH*
• **apostrophe**	apostrophe (*f*)	*a-pus-truf*
• **asterisk**	astérisque (*m*)	*as-tay-reesk*
• **bracket**	crochet (*m*)	*krush-eh*
• **capital letter**	lettre majuscule (*f*)	*leht-re ma-zh-ews-kewl*
• **colon**	deux points (*m, pl*)	*duh pwEH*
• **comma**	virgule (*f*)	*veerg-ewl*
• **exclamation mark**	point (*m*) d'exclamation	*pwEH dehks-kla-mas-yOH*
• **hyphen**	tiret (*m*)	*teer-eh*
	trait (*m*) d'union	*trehd-ew-ny-OH*
• **italics**	en italique (*m*)	*AH nee-ta-leek*
• **parenthesis**	parenthèse (*f*)	*par-AH-tehz*
• **period**	point (*m*)	*pwEH*

• **question mark**	point (*m*) d'interrogation	*pwEH-dEH-tay-rug-as-yOH*
• **quotation mark**	guillemet (*m*)	*gee-y-meh*
• **semicolon**	point (*m*) virgule (*f*)	*pwEH veerg-ewl*
• **small letter**	lettre minuscule (*f*)	*leht-re meen-ews-kewl*
• **square bracket**	crochet (*m*)	*krush-eh*
• **underlining**	soulignement (*m*)	*soo-lee-ny-mAH*
salutation	formule (*f*) initiale	*for-mew-lee-nees-yal*
sentence	phrase (*f*)	*frahz*
signature	signature (*f*)	*see-ny-a-tewr*
• **sign**	signer (*v*)	*see-ny-ay*
spelling	orthographe (*f*)	*or-tug-raf*
text	texte (*m*)	*tehkst*
• **abbreviation**	abréviation (*f*)	*ab-rayv-y-as-yOH*
• **letter** *(of the alphabet)*	lettre (*f*)	*leht-re*
• **line**	ligne (*f*)	*lee-ny*
• **margin**	marge (*f*)	*mar-zh*
• **P.S.**	P.S.	*pay-ehs*
	post-scriptum (*m*)	*pust-skreep-tum*
• **paragraph**	paragraphe (*m*)	*pa-ra-graf*
• **phrase**	phrase (*f*)	*frahz*
word	mot (*m*)	*moh*

d. WRITING MATERIALS AND ACCESSORIES

adhesive tape	ruban (*m*) adhésif transparent	*rewbAH ad-ay-zeef trAHs-par-AH*
	du skotch (*m*)	*dew skutch*
clip	trombone (*m*)	*trOH-bun*
envelope	enveloppe (*f*)	*AH-vlup*
eraser	gomme (*f*)	*gum*
glue	colle (*f*)	*kul*
ink	encre (*f*)	*AH-kre*
letter	lettre (*f*)	*leht-re*
letterhead	papier (*m*) à en-tête	*pap-yay a AH-teht*
marker	marqueur (*m*)	*mark-ur*
	crayon-feutre (*m*)	*kray-yOH fuh-tr*
pad	bloc-notes (*m*)	*bluk nut*
page	page (*f*)	*pazh*
paper	papier (*m*)	*pap-yay*
pen	stylo (*m*)	*stee-loh*
• **ballpoint pen**	stylo (*m*) à bille	*stee-loh a bee-y*
• **felt-tip pen**	stylo-feutre (*m*)	*stee-loh fuh-tr*
pencil	crayon (*m*)	*kray-yOH*
ruler	règle (*f*)	*reh-gle*
scissors	ciseaux (*m, pl*)	*see-zoh*

FOCUS: Letters

Formal

Lieu et date	Paris, le premier juin 19 . . .
Destinataire	M. Charles DURAND, Directeur Institut de Beauté 2, Square Henri Delormel 75014 Paris
Formule (Salutation) initiale	Monsieur le Directeur,
le contenu (le corps)	Voudriez-vous m'envoyer . . . .
Formule (Salutation) finale	Veuillez agréer, Monsieur, l'expression de mes sentiments distingués.
Signature	____________________
Destinateur	Monique PAULY 29, rue des Jardins 75008 Paris

Familiar

Paris, le 2 juin 19 . . .

Chers amis,

J'écris ces quelques mots pour . . . .
. . . .

Grosses bises,

Dominique

staple	agrafe (*f*)	*ag-raf*
• **stapler**	agrafeuse (*f*)	*ag-gra-fuhz*
string	ficelle (*f*)	*fee-sehl*
typewriter	machine (*f*) à écrire	*ma-sheen a ay-kreer*
• **carriage**	chariot (*m*)	*shar-ee-oh*
• **keyboard**	clavier (*m*)	*klav-yay*
• **ribbon**	ruban (*m*)	*rewb-AH*
• **space bar**	barre (*f*) d'espacement	*bar-dehs-pas-mAH*
• **tab**	tabulateur (*m*)	*ta-bew-la-tur*
• **type**	taper (*v*) à la machine	*ta-pay a la ma-sheen*

For more information on computer terminology, see Section 42.

e. AT THE POST OFFICE

abroad	à l'étranger	*al-ay-trAH-zh-ay*
address	adresse (*f*)	*ad-rehs*
• **return address**	adresse (*f*) de l'expéditeur	*ad-rehs de lehks-pay-dee-tur*
addressee	destinataire (*m*)	*day-steen-a-tehr*
airmail	par avion	*par av-yOH*
business letter	lettre (*f*) commerciale	*leht-re kum-ehrs-yal*
clerk	commis (*m*)	*kum-ee*
	employé(e) (*m, f*)	*AH-plwa-yay*
clerk's window	guichet (*m*)	*geesh-eh*
correspondence	correspondance (*f*)	*kor-ehs-pOH-dAH-ss*
• **envelope**	enveloppe (*f*)	*AH-vlup*
general delivery	poste (*f*) restante	*pust rehstAHt*
invitation	invitation (*f*)	*EH-veet-as-yOH*
• **wedding/other**	faire-part (*m*)	*fehr-par*
letter carrier	facteur (*m*) (de lettres)	*fak-tur (de leht-re)*
mail	courrier (*m*)	*koor-yay*
	poste (*f*)	*pust*
• **mail**	mettre (*v*) une lettre à la poste	*meht-re ewn leht-re a la pust*
mail delivery	distribution (*f*) du courrier	*dees-tree-bews-yOH dew koor-yay*
mailbox (slot)	boîte (*f*) à lettres	*bwat a leht-re*
money order	mandat (*m*) de paiement	*mAHda de pehmAH*
note	billet (*m*)	*beey-eh*

package	colis (*m*)	*kul-ee*
	paquet (*m*)	*pa-kay*
post office	bureau (*m*) de poste	*bew-rohd pust*
postage	affranchissement (*m*)	*a-frAH-shees-mAH*
• meter	vignette (*f*)	*vee-ny-eht*
postal box	case (*f*) postale	*kahz pus-tal*
	boîte (*f*) postale	*bwat pus-tal*
postal code	code (*m*) postal	*kud pus-tal*
postal rate	tarif (*m*)	*tar-eef*
postcard	carte (*f*) postale	*kart pus-tal*
printed matter	imprimés (*m, pl*)	*EH-pree-may*
receive	recevoir (*v*)	*res-vwar*
registered letter	lettre (*f*) recommandée	*leht-re re-kum-AH-day*
reply	réponse (*f*)	*raypOHs*
• reply	répondre (*v*)	*rayp-OH-dre*
send	expédier (*v*)	*ehks-payd-yay*
	envoyer (*v*)	*AH-vwa-yay*
sender	expéditeur (*m*)	*ehks-pay-dee-tur*
special delivery	expédition (*f*) express	*ehks-payd-ees-yOH ehks-press*
stamp (postage)	timbre-poste (*m*)	*tEH-bre pust*
wait for	attendre (*v*)	*at-AH-dre*
write	écrire (*v*)	*ay-kreer*

20. THE MEDIA

a. PRINT MEDIA

advertising	publicité (*f*)	*pew-blee-see-tay*
appendix	appendice (*m*)	*ap-AH-deess*
atlas	atlas (*m*)	*at-lahss*
author	auteur (*m*)	*oh-tur*
	femme (*f*) auteur	*fahm oh-tur*
book	livre (*m*)	*leev-re*
comics	bande (*f*) dessinée	*bAHd day-see-nay*
cover	couverture (*f*)	*koo-vehr-tewr*
essay	essai (*m*)	*ay-seh*
fiction	ouvrage (*m*) de fiction	*oov-ra-zh de feeks-yOH*
• nonfiction	ouvrage (*m*) de réalité	*oov-ra-zh de ray-al-ee-tay*
• science fiction	science-fiction (*f*)	*syAHs-feeks-yOH*
index	index (*m*)	*EH-dehks*
magazine	magazine (*m*)	*ma-ga-zeen*
	revue (*f*)	*re-vew*

newspaper	journal (*m*)	*zh-oor-nal*
• **article**	article (*m*)	*ar-teekl*
• **criticism**	critique (*f*)	*kree-teek*
• **daily newspaper**	quotidien (*m*)	*kut-eed-y-EH*
• **editor**	rédacteur (*m*)	*ray-dak-tur*
	rédactrice (*f*)	*ray-dak-treess*
• **editorial**	éditorial (*m*)	*ay-dee-tor-yal*
• **front page**	la une	*la-ewn*
	première page (*f*)	*prem-yehr pazh*
• **headline**	manchette (*f*)	*mAH-sh-eht*
• **illustration**	illustration (*f*)	*eel-ew-stras-yOH*
• **interview**	interview (*f*)	*EH-tehr-vew*
• **journalist**	journaliste (*m/f*)	*zh-oor-nal-eest*
• **news**	actualités (*f*)	*ak-tew-a-leet-ay*
• **obituary**	notice (*f*)	*nut-eess*
	nécrologique	*nay-kru-lu-zheek*
• **photo**	photo(graphie) (*f*)	*fu-tu(graf-ee)*
• **reader**	lecteur (*m*)	*lehk-tur*
	lectrice (*f*)	*lehk-treess*
• **reporter**	reporter (*m/f*)	*re-port-ehr*
• **review**	critique (*f*)	*kree-teek*
• **weekly periodical**	hebdomadaire (*adj/n, m, f*)	*ehb-dum-a-dehr*
note	note (*f*)	*nut*
• **footnote**	note (*f*) en bas de page	*nut-AH-bahd-pazh*
novel	roman (*m*)	*rum-AH*
• **adventure**	d'aventure	*dav-AH-tewr*
• **best-seller**	best-seller (*m*)	*behst-sehl-ur*
• **mystery**	policier (*adj*)	*pul-ees-yay*
• **plot**	intrigue (*f*)	*EH-treeg*
• **romance**	d'amour	*da-moor*
page	page (*f*)	*pazh*
pamphlet, brochure	dépliant (*m*)	*day-plee-yAH*
	brochure (*f*)	*brush-ewr*
play	pièce (*f*) de théâtre	*pee-ehss de tay-ah-tre*
• **comedy**	comédie (*f*)	*kum-ay-dee*
• **drama**	drame (*m*)	*drahm*
• **tragedy**	tragédie (*f*)	*tra-zh-ay-dee*
pocket book	livre (*m*) de poche	*leev-re de push*
poem, poetry	poème (*m*)	*pu-ehm*
	poésie (*f*)	*pu-ay-zee*
print medium	imprimerie (*f*)	*EH-preem-ree*
• **print**	imprimer (*v*)	*EH-preem-ay*
• **printing, typography**	typographie (*f*)	*teep-ug-raf-ee*
publish	publier (*v*)	*pew-blee-yay*
• **publisher**	éditeur (*m*)	*ay-deet-ur*

read	lire (*v*)	*leer*
reference book	ouvrage (*m*) de référence	*oov-ra-zh de ray-fayr-AH-s*
• **definition**	définition (*f*)	*day-fee-nees-yOH*
• **dictionary**	dictionnaire (*m*)	*deek-see-yun-ehr*
• **encyclopedia**	encyclopédie (*f*)	*AH-see-klup-ay-dee*
science fiction	science-fiction (*f*)	*syAHs-feeks-yOH*
short story	conte (*m*)	*kOHt*
	nouvelle (*f*)	*noo-vehl*
text	texte (*m*)	*tehkst*
title	titre (*m*)	*teet-re*
turn pages, leaf through	tourner (*v*) la page	*toor-nay la pahzh*
	feuilleter (*v*)	*fuh-y-tay*
write	écrire (*v*)	*ay-kreer*

b. ELECTRONIC MEDIA

antenna	antenne (*f*)	*AH-tehn*
audio-visual equipment	appareils (*m, pl*) audio-visuels	*a-pa-reh-y ohd-yuh vee-zew-ehl*
• **blank cassette**	cassette vierge (*f*)	*kas-eht vee-er-zh*
• **cassette**	cassette (*f*)	*kas-eht*
• **compact disc**	disque compact (*m*)	*deesk-kOH-pakt*
• **headphones**	casque (*m*) à écouteurs	*kask-a-ay-koo-tur*
• **loudspeaker**	haut-parleur (*m*)	*oh-par-lur*
• **microphone**	microphone (*m*)	*meek-ruf-un*
• **play a record**	passer un disque	*pah-say UH deesk*
• **receiver, tuner**	dispositif (*m*) d'accord	*dees-poh-zee-teef dak-or*
• **record**	disque (*m*)	*deesk*
	enregistrer (*v*)	*AH-re-zh-ees-tray*
• **record player**	tourne-disque (*m*)	*toorn-deesk*
• **speaker**	caisse (*f*) acoustique	*kehs-akoos-teek*
	baffle (*m*)	*bah-fle*
• **stereo**	stéréo(phonique) (*adj*)	*stay-ray-u-(fun-eek)*
• **tape**	bande (*f*) magnétique	*bAHd ma-ny-ay-teek*
• **tape recorder**	magnétophone (*m*)	*ma-ny-ay-tu-fun*
program	programme (*m*)	*prug-ram*
projector	projecteur (*m*)	*pruzh-ehk-tur*
• **slide projector**	pour diapositives (*f*)	*poor dee-a-poh-zee-teev*
radio	radio (*f*)	*rad-yo*
	T.S.F. (*f*)	*tay-ehs-ehf*
• **car radio**	autoradio (*m*)	*u-tu-rad-yo*
• **listen to**	écouter (*v*)	*ay-koo-tay*
• **news report**	nouvelles (*f, pl*) du jour	*noo-vehl dew zh-oor*

• **newscast**	journal (*m*) parlé	*zh-oor-nal par-lay*
• **pocket radio**	poste (*m*) à transistors de poche	*pust a trAH-zees-tor de push*
• **portable radio**	radio portative (*f*)	*rad-yo port-a-teev*
• **station**	indicatif (*m*) d'appel	*EH-dee-ka-teef dap-ehl*
show	spectacle (*m*)	*spehk-tak-le*
television	télévision (*f*)	*tay-lay-veez-yOH*
• **channel**	canal (*m*)	*ka-nal*
	chaîne (*f*)	*sh-ehn*
• **closed circuit**	circuit fermé (*m*)	*seer-kew-ee fehrm-ay*
• **commercial**	publicité (*f*)	*pew-blee-see-tay*
• **documentary**	documentaire (*m*)	*duk-ewm-AH-tehr*
• **interview**	interview (*f*)	*EH-tehr-vew*
• **look at, watch**	regarder (*v*)	*re-gar-day*
• **network**	réseau (*m*)	*ray-zoh*
• **news report**	actualités (*f*)	*ak-tew-a-leet-ay*
• **newscast**	journal (*m*) télévisé	*zh-oor-nal tay-lay-vee-zay*
• **on the air**	en émission	*AH-nay-mees-yOH*
• **remote control**	télécommande (*f*)	*tay-lay-kum-AH-d*
• **series**	série (*f*) d'émissions	*say-ree day-mees-yOH*
• **soap opera**	mélo (*m*)	*may-lo*
• **television set**	téléviseur (*m*)	*tay-lay-veez-ur*
• **transmission**	émission (*f*)	*ay-mees-yOH*
• **TV**	télé (*f*)	*tay-lay*
• **TV movie**	téléfilm (*m*)	*tay-lay feelm*
• **VCR**	système (*m*) d'enregistrement (*m*) à vidéocassettes	*sees-tehm dAH-re-zh-eestremAH a vee-day-o kas-eht*
	magnétoscope (*m*)	*man-yay-tus-kup*
	VCR (*m*)	*vay-say-ehr*
• **VHS/SECAM/TV**	VHS/SECAM/TV (*m*)	*vay-ash-ehs say-kahm tay-vay*
	système (*m*) séquentiel à mémoire	*sees-tehm say-kAH-syehl a may-mwar*
• **video game**	jeu-vidéo (*m*)	*zh-uh vee-day-o*
• **videocassette**	vidéocassette (*f*)	*vee-day-o kas-eht*
• **videorock**	vidéorock (*m*)	*vee-day-o ruk*
• **videotape**	bande (*f*) magnétique	*bAHd ma-ny-ay-teek*
• **volume control**	réglage (*m*) de volume	*ray-glazh de vul-ewm*
turn off	éteindre (*v*)	*ayt-EH-dre*
turn on	allumer (*v*)	*al-ew-may*
walkie-talkie	talkie-walkie (*m*)	*tuk-ee-wuk-ee*

FOCUS: Colloquial Expressions

Relevant idiomatic expressions are handled in the vocabulary lists throughout the book. In addition, there are several FOCUS boxes dealing with special groups of idioms. Here are a few idioms dealing with ways of expressing displeasure:

Come on!	allons donc!	*al-OH dOH*
Cut it out!	arrêtez!	*a-reht-ay*
Damn it!	Zut!	*zewt*
"dirty word"	"mot grossier (*m*)"	*moh gros-yay*
Get lost!	Allez-vous en!	*a-lay-vooz-AH*
No way!	Pas de moyen!	*pahd mwa y-EH*
Yuch!	Quel dégoût!	*kehl day-goo*

21. FEELINGS

a. MOODS/ATTITUDES/EMOTIONS

affection	affection (*f*)	*af-ehks-yOH*
agree	être (*v*) d'accord	*eh-tre dak-or*
anger	colère (*f*)	*kul-ehr*
• **angry**	fâché(e) (*adj, m, f*)	*fah-shay*
anxiety, anxiousness	anxiété (*f*)	*AHks-yay-tay*
• **anxious**	anxieux (*adj, m*)	*AHks-yuh*
	anxieuse (*adj, f*)	*AHks-yuhz*
assure	assurer (*v*)	*a-sewr-ay*
attitude	attitude (*f*)	*a-tee-tewd*
be able to	pouvoir (*v*)	*poo-vwar*
be down	être (*v*) à plat	*eh-tre a pla*
be up	être (*v*) remonté(e)	*eh-tre rem-OH-tay*
bore	ennuyer (*v*)	*AH-new-ee-yay*
• **become bored**	s'ennuyer (*v*)	*sAH-new-ee-yay*
• **feel bored**	crever (*v*) d'ennui	*kre-vay dAH-new-ee*
• **boredom**	ennui (*m*)	*AH-new-ee*
complain	se plaindre (*v*)	*se-plEH-dre*
• **complaint**	plainte (*f*)	*plEHt*
cry (weep)	pleurer (*v*)	*plur-ay*
• **tears**	larmes (*f*)	*larm*
depressed	déprimé(e) (*adj, m, f*)	*day-preem-ay*
• **depression**	dépression (*f*)	*day-prays-yOH*
desperate	désespéré(e) (*adj, m, f*)	*dayz-ehs-pay-ray*
• **desperation**	désespoir (*m*)	*dayz-ehs-pwar*
disagree	être (*v*) en désaccord	*eh-tre AH day-za-kor*

• **disagreement**	désaccord (*m*)	*day-za-kor*
• **be against**	être (*v*) contre	*eh-tre kOHtre*
disappoint	décevoir (*v*)	*day-svwar*
• **disappointed**	déçu(e) (*adj/m, f*)	*dayss-ew*
disappointment	déception (*f*)	*day-sehp-syOH*
dissatisfaction	insatisfaction (*f*)	*EH-sa-tees-faks-yOH*
• **dissatisfied**	insatisfait(e) (*adj, m, f*)	*EH-sa-tees-feh(t)*
encourage	encourager (*v*)	*AH-koor-azh-ay*
• **encouragement**	encouragement (*m*)	*AH-koor-azh-mAH*
faith, trust	confiance (*f*)	*kOH-fy-AH-s*
• **trust**	avoir (*v*) confiance en	*avwar kOH-fy-AH-s AH*
fear	peur (*f*)	*pur*
• **be afraid**	avoir (*v*) peur	*avwar pur*
feel	sentir (*v*)	*sAH-teer*
• **feel like**	avoir (*v*) envie de	*avwar AH-vee-de*
flatter	flatter (*v*)	*flat-ay*
• **flattery**	flatterie (*f*)	*flat-ree*
fun, enjoyment	amusement (*m*)	*a-mewz-mAH*
• **have fun, enjoy oneself**	s'amuser (*v*)	*sa-mewz-ay*
happiness	bonheur (*m*)	*bun-ur*
• **happy**	heureux (*adj, m*)	*ur-uh*
	heureuse (*adj, f*)	*ur-huz*
	content(e) (*adj, m, f*)	*kOHt-AH(t)*
have to, must	devoir (*v*)	*de-vwar*
hope	espoir (*m*)	*ehs-pwar*
• **hope**	espérer (*v*)	*ehs-pay-ray*
indifference	indifférence (*f*)	*EH-dee-fay-rAH-s*
• **indifferent**	indifférent(e) (*adj, m, f*)	*EH-dee-fay-rAH(t)*
joy	joie (*f*)	*zh-wa*
laugh	rire (*v*)	*reer*
• **laughter**	rire (*m*)	*reer*
matter	importer (*v*)	*EH-por-tay*
mood	humeur (*f*)	*ew-mur*
• **bad mood**	mauvaise humeur	*muv-ehz ew-mur*
• **good mood**	bonne humeur	*bun ew-mur*
need	besoin (*m*)	*be-zwEH*
• **need**	avoir (*v*) besoin de	*avwar be-zwEH de*
patience	patience (*f*)	*pas-yAHs*
• **have patience**	avoir (*v*) de la patience	*avwar-dla-pas-yAHs*
relief	soulagement (*m*)	*sool-azh-mAH*

• **sigh of relief**	soupir (*m*) de soulagement	*soo-peer de sool-azh-mAH*
sad	triste (*adj*)	*treest*
• **sadness**	tristesse (*f*)	*treest-ehs*
satisfaction	satisfaction (*f*)	*sa-tees-faks-yOH*
• **satisfied**	satisfait(e) (*adj, m, f*)	*sa-tees-feh(t)*
shame	honte (*f*)	*OHt*
• **be ashamed**	avoir (*v*) honte	*avwar OHt*
smile	sourire (*v* & *n, m*)	*soo-reer*
sorrow	chagrin (*m*)	*shag-rEH*
surprise	surprise (*f*)	*sewr-preez*
• **surprise**	surprendre (*v*)	*sewr-prAH-dre*
• **surprised**	surpris(e) (*adj, m, f*)	*sewr-pree(z)*
sympathy	compassion (*f*)	*kOH-pahs-yOH*
• **sympathetic**	compatissant(e) (*adj, m, f*)	*kOH-pa-tees-AH(t)*
thankfulness	gratitude (*f*)	*gra-tee-tewd*
	reconnaissance (*f*)	*re-kun-ehs-AH-s*
• **thankful**	reconnaissant(e) (*adj, m, f*)	*re-kun-ehs-AH(t)*
• **thank**	remercier (*v*)	*re-mehr-see-yay*
tolerance	tolérance (*f*)	*tul-ay-rAH-s*
• **tolerate**	tolérer (*v*)	*tul-ay-ray*
want to	vouloir (*v*)	*vool-war*
	désirer (*v*)	*day-zee-ray*

b. LIKES AND DISLIKES

accept	accepter (*v*)	*aks-ehp-tay*
• **acceptable**	acceptable (*adj*)	*aks-ehp-ta-ble*
• **unacceptable**	inacceptable (*adj*)	*een-aks-ehp-ta-ble*
approval	approbation (*f*)	*ap-rub-ahs-yOH*
• **approve**	approuver (*v*)	*ap-roov-ay*
be fond of	avoir (*v*) une passion pour	*avwar ewn pahs-yOH poor*
detest	détester (*v*)	*day-tehst-ay*
disgust	dégoût (*m*)	*day-goo*
• **disgusted**	dégoûté(e) (*adj, m, f*)	*day-goo-tay*
hate	haïr (*v*)	*a-eer*
• **hatred**	haine (*f*)	*ehn*
I can't stand him (her)!	Je ne peux pas le (la) supporter!	*zhen puh pahl(la) sew-por-tay*
kiss	embrasser (*v*)	*AH-bra-say*

like	aimer (*v*) bien	*ay-may byEH*
• **liking (*taste*)**	penchant (*m*)	*pAH-shAH*
	goût (*m*)	*goo*
• **dislike (not to like)**	ne pas aimer (*v*)	*ne-pah-zay-may*
love	amour (*m*)	*a-moor*
• **love**	aimer (*v*)	*ay-may*
mediocre	médiocre (*adj*)	*mayd-y-uk-re*
pleasant	agréable (*adj*)	*a-gray-abl*
• **unpleasant**	désagréable (*adj*)	*dayz-a-gray-abl*
prefer	préférer (*v*)	*pray-fay-ray*
Too bad!	Dommage!	*dum-azh*

c. EXPRESSING EMOTIONS

Are you joking?	Vous plaisantez? (*pol*)	*voo-pleh-zAH-tay*
	Tu plaisantes? (*fam*)	*tew-pleh-zAHt*
Be careful!	Attention!	*atAHs-yOH*
Enough!	Assez!	*a-say*
Fortunately!	Heureusement! (*adv*)	*ur-uhz-mAH*
Good heavens!/Oh my!	Oh! là! là!	*oh-la-la*
I don't believe it!	Je ne le crois pas!	*zhen le krwah pah*
I don't feel like . . .	Je n'ai pas envie de	*zhen ay pah AH-vee de*
I wish! (If only . . . !)	Si seulement . . . .!	*see sulmAH*
I'm serious!	Je suis sérieux (*m*) sérieuse (*f*)	*zhe swee say-ry-uh (say-ry-uhz)*
I'm sorry!	Je regrette!	*zher-greht*
Impossible!	Pas possible!	*pah-pus-eebl*
It doesn't matter!	Peu importe!	*puh EH-port*
My God!	Mon Dieu!	*mOH dy-uh*
Poor man!	Pauvre homme!	*poh-vr um*
Poor woman!	Pauvre femme!	*poh-vr fahm*
Quiet!	Silence!	*seel-AHs*
Really?	Vraiment?	*vrehm-AH*
Shut up!	Taisez-vous!	*teh-zay-voo*
	Tais-toi! (*fam*)	*teh-twa*
Thank goodness!	Grâce à Dieu!	*grahss a dy-uh*
Ugh!	Pouah!	*pwa*
Unbelievable!	Incroyable!	*EH-krwa-yabl*
Unfortunately!	Malheureusement!	*mal-ur-uhz-mAH*
What a bore!	Quel raseur! (*m*)	*kehl rahz-ur*
	Quelle raseuse! (*f*)	*kehl rahz-uhz*

22. *THINKING*

a. DESCRIBING THOUGHT

complicated	compliqué(e) (*adj, m, f*)	*kOH-plee-kay*
concept	concept (*m*)	*kOH-sehpt*
conscience	conscience (*f*)	*kOH-sy-AHs*
conscientious	consciencieux (*adj, m*)	*kOH-sy-AHs-yuh*
	consciencieuse (*f*)	*kOH-sy-AHs-yuhz*
difficult	difficile (*adj*)	*dee-fee-seel*
doubt	doute (*m*)	*doot*
easy	facile (*adj*)	*fa-seel*
existence	existence (*f*)	*ehg-zees-tAHs*
hypothesis	hypothèse (*f*)	*ee-pu-tehz*
idea	idée (*f*)	*ee-day*
ignorant	ignorant(e) (*adj, m, f*)	*ee-ny-or-AH(t)*
imagination	imagination (*f*)	*ee-ma-zh-ee-nas-yOH*
interesting	intéressant(e) (*adj, m, f*)	*EH-tay-rehs-AH(t)*
judgment	jugement (*m*)	*zh-ew-zh-mAH*
justice	justice (*f*)	*zh-ewss-teess*
knowledge	connaissance (*f*)	*kun-ehs-AHs*
knowledgeable	connaisseur (*adj, m*)	*kun-ehs-ur*
	connaisseuse (*f*)	*kun-ehs-uhz*
mind	esprit (*m*)	*ehs-pree*
opinion	opinion (*f*)	*up-ee-ny-OH*
• in my opinion	à mon opinion	*a-mOH-nup-ee-ny-OH*
problem	problème (*m*)	*prub-lehm*
• No problem!	Pas de problème!	*pahd-prub-lehm*
reason	raison (*f*)	*reh-zOH*
simple	simple (*adj*)	*sEH-pl*
thought	pensée (*f*)	*pAH-say*
wisdom	sagesse (*f*)	*sa-zh-ehs*

b. BASIC THOUGHT PROCESSES

agree	être (*v*) d'accord	*eh-tre dak-or*
be interested in	s'intéresser (*v*) à	*sEH-tay-ray-say a*
be right	avoir (*v*) raison	*avwar rehz-OH*
be wrong	avoir (*v*) tort	*avwar tor*
believe	croire (*v*)	*krwar*
convince	convaincre (*v*)	*kOH-vEH-kre*
demonstrate	démontrer (*v*)	*day-mOH-tray*
doubt	douter (*v*)	*doo-tay*

forget	oublier (*v*)	*oobl-yay*
imagine	imaginer (*v*)	*ee-ma-zh-een-ay*
know	savoir (*v*)	*sav-war*
	connaître (*v*)	*kun-eht-re*
learn	apprendre (*v*)	*ap-rAH-dre*
persuade	persuader (*v*)	*pehr-sew-a-day*
reason	raisonner (*v*)	*reh-zun-ay*
reflect	réfléchir (*v*)	*ray-flay-sheer*
remember	se rappeler (*v*)	*se-rap-lay*
	se souvenir de	*se-soov-neer de*
study	étudier (*v*)	*ay-tewd-yay*
think	penser (*v*)	*pAH-say*
understand	comprendre (*v*)	*kOH-prAH-dre*
• **What do you think?**	Qu'en pensez-vous? (*pol*)	*kAH-pAH-say-voo*
	Qu'en penses-tu? (*fam*)	*kAH-pAH-s tew*

DAILY LIFE

23. AT HOME

a. PARTS OF THE HOUSE

attic	grenier (*m*)	*gren-yay*
basement	sous-sol (*m*)	*soo-sul*
bathtub	baignoire (*f*)	*beh-ny-war*
ceiling	plafond (*m*)	*plafOH*
chimney	cheminée (*f*)	*shmeen-ay*
corridor	couloir (*m*)	*kool-war*
door	porte (*f*)	*port*
doorbell	bouton (*m*) de sonnette	*bootOH de sun-eht*
entrance	entrée (*f*)	*AHtray*
faucet	robinet (*m*)	*rub-een-ay*
fireplace	âtre (*m*)	*ah-tre*
floor	plancher (*m*)	*plAH-shay*
	parquet (*m*)	*par-kay*
floor (*level*)	étage (*m*)	*ay-ta-zh*
garage	garage (*m*)	*gar-azh*
garden	jardin (*m*)	*zh-ard-EH*
ground floor	rez-de-chaussée (*m*)	*rayd-sh-oh-say*
house	maison (*f*)	*meh-zOH*
mailbox	boîte (*f*) à lettres	*bwat-a-leht-re*
porch	porche (*m*)	*porsh*
	véranda (*f*)	*vay-rAH-da*
roof	toit (*m*)	*twa*
shelf	étagère (*f*)	*ay-ta-zh-ehr*
shower	douche (*f*)	*doosh*
sink	évier (*m*)	*ayv-yay*
	lavabo (*m*) (*in a bathroom*)	*la-va-boh*
stairs	escalier (*m*)	*ehs-kal-yay*
switch	interrupteur (*m*)	*EH-tehr-ewp-tur*
terrace	terrasse (*f*)	*tehr-ahs*
wall	mur (*m*)	*mewr*
window	fenêtre (*f*)	*fneht-re*
window sill	rebord (*m*) de la fenêtre	*re-bor-dla-fneht-re*

b. ROOMS

bathroom	salle (*f*) de bains	*sal de bEH*
bedroom	chambre (*f*) à coucher	*shAH-br a koo-shay*

closet	armoire (*f*)	*arm-war*
	placard (*m*)	*plak-ar*
dining room	salle (*f*) à manger	*sal a mAHzh-ay*
kitchen	cuisine (*f*)	*kew-ee-zeen*
living room	salon (*m*)	*salOH*
	salle (*f*) de séjour	*sal de say-zh-oor*
room	pièce (*f*)	*py-ehs*
wine cellar	cave (*f*) à vin	*kav a vEH*

c. FURNITURE AND DECORATION

armchair	fauteuil (*m*)	*foh-tuh-y*
bed	lit (*m*)	*lee*
bedside table	table (*f*) de chevet	*ta-bl de sh-veh*
	table (*f*) de nuit	*ta-bl-de-new-ee*
bookcase	étagère (*f*) à livres	*ay-ta-zh-er a leevr*
carpet, rug	tapis (*m*)	*ta-pee*
chair	chaise (*f*)	*sh-ehz*
chest of drawers, dresser	commode (*f*)	*kum-ud*
curtains	rideaux (*m*)	*reed-oh*
decorating	décoration (*f*)	*day-kor-as-yOH*
drawer	tiroir (*m*)	*teer-war*
furniture	meuble (*m*)	*muh-bl*
lamp	lampe (*f*)	*lAHp*
mirror	miroir (*m*)	*meer-war*
painting	tableau (*m*)	*tab-loh*
sofa	canapé (*m*)	*ka-na-pay*
stool	tabouret (*m*)	*tab-oor-eh*
table	table (*f*)	*tabl*
wall-to-wall carpeting	moquette (*f*)	*muk-eht*
writing desk	secrétaire (*m*)	*sek-ray-tehr*

d. APPLIANCES AND COMMON HOUSEHOLD ITEMS

bag	sac (*m*)	*sak*
• **shopping bag**	sac à provisions	*sak-a-pru-veez-yOH*
barrel	tonneau (*m*)	*tun-oh*
basket	corbeille (*f*)	*kor-bay*
	panier (*m*)	*pan-yay*
bedspread	couvre-lit (*m*)	*koo-vre-lee*
blanket	couverture (*f*)	*koov-ehr-tewr*
bottle	bouteille (*f*)	*boo-tay*
box	boîte (*f*)	*bwat*
broom	balai (*m*)	*bal-eh*

case	douille (*f*)	*doo-y*
	bac (*m*)	*bak*
clothes hanger	cintre (*m*)	*sEH-tre*
coffee machine	cafetière (*f*) électrique	*kaf-tyehr ay-lehk-treek*
	percolateur (*m*)	*pehrk-u-la-tur*
coffee pot	cafetière (*f*)	*kaf-tyehr*
cup	tasse (*f*)	*tas*
dishwasher	lave-vaisselle (*m*)	*lav-veh-sehl*
dryer	sèche-linge (*m*)	*sesh-lEH-zh*
fork	fourchette (*f*)	*foorsh-eht*
freezer	congélateur (*m*)	*kOHzh-ay-la-tur*
glass (*drinking*)	verre (*m*)	*vehr*
kettle	bouilloire (*f*)	*boo-y-war*
key	clef (*f*)	*klay*
knife	couteau (*m*)	*koo-toh*
• **blade**	lame (*f*)	*lahm*
• **handle**	manche (*m*)	*mAH-sh*
ladle	louche (*f*)	*loosh*
lid	couvercle (*m*)	*koov-ehr-kl*
microwave oven	four (*m*) à micro-onde (*f*)	*foor a meek-ro-OHd*
napkin	serviette (*f*)	*sehrv-yeht*
pail	seau (*m*)	*soh*
pan	casserole (*f*)	*kas-rul*
	sauteuse (*f*)	*soh-tuhz*
pillow	oreiller (*f*)	*or-ay-yay*
pillowcase	taie (*f*) d'oreiller	*teh dor-ay-yay*
plate	assiette (*f*)	*as-yeht*
pot	faitout (*m*)	*feh-too*
radio	radio (*f*)	*rad-yo*
refrigerator	frigo (*m*)	*free-go*
	refrigérateur (*m*)	*re-free-zh-ay-ra-tur*
saucer	soucoupe (*f*)	*soo-koop*
sewing machine	machine (*f*) à coudre	*ma-sheen-a-kood-re*
sheet (*bed*)	drap (*m*)	*dra*
spoon	cuiller (*f*)	*kew-ee-yehr*
• **teaspoon**	cuiller (*f*) à café	*kew-ee-yehr-a-ka-fay*
stove	cuisinière (*f*) électrique	*kew-ee-zeen-yehr ay-lekh-treek*
	cuisinière (*f*) à gaz	*kew-ee-zeen-yehr a gaz*
tablecloth	nappe (*f*)	*nap*
tableware	ustensiles (*m, pl*) à table	*ewst-AH-seel-a-tabl*
teapot	théière (*f*)	*tay-yehr*
television set	téléviseur (*m*)	*tay-lay-veez-ur*
toaster	grille-pain (*m*)	*gree-y pEH*

tools	outils (*m, pl*)	*oo-tee*
tray	plateau (*m*) à servir	*pla-toh a sehr-veer*
vacuum cleaner	aspirateur (*m*)	*as-pee-ra-tur*
washing machine	lave-linge (*m*)	*lav-lEH-zh*
	machine (*f*) à laver (*v*)	*ma-sheen a la-vay*

e. SERVICES

air conditioning	climatisation (*f*)	*klee-ma-tee-zass-yOH*
• **air conditioner**	climatiseur (*m*)	*klee-ma-tee-zuhr*
electricity	électricité (*f*)	*ay-lehk-tree-see-tay*
furnace	chaudière (*f*)	*sh-ohd-yehr*
gas	gaz (*m*)	*gaz*
heating	chauffage (*m*) central	*sh-oh-fazh sAH-tral*
light, power	éclairage (*m*)	*ay-klehr-azh*
telephone	téléphone (*m*)	*tay-lay-fun*
water	eau (*f*)	*oh*

f. ADDITIONAL HOUSEHOLD VOCABULARY

at home	à la maison	*a-la-mehz-OH*
	chez soi	*shay-swa*
build	construire (*v*)	*kOH-strew-eer*
buy	acheter (*v*)	*ash-tay*
clean	nettoyer (*v*)	*neht-wa-yay*
clear the table	desservir (*v*) la table	*day-sehr-veer la ta-bl*
live (in)	habiter (*v*)	*a-bee-tay*
make the bed	faire (*v*) le lit	*fehr le lee*
move (*out of a house*)	déménager (*v*)	*day-may-na-zh-ay*
paint	peindre (*v*)	*pEH-dr*
put a room in order	mettre (*v*) une pièce en ordre	*meh-tr ewn py-ehs AH-nor-dr*
restore	restaurer (*v*)	*re-sto-ray*
sell	vendre (*v*)	*vAH-dr*
set the table	mettre (*v*) le couvert	*meh-tr le koo-vehr*
wash	laver (*v*)	*la-vay*
• **wash the clothes**	laver (*v*) le linge	*la-vay-le-lEHzh*
• **wash the dishes**	faire (*v*) la vaisselle	*fehr la veh-sehl*

g. LIVING IN AN APARTMENT

apartment	appartement (*m*)	*a-par-tem-AH*
apartment building	immeuble (*m*)	*eem-uh-bl*
building	édifice (*m*)	*ay-dee-feess*

condominium	immeuble (*m*) en copropriété (*f*)	*eem-uh-bl AH ko-pro-pree-ay-tay*
elevator	ascenseur (*m*)	*ass-AH-sur*
ground floor	rez-de-chaussée (*m*)	*rayd-sh-oh-say*
landlord	propriétaire (*m/f*)	*prup-pree-yay-tehr*
rent	loyer (*m*)	*lwa-yay*
• rent	louer (*v*)	*lway*
superintendent (*of apartment building*)	concierge (*m/f*)	*kOH-see-ehr-zh*
tenant	locataire (*m/f*)	*luk-a-tehr*

24. EATING AND DRINKING

a. MEALS

breakfast	petit déjeuner (*m*)	*ptee day-zh-un-ay*
dinner	dîner (*m*)	*dee-nay*
food	nourriture (*f*)	*noo-ree-tewr*
lunch	déjeuner (*m*)	*day-zh-un-ay*
meal	repas (*m*)	*re-pah*
snack	casse-croûte (*m*)	*kass-kroot*
	goûter (*m*)	*goo-tay*

b. PREPARATION

broiled, grilled	grillé(e) (*adj, m, f*)	*gree-yay*
cooking, cuisine	cuisine (*f*)	*kew-ee-zeen*
marinated	mariné(e) (*adj, m, f*)	*ma-ree-nay*
medium	à point	*a-pwEH*
rare	saignant(e) (*adj, m, f*)	*seh-ny-AH(t)*
roast	rôti(e) (*adj, m, f*)	*roh-tee*
well-done	bien cuit(e) (*adj, m, f*)	*byEH kwee(t)*
with sauce (gravy)	au jus	*oh-zh-ew*

c. MEAT AND POULTRY

bacon	bacon (*m*)	*bay-kun*
beef	bœuf (*m*)	*buhf*
bologna	saucisson (*m*)	*so-see-sOH*
chicken	poulet (*m*)	*poo-lay*
cold cuts	charcuterie (*f*)	*shar-kew-tree*
duck	canard (*m*)	*kan-ar*
ham	jambon (*m*)	*zh-AH-bOH*

lamb	agneau (*m*)	*a-ny-oh*
liver	foie (*m*)	*fwa*
meat	viande (*f*)	*vee-y-AHd*
pork	porc (*m*)	*por*
salami	salami (*m*)	*sa-la-mee*
sausage	saucisse (*f*)	*so-seess*
turkey	dindon (*m*)	*dEH-dOH*
veal	veau (*m*)	*voh*

d. FISH, SEAFOOD, AND SHELLFISH

anchovy	anchois (*m*)	*AH-sh-wa*
clam	palourde (*f*)	*pa-loord*
cod	morue (*f*)	*mu-rew*
dried cod	merluche (*f*)	*mehr-lewsh*
eel	anguille (*f*)	*AH-gee-y*
fish	poisson (*m*)	*pwassOH*
herring	hareng (*m*)	*ar-AH*
lobster	homard (*m*)	*um-ar*
	langouste (*f*)	*lAH-goost*
mussels	moule (*f*)	*mool*
oyster	huître (*f*)	*ew-eet-re*
prawn	langoustine (*f*)	*lAH-goos-teen*
salmon	saumon (*m*)	*so-mOH*
sardine	sardine (*f*)	*sar-deen*
seafood	fruits de mer (*m, pl*)	*frew-eed-mehr*
shellfish	crustacés (*m, pl*)	*krew-sta-say*
shrimp	crevette (*f*)	*kre-veht*
sole	sole (*f*)	*sul*
squid	calmar (*m*)	*kal-mar*
trout	truite (*f*)	*trew-eet*
tuna	thon (*m*)	*tOH*

e. VEGETABLES

artichoke	artichaut (*m*)	*ar-tee-sh-oh*
asparagus	asperge (*f*)	*as-pehr-zh*
bean	fève (*f*)	*fehv*
	haricot (*m*)	*a-ree-koh*
beet	betterave (*f*)	*beht-rav*
broccoli	brocoli (*m*)	*bruk-ul-ee*
cabbage	chou (*m*)	*shoo*
carrot	carotte (*f*)	*kar-ut*
cauliflower	chou-fleur (*m*)	*shoo-flur*
celery	céleri (*m*)	*sayl-ree*
cucumber	concombre (*m*)	*kOH-kOH-br*

eggplant	aubergine (*f*)	*oh-behr-zh-een*
lettuce	laitue (*f*)	*leht-ew*
mushroom	champignon (*m*)	*shAM-pee-ny-OH*
olive	olive (*f*)	*ul-eev*
onion	oignon (*m*)	*u-ny-OH*
peas	pois (*m*); petits pois (*m, pl*)	*pwa; ptee pwa*
potato	pomme (*f*) de terre	*pum-de-tehr*
potato salad	salade (*f*) de pommes de terre	*sa-lad-de-pum-de-tehr*
spinach	épinards (*m, pl*)	*ay-pee-nar*
string bean	haricot vert (*m*)	*a-ree-koh vehr*
tomato	tomate (*f*)	*tum-at*
vegetables	légumes (*m, pl*)	*lay-gewn*

f. FRUITS

apple	pomme (*f*)	*pum*
apricot	abricot (*m*)	*a-bree-ko*
banana	banane (*f*)	*ba-nan*
blueberry	myrtille (*f*)	*meer-tee-y*
cherry	cerise (*f*)	*sreez*
date	datte (*f*)	*daht*
fig	figue (*f*)	*feeg*
fruit	fruit (*m*)	*frew-ee*
grapefruit	pamplemousse (*m*)	*pAH-ple-mooss*
grapes	raisins (*m, pl*)	*reh-zEH*
lemon	citron (*m*)	*seet-rOH*
mandarin orange	mandarine (*f*)	*mAH-da-reen*
orange	orange (*f*)	*or-AH-zh*
peach	pêche (*f*)	*peh-sh*
peanut	arachide (*f*)	*a-rash-eed*
	cacahouète (*f*)	*ka-ka-weht*
pineapple	ananas (*m*)	*a-na-nass*
plum	prune (*f*)	*prewn*
prune	pruneau (*m*)	*prewn-oh*
raisin	raisin scc (*m*)	*reh-zEH sehk*
raspberry	framboise (*f*)	*frAH-bwahz*
strawberry	fraise (*f*)	*frehz*
walnut	noix (*f*)	*nwa*
watermelon	pastèque (*f*)	*pas-tehk*

g. MEAL AND MENU COMPONENTS

aperitif	apéritif (*m*)	*a-pay-ree-teef*
appetizer	hors-d'œuvre variés (*m, pl*)	*or-duh-vre va-ree-yay*

broth	bouillon (*m*)	*boo-yOH*
cake	gâteau (*m*)	*gah-toh*
cutlet	côtelette (*f*)	*koht-leht*
dessert	dessert (*m*)	*day-sehr*
dumpling	boulette (*f*)	*boo-leht*
filet	filet (*m*)	*fee-leh*
fish stew	bouillabaisse (*f*)	*boo-ya-behss*
French fries	frites (*f, pl*)	*freet*
fruit tartlet	tartelette (*f*) aux fruits	*tart-leht oh frew-ee*
garlic	ail (*m*)	*a-y*
menu	carte (*f*)	*kart*
	menu (*m*)	*me-new*
of the day	du jour	*dew zh-oor*
pancake	crêpe (*f*)	*krehp*
pasta	pâte (*f*)	*paht*
pie	tarte (*f*)	*tart*
• **apple**	aux pommes	*oh pum*
• **cherry**	aux cerises	*oh sreez*
• **chocolate**	au chocolat	*oh sh-uk-ul-a*
• **peach**	aux pêches	*oh peh-sh*
quiche	quiche (*f*)	*keesh*
• **cheese**	au fromage	*oh frum-azh*
• **ham**	au jambon	*oh zh-AH-bOH*
rice with vegetables	riz (*m*) aux légumes	*ree oh layg-ewm*
roast beef	rosbif (*m*)	*rohs-beef*
salad	salade (*f*)	*sa-lad*
sandwich	sandwich (*m*)	*sAHd-weesh*
• **cheese**	au fromage	*oh frum-azh*
• **ham**	au jambon	*oh zh-AH-bOH*
sherbet	sorbet (*m*)	*sor-beh*
snails	escargots (*m, pl*)	*ehs-kar-go*
soup	soupe (*f*)	*soop*
	potage (*m*)	*pu-tazh*
• **fish**	au poisson	*oh pwass-OH*
• **onion**	à l'oignon	*al-u-ny-OH*
• **thick**	purée	*pew-ray*
steak	bifteck (*m*)	*beef-tehk*

h. DAIRY PRODUCTS, EGGS, AND RELATED FOODS

butter	beurre (*m*)	*bur*
cheese	fromage (*m*)	*frum-azh*
• **grated**	au gratin	*oh grat-EH*
• **melted**	fondu	*fOHdew*
• **puffed**	soufflé	*soo-flay*
cream	crème (*f*)	*krehm*
• **whipped**	crème Chantilly	*krehm shAH-tee-yee*

dairy product	produit (*m*) laitier	*prud-ew-ee leht-yay*
egg	œuf (*m*)	*uhf*
• two eggs	deux œufs	*duh-zuh*
• fried	sur le plat	*sewr le pla*
• hard-boiled	dur	*dewr*
• in aspic	en gelée	*AH zh-lay*
• omelette	omelette	*um-leht*
• cheese	au fromage	*oh frum-azh*
• ham	au jambon	*oh zhAH-bOH*
• whipped cream	omelette mousseline	*um-leht moos-leen*
• poached	poché	*pu-shay*
• soft-boiled	à la coque	*a la kuk*
• stuffed	œuf dur farci	*uhf dewr far-see*
ice cream	glace (*f*)	*glass*
	crème (*f*) glacée	*krehm gla-say*
• cone	cornet (*m*)	*kor-neh*
• chocolate	au chocolat	*oh shuk-ul-a*
• strawberry	aux fraises	*oh frehz*
• vanilla	à la vanille	*a la van-ee-y*
milk	lait (*m*)	*leh*
• buttermilk	babeurre (*m*)	*ba-bur*
	lait de beurre	*lehd-bur*
• skimmed	écrémé	*ay-kray-may*
pudding	crème (*f*)	*krehm*
• caramel	au caramel	*oh ka-ra-mehl*
• coffee	au café	*oh ka-fay*
• custard	flan	*flAH*
• rice	de riz	*de ree*
• tapioca	tapioca au lait	*ta-pee-uk-a oh leh*
yogurt	yaourt (*m*)	*ya-oor*

FOCUS: A Few Popular French Cheeses

brie (*m*)	*bree*	gruyère (*m*)	*grew-yehr*
camembert (*m*)	*kamAH-behr*	port-salut (*m*)	*pohr-sa-lew*
cantal (*m*)	*kAH-tal*	reblochon (*m*)	*re-blu-shOH*
chèvre (*m*)	*sh-ehv-re*	roquefort (*m*)	*ruk-for*

i. GRAINS AND GRAIN PRODUCTS

barley	orge (*f*)	*or-zh*
bread	pain (*m*)	*pEH*
cookie	sablé (*m*)	*sa-blay*
	petit-beurre (*m*)	*ptee-bur*
	gâteau sec (*m*)	*gah-toh sehk*

corn	maïs (*m*)	*ma-eess*
crouton	croûton (*m*)	*kroot-OH*
crumb	mie (*f*)	*mee*
crust	croûte (*f*)	*kroot*
flour	farine (*f*)	*fa-reen*
oat	avoine (*f*)	*av-wan*
pastry	pâtisserie (*f*)	*pah-tee-sree*
rice	riz (*m*)	*ree*
wheat	blé (*m*)	*blay*

FOCUS: French Breads

breads	les pains (*m*)	*lay pEH*
brioche	brioche (*f*)	*bree-yush*
croissant	croissant (*m*)	*krwasAH*
double roll	petit pain (*m*) double	*ptee pEH doobl*
gingerbread	pain (*m*) d'épices	*pEH day-peess*
long loaf of bread	pain (*m*) long	*pEH lOH*
long stick of bread	baguette (*f*)	*bag-eht*
	flûte (*f*)	*flewt*
pretzel	bretzel (*m*)	*bred-zehl*
pumpernickel	pain (*m*) noir	*pEH nwar*
roll	petit pain (*m*) chapelet	*ptee pEH shap-leh*
round bread	pain (*m*) rond	*pEH rOH*
rusk (Melba toast)	biscotte (*f*)	*beess-kut*
rye and wheat bread	pain (*m*) de campagne	*pEHd-kAH-pan-y*
rye bread	pain (*m*) au seigle	*pEH oh sehgl*
small round loaf of bread	petite boule (*f*)	*pteet bool*
whole wheat bread	pain (*m*) complet	*pEH kOH-pleh*

FOCUS: French Pastries

pastries	pâtisseries (*f*)	*pah-teess-ree*
cheesecake	gâteau (*m*) au fromage	*gah-toh oh frum-azh*
coconut macaroon	macaron (*m*)	*ma-karOH*
cream cake (pie)	gâteau (*m*) à la crème	*gah-toh a la krehm*
cream puff	chou (*m*) à la crème	*shoo a la krehm*
creamed horn	cornet (*m*) feuilleté à la crème	*korn-eh fu-y-tay a la krehm*
eclair	éclair (*m*)	*ay-klehr*
fruit flan	flan (*m*) aux fruits	*flAH oh frew-ee*
iced bun	gâteau (*m*) américain	*gah-toh amay-reek-EH*
icing, iced, glazed	glacé(e) (*adj*)	*gla-say*
jelly roll	roulé (*m*)	*roo-lay*
meringue	meringue (*f*)	*me-rEHg*
napoleon	millefeuille (*m*)	*meel-fu-y*
slice of cream cake	tranche (*f*) de gâteau à la crème	*trAHsh de gah-toh a la krehm*
tartlet	tartelette (*f*)	*tart-leht*
twist bun	tresse (*f*)	*trehss*
wafer	gaufrette (*f*)	*go-freht*
waffle	gaufre (*f*)	*go-fr*

j. CONDIMENTS AND SPICES

basil	basilic (*m*)	*ba-zee-leek*
garlic	ail (*m*)	*a-y*
herb	herbe (*f*)	*ehrb*
honey	miel (*m*)	*mee-yehl*
jam (*preserves*)	confiture (*f*)	*kOH-fee-tewr*
jelly	gelée (*f*)	*zh-lay*
marmalade	confiture d'oranges	*kOH-fee-tewr dor-AH-zh*
mint	menthe (*f*)	*mAHt*
oil	huile (*f*)	*ew-eel*
parsley	persil (*m*)	*pehr-see*
pepper	poivre (*m*)	*pwa-vre*
rosemary	romarin (*m*)	*rum-ar-EH*
salt	sel (*m*)	*sehl*
spice	épice (*f*)	*ay-peess*
sugar	sucre (*m*)	*sew-kre*
vinegar	vinaigre (*m*)	*veen-ehg-re*

k. DRINKS

alcoholic beverage	boisson (*f*) alcoolique (adj)	*bwass-OH al-ku-(u)-leek*
beer	bière (*f*)	*bee-yehr*
camomile	camomille (*f*)	*ka-mum-eel*
coffee	café (*m*)	*kafay*
• **black**	noir	*nwar*
• **light (half-and-half)**	au lait	*oh-leh*
• **with cream**	café-crème	*kafay-krehm*
drink	boisson (*f*)	*bwass-OH*
juice	jus (*f*)	*zh-ew*
liqueur	liqueur (*f*)	*lee-kur*
mineral water	eau (*f*) minérale	*oh mee-nay-ral*
soft drink	gazeuse (*f*)	*gaz-uhz*
tea	thé (*m*)	*tay*
water	eau (*f*)	*oh*
wine	vin (*m*)	*vEH*

l. AT THE TABLE

bottle	bouteille (*f*)	*boo-tay*
bowl	bol (*m*)	*bul*
	assiette (*f*) creuse	*ass-ee-yeht kruhz*
cup	tasse (*f*)	*tass*
fork	fourchette (*f*)	*foorsh-eht*
glass (drinking)	verre (*m*)	*vehr*
knife	couteau (*m*)	*koo-toh*
napkin	serviette (*f*)	*sehr-vee-yeht*
plate	assiette (*f*)	*ass-ee-yeht*
saucer	soucoupe (*f*)	*soo-koop*
spoon	cuiller (*f*)	*kew-ee-yehr*
	cuillère (*f*)	*kew-ee-yehr*
table	table (*f*)	*ta-bl*
tablecloth	nappe (*f*)	*nap*
tableware	ustensiles (*m, pl*) de table	*ewst-AH-seel de ta-bl*
	couvert (*m*)	*koo-vehr*
teaspoon	cuiller (*f*) à café	*kew-ee-yehr a kafay*
toothpick	cure-dent (*m*)	*kewr-dAH*
tray (serving)	plateau (*m*) à servir	*pla-toh a sehr-veer*
wineglass	verre (*m*) à vin	*vehr a vEH*

Cheers!	À votre santé!	*a-vutr-sAH-tay*
Enjoy your meal!	Bon appétit!	*bun-a-pay-tee*

m. DINING OUT

bartender	barman (*m*)	*bar-man*
bill, check	addition (*f*)	*a-dee-syOH*
cafeteria	restaurant (*m*) self-service	*rehs-tor-AH sehlf-sehr-veess*
cover charge	couvert (*m*)	*koo-vehr*
fixed price	prix (*m*) fixe	*pree-feeks*
pizza parlor	pizzeria (*f*)	*peed-zayr-ya*
price	prix (*m*)	*pree*
reservation	réservation (*f*)	*ray-zehr-vas-yOH*
• reserved	réservé(e) (*adj, m, f*)	*ray-zehr-vay*
restaurant	restaurant (*m*)	*rehs-tor-AH*
• informal restaurant	bistro, bistrot (*m*)	*bee-stro*
service	service (*m*)	*sehr-veess*
snack bar	buffet (*m*)	*bew-feh*
take-out	à emporter (*v*)	*a-AH-por-tay*
tip	pourboire (*m*)	*poor-bwar*
• tip	donner (*v*) un pourboire	*dun-ay UH poor-bwar*
waiter	serveur (*m*)	*sehr-vur*
waitress	serveuse (*f*)	*sehr-vuhz*

n. BUYING FOOD AND DRINK

bakery	boulangerie (*f*)	*bool-AH-zh-ree*
butcher (shop)	boucherie (*f*)	*boosh-ree*
dairy	laiterie (*f*)	*leht-ree*
delicatessen	charcuterie (*f*)	*shar-kew-tree*
fish store	poissonnerie (*f*)	*pwa-sun-ree*
grocery store	épicerie (*f*)	*ay-peess-ree*
market	marché (*m*)	*marsh-ay*
pastry shop	pâtisserie (*f*)	*pah-tee-sree*
produce market	marché (*m*) aux légumes et fruits	*marsh-ay oh layg-ewm ay-frew-ee*
supermarket	supermarché (*m*)	*sew-pehr-marsh-ay*

o. FOOD AND DRINK: ACTIVITIES

add up the bill	faire (*v*) l'addition	*fehr la-dee-syOH*
be hungry	avoir (*v*) faim	*avwar fEH*
be thirsty	avoir (*v*) soif	*avwar swaf*
clear the table	desservir (*v*) la table	*day-sehr-veer la ta-ble*
cook	cuire (*v*)	*kew-eer*
	faire (*v*) la cuisine	*fehr la kew-ee-zeen*

cost	coûter (*v*)	*koo-tay*
cut	couper (*v*)	*koo-pay*
drink	boire (*v*)	*bwar*
eat	manger (*v*)	*mAH-zh-ay*
have a snack	prendre (*v*) un goûter	*prAH-dre UH goo-tay*
have dinner	dîner (*v*)	*dee-nay*
have lunch	déjeuner (*v*)	*day-zh-un-ay*
order	commander (*v*)	*kumAH-day*
peel	éplucher (*v*)	*ay-plew-shay*
pour	verser (*v*)	*vehr-say*
serve	servir (*v*)	*sehr-veer*
set the table	mettre (*v*) la table	*meht-re la ta-ble*
shop for food	acheter (*v*) des provisions	*ash-tay day pru-veez-yOH*
slice	trancher (*v*)	*trAH-shay*
take out (food to go)	emporter (*v*)	*AH-por-tay*
toast	griller (*v*)	*gree-yay*
weigh	peser (*v*)	*pe-zay*

p. DESCRIBING FOOD AND DRINK

appetizing	appétissant(e) (*adj, m, f*)	*a-pay-tee-sAH(t)*
bad	mauvais(e) (*adj*)	*muv-eh(z)*
baked	au four	*oh-foor*
bitter	amer, amère (*adj, m, f*)	*a-mehr*
cheap	à bon marché	*a-bOH marsh-ay*
	économe (*adj*)	*ay-kun-um*
cold	froid(e) (*adj, m, f*)	*frwa(d)*
expensive	cher, chère, (*adj, m, f*)	*sh-ehr*
	coûteux(-euse) (*adj, m, f*)	*koo-tuh(-tuhz)*
fried	frit(e) (*adj*)	*free(t)*
good	bon (*adj, m*)	*bOH*
	bonne (*f*)	*bun*
hot	chaud(e) (*adj, m, f*)	*sh-oh(d)*
mild	tiède (*adj*)	*tee-yehd*
salty	salé(e) (*adj, m, f*)	*sal-ay*
sour	aigre (*adj*)	*eh-gr*
spicy	épicé(e) (*adj, m, f*)	*ay-pee-say*
sweet	doux (*adj, m*)	*doo*
	douce (*f*)	*dooss*
tasty	savoureux(-euse) (*adj, m, f*)	*sa-voor-uh(-uhz)*
with ice	avec glaçons (*m, pl*)	*a-vehk glasOH*

25. SHOPPING AND ERRANDS

a. GENERAL VOCABULARY

bag (*shopping*)	sac (*m*) à provisions	*sak a pru-veez-yOH*
become	devenir (*v*)	*de-vneer*
bill (*from cash register*)	fiche (*f*) de caisse (*f*)	*feesh de kehss*
• **bill (invoice)**	facture (*f*)	*fak-tewr*
bring	apporter (*v*)	*a-port-ay*
buy	acheter (*v*)	*ash-tay*
cash register	caisse (*f*)	*kehss*
• **cashier**	caissier (*m*)	*kehs-yay*
	caissière (*f*)	*kehs-yehr*
change (*money*)	monnaie (*f*)	*mun-eh*
	rendu (*m*)	*rAH-dew*
• **change**	changer (*v*)	*sh-AH-zh-ay*
cost	coût (*m*)	*koo*
	prix (*m*)	*pree*
• **cost**	coûter (*v*)	*koo-tay*
• **How much does it cost?**	Ça coûte combien?	*sa koot kOH-byEH*
• **How much does it come to?**	Ça fait combien?	*sa feh kOH-byEH*
• **How much is it?**	C'est combien?	*seh kOH-byEH*

> **It costs an arm and a leg!** = Cela coûte les yeux de la tête (*lit.*, It costs both eyes from the head)! *sla koot lay-zyuhd la teht*

counter	comptoir (*m*)	*kOHtwar*
customer	client(e) (*m, f*)	*klee-yAH(t)*
department (*of a store*)	rayon (*m*)	*ray-yOH*
entrance	entrée (*f*)	*AHtray*
exchange	échanger (*v*)	*ay-shAHzh-ay*
exit	sortie (*f*)	*sor-tee*
gift	cadeau (*m*)	*ka-doh*
lack	manquer (à) (*v*)	*mAH-kay (a)*
look for something	chercher (*v*)	*sh-ehr-shay*
package	colis (*m*)	*kul-ee*
	paquet (*m*)	*pa-kay*
pay	payer (*v*)	*pay-yay*
• **cash**	en espèces	*AH-nehs-pehss*
• **with a check**	en chèque	*AH-sh-ehk*
• **with a credit card**	carte (*f*) de crédit	*kart de kray-dee*

price	prix (*m*)	*pree*
• **discount**	rabais (*m*)	*ra-beh*
	remise (*f*)	*re-meez*
• **expensive**	cher, chère (*adj, m, f*)	*sh-ehr*
	coûteux(-euse) (*adj, m, f*)	*koo-tuh(-tuhz)*
• **fixed price**	prix (*m*) fixe	*pree-feeks*
• **inexpensive**	à bon marché	*a-bOH marsh-ay*
	économe (*adj*)	*ay-kun-um*
• **price tag, label**	étiquette (*f*)	*ay-tee-keht*
• **reduced price**	prix (*m*) réduit	*pree ray-dew-ee*
purchase	achat (*m*)	*a-sha*
	acheter (*v*)	*ash-tay*
refund	rembourser (*v*)	*rAH-boor-say*
	rendre (*v*)	*rAH-dr*
sale	vente (*f*)	*vAHt*
• **for sale**	à vendre (*v*)	*a-vAH-dr*
• **on sale**	en vente (*f*)	*AH vAHt*
• **sell**	vendre (*v*)	*vAH-dre*
shop	boutique (*f*)	*boo-teek*
• **shop**	faire (*v*) des achats (*m, pl*)	*fehr day za-sha*
	faire (*v*) des emplettes (*f, pl*)	*fehr day zAH-pleht*
	faire (*v*) du shopping (*m*)	*fehr dew shup-een*
spend (*money*)	dépenser (*v*)	*day-pAH-say*
store	magasin (*m*)	*ma-gaz-EH*
• **closed**	fermé (*adj*)	*fehr-may*
• **deparment store**	grand magasin (*m*)	*grAH ma-gaz-EH*
• **open**	ouvert (*adj*)	*oo-vehr*
• **store clerk**	employé(e) (*m, f*)	*AH-plwa-yay*
• **store hours**	heures (*f, pl*)	*ur*
• **opening hours**	heures d'ouverture (*f*)	*ur doov-ehr-tewr*
• **closing hours**	heures de fermeture (*f*)	*ur de fehrm-tewr*
• **store/shop window**	vitrine (*f*)	*vee-treen*
take	prendre (*v*)	*prAH-dr*
• **take back (return an item)**	rendre (*v*)	*rAH-dr*

b. HARDWARE

battery	pile (*f*)	*peel*
cable	câble (*m*)	*kah-ble*

clamp	étau (*m*)	*ay-toh*
drill	foreuse (*f*)	*for-uhz*
electrical	électrique (*adj*)	*ay-lehk-treek*
file	lime (*f*)	*leem*
flashlight	lampe (*f*) de poche	*lAHp de pu-sh*
fuse	fusible (*m*)	*few-zee-bl*
	plomb (*m*) fusible	*plOH few-zee-bl*
hammer	marteau (*m*)	*mar-toh*
hardware store	quincaillerie (*f*)	*kEH-kah-y-ree*
insulation	isolant (*m*)	*ee-zul-AH*
light bulb	ampoule (*f*)	*AH-pool*
• **fluorescent**	fluorescent(e) (*adj, m, f*)	*flew-or-ay-sAH(t)*
• **neon**	au néon	*oh-nay-OH*
masking tape	papier (*m*) cache	*pap-yay kash*
mechanical	mécanique (*adj*)	*may-kan-eek*
nail	clou (*m*)	*kloo*
outlet	prise (*f*)	*preez*
pick	pic (*m*)	*peek*
	pioche (*f*)	*pee-yush*
plane	rabot (*m*)	*ra-boh*
pliers	pinces (*f, pl*)	*pEHss*
	tenailles (*f, pl*)	*ten-ah-y*
plug	fiche (*f*) de prise (*f*) de courant	*feesh de preez de koor-AH*
plumbing	plomberie (*f*)	*plOHbree*
punch	poinçon (*m*)	*pwEH-sOH*
saw	scie (*f*)	*see*
screw	vis (*f*)	*veess*
screwdriver	tournevis (*m*)	*toorn-veess*
shovel	pelle (*f*)	*pehl*
tool	outil (*m*)	*oo-tee*
transformer	transformateur (*m*)	*trAHs-form-at-ur*
wire	fil (*m*) métallique	*feel may-ta-leek*
wrench	pince (*f*) universelle	*pEHss ew-nee-vehr-sehl*

c. STATIONERY

adhesive tape	ruban (*m*) adhésif	*rewbAH ad-ay-zeef*
ballpoint pen	stylo (*m*) à bille	*stee-lo a bee-y*
briefcase	serviette (*f*)	*sehr-vee-yeht*
envelope	enveloppe (*f*)	*AHvlup*
marker	marqueur (*m*)	*mark-ur*
paper	papier (*m*)	*pap-yay*
pen	stylo (*m*)	*stee-lo*
pencil	crayon (*m*)	*kreh-yOH*

sheet (*of paper*)	feuille (*f*) de papier (*m*)	*fuh-y de pap-yay*
staple	agrafe (*f*)	*ag-raf*
stapler	agrafeuse (*f*)	*ag-ra-fuhz*
stationery store	papeterie (*f*)	*pap-tree*
string	ficelle (*f*)	*fee-sehl*
writing/note pad	bloc-notes (*m*)	*bluk-nut*

d. PHOTO/CAMERA

camera	appareil (*m*) de photo	*a-pa-reh-yd foto*
• **movie camera**	caméra (*f*)	*ka-may-ra*
	appareil cinématographique	*a-pa-reh-y see-nay-ma-tu-gra-feek*
• **video camera**	caméra vidéo (*f*)	*ka-may-ra vee-day-o*
camera shop	magasin (*m*) de photo	*ma-gaz-EH de foto*
film	film (*m*)	*feelm*
• **roll of film**	rouleau (*m*) de film	*roo-lohd feelm*
	rouleau (*m*) de pellicule (*f*)	*roo-lohd pay-leek-ewl*
	pellicule (*f*)	*pay-leek-ewl*
flash	flash (*m*)	*flash*
lens	optique (*f*) de prise de vues	*up-teek de preez de vew*
light bulb	ampoule (*f*)	*AH-pool*
photo, picture	photo(graphie) (*f*)	*foto(gra-fee)*
• **clear (picture)**	photo (*f*) nette	*foto neht*
• **out of focus**	photo (*f*) floue	*foto floo*
• **color (picture)**	en couleur (*f*)	*AH koo-lur*
• **focus**	mettre (*v*) en mise au point	*meht-r AH meez oh pwEH*
• **in black and white**	en noir et blanc	*AH nwar ay blAH*
• **take a picture**	prendre (*v*) une photo	*prAH-dr ewn foto*
• **The picture turned out badly.**	La photo a mal réussi.	*la foto a mal ray-ew-see*
• **The picture turned out well.**	La photo a bien réussi.	*la foto a byEH ray-ew-see*
screen	écran (*m*)	*ay-krAH*
slide	diapositive (*f*)	*dya-po-zee-teev*
zoom	zoom (*m*)	*zoom*

e. TOBACCO

card	carte (*f*)	*kart*
cigar	cigare (*m*)	*see-gar*
cigarette	cigarette (*f*)	*see-gar-eht*
lighter	briquet (*m*)	*breek-eh*
matches	allumettes (*f*)	*a-lew-meht*
pipe	pipe (*f*)	*peep*
smoke shop	bureau (*m*) de tabac	*bew-rohd ta-ba*
tobacco	tabac (*m*)	*ta-ba*
tobacconist	buraliste (*m, f*)	*bewr-al-eest*

f. COSMETICS/TOILETRIES

bath oil	huile (*f*) de bain	*ew-eeld bEH*
blade	lame (*f*)	*lam*
brush	brosse (*f*)	*bruss*
cologne	eau (*f*) de cologne	*ohd ku-lu-ny*
comb	peigne (*m*)	*peh-ny*
cosmetics/perfume shop	parfumerie (*f*)	*par-fewm-ree*
cream	crème (*f*)	*krehm*
curler	bigoudi (*m*)	*bee-goo-dee*
deodorant	déodorant (*m*)	*day-ud-u-rAH*
electric razor	rasoir (*m*) électrique	*rahz-war ay-lehk-treek*
face powder	poudre (*f*)	*pood-re*
hair dryer	séchoir (*m*) à cheveux	*say-sh-war a sh-vuh*
lipstick	rouge (*m*) à lèvres	*roo-zh a leh-vre*
	fard (*m*) à lèvres	*far a leh-vre*
lotion	lotion (*f*)	*loh-syOH*
mascara	fard (*m*) pour les yeux	*far poor layz-yuh*
nail polish	vernis (*m*) à ongles	*vehr-nee a OHgle*
perfume	parfum (*m*)	*parfUH*
make-up	maquillage (*m*)	*ma-kee-ya-zh*
razor	rasoir (*m*)	*rahz-war*
shampoo	shampooing (*m*)	*sh-AH-pwEH*
shaving cream	crème (*f*) à raser	*krehm a rah-zay*
soap	savon (*m*)	*savOH*
talcum powder	talc (*m*)	*tal-k*

g. LAUNDRY

button	bouton (*m*)	*bootOH*
clean	propre (*adj*)	*prup-r*

clothes	vêtements (*m, pl*)	*veht-mAH*
• **clothes basket**	panier (*m*) à linge	*pan-yay a lEHzh*
• **clothespin**	pince (*f*) à linge	*pEHss a lEHzh*
dirty	sale (*adj*)	*sal*
dry cleaner	nettoyage (*m*) à sec	*neht-wa-ya-zh a sehk*
hole	trou (*m*)	*troo*
iron	fer (*m*) à repasser	*fehr a re-pah-say*
• **iron**	repasser (*v*)	*re-pah-say*
laundry	linge (*m*)	*lEHzh*
	lessive (*f*)	*leh-seev*
mend	raccommoder (*v*)	*ra-kum-ud-ay*
pocket	poche (*f*)	*pu-sh*
sew	coudre (*v*)	*koo-dr*
sleeve	manche (*f*)	*mAHsh*
soap powder	savon (*m*) en poudre	*savOH AH poo-dr*
spot, stain	tache (*f*)	*tash*
starch	amidon (*m*)	*a-meed-OH*
stitch	point (*m*)	*pwEH*
wash	laver (*v*)	*la-vay*
• **washable**	lavable (*adj*)	*la-va-bl*
zipper	fermeture (*f*) à glissière	*fehrm-tewr a gleess-yehr*
	fermeture (*f*) éclair	*fehrm-tewr ay-klehr*

h. PHARMACY/DRUGSTORE

adhesive plastic strip	sparadrap (*m*)	*spa-ra-dra*
antibiotic	antibiotique (*m*)	*AH-tee-byu-teek*
aspirin	aspirine (*f*)	*as-pee-reen*
bandage	pansement (*m*)	*pAHs-mAH*
cortisone	cortisone (*f*)	*kor-tee-zun*
drugstore/pharmacy	pharmacie (*f*)	*farma-see*
injection	injection (*f*)	*EH-zh-ehks-yOH*
	piqûre (*f*)	*peek-ewr*
insulin	insuline (*f*)	*EH-sewl-een*
medicine	médicament (*m*)	*may-deek-am-AH*
ointment	pommade (*f*)	*pum-ad*
penicillin	pénicilline (*f*)	*pay-nee-see-leen*
pharmaceutical drug	remède (*m*)	*re-mehd*
	médicament (*m*)	*may-deek-am-AH*
pharmacist	pharmacien (*m*)	*farm-ass-yEH*
	pharmacienne (*f*)	*farm-ass-yehn*
pill	pilule (*f*)	*peel-ewl*
powder	poudre (*f*)	*poo-dre*
prescription	ordonnance (*f*)	*or-dun-AH-ss*
sodium bicarbonate	bicarbonate (*m*) de soude (*f*)	*bee-kar-bun-at de sood*

sodium citrate	citrate (*m*) de soude (*f*)	*see-trat de sood*
syrup	sirop (*m*)	*see-roh*
tablet	comprimé (*m*)	*kOHpree-may*
thermometer	thermomètre (*m*)	*tehr-mum-eht-re*
tincture of iodine	teinture (*f*) d'iode (*m*)	*tEHtewr dy-ud*
tissue	mouchoir (*m*) de papier (*m*)	*moosh-war de pap-yay*
toothbrush	brosse (*f*) à dents	*bruss a dAH*
toothpaste	dentifrice (*m*)	*dAHtee-freess*
vitamin	vitamine (*f*)	*vee-ta-meen*

i. JEWELRY

artificial	artificiel(le) (*adj, m, f*)	*ar-tee-fee-sy-ehl*
bracelet	bracelet (*m*)	*bras-leh*
brooch	broche (*f*)	*brush*
carat	carat (*m*)	*ka-ra*
chain	chaîne (*f*)	*sh-ehn*
diamond	diamant (*m*)	*dy-am-AH*
earring	boucle (*f*) d'oreille (*f*)	*book-l dor-ay*
emerald	émeraude (*f*)	*ehm-rohd*
false	faux (*adj, m*)	*foh*
	fausse (*f*)	*foh-ss*
fix, repair	ajuster (*v*)	*a-zh-ew-stay*
	réparer (*v*)	*ray-pa-ray*
gold	or (*m*)	*or*
jewel	bijou (*m*)	*bee-zh-oo*
jewelry store	bijouterie (*f*)	*bee-zh-oo-tree*
	joaillerie (*f*)	*zh-u-ah-y-ree*
necklace	collier (*m*)	*kul-yay*
opal	opale (*f*)	*up-al*
pearl	perle (*f*)	*pehrl*
precious	précieux (*adj, m*)	*pray-sy-uh*
	précieuse (*f*)	*pray-sy-uhz*
ring	bague (*f*)	*bag*
	anneau (*m*)	*an-oh*
ruby	rubis (*m*)	*rew-bee*
sapphire	saphir (*m*)	*sa-feer*
silver	argent (*m*)	*ar-zh-AH*
topaz	topaze (*f*)	*tup-ahz*
watch	montre (*f*)	*mOH-tr*
• alarm clock	réveille-matin (*m*)	*ray-veh-y-matEH*
• clock	horloge (*f*)	*or-lu-zh*

• **dial**	cadran (*m*)	*kad-rAH*
• **hand**	aiguille (*f*)	*ehg-ew-ee-y*
• **spring**	ressort (*m*)	*re-sor*
• **watchband**	bracelet (*m*) d'une montre	*bra-sleh dewn mOHtr*
• **wind**	remonter (*v*)	*re-mOH-tay*
• **wristwatch**	bracelet-montre (*m*)	*bra-sleh-mOHtr*
	montre-bracelet (*f*)	*mOHtr bra-sleh*

j. MUSIC

cassette	cassette (*f*)	*kaseht*
classical music	musique (*f*) classique	*mew-zeek kla-seek*
compact disc	disque compact (*m*)	*deesk-kOH-pakt*
composer	compositeur (*m*)	*kOH-po-zeet-ur*
	compositrice (*f*)	*kOH-po-zeet-reess*
dance music	musique (*f*) de danse (*f*)	*mew-zeek de dAHs*
jazz	jazz (*m*)	*dzh-ahz*
music	musique (*f*)	*mew-zeek*
record	disque (*m*)	*deesk*
rock music	musique (*f*) rock	*mew-zeek ruk*
singer	chanteur (*m*)	*shAHtur*
	chanteuse (*f*)	*shAHtuhz*
song	chanson (*f*)	*shAH-sOH*
tape	bande (*f*)	*bAHd*

k. CLOTHING

bathing suit	maillot (*m*) de bain (*m*)	*ma-yod bEH*
belt	ceinture (*f*)	*sEH-tewr*
blouse	chemisier (*m*)	*sh-em-eez-yay*
bra	soutien-gorge (*m*)	*soot-y-EH gohr-zh*
cardigan	chandail (*m*)	*sh-AH-da-y*
clothing	habillement (*m*)	*ab-ee-y-mAH*
	vêtements (*m, pl*)	*veht-mAH*
coat (suit)	veste (*f*)	*vehst*
	veston (*m*)	*vehstOH*
dress	robe (*f*)	*rub*
dressing room	cabine (*f*)	*ka-been*
fashion	mode (*f*)	*mud*
fur coat	manteau (*m*) de fourrure	*mAH-toh de foor-ewr*
glove	gant (*m*)	*gAH*

handkerchief	mouchoir (*m*)	*moosh-war*
hat	chapeau (*m*)	*sha-poh*
jacket	veste (*f*)	*vehst*
	veston (*m*)	*vehstOH*
men's shop/clothing	magasin (*m*) d'habillement masculin	*ma-gaz-EH dab-ee-y-mAH mas-kewl-EH*
pajamas	pyjama (*m*)	*pee-zha-ma*
pants	pantalon (*m*)	*pAH-tal-OH*
raincoat	imperméable (*m*)	*EH-pehr-may-abl*
scarf	écharpe (*f*)	*ay-sharp*
shirt	chemise (*f*)	*shmeez*
size, fit	taille (*f*)	*ta-y*
	mesure (*f*)	*me-zewr*
skirt	jupe (*f*)	*zh-ewp*
slip	jupon (*m*)	*zh-ewp-OH*
	fond (*m*) de robe	*fOH de rub*
	combinaison (*f*)	*kOH-been-ehzOH*
smock	blouse (*f*)	*blooz*
suit	costume (*m*)	*kus-tewm*
	complet (*m*)	*kOHpleh*
sweater	tricot (*m*)	*tree-koh*
	sweater (*m*)	*sweht-ehr*
	pull-over (*m*)	*pewl-uv-ehr*
tailored suit (*woman's*)	costume (*m*) tailleur	*kus-tewm ta-y-ur*
T-shirt	T-shirt (*m*)	*tee-sh-ehrt*
tie	cravate (*f*)	*kra-vat*
underwear	sous-vêtements (*m, pl*)	*soo-veht-mAH*
vest	gilet (*m*)	*zh-ee-leh*
windbreaker	blouson (*m*)	*blooz-OH*
women's shop/clothing	magasin (*m*) d'habillement féminin	*ma-gaz-EH dab-ee-y-mAH fay-meen-EH*

1. DESCRIBING CLOTHING

For colors, see section 7.

beautiful	beau (*m*)	*boh*
	bel (*m,s*)	*behl*
	belle (*f,s,pl*)	*behl*
big	grand	*grAH*
	grande (*f*)	*grAHd*

cotton	coton (*m*)	*kutOH*
elegant	élégant(e)	*ay-lay-gAH(t)*
fabric	tissu (*m*)	*teess-ew*
in the latest style/fashion	à la mode	*a-la-mud*
	au dernier cri	*oh dehrn-yay kree*
leather	cuir (*m*)	*kew-eer*
loose	vague (*adj*)	*vag*
	non-ajusté(e) (*adj, m, f*)	*nOH a-zh-ew-stay*
	ample (*adj*)	*AHpl*
nylon	nylon (*m*)	*neelOH*
polyester	polyester (*m*)	*pu-lee-ehs-tehr*
silk	en soie (*f*)	*AHswa*
small	petit(e) (*adj, m, f*)	*ptee(t)*
striped	rayé(e) (*adj, m, f*)	*ray-yay*
This looks bad on me.	Ceci ne me va pas bien.	*se-see nem va pah byEH*
This looks nice on me.	Ceci me va bien.	*se-see me va byEH*
tight	serré(e) (*adj, m, f*)	*sehr-ay*
ugly	laid(e) (*adj, m, f*)	*leh(d)*
wool	en laine (*f*)	*AH lehn*

m. CLOTHING: ACTIVITIES

enlarge	faire (*v*) élargir (*v*)	*fehr ay-lar-zh-eer*
get dressed	s'habiller (*v*)	*sa-bee-yay*
lengthen	faire (*v*) allonger (*v*)	*fehr al-OH-zh-ay*
put on	(se) mettre (*v*)	*(se) meht-r*
shorten	faire (*v*) accourcir (*v*)	*fehr a-koor-seer*
take off	enlever (*v*)	*AH-lvay*
tighten	faire (*v*) serrer (*v*)	*fehr sehr-ay*
try on	essayer (*v*)	*ay-say-yay*
undress	se déshabiller (*v*)	*se day-za-bee-yay*
wear	porter (*v*)	*por-tay*

n. SHOES

boot	botte (*f*)	*but*
pair	paire (*f*)	*pehr*
shoe	chaussure (*f*)	*sh-oh-sewr*
shoe repair store	cordonnerie (*f*)	*kor-dun-ree*
shoe store	magasin (*m*) de chaussures (*f*)	*ma-gaz-EH de sh-oh-sewr*
shoelace	lacet (*m*)	*la-seh*

size (*of shoe*)	pointure (*f*)	*pwEH-tewr*
slipper	pantoufle (*f*)	*pAH-too-fle*
	chausson (*m*)	*sh-oh-sOH*
sock	chaussette (*f*)	*sh-oh-seht*
stocking	bas (*m*)	*bah*

o. BOOKS

book	livre (*m*)	*lee-vr*
best-seller	best-seller (*m*)	*behst-sehl-ehr*
bookstore	librairie (*f*)	*lee-breh-ree*
book of adventure	livre (*m*) d'aventure (*f*)	*lee-vr dav-AH-tewr*
comics	bandes (*f, pl*) dessinées	*bAHd day-seen-ay*
dictionary	dictionnairc (*m*)	*deek-see-yun-ehr*
encyclopedia	encyclopédie (*f*)	*AH-see-klup-ay-dee*
guidebook	guide (*m*)	*geed*
magazine	magazine (*m*)	*ma-gaz-een*
	revue (*f*)	*re-vew*
mystery novel	roman (*m*) policier	*rumAH pul-eess-yay*
newspaper	journal (*m*)	*zh-oor-nal*
novel	roman (*m*)	*rumAH*
poetry	poésie (*f*)	*pu-ay-zee*
reference book	ouvrage (*m*) de référence (*f*)	*oov-ra-zh de ray-fayr-AH-s*
romance book	livre (*m*) d'amour	*lee-vr dahm-oor*
science-fiction book	livre (*m*) de science-fiction	*lee-vr de see-AH-s-feeks-yOH*
technical book	livre (*m*) de technologie (*f*)	*lee-vr de tehk-nu-lu-zh-ee*
textbook	livre (*m*) de classe (*f*)	*lee-vr de klahs*
	livre (*m*) d'étude (*f*)	*lee-vr day-tewd*

26. *BANKING AND COMMERCE*

For numerical concepts, see section 1.

account	compte (*m*)	*kOHt*
• **close an account**	arrêter (*v*) un compte	*ar-eh-tay UH kOHt*
	clore (*v*) un compte	*klor UH kOHt*

• open an account	ouvrir (*v*) un compte	*oov-reer UH kOHt*
bank	banque (*f*)	*bAHk*
• head office	siège (*m*) central	*see-yeh-zh sAHtral*
• work in a bank	travailler (*v*) dans une banque	*tra-va-yay dAH zewn bAHk*
bank book	carnet (*m*) de banque	*kar-neh de bAHk*
bank rate	taux (*m*) bancaire	*toh bAH-kehr*
• fixed	fixe (*adj*)	*feeks*
• variable	variable (*adj*)	*va-ree-abl*
bill, banknote	billet (*m*) de banque	*bee-yeh de bAHk*
• dollar	dollar (*m*)	*dul-ar*
• French Franc	franc français	*frAH frAH-seh*
• large bill	gros billet (*m*)	*groh bee-yeh*
• small bill	petit billet (*m*)	*ptee bee-yeh*
bond	obligation (*f*)	*ub-lee-gas-yOH*
budget	budget (*m*)	*bewd-zh-eh*
cash	en espèces	*AH-nehs-pehs*
• cash a check	toucher (*v*) un chèque	*too-shay UH sh-ehk*
• cash desk	caisse (*f*)	*kehss*
cashier, teller	caissier (*m*)	*kehs-yay*
	caissière (*f*)	*kehs-yehr*
check	chèque (*m*)	*sh-ehk*
• checkbook	carnet (*m*) de chèques	*kar-neh de sh-ehk*
cost of living	coût (*m*) de la vie	*koo de la vee*
credit	crédit (*m*)	*kray-dee*
• credit card	carte (*f*) de crédit	*kart de kray-dee*
currency	billets (*m*) de banque	*bee-yeh de bAHk*
	monnaie (*f*) fiduciaire	*mun-eh fee-dew-see-yehr*
current account	compte (*m*) courant	*kOHt koor-AH*
customer	client(e) (*m, f*)	*klee-yAH(t)*
debit	débit (*m*)	*day-bee*
debt	dette (*f*)	*deht*
deposit	versement (*m*)	*vehrs-mAH*
• deposit	verser (*v*) une somme au compte	*vehr-say ewn sum oh kOHt*
deposit slip	fiche (*f*) de versement	*feesh de vehrs-mAH*
	fiche (*f*) de dépôt bancaire	*feesh de day-poh bAH-kehr*
draft, promissory note	billet (*m*) à ordre	*bee-yeh a or-dre*

employee	employé(e) (*m, f*)	*AH-plwa-yay*
endorse	endosser (*v*)	*AH-doh-say*
• endorsement	endossement (*m*)	*AH-dohs-mAH*
	endos (*m*)	*AH-doh*
exchange	change (*m*)	*shAH-zh*
• exchange	changer (*v*)	*shAH-zh-ay*
• exchange rates	cours (*m*) du change	*koor dew shAH-zh*
expiry (date)	échéance (*f*)	*ay-shay-AH-s*
income	revenu (*m*)	*rev-new*
insurance	assurance (*f*)	*as-ew-rAHs*
interest	intérêt (*m*)	*EH-tay-reh*
• interest rate	taux (*m*) d'intérêt	*toh dEH-tay-reh*
invest	investir (*v*)	*EH-vehs-teer*
• investment	investissement (*m*)	*EH-vehs-tees-mAH*
line	queue (*f*)	*kuh*
• line up	faire (*v*) la queue	*fehr la kuh*
loan	prêt (*m*)	*preh*
• get a loan	obtenir (*v*) un prêt	*up-te-neer UH preh*
loose change	monnaie (*f*)	*mun-eh*
manager	directeur(-trice) (*m, f*)	*dee-rehk-tur(-trice)*
money	argent (*m*)	*ar-zh-AH*
money order	mandat (*m*) de paiement (*m*)	*mAHda de peh-mAH*
mortgage	hypothèque (*f*)	*ee-pu-tehk*
pay	payer (*v*)	*pay-yay*
• pay off	acquitter (*v*)	*a-kee-tay*
• payment	paiement (*m*)	*peh-mAH*
postdate	postdater (*v*)	*pust-da-tay*
receipt	reçu (*m*)	*res-ew*
	acquit (*m*)	*a-kee*
	récépissé (*m*)	*ray-say-pee-say*
safe	coffre-fort (*m*)	*kuf-re-for*
• safety deposit box	coffre (*m*) de sécurité	*kuf-re de say-kew-ree-tay*
salary	salaire (*m*)	*sal-ehr*
save	économiser (*v*)	*ay-kun-um-ee-zay*
	épargner (*v*)	*ay-parn-yay*
• savings	épargne (*f*)	*ay-parn-y*
sign	signer (*v*)	*seen-yay*
• signature	signature (*f*)	*seen-ya-tewr*
stock, share	action (*f*)	*aks-yOH*
• stock market/exchange	Bourse (*f*)	*boorss*
teller's window	guichet (*m*)	*geesh-eh*
traveler's check	chèque (*m*) de voyage	*sh-ehk de vwa-ya-zh*

withdraw	prélever (*v*)	*prayl-vay*
• **withdrawal**	prélèvement (*m*)	*pray-lehv-mAH*
• **withdrawal slip**	fiche (*f*) de prélèvement (*m*)	*feesh de pray-lehv-mAH*

27. GAMES AND SPORTS

a. GAMES, HOBBIES, AND PHYSICAL FITNESS

bingo	bingo (*m*)	*been-go*
• **bingo card**	fiche (*f*)	*feesh*
billiards, to play	jouer (*v*) au billard (*m*)	*zh-oo-ay oh bee-yar*
• **billiard ball**	bille (*f*)	*bee-y*
• **billiard table**	table (*f*) de billard (*m*)	*ta-bl de bee-yar*
• **cue**	queue (*f*) de billard (*m*)	*kuh de bee-yar*
• **cushion**	rebord (*m*) élastique	*re-bor ay-las-teek*
• **pocket**	trou (*m*)	*troo*
checkers (to play)	jouer (*v*) aux dames	*zh-oo-ay oh dahm*
• **checkerboard**	damier (*m*)	*dahm-yay*
• **checker piece**	pion (*m*)	*pee-yOH*
chess (to play)	jouer (*v*) aux échecs	*zh-oo-ay oh zay-sh-ehk*
• **bishop**	fou (*m*)	*foo*
• **chessboard**	échiquier (*m*)	*ay-sheek-yay*
• **king**	roi (*m*)	*rwa*
• **knight**	cavalier (*m*)	*ka-val-yay*
• **pawn**	pion (*m*)	*pee-yOH*
• **queen**	dame (*f*)	*dahm*
• **rook**	tour (*f*)	*toor*
coin	monnaie (*f*)	*mun-eh*
• **coin collecting**	numismatique (*f*)	*new-mees-ma-teek*
dice, to play	jouer (*v*) aux dés (*m, pl*)	*zh-oo-ay oh day*
game	jeu (*m*)	*zh-uh*
	partie (*f*)	*par-tee*
hobby	passe-temps (*m*)	*pahs-tAH*
jog	faire (*v*) du jogging (*m*)	*fehr dew dzh-ug-een*
• **jogging**	jogging (*m*)	*dzhug-een*
play cards	jouer (*v*) aux cartes (*f, pl*)	*zh-oo-ay oh kart*
• **ace**	as (*m*)	*ahss*
• **ace of spades**	as (*m*) de pique (*f*)	*ahss de peek*
• **clubs**	trèfle (*m*)	*treh-fl*
• **diamonds**	carreau (*m*)	*kar-oh*

• **hearts**	cœur (*m*)	*kur*
• **joker**	joker (*m*)	*zh-uk-ur*
• **king**	roi (*m*)	*rwa*
• **queen**	reine (*f*)	*rehn*
	dame (*f*)	*dahm*
• **spades**	pique (*f*)	*peek*
• **tarot**	tarot (*m*)	*tar-oh*
stamp (postage)	timbre-poste (*m*)	*tEHbr-pust*
• **stamp collecting**	collection (*f*) de timbres	*kul-ehks-yOH de tEHbr*

b. SPORTS

amateur	amateur (*m*)	*a-ma-tur*
	dilettante (*m/f*)	*deel-ehtAHt*
athlete	athlète (*m/f*)	*at-leht*
ball	balle (*f*)	*bal*
• **catch**	attraper (*v*)	*a-trap-ay*
• **hit**	battre (*v*)	*bat-r*
• **kick**	donner (*v*) un coup de pied	*dun-ay UH kood pee-yay*
• **pass**	passer (*v*)	*pah-say*
• **throw**	lancer (*v*)	*lAH-say*
baseball	base-ball (*m*)	*behz-bol*
• **ball**	balle (*f*)	*bal*
• **base**	base (*f*)	*bahz*
• **bat**	batte (*f*)	*bat*
• **batter**	batteur (*m*)	*ba-tur*
• **catcher's mask**	masque (*m*) du receveur	*mask dew re-se-vur*
• **foul line**	ligne (*f*) de pénalité	*lee-ny de pay-na-lee-tay*
• **glove**	gant (*m*)	*gAH*
• **home base**	base (*f*) du batteur	*bahz dew ba-tur*
• **pitcher**	lanceur (*m*)	*lAH-sur*
basketball	basket(-ball) (*m*)	*bas-keht(-bol)*
• **ball**	ballon (*m*) de basket	*ba-lOH de bas-keht*
• **basket**	panier (*m*)	*pan-yay*
bicycle racing	courses (*f*) cyclistes	*koorss see-kleest*
body building	culturisme (*m*)	*kewl-tewr-ees-me*
• **weight lifting**	haltérophilie (*f*)	*al-tay-ru-feel-ee*
bowling	bowling (*m*)	*bul-een-y*
• **bowl**	jouer (*v*) au bowling (*m*)	*zh-oo-ay oh bul-een-y*
• **bowling alley**	piste (*f*)	*peest*
• **bowling ball**	boule (*f*)	*bool*
• **bowling pin**	quille (*f*)	*kee-y*

boxing	boxe (*f*)	*buks*
• **boxing glove**	gant (*m*) de boxe	*gAH de buks*
• **boxing ring**	ring (*m*)	*ree-ny*
• **ropes**	cordes (*f*, *pl*)	*kord*
car racing	courses (*f*) de voitures	*koorss de vwa-tewr*
coach	entraîneur (*m*/*f*)	*AH-trehn-ur*
competition	concours (*m*)	*kOHkoor*
fencing	escrime (*f*)	*ehs-kreem*
• **fence**	faire (*v*) de l'escrime	*fehr de lehs-kreem*
• **French foil**	fleuret (*m*) français	*flur-eh frAHseh*
• **mask**	masque (*m*)	*mask*
• **On guard!**	En garde (*f*)!	*AH gard*
• **saber (light)**	sabre (*m*) d'escrime (*f*)	*sah-br dehs-kreem*
• **Touché!**	Touché!	*too-shay*
field	champ (*m*)	*shAH*
football	football (*m*) américain	*foot-bohl a-may-reek-EH*
game, match	jeu (*m*)	*zh-uh*
	match (*m*)	*mat-sh*
	partie (*f*)	*par-tee*
goal	but (*m*)	*bew(t)*
• **goalie**	gardien(-ienne) (*m*, *f*) de but	*gard-yEH(-yehn) de bew(t)*
golf (to play)	jouer (*v*) au golf (*m*)	*zh-oo-ay oh gulf*
gymnasium	gymnase (*m*)	*zh-eem-nahz*
• **work out**	pratiquer (*v*) les exercices du corps	*pra-tee-kay lay zehg-zehr-seess dew kor*
helmet	casque (*m*)	*kask*
hockey	hockey (*m*) sur glace	*uk-eh sewr glahss*
• **hockey player**	joueur(-euse) (*m*, *f*) de hockey	*zh-oo-ur(-uhz) de uk-eh*
• **hockey stick**	crosse (*f*)	*kruss*
	stick (*m*)	*steek*
• **puck**	palet (*m*)	*pal-eh*
	puck (*m*)	*puk*
• **skate**	patin (*m*) à glace	*patEH a glahss*
mountain climbing	alpinisme (*m*)	*alp-een-ees-me*
• **knapsack**	sac (*m*) à dos (*m*)	*sak a doh*
• **mountain boot**	chaussure (*f*) d'escalade (*f*)	*sho-sewr dehs-ka-lad*
• **rope**	corde (*f*) d'alpinisme (*m*)	*kord dalp-een-ees-me*
• **snow goggles**	lunettes (*f*, *pl*) de glacier (*m*)	*lew-neht de glas-yay*

net	but (*m*)	*bew(t)*
penalty	pénalité (*f*)	*pay-nal-ee-tay*
play	jeu (*m*)	*zh-uh*
• player	joueur (*m*)	*zh-oo-ur*
	joueuse (*f*)	*zh-oo-uhz*
point	marque (*f*)	*mark*
professional	professionel(-elle) (*m, f*)	*pruf-ehs-ee-yun-ehl*
race	course (*f*)	*koorss*
• horse racing	course (*f*) au galop	*koorss oh gal-oh*
	courses (*f*) de chevaux	*koorss de shvoh*
referee	arbitre (*m/f*)	*ar-beet-r*
run	courir (*v*)	*koo-reer*
score	marque (*f*)	*mark*
• draw, tie	match (*m*) nul	*mat-sh newl*
• draw	terminer (*v*) à match nul	*tehr-mee-nay a mat-sh newl*
	terminer (*v*) à égalité	*tehr-mee-nay a ay-gal-ee-tay*
• lose	perdre (*v*)	*pehr-dr*
• loss	perte (*f*)	*pehrt*
• win	gain (*m*)	*gEH*
	gagner (*v*)	*gan-yay*
skate	patiner (*v*)	*pa-teen-ay*
• to ice skate	patiner (*v*) sur glace	*pa-teen-ay sewr glahss*
• to roller skate	patiner (*v*) à roulettes	*pa-teen-ay a roo-leht*
ski	skier (*v*)	*skee-yay*
	faire (*v*) du ski	*fehr dew skee*
• ski	ski (*m*)	*skee*
• skier	skieur (*m*)	*skee-ur*
	skieuse (*f*)	*skee-uhz*
• water skiing	ski (*m*) nautique	*skee noh-teek*
soccer	foot (*m*)	*foot*
• play soccer	jouer (*v*) au foot	*zh-oo-ay oh foot*
• soccer ball	ballon (*m*)	*balOH*
sport	sport (*m*)	*spor*
• practice a sport	faire (*v*) du sport (*m*)	*fehr dew spor*
• sports fan	fan (*m*)	*fahn*
	fanatique (*m/f*) du sport	*fan-a-teek dew spor*
	enthousiaste (*m/f*) du sport	*AH-too-zee-ast dew spor*
stadium	stade (*m*)	*stad*
swim	nager (*v*)	*na-zh-ay*

• swimming	natation (*f*)	*na-tas-yOH*
• swimming pool	piscine (*f*)	*pee-seen*
team	équipe (*f*)	*ay-keep*
tennis (*to play*)	jouer (*v*) au tennis	*zh-oo-ay oh tehn-eess*
• racket	raquette (*f*)	*ra-keht*
ticket	billet (*m*)	*bee-yeh*
	ticket (*m*)	*teek-eh*
track	piste (*f*)	*peest*
volleyball	volley-ball (*m*)	*vul-eh-bol*
water polo	water-polo (*m*)	*wa-tehr-pu-loh*
wrestling	lutte (*f*)	*lewt*

28. THE ARTS

a. CINEMA

actor	acteur (*m*)	*ak-tur*
actress	actrice (*f*)	*ak-treess*
aisle	allée (*f*)	*alay*
box office	guichet (*m*)	*geesh-eh*
cinema	cinéma (*m*)	*see-nay-ma*
	ciné (*m*)	*see-nay*
lobby	foyer (*m*)	*fwa-yay*
movie, film	film (*m*)	*feelm*
• make a movie	tourner (*v*) un film	*toor-nay UH feelm*
• premiere showing	première (*f*) représentation (*f*)	*prem-yehr re-prayz-AH-tas-yOH*
movie director	réalisateur (*m*)	*ray-al-eez-at-ur*
	metteur (*m*) en scène (*f*)	*meht-ur AH sehn*
movies	cinéma (*m*)	*see-nay-ma*
row	rang (*m*)	*rAH*
screen	écran (*m*)	*ay-krAH*
seat	place (*f*)	*plass*
	siège (*m*)	*see-yeh-zh*
soundtrack	piste (*f*) sonore	*peest sun-or*

FOCUS: Some Well-Known French Cinema Directors

Jean Cocteau (1889–1963)	*Orphée (Orpheus)* *La Belle et la Bête (Beauty and the Beast)* *Le Sang du poète (Blood of a Poet)*
Jean Renoir (1894–1979)	*La Grande illusion (Grand Illusion)*
François Truffaut (1932–1984)	*Les Quatre cent coups (400 Blows)* *Jules et Jim (Jules and Jim)*

b. ART/SCULPTURE/ARCHITECTURE

architecture	architecture (*f*)	*arsh-ee-tehk-tewr*
• blueprint	copie (*f*) cyanotype	*kup-ee see-ano-teep*
art	art (*m*)	*ar*
artist	artiste (*m/f*)	*ar-teest*
brush	pinceau (*m*)	*pEHsoh*
easel, tripod	chevalet (*m*)	*sh-val-eh*
exhibition	exposition (*f*)	*ehks-poh-zees-yOH*
fresco painting	fresque (*f*)	*frehsk*
masterpiece	chef (*m*) d'œuvre (*f*)	*shay duv-re*
paint	peindre (*v*)	*pEH-dr*
• painter	peintre (*m/f*)	*pEH-tr*
	artiste-peintre (*m/f*)	*ar-teest pEH-tr*
• painting	peinture (*f*)	*pEH-tewr*
	tableau (*m*)	*tab-loh*
palette	palette (*f*)	*pal-eht*
pastel	pastel (*m*)	*pas-tehl*
portrait	portrait (*m*)	*port-reh*
sculpt	sculpter (*m*)	*skewl-tay*
• sculptor	sculpteur (*m*)	*skewl-tur*
• sculptress	femme sculpteur (*f*)	*fahm skewl-tur*
• sculpture	sculpture (*f*)	*skewl-tewr*
watercolor	aquarelle (*f*)	*ak-wa-rehl*

FOCUS: Some Well-Known French Artists

Edgar Degas (1834–1917)	*Le Ballet (The Ballet)* *Danseuse (Dancer)* *Danseuse saluant (Dancer Taking a Bow)* *Scène de Ballet (Ballet Scene)*
Raoul Dufy (1877–1953)	*La Plage à Sainte-Adresse (The Beach at Sainte-Adresse)* *Baigneuses (Bathers)*
Jean-Honoré Fragonard (1732–1806)	*La Liseuse (Girl Reading a Book)*
Henri de Toulouse-Lautrec (1864–1901)	*Au Moulin de la Galette (At the Moulin de la Galette)*

c. MUSIC/DANCE

accordion	accordéon (*m*)	*ak-or-day-OH*
ballet	ballet (*m*)	*bal-eh*
brass instruments	cuivres (*m, pl*)	*kew-eevre*
• **horn**	cor (*m*)	*kor*
• **trombone**	trombone (*m*)	*trOH-bun*
• **trumpet**	trompette (*f*)	*trOH-peht*
• **tuba**	tuba (*m*)	*tew-ba*
classical music	musique (*f*) classique	*mew-zeek kla-seek*
composer	compositeur (*m*)	*kOH-po-zee-tur*
	femme compositeur (*f*)	*fahm kOH-po-zee-tur*
• **composition**	composition (*f*)	*kOH-po-zees-yOH*
concert	concert (*m*)	*kOH-sehr*
dance	bal (*m*)	*bal*
• **dance**	danser (*v*)	*dAH-say*
• **dancer**	danseur (*m*)	*dAH-sur*
	danseuse (*f*)	*dAH-suhz*
folk music	musique (*f*) folklorique	*mew-zeek fulk-lur-eek*
guitar	guitare (*f*)	*geet-ar*
• **guitarist**	guitariste (*m, f*)	*geet-ar-eest*
harmony	harmonie (*f*)	*arm-un-ee*
harp	harpe (*f*)	*arp*

instrument	instrument (*m*)	*EH-strew-mAH*
• **play an instrument**	jouer (*v*) de (du, de l', de la)	*zh-oo-ay de (dew, del, de la)*
jazz	jazz (*m*)	*dzh-ahz*
keyboard instruments	instruments (*m/pl*) à clavier (*m*)	*EH-strew-mAH a klav-yay*
• **grand piano**	piano (*m*) à queue (*f*)	*pee-yan-oh a kuh*
• **harpsichord**	clavecin (*m*)	*klav-sEH*
• **organ**	orgue (*m*)	*urg*
• **pianist**	pianiste (*m, f*)	*pee-yan-eest*
• **piano**	piano (*m*)	*pee-yan-oh*
• **synthesizer**	synthétiseur (*m*)	*sEH-tay-teez-ur*
• **upright piano**	piano (*m*) droit	*pee-yan-oh drwa*
light music	musiquc (*f*) légère	*mew-zeek lay-zh-ehr*
mandolin	mandoline (*f*)	*mAH-dul-een*
music	musique (*f*)	*mew-zeek*
• **musician**	musicien (*m*)	*mew-zees-yEH*
	musicienne (*f*)	*mew-zees-yehn*
note	note (*f*)	*nut*
opera	opéra (*m*)	*up-ay-ra*
orchestra	orchestre (*m*)	*or-kehs-tre*
orchestra conductor	chef (*m*) d'orchestre (*m*)	*sh-ehf dor-kehs-tre*
percussion instruments	instruments (*m, pl*) à percussion (*f*)	*EH-strew-mAH a pehr-kewss-yOH*
• **bass drum**	grosse caisse (*f*)	*groh-ss kehss*
• **cymbals**	cymbales (*f, pl*)	*sEH-bal*
• **drum**	caisse (*f*)	*kehss*
• **set of drums**	batterie (*f*)	*bat-ree*
• **timpani**	timbale (*f*)	*tEH-bal*
player	joueur (*m*)	*zh-oo-ur*
	joueuse (*f*)	*zh-oo-uhz*
rhythm	rythme (*m*)	*reet-me*
show	spectacle (*m*)	*spehk-takl*
song	chanson (*f*)	*shAH-sOH*
• **sing**	chanter (*v*)	*shAH-tay*
• **singer**	chanteur (*m*)	*shAH-tur*
	chanteuse (*f*)	*shAH-tuhz*
stringed instruments	instruments (*m, pl*) à cordes (*f*)	*EH-strewm-AH a kord*
• **bow**	archet (*m*) de violon (*m*)	*arsh-eh de vee-yulOH*
• **cello**	violoncelle (*m*)	*vee-yulOH-sehl*
• **double bass**	contrebasse (*f*)	*kOH-tre-bahss*
• **string**	corde (*f*)	*kord*
• **viola**	viole (*f*)	*vee-yul*

• **violin**	violon (*m*)	*vee-yulOH*
• **violinist**	violoniste (*m, f*)	*vee-yul-un-eest*
symphony	symphonie (*f*)	*sEH-fun-ee*
wind instruments	instruments (*m, pl*) à vent (*m*)	*EH-strew-mAH a vAH*
• **bagpipes**	cornemuse (*f*)	*korn-mewz*
• **bassoon**	basson (*m*)	*bahsOH*
• **clarinet**	clarinette (*f*)	*kla-reen-eht*
• **flute**	flûte (*f*)	*flewt*
• **oboe**	hautbois (*m*)	*oh-bwah*
• **saxophone**	saxophone (*m*)	*saks-uf-un*

FOCUS: Some Well-Known French Composers

Georges Bizet (1838–1875)	*Carmen*
Gustave Charpentier (1860–1956)	*Louise*
Jules Massenet (1842–1912)	*Manon*

d. LITERATURE

appendix	appendice (*m*)	*ap-EH-deess*
autobiography	autobiographie (*f*)	*ut-ub-yug-ra-fee*
biography	biographie (*f*)	*bee-yug-ra-fee*
chapter	chapitre (*m*)	*sh-ap-eet-re*
character (in *a novel, play*)	personnage (*m*)	*pehr-sun-azh*
criticism	critique (*f*)	*kree-teek*
fable	fable (*f*)	*fah-bl*
fairy tale	conte (*m*) de fées (*f*)	*kOHt de fay*
fiction	livre (*m*) de fiction (*f*)	*lee-vre de feeks-yOH*
genre	genre (*m*)	*zh-AH-re*
literature	littérature (*f*)	*lee-tay-ra-tewr*
myth	mythe (*m*)	*meet*
mythology	mythologie (*f*)	*meet-ul-u-zh-ee*
novel	roman (*m*)	*rumAH*
plot	intrigue (*f*)	*EH-treeg*
poet	poète (*m*)	*pu-eht*
	femme (*f*) poète	*fahm pu-eht*
poetry	poésie (*f*)	*pu-ay-zee*
preface	préface (*f*)	*pray-fass*
rhetoric	rhétorique (*f*)	*ray-tu-reek*

short story	conte (*m*)	*kOHt*
	nouvelle (*f*)	*noo-vehl*
style	style (*m*)	*steel*
theme	thème (*m*)	*tehm*
work (*literary*)	ouvrage (*m*)	*oov-razh*
writer	écrivain (*m*)	*ay-kreev-EH*
	femme (*f*) écrivain	*fahm ay-kreev-EH*

FOCUS: Some Well-Known French Writers

Gustave Flaubert (1821–1880)	*Madame Bovary*
Michel de Montaigne (1533–1592)	*Les Essais* (*The Essays*)
Jean-Paul Sartre (1905–1980)	*Les Mots* (*The Words*)
Simone de Beauvoir (1908–1986)	*Les Mandarins* (*The Mandarins*)
Albert Camus (1913–1960)	*L'Étranger* (*The Stranger*)

e. THEATER

act	acte (*m*)	*akt*
• **act**	jouer (*v*) dans une pièce	*zh-oo-ay dAH zewn pee-yehs*
applause	applaudissement (*m*)	*ap-loh-dees-mAH*
• **applaud**	applaudir (*v*)	*ap-loh-deer*
audience	spectateurs (*m, pl*)	*spehk-ta-tur*
comedian	acteur(-trice)(*m, f*) comique	*ak-tur(-treess) kum-eek*
comedy	comédie (*f*)	*kum-ay-dee*
curtain	rideau (*m*) de scène (*f*)	*reed-oh de sehn*
drama	drame (*m*)	*drahm*
hero	héros (*m*)	*ay-roh*
heroine	héroïne (*f*)	*ay-ru-een*
intermission	entracte (*m*)	*AH-trakt*
mime	mime (*m, f*)	*meem*
pantomime	pantomime (*f*)	*pAH-tum-eem*
play	pièce (*f*) de théâtre (*m*)	*pee-yehs de tay-ah-tr*

playwright	dramaturge (*m, f*)	*dra-ma-tewr-zh*
	auteur (*m*) dramatique	*oh-tur dra-ma-teek*
	femme (*f*) auteur dramatique	*fahm oh-tur dra-ma-teek*
plot	intrigue (*f*)	*EH-treeg*
program	programme (*m*)	*prug-ram*
scene	scène (*f*)	*sehn*
scenery	mise (*f*) en scène (*f*)	*meez AH sehn*
stage	scène (*f*)	*sehn*
theater	théâtre (*m*)	*tay-ah-tr*
tragedy	tragédie (*f*)	*tra-zh-ay-dee*

FOCUS: Some Well-Known French Playwrights

Paul Claudel (1868–1955)	*L'Annonce faite à Marie* (*Tidings Brought to Mary*)
Jean Giraudoux (1882–1949)	*La Folle de Chaillot* (*The Madwoman of Chaillot*)
Jean-Baptiste Poquelin Molière (1622–1673)	*L'Avare* (*The Miser*) *Le Malade imaginaire* (*The Imaginary Invalid*) *Le Bourgeois gentilhomme* (*The Would-Be Gentleman*)
Jean-Paul Sartre (1905–1980)	*Huis Clos* (*No Exit*)

29. HOLIDAYS AND GOING OUT

a. HOLIDAYS/SPECIAL OCCASIONS

anniversay	anniversaire (*m*)	*a-nee-vehr-sehr*
Bastille Day (July 14)	La Prise de la Bastille	*la preez dla bastee-y*
birthday	anniversaire (*m*) de naissance (*f*)	*a-nee-vehr-sehr de neh-sAHss*
Christmas	Noël (*m*)	*nu-ehl*
Easter	Pâques (*f, pl*)	*pahk*
engagement	fiançailles (*f, pl*)	*fee-yAH-sah-y*

Feast of the Assumption (Aug. 15)	Assomption (*f*)	*a-sOH-ps-yOH*
holiday (official)	jour (*m*) férié	*zh-oor fay-ree-yay*
holidays	jours (*m, pl*) de fête (*f*)	*zh-oor de feht*
name day	fête (*f*)	*feht*
New Year's Day	le Jour de l'An (*m*)	*le zh-oor de lAH*
New Year's Eve	la veille du Jour de l'An	*la veh-y dew zh-oor de lAH*
picnic	pique-nique (*m*)	*peek-neek*
vacation	vacances (*f, pl*)	*va-kAH-ss*
wedding	mariage (*m*)	*mar-ee-yazh*
	noces (*f, pl*)	*nuss*

b. GOING OUT

dance	bal (*m*)	*bal*
• dance	danser (*v*)	*dAH-say*
disco	discothèque (*f*)	*dees-kut-ehk*
go out	sortir (*v*)	*sor-teer*
have fun	s'amuser (*v*)	*sam-ew-zay*
party	fête (*f*)	*feht*
remain	rester (*v*)	*rehs-tay*
return	retourner (*v*)	*re-toor-nay*
	revenir (*v*)	*rev-neer*
visit (*friends, relatives*)	faire (*v*) une visite à	*fehr ewn vee-zeet a*

c. SPECIAL GREETINGS

Best wishes!	Meilleurs vœux! (*m, pl*)	*meh-yur vuh*
Compliments!	Mes compliments! (*m, pl*)	*may kOH-pleem-AH*
Congratulations!	Félicitations! (*f, pl*)	*fay-lee-see-tas-yOH*
Happy Birthday!	Bon anniversaire! (*m*)	*bun-a-nee-vehr-sehr*
Happy Easter!	Bonnes Pâques! (*f, pl*)	*bun pahk*
Happy New Year!	Bonne année! (*f*)	*bun-a-nay*
	Heureuse année! (*f*)	*ur-uhz a-nay*
Have a good holiday!	Bonnes vacances! (*f, pl*)	*bun va-kAH-ss*
Have a nice day!	Bonne journée! (*f*)	*bun-zh-oor-nay*
Have fun!	Amusez-vous! (*pol*)	*a-mew-zay voo*
	Amuse-toi! (*fam*)	*a-mewz twa*
Merry Christmas!	Joyeux Noël! (*m*)	*zh-wa-yuh nu-ehl*

TRAVEL

30. CHOOSING A DESTINATION

For more related vocabulary, see section 13.

a. AT THE TRAVEL AGENCY

abroad	à l'étranger	*al-ay-trAH-zh-ay*
brochure	brochure (*f*)	*brush-ewr*
charter flight	avion charter (*m*)	*av-yOH shar-tehr*
city	ville (*f*)	*veel*
• **capital city**	capitale (*f*)	*kap-ee-tal*
class	classe (*f*)	*klahss*
• **first class**	en première	*AH prem-yehr*
• **economy class**	en touriste	*AH toor-eest*
continent	continent (*m*)	*kOH-teen-AH*
country	pays (*m*)	*peh-ee*
downtown	en ville	*AH veel*
	centre (*m*) de la ville	*sAH-tre de la veel*
excursion	excursion (*f*)	*ehks-kewrs-yOH*
insurance	assurance (*f*)	*ass-ewr-AHss*
nation	nation (*f*)	*nahss-yOH*
outskirts, suburbs	environs (*m, pl*)	*AH-veerOH*
	banlieue (*f*)	*bAHl-yuh*
see	voir (*v*)	*vwar*
ticket	billet (*m*)	*bee-yeh*
• **by boat**	en bateau (*m*)	*AH ba-toh*
• **by plane**	en avion (*m*)	*AH nav-yOH*
• **by train**	par le train	*parl trEH*
• **buy a ticket**	acheter (*v*) un billet	*ash-tay UH bee-yeh*
• **one-way ticket**	billet d'aller	*bee-yeh dal-ay*
• **round-trip ticket**	billet d'aller et retour	*bee-yeh dal-ay ay r-toor*
tour	voyage (*m*) organisé	*vwa-yazh organ-ee-zay*
tour bus	autocar (*m*) de tourisme	*u-toh-kar de toor-eesm*
	autocar (*m*) d'excursion	*u-toh-kar dehks-kewrs-yOH*
tour guide	guide (*m, f*)	*geed*

tourist	touriste (*m, f*)	*toor-eest*
travel	voyager (*v*)	*vwa-ya-zh-ay*
• travel agency	agence (*f*) de voyages	*azh-AH-ss de vwa-ya-zh*
trip, journey	voyage (*m*)	*vwa-ya-zh*
• Have a nice trip!	Bon voyage!	*bOH vwa-ya-zh*
• take a trip	faire (*v*) un voyage	*fehr UH vwa-ya-zh*
visit	visiter (*v*)	*vee-zee-tay*
world	monde (*m*)	*mOHd*

b. COUNTRIES AND CONTINENTS

Africa	Afrique (*f*)	*af-reek*
America	Amérique (*f*)	*a-may-reek*
• Latin America	Amérique (*f*) Latine	*a-may-reek la-teen*
• North America	Amérique (*f*) du Nord	*a-may-reek dew nor*
• South America	Amérique (*f*) du Sud	*a-may-reek dew sewd*
Asia	Asie (*f*)	*a-zee*
Australia	Australie (*f*)	*us-tra-lee*
Austria	Autriche (*f*)	*oh-treesh*
Belgium	Belgique (*f*)	*behl-zh-eek*
Brazil	Brésil (*m*)	*bray-zeel*
Canada	Canada (*m*)	*ka-na-da*
China	Chine (*f*)	*sheen*
Denmark	Danemark (*m*)	*dahn-mark*
Egypt	Egypte (*f*)	*ay-zh-eept*
England	Angleterre (*f*)	*AH-gle-tehr*
Europe	Europe (*f*)	*ur-up*
France	France (*f*)	*frAHs*
Germany	Allemagne (*f*)	*al-ma-ny*
Greece	Grèce (*f*)	*greh-ss*
Holland	Hollande (*f*)	*ul-AHd*
Ireland	Irlande (*f*)	*eer-lAHd*
Israel	Israël (*m*)	*ees-ra-ehl*
Italy	Italie (*f*)	*ee-ta-lee*
Japan	Japon (*m*)	*zh-ap-OH*
Mexico	Mexique (*m*)	*mehk-seek*
New Zealand	Nouvelle-Zélande (*f*)	*noo-vehl zayl-AHd*
Norway	Norvège (*f*)	*nor-veh-zh*
Poland	Pologne (*f*)	*pu-lu-ny*
Portugal	Portugal (*m*)	*por-tew-gal*
Russia	Russie (*f*)	*rew-see*
Spain	Espagne (*f*)	*ehs-pa-ny*
Sweden	Suède (*f*)	*sew-ed*

Switzerland	Suisse (*f*)	*sweess*
Thailand	Thaïlande (*f*)	*tah-y-lAHd*
United States of America	États-Unis (*m, pl*) d'Amérique	*ay-ta-zew-nee da-may-reek*

c. A FEW CITIES

Barcelona	Barcelone	*bar-se-lun*
Beijing/Peking	Béjing/Pékin	*bay-zheen/pay-keen*
Berlin	Berlin	*behrlEH*
Florence	Florence	*flu-rAH-ss*
Frankfurt	Francfort	*frAH-for*
London	Londres	*loH-dre*
Marseilles	Marseille	*mar-seh-y*
Milan	Milan	*meel-AH*
Moscow	Moscou	*mus-koo*
Naples	Naples	*nap-le*
Paris	Paris	*pah-ree*
Rome	Rome	*rum*
Venice	Venise	*vneez*

to + country	aller (*v*) + prep. + country	
• **to France**	aller (*v*) en France	*a-lay AH frAHs*
to + city	aller (*v*) + à + city	
• **to Paris**	aller (*v*) à Paris	*a-lay a pah-ree*

d. NATIONALITIES AND LANGUAGES

Gender has not been provided for the names of languages, which are invariably masculine in French. Pronunciation has not been provided for the names of languages when it is the same as that of the masculine form of the nationality.

American	Américain (*m*)	*a-may-reekEH*
	Américaine (*f*)	*a-may-reek-ehn*
	(*language:* **English** anglais;	*AH-gleh;*
	American américain)	*a-may-reekEH*
Arab	Arabe (*m, f*)	*a-rab*
	(*language:* **Arabic** arabe)	

Australian	Australien (*m*)	*us-tral-yEH*
	Australienne (*f*)	*us-tral-yehn*
	(*language:* **English** anglais)	
Austrian	Autrichien (*m*)	*oh-treesh-yEH*
	Autrichienne (*f*)	*oh-treesh-yehn*
	(*language:* **German** allemand)	*almAH*
Belgian	Belge (*m, f*)	*behl-zh*
	(*languages*: **French** français;	*frAH-seh*
	Flemish flamand)	*fla-mAH*
Brazilian	Brésilien (*m*)	*bray-zeel-yEH*
	Brésilienne (*f*)	*bray-zeel-yehn*
	(*language:* **Portuguese** portugais)	*por-tew-geh*
Canadian	Canadien (*m*)	*kan-ad-yEH*
	Canadienne (*f*)	*kan-ad-yehn*
	(*languages*: **English** anglais;	*AH-gleh*
	French français)	*frAH-seh*
Chinese	Chinois (*m*)	*sheen-wa*
	Chinoise (*f*)	*sheen-waz*
	(*language:* **Chinese** chinois)	
Danish	Danois (*m*)	*dan-wa*
	Danoise (*f*)	*dan-waz*
	(*language:* **Danish** danois)	
Dutch	Hollandais (*m*)	*ul-AH-deh*
	Hollandaise (*f*)	*ul-AH-dehz*
	(*language:* **Dutch** hollandais)	
English	Anglais (*m*)	*AH-gleh*
	Anglaise (*f*)	*AH-glehz*
	(*language:* **English** anglais)	
French	Français (*m*)	*frAH-seh*
	Française (*f*)	*frAH-sehz*
	(*language:* **French** français)	
German	Allemand (*m*)	*al-mAH*
	Allemande (*f*)	*al-mAHd*
	(*language:* **German** allemand)	

Greek	Grec (*m*)	*grehk*
	Grecque (*f*)	*grehk*
	(*language:* **Greek** grec)	
Irish	Irlandais (*m*)	*eer-lAH-deh*
	Irlandaise (*f*)	*eer-lAH-dehz*
	(*languages:* **English** anglais	*AH-gleh*
	Gaelic gaélique)	*ga-ay-leek*
Israeli	Israélite (*m, f*)	*ees-ra-ay-leet*
	(*languages:* **Hebrew** hébreu	*ay-bruh*
	Arabic arabe	*a-rab*
	English anglais)	*AH-gleh*
Italian	Italien (*m*)	*ee-ta-lee-yEH*
	Italienne (*f*)	*ee-ta-lee-yehn*
	(*language:* **Italian** italien)	
Japanese	Japonais (*m*)	*zh-ap-un-eh*
	Japonaise (*f*)	*zh-ap-un-ehz*
	(*language:* **Japanese** japonais)	
Norwegian	Norvégien (*m*)	*nor-vay-zh-yEH*
	Norvégienne (*f*)	*nor-vay-zh-yehn*
	(*language:* **Norwegian** norvégien)	
Polish	Polonais (*m*)	*pul-un-eh*
	Polonaise (*f*)	*pul-un-ehz*
	(*language:* **Polish** polonais)	
Portuguese	Portugais (*m*)	*por-tew-geh*
	Portugaise (*f*)	*por-tew-gehz*
	(*language:* **Portuguese** portugais)	
Russian	Russe (*m, f*)	*rewss*
	(*language:* **Russian** russe)	
Spanish	Espagnol (*m*)	*ehs-pan-yul*
	Espagnole (*f*)	*ehs-pan-yul*
	(*language:* **Spanish** espagnol)	
Swede	Suédois (*m*)	*sew-ay-dwa*
	Suédoise (*f*)	*sew-ay-dwaz*
	(*language:* **Swedish** suédois)	

Swiss	Suisse (*m, f*) (*languages:* **French** français **German** allemand **Italian** italien)	*sweess*

31. PACKING AND GOING THROUGH CUSTOMS

baggage, luggage	bagages (*m, pl*)	*ba-ga-zh*
• **hand luggage**	bagages (*m, pl*) à main	*ba-ga-zh a mEH*
border	frontière (*f*)	*frOHt-yehr*
carry	porter (*v*)	*por-tay*
carry-on	sac (*m*) de voyage	*sak de vwa-ya-zh*
customs	douane (*f*)	*dwan*
• **customs officer**	douanier (*m, f*)	*dwan-yay*
declare	déclarer (*v*)	*day-kla-ray*
• **nothing to declare**	rien à déclarer	*ree-yEH a day-kla-ray*
• **something to declare**	quelque chose (*pron*) à déclarer	*kehl-ke sh-oh-z a day-kla-ray*
documents	documents (*m, pl*)	*duk-ewm-AH*
duty tax	tarif (*m*) douanier	*tar-eef dwan-yay*
• **pay customs/duty**	payer (*v*) les droits de douane	*pay-ay lay drwa de dwan*
foreign currency	monnaie (*f*) étrangère	*mun-eh ay-trAH-zh-ehr*
foreigner	étranger (*m*) étrangère (*f*)	*ay-trAH-zh-ay* *ay-trAH-zh-ehr*
form (*to fill out*)	formule (*f*)	*form-ewl*
identification (*paper*)	carte (*f*) d'identité	*kart deed-AH-tee-tay*
import	importer (*v*)	*EH-por-tay*
knapsack	sac (*m*) à dos	*sak a doh*
pack (one's bags/luggage)	faire (*v*) les bagages	*fehr lay ba-ga-zh*
passport	passeport (*m*)	*pahs-por*
passport control	contrôle (*m*) de passeports	*kOH-trohl de pahs-por*
suitcase, piece of luggage	valise (*f*)	*val-eez*
tariff	tarif (*m*)	*tar-eef*
visa	visa (*m*)	*vee-za*
weight	poids (*m*)	*pwa*
• **heavy**	lourd(e) (*adj, m, f*)	*loor(d)*
• **light**	léger (*adj, m*) légère (*f*)	*lay-zh-ay* *lay-zh-ehr*
• **maximum**	maximum (*m*)	*maks-ee-mum*

32. TRAVELING BY AIR

a. IN THE TERMINAL

airline	ligne (*f*) aérienne	*lee-ny a-ayr-yehn*
airport	aéroport (*m*)	*a-ay-rup-or*
arrival	arrivée (*f*)	*a-ree-vay*
go on board	monter (*v*) à bord	*mOHtay a bor*
• **boarding**	embarquement (*m*)	*AH-bark-mAH*
• **boarding pass**	carte (*f*) d'embarquement	*kart dAH-bark-mAH*
connection	correspondance (*f*)	*kor-ehsp-OH-dAH-s*
departure	départ (*m*)	*day-par*
economy class	classe (*f*) touriste	*klahss toor-eest*
flight	vol (*m*)	*vul*
first class	première classe (*f*)	*prem-yehr klahss*
gate	porte (*f*)	*port*
information desk	bureau (*m*) de renseignements	*bew-roh de rAH-seh-ny-mAH*
lost and found	objets (*m, pl*) perdus	*ub-zh-eh pehr-dew*
no smoking	défense de fumer	*dayf-AHs de few-may*
porter	porteur (*m*)	*por-tur*
reservation	réservation (*f*)	*ray-zehr-vas-yOH*
terminal	terminal (*m*)	*tehr-meen-al*
ticket	billet (*m*)	*bee-yeh*
ticket window	guichet (*m*)	*geesh-eh*
waiting room	salle (*f*) d'attente (*f*)	*sal dat-AHt*

b. FLIGHT INFORMATION

canceled flight	vol (*m*) annulé	*vul an-ew-lay*
early	tôt (*adv*)	*toh*
	en avance	*AH-nav-AH-s*
late	en retard	*AH re-tar*
on time	à l'heure	*al-ur*

c. ON THE PLANE

airplane	avion (*m*)	*av-yOH*
aisle	passage (*m*)	*pahs-azh*
	allée (*f*)	*alay*
cabin	cabine (*f*)	*kabeen*
co-pilot	copilote (*m, f*)	*kup-ee-lut*
crew	équipe (*f*)	*ay-keep*

flight attendant	hôtesse (*f*) de l'air	*oh-tehss de lehr*
	steward (*m*)	*stew-ar*
headphones	écouteur (*m*) auriculaire	*ay-koot-ur u-ree-kew-lehr*
land	atterrir (*v*)	*a-tay-reer*
• **landing**	atterrissage (*m*)	*a-tay-rees-azh*
lifejacket	gilet (*m*) de sauvetage	*zh-ee-leh de sohv-tazh*
passenger	passager (*m*)	*pah-sa-zh-ay*
	passagère (*f*)	*pah-sa-zh-ehr*
runway	piste (*f*)	*peest*
seat	place (*f*)	*plahss*
• **aisle**	côté passage (*m*)	*koh-tay pahs-azh*
• **window**	côté (*m*) fenêtre	*koh-tay fneh-tre*
seat belt	ceinture (*f*)	*sEH-tewr*
• **buckle up, fasten**	boucler (*v*)	*boo-klay*
sit down	s'asseoir (*v*)	*sa-swar*
take off	décollage (*m*)	*day-kul-azh*
	décoller (*v*)	*day-kul-ay*
toilet	toilettes (*f, pl*)	*twa-leht*
tray	plateau (*m*)	*pla-toh*
turbulence	turbulence (*f*)	*tewr-bewlAHss*
wheel, landing gear	train (*m*) d'atterrissage	*trEH da-tay-rees-azh*
wing	aile (*f*)	*ehl*

33. ON THE ROAD

a. VEHICLES

ambulance	ambulance (*f*)	*AHbewlAHss*
automobile	automobile (*f*)	*u-tum-u-beel*
	auto (*f*)	*u-toh*
bicycle	bicyclette (*f*)	*bee-see-kleht*
• **brake**	frein (*m*)	*frEH*
• **chain guard**	couvre-chaîne (*m*)	*koov-re sh-ehn*
• **handlebar**	guidon (*m*)	*geed-OH*
• **pedal**	pédale (*f*)	*pay-dal*
• **spoke**	rayon (*m*)	*reh-yOH*
• **seat**	selle (*f*)	*sehl*
• **tire**	pneu (*m*)	*pnuh*
bus	autobus (*m*)	*u-toh-bewss*
• **streetcar**	tram (*m*)	*tram*
	tramway (*m*)	*tram-weh*
• **trolley**	trolley (*m*)	*trul-eh*

car	auto (*f*)	*u-toh*
	voiture (*f*)	*vwa-tewr*
• **rented car**	auto (*f*) en location	*u-toh AH luk-as-yOH*
• **sports car**	voiture (*f*) de sport	*vwa-tewr de spor*
compact car	voiture (*f*) compacte	*vwa-tewr kOHpakt*
motorcycle	motocyclette (*f*)	*mu-tu-see-kleht*
	moto (*f*)	*mut-oh*
• **driver**	motocycliste (*m*, *f*)	*mu-tu-see-kleest*
• **scooter**	scooter (*m*)	*skoot-ehr*
taxi	taxi (*m*)	*tak-see*
trailer	remorque (*f*)	*re-mork*
truck	camion (*m*)	*kam-yOH*
• **dump**	à triple mouvement	*a-treeple-moov-mAH*
• **fire**	fourgon-pompe (*m*)	*foorgOH-pOHp*
• **garbage**	de collecte	*de-kul-ehkt*
• **tanker**	camion-citerne (*m*)	*kam-yOH-see-tehrn*
• **tow**	dépanneuse (*f*)	*day-pan-uhz*
• **tractor**	camion-tracteur (*m*)	*kam-yOH-trak-tur*
• **transport**	des marchandises	*day marsh-AH-deez*
van	fourgon (*m*)	*foorgOH*
• **passenger van**	fourgon (*m*) automobile	*foorgOH u-tum-u-beel*
vehicle	véhicule (*m*)	*vay-ee-kewl*

b. DRIVING: PEOPLE AND DOCUMENTS

driver (*of a car*)	chauffeur (*m*)	*shoh-fur*
	automobiliste (*m*, *f*)	*u-tum-u-beel-eest*
• **to drive**	conduire (*v*)	*kOH-dew-eer*
driver's license	permis (*m*) de conduire	*pehr-mee de kOH-dew-eer*
insurance card	carte (*f*) d'assurance	*kart das-ewr-AH-s*
ownership papers	documents (*m*) de propriété	*duk-ewm-AH de prup-ree-yay-tay*
passenger	passager (*m*)	*pah-sa-zh-ay*
	passagère (*f*)	*pah-sa-zh-ehr*
pedestrian	piéton (*m*)	*pee-yay-tOH*
	piétonne (*f*)	*pee-yay-tun*
police	police (*f*)	*pul-eess*
• **highway police**	agent (*m*) de police routier	*azh-AHd pul-eess root-yay*
• **policeman**	agent (*m*) de police	*azh-AHd pul-eess*
• **policewoman**	auxiliaire féminine de police	*uks-eel-yehr fay-meen-een de pul-eess*
• **traffic police**	agent (*m*) de patrouille	*azh-AHd pa-troo-y*

registration papers	carte (*f*) grise	*kart greez*
road map	carte (*f*) routière	*kart root-yehr*

c. DRIVING

accident	accident (*m*)	*ak-seed-AH*
back up	reculer (*v*)	*re-kew-lay*
brake	freiner (*v*)	*fray-nay*
breakdown	en panne	*AH pahn*
bridge	pont (*m*)	*pOH*
corner (street)	coin (*m*) de la rue	*kwEHd la rew*
curve	courbe (*f*)	*koorb*
distance	distance (*f*)	*deest-AH-s*
drive	conduire (*v*)	*kOH-dew-eer*
fine, ticket	contravention (*f*)	*kOH-trav-AH-syOH*
gas station	station-service (*f*)	*stas-yOH-sehr-veess*
• **check the oil**	vérifier (*v*) l'huile	*vay-reef-yay lew-eel*
• **fill up**	faire (*v*) le plein	*fehr le plEH*
• **fix**	réparer (*v*)	*ray-pa-ray*
• **gas**	essence (*f*)	*ay-sAH-ss*
• **leaded gas**	essence (*f*) plombée	*ay-sAH-ss plOH-bay*
• **mechanic**	mécanicien (*m*) mécanicienne (*f*)	*may-ka-nees-yEH* *may-ka-nees-yehn*
• **self-service**	self-service (*m*)	*sehlf-sehr-veess*
• **tools**	outils (*m, pl*)	*oo-tee*
• **unleaded gas**	essence (*f*) non-plombée	*ay-sAH-ss nOH-plOH-bay*
gears change	changer (*v*) de vitesse (*f*)	*sh-AH-zh-ay de veet-ehss*
go forward	avancer (*v*)	*av-AH-say*
highway	autoroute (*f*)	*u-toh-root*
intersection	carrefour (*m*) croisement (*m*)	*kar-foor* *krwaz-mAH*
lane (traffic)	piste (*f*)	*peest*
park	stationner (*v*)	*stas-yun-ay*
• **parking**	stationnement (*m*)	*stas-yun-mAH*
• **public parking**	stationnement (*m*) public	*stas-yun-mAH pew-bleek*
pass	dépasser (*v*)	*day-pah-say*
pedestrian crossing	passage (*m*) pour piétons passage (*m*) piétonnier	*pahs-azh poor pee-yay-tOH* *pahs-azh pee-yay-tun-yay*
ramp	rampe (*f*)	*rAHp*
road	chemin (*m*)	*sh-mEH*
rush hours	les heures (*f, pl*) d'affluence	*lay-zur daf-lew-AH-s*
signal	signal (*m*)	*seen-yal*

No U-turn

No passing

Border crossing

Traffic signal ahead

Speed limit

Traffic circle (roundabout) ahead

Minimum speed limit

All traffic turns left

End of no passing zone

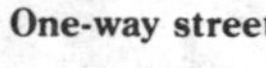
One-way street

DEVIATION

Detour

Danger ahead

Entrance to expressway

Expressway ends

Guarded railroad crossing

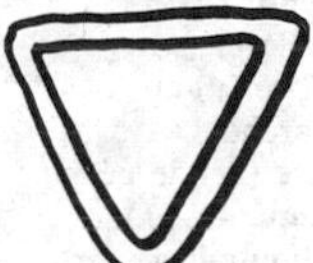

Yield

Stop

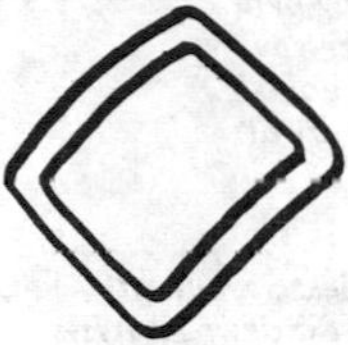

Right of way

Dangerous intersection ahead

Gasoline (petrol) ahead

Parking

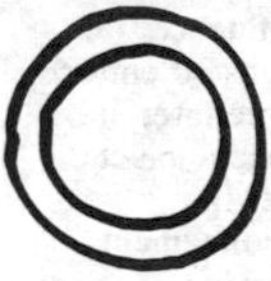

No vehicles allowed

Dangerous curve

Pedestrian crossing

Oncoming traffic has right of way

No bicycles allowed

No parking allowed

No entry

No left turn

speed	vitesse (*f*)	*veet-ehs*
• **slow down**	ralentir (*v*)	*ral-AH-teer*
• **speed up**	accélérer (*v*)	*aks-ay-lay-ray*
start (*car*)	mettre (*v*) en marche	*meht-re AH marsh*
toll booth	poste (*m*) de péage	*pust de pay-azh*
traffic	circulation (*f*)	*seer-kew-las-yOH*
• **traffic jam**	embouteillage (*m*)	*AHboo-teh-yazh*
	encombrement (*m*)	*AH-kOH-bre-mAH*
traffic lights	les feux (*m, pl*)	*lay fuh*
tunnel	tunnel (*m*)	*tew-nehl*
turn	virer (*v*)	*vee-ray*
• **(to the) left**	à gauche	*a goh-sh*
• **(to the) right**	à droite	*a drwat*

d. ROAD SIGNS

Bicycle Path	Piste cycliste	*peest seek-leest*
Emergency Lane	Piste d'urgence	*peest dewr-zh-AH-s*
Intersection	Carrefour	*kar-foor*
Level Crossing	Passage à niveau	*pahs-azh a neev-oh*
Merge	Confluence	*kOH-flew-AH-s*
No Entry	Défense d'entrer	*dayf-AH-s dAH-tray*
	Entrée interdite	*AH-tray EH-tehr-deet*
No Left Turn	Virage à gauche interdit	*veer-azh a goh-sh EH-tehr-dee*
No Parking	Stationnement interdit	*stas-yun-mAH EH-tehr-dee*
No Passing	Interdiction de dépasser	*EH-tehr-deeks-yOH de day-pah-say*
No Right Turn	Virage à droite interdit	*veer-azh a drwat EH-tehr-dee*
No Stopping	Arrêt interdit	*a-reh EH-tehr-dee*
No Thoroughfare	Circulation interdite	*seer-kew-las-yOH EH-tehr-deet*
No U-Turn	Virage U interdit	*veer-azh ew EH-tehr-dee*
One Way	Sens unique	*sAHs ew-neek*
Passing Lane	Piste pour dépasser (doubler)	*peest poor day-pah-say (doo-blay)*
Slippery When Wet	Chaussée glissante	*sho-say glees-AHt*
Speed Limit	Vitesse maximum	*veet-ehs mak-see-mum*
Stop	Arrêt	*a-reh*
	Stop	*stup*
Toll	Péage	*pay-azh*
Tow-Away Zone	Zone de remorquage	*zohn de re-mork-azh*
Work in Progress	Travaux	*tra-voh*
Yield	Cédez	*say-day*

e. THE CAR

air conditioner	climatiseur (*m*)	*klee-ma-tee-zuhr*
battery	batterie (*f*)	*bat-ree*
brake	frein (*m*)	*frEH*
bumper	pare-chocs (*m*)	*par-shuk*
car body	carrosserie (*f*)	*ka-russ-ree*
car window	vitre (*f*)	*veet-re*
carburetor	carburateur (*m*)	*kar-bew-ra-tur*
choke	volet (*m*) de départ	*vul-eh de day-par*
	starter (*m*)	*star-tehr*
clutch (pedal)	pédale (*f*) d'embrayage	*pay-dal dAH-breh-ya-zh*
dashboard	tableau (*m*) de bord	*tab-loh de bor*
door	portière (*f*)	*port-yehr*
fender	pare-chocs intégré (*m*)	*par-sh-uk EH-tay-gray*
filter	filtre (*m*)	*feel-tre*
gas pedal	pédale (*f*) d'accélérateur	*pay-dal dak-say-lay-ra-tur*
gas tank	réservoir (*m*) d'essence	*ray-zehr-vwar day-sAH-ss*
gearshift	levier (*m*) de changement de vitesse	*lev-yay de sh-AH-zh-mAH de veet-ehss*
glove compartment	boîte (*f*) à gants	*bwat a gAH*
	vide-poches (*m*)	*veed-pu-sh*
handle	poignée (*f*)	*pwan-yay*
hazard flash	feux (*m, pl*) de détresse	*fuh de day-trehss*
heater	système (*m*) de chauffage	*sees-tehm de sh-oh-fazh*
hood	capot (*m*)	*ka-poh*
horn	klaxon (*m*)	*klak-sun*
	avertisseur (*m*) sonore	*a-vehr-tees-ur sun-or*
horsepower	cheval-vapeur (*m*)	*sh-val vap-ur*
license plate	plaque (*f*)	*plak*
lights	phares (*m, pl*)	*far*
	projecteurs (*m, pl*)	*pru-zh-ehkt-ur*
motor	moteur (*m*)	*mut-ur*
• **fan**	ventilateur (*m*) d'aération	*vAH-tee-lat-ur da-ay-ras-yOH*
• **gas pump**	pompe (*f*) à essence	*pOHp-a-ay-sAH-ss*
• **generator**	dynamo (*f*)	*dee-na-moh*
• **piston**	piston (*m*)	*peest-OH*
• **shaft**	arbre-moteur (*m*)	*ar-bre-mut-ur*
	arbre de couche	*ar-bre de koosh*

• spark plug	bougie (*f*)	*boo-zh-ee*
• valve	soupape (*f*)	*soo-pap*
	clapet (*m*)	*klap-eh*
muffler	pot (*m*) d'échappement	*poh day-shap-mAH*
oil	huile (*f*)	*ew-eel*
oil filter	filtre (*m*) à huile	*feel-tre-a-ew-eel*
power brake	servofrein (*m*)	*sehr-vu-frEH*
power steering	servodirection (*f*)	*sehr-vu-deer-ehks-yOH*
power window	vitre (*f*) à commande automatique	*veet-re-a-kum-AHd ut-um-at-eek*
radiator	radiateur (*m*)	*rad-yat-ur*
rear window	lunette (*f*) arrière	*lew-neht ar-yehr*
rearview mirror	rétroviseur (*m*) intérieur	*ray-truv-eez-ur EH-tayr-yuhr*
roof	toit (*m*)	*twa*
seat	siège (*m*)	*see-yeh-zh*
seat belt	ceinture (*f*)	*sEH-tewr*
side mirror	rétroviseur (*m*) extérieur	*ray-truv-eez-ur ehks-tayr-yuhr*
speedometer	compteur (*m*) de vitesse	*kOH-tur de veet-ehss*
steering wheel	volant	*vul-AH*
tire	pneu(matique) (*m*)	*pnuh(ma-teek)*
trunk	coffre (*m*)	*kuf-re*
turn signal	clignateur (*m*)	*kleen-yat-ur*
vent	trou (*m*) d'aération (*f*)	*troo-da-ay-ras-yOH*
wheel	roue (*f*)	*roo*
windshield	pare-brise (*m*)	*par-breez*
• windshield wiper	essuie-glace (*m*)	*ehs-ew-ee-glahs*
	essuie-vitre (*m*)	*ehs-ew-ee-veet-re*

34. TRAIN, BUS, AND SUBWAY

bus (*long-distance travel*)	autocar (*m*)	*ut-oh-kar*
	car (*m*) de voyage	*kar de vwa-ya-zh*
• driver	chauffeur (*m, f*)	*sh-oh-fur*
• station, depot	station (*f*)	*stas-yOH*
	gare (*f*)	*gahr*
coach	voiture (*f*)	*vwa-tewr*
	wagon (*m*)	*vag-OH*

compartment	compartiment (*m*)	*kOH-par-teem-AH*
• nonsmoking	non-fumeurs	*nOH fewm-ur*
• smoking	fumeurs	*fewm-ur*
conductor	conducteur (*m*)	*kOH-dewk-tur*
	conductrice (*f*)	*kOH-dewk-treess*
connection	correspondance (*f*)	*kur-ehs-pOHd-AH-s*
direct train	train (*m*) direct	*trEH deer-ehkt*
express bus	autocar (*m*) express	*ut-oh-kar ehks-prehss*
express train	train (*m*) express	*trEH ehks-prehss*
leave, depart	partir (*v*)	*par-teer*
local train	train (*m*) omnibus	*trEH um-nee-bewss*
miss (*the train, etc.*)	manquer (*v*)	*mAH-kay*
	rater (*v*)	*ra-tay*
newsstand	kiosque (*m*) à journaux	*kee-usk a zh-oor-noh*
porter	porteur (*m*)	*port-ur*
railroad	chemin (*m*) de fer	*shmEHd fehr*
• station	gare (*f*)	*gar*
schedule	horaire (*m*)	*or-ehr*
• early	tôt (*adv*)	*toh*
	en avance	*AH-nav-AH-s*
• late	en retard	*AH re-tar*
• on time	à l'heure	*al-ur*
seat	place (*f*)	*plahss*
• economy	en classe touriste	*AH klahss toor-eest*
• first class	en première classe	*AH prem-yehr klahss*
stop	arrêt (*m*)	*ar-eh*
subway	métro (*m*)	*may-troh*
• subway station	station (*f*)	*stas-yOH*
take/catch the train, *etc.*	prendre (*v*)	*prAH-dre*
ticket	billet (*m*)	*bee-yeh*
• buy a ticket	acheter (procurer) (*v*) un billet	*ash-tay (pruk-ew-ray) UH bee-yeh*
• ticket cancelling machine	composteur (*m*) de billets	*kOH-pust-ur de bee-yeh*
• ticket counter	délivrance (*f*) des billets (*m, pl*)	*day-leev-rAH-s day bee-yeh*
track	voie (*f*)	*vwa*
train	train (*m*)	*trEH*
• All aboard!	En voiture!	*AH vwa-tewr*
• coach	wagon (*m*)	*vagOH*
	voiture (*f*)	*vwa-tewr*
• train sation	gare (*f*)	*gahr*
wait for (the train, *etc.*)	attendre (*v*)	*atAH-dre*

35. HOTELS

a. LODGING

boarding house	pension (*f*)	*pAHs-yOH*
chalet	chalet (*m*)	*shal-eh*
hotel	hôtel (*m*)	*oh-tehl*
• **luxury hotel**	hôtel (*m*) de luxe	*oh-tehl de lewks*
motel	motel (*m*)	*mut-ehl*
youth hostel	auberge (*f*) de la jeunesse	*oh-behr-zh de la zh-uh-nehs*

b. STAYING IN HOTELS

bill	compte (*m*)	*kOHt*
• **ask for the bill**	demander (*v*) le compte	*demAH-dayl kOHt*
• **Charge it to my bill.**	Mettez-le sur mon compte.	*meht-ay le sewr mOH kOHt*
bellhop	porteur (*m*)	*port-ur*
breakfast	petit déjeuner (*m*)	*ptee day-zh-un-ay*
• **breakfast included**	compris (*adj*)	*kOH-pree*
call for a taxi	appeler (*v*) un taxi	*a-play UH tak-see*
complain	se plaindre (*v*)	*se-plEH-dre*
• **complaint**	plainte (*f*)	*plEHt*
doorman	portier (*m*)	*port-yay*
elevator	ascenseur (*m*)	*ass-AH-sur*
entrance	entrée (*f*)	*AH-tray*
exit	sortie (*f*)	*sor-tee*
floor (*level*)	étage (*m*)	*ay-ta-zh*
garage	garage (*m*)	*gar-azh*
hotel clerk	employé (*m*)	*AH-plwa-yay*
	employée (*f*)	*AH-plwa-yay*
identification card	carte (*f*) d'identité	*kart deed-AH-tee-tay*
key	clef (*f*)	*klay*
• **give back the room key before leaving**	rendre (*v*) la clef de la chambre avant de partir	*rAH-dre la klayd la sh-AH-bre avAH de par-teer*
lobby	foyer (*m*)	*fwa-yay*
• **main door**	porte (*f*) principale	*port prEH-see-pal*
• **main floor**	rez-de-chaussée (*m*)	*rayd-sh-oh-say*
luggage	bagages (*m, pl*)	*ba-ga-zh*
maid	bonne (*f*)	*bun*
	domestique (*f*)	*dum-ehs-teek*

manager	gérant (*m*)	*zh-ayrAH*
	gérante (*f*)	*zh-ayrAHt*
	directeur (*m*)	*dee-rehkt-ur*
	directrice (*f*)	*dee-rehkt-reess*
message	message (*m*)	*mehs-azh*
passport	passeport (*m*)	*pahs-por*
pay	payer (*v*)	*pay-ay*
• **cash**	en espèces	*AH-nehs-pehs*
• **check**	chèque (*m*)	*sh-ehk*
• **credit card**	carte (*f*) de crédit	*kart de kray-dee*
• **traveler's check**	chèque (*m*) de voyage	*sh-ehk de vwa-ya-zh*
price, rate	tarif (*m*)	*ta-reef*
• **low season**	basse saison (*f*)	*bahss-sehz-OH*
• **peak season**	haute saison (*f*)	*oht-sehz-OH*
pool	piscine (*f*)	*pee-seen*
porter	porteur (*m*)	*port-ur*
• **give the porter a tip**	donner (*v*) un pourboire au porteur	*dun-ay UH poor-bwar oh port-ur*
receipt	reçu (*m*)	*res-ew*
reservation	réservation (*f*)	*ray-zehr-vas-yOH*
• **reserve**	réserver (*v*)	*ray-zehr-vay*
room	chambre (*f*)	*sh-AH-bre*
• **Do you have a vacant room?**	Avez-vous une chambre libre?	*avay-voo-ewn sh-AH-bre lee-bre*
• **double room**	chambre (*f*) double	*sh-AH-bre dooble*
• **have baggage taken to one's room**	faire (*v*) porter (*v*) les bagages dans la chambre	*fehr por-tay lay ba-ga-zh dAH la sh-AH-bre*
• **bridal suite**	chambre (*f*) matrimoniale	*sh-AH-bre ma-tree-mun-yal*
• **room with bath**	avec bain (*m*)	*a-vehk bEH*
• **room with two beds**	à deux lits (*m, pl*)	*a-duh lee*
• **single room**	à un lit (*m*)	*a UH lee*
services	services (*m, pl*)	*sehr-veess*
stairs	escalier (*m*)	*ehs-kal-yay*
view	vue (*f*)	*vew*
wake-up call	réveil (*m*) par téléphone	*ray-veh-y par tay-lay-fun*

c. THE HOTEL ROOM

See also Section 23.

armchair	fauteuil (*m*)	*foh-tuh-y*
balcony	balcon (*m*)	*balk-OH*
• sliding door	porte (*f*) coulissante	*port kool-ee-sAHt*
bathroom	salle (*f*) de bains	*sal de bEH*
bathtub	baignoire (*f*)	*beh-ny-war*
bed	lit (*m*)	*lee*
• double bed	grand lit (*m*)	*grAH lee*
bedside table	table (*f*) de nuit (*f*)	*ta-ble de new-ee*
blanket	couverture (*f*)	*koo-vehr-tewr*
chest of drawers	commode (*f*)	*kum-ud*
closet	armoire (*f*)	*arm-war*
clothes hanger	cintre (*m*)	*sEH-tre*
curtains	rideaux (*m, pl*)	*ree-doh*
dresser	commode (*f*)	*kum-ud*
faucet	robinet (*m*)	*rub-ee-neh*
lamp	lampe (*f*)	*lAHp*
lights	lumières (*f, pl*)	*lewm-yehr*
• current	courant (*m*)	*koorAH*
• switch	interrupteur (*m*)	*EH-tehr-ewp-tur*
• turn off	éteindre (*v*)	*ay-tEH-dr*
• turn on	allumer (*v*)	*al-ew-may*
mirror	miroir (*m*)	*meer-war*
	glace (*f*)	*glahss*
pillow	oreiller (*m*)	*or-ay-yay*
radio	radio (*f*)	*rad-yo*
soap	savon (*m*)	*savOH*
shampoo	shampooing (*m*)	*sh-AH-pwEH*
sheets	draps (*m, pl*)	*dra*
shower	douche (*f*)	*doosh*
sink, wash basin	lavabo (*m*)	*la-va-boh*
• cold water	eau (*f*) froide	*oh frwad*
• hot water	eau (*f*) chaude	*oh sh-ohd*
table	table (*f*)	*ta-bl*
telephone	téléphone (*m*)	*tay-lay-fun*
television set	téléviseur (*m*)	*tay-lay-veez-ur*
thermostat	thermostat (*m*)	*tehrm-us-ta*
toilet	toilette (*f*)	*twa-leht*
	W.C.	*doo-ble-vay-say*
• toilet paper	papier (*m*) hygiénique	*pap-yay ee-zh-yay-neek*
towel	serviette (*f*) de bain	*sehrv-yeht de bEH*

36. ON VACATION

a. SIGHTSEEING

amphitheater	amphithéâtre (*m*)	*AH-feet-ay-ah-tre*
art gallery	galerie (*f*) d'art	*gal-ree dar*

avenue	avenue (*f*)	*av-new*
basilica	basilique (*f*)	*ba-zee-leek*
bell tower	campanile (*m*)	*kAH-pa-neel*
	clocher (*m*)	*klush-ay*
bridge	pont (*m*)	*pOH*
castle	château (*m*)	*sh-ah-toh*
cathedral	cathédrale (*f*)	*ka-tay-dral*
church	église (*f*)	*ay-gleez*
city	ville (*f*)	*veel*
city map	carte (*f*) de la ville	*kart de la veel*
corner	coin (*m*)	*kwEH*
downtown	en ville	*AH veel*
	centre (*m*) de la ville	*sAH-tre de la veel*
garbage bin	poubelle (*f*)	*poo-behl*
guide	guide (*m, f*)	*geed*
intersection	croisement (*m*)	*krwaz-mAH*
	carrefour (*m*)	*kar-foor*
kiosk	kiosque (*m*) à journaux	*kee-usk a zh-oor-noh*
monument	monument (*m*)	*mun-ewm-AH*
museum	musée (*m*)	*mew-zay*
park	parc (*m*)	*park*
park bench	banc (*m*)	*bAH*
parking meter	parcmètre (*m*)	*park-meht-r*
pedestrian crosswalk	passage (*m*) pour piétons	*pahs-azh poor pee-yay-tOH*
public garden	jardin (*m*) public	*zh-ard-EH pew-bleek*
public notices	affiches (*f, pl*) publiques	*a-feesh pew-bleek*
public phone	téléphone (*m*) public	*tay-lay-fun pew-bleek*
public washroom	toilettes (*f, pl*) publiques	*twa-leht pew-bleek*
railway crossing	passage (*m*) à niveau gardé	*pahs-azh a nee-voh gar-day*
sidewalk	trottoir (*m*)	*trut-war*
square	place (*f*)	*plahss*
street	rue (*f*)	*rew*
• **street sign**	plaque (*f*) de nom (*m*) de rue (*f*)	*plak de nOH de rew*
take an excursion	faire (*v*) une excursion	*fehr ewn eks-kewrs-yOH*
temple	temple (*m*)	*tAH-ple*
tower	tour (*f*)	*toor*
traffic lights	feux (*m, pl*)	*fuh*
water fountain	fontaine (*f*)	*fOH-tehn*

b. GETTING OUT OF THE CITY

beach	plage (*f*)	*plazh*
• at the beach	à la plage (*f*)	*a la plazh*
• get a suntan	se bronzer (*v*)	*se brOH-zay*
• on vacation	en vacances (*f, pl*)	*AH va-kAH-ss*
• get some sun	prendre (*v*) un peu de soleil	*prAHdr UH puhd sul-ay*
• take a holiday	avoir (*v*) congé	*avwar kOH-zh-ay*
boat	bateau (*m*)	*ba-toh*
brook	ruisseau (*m*)	*rew-ee-soh*
camping area	camping (*m*)	*kAH-peen*
canoe	canoë (*m*)	*kan-u-ay*
cap	casquette (*f*)	*kas-keht*
cruise	croisière (*f*)	*krwaz-yehr*
fishing	pêche (*f*)	*peh-sh*
in the country	à la campagne	*a-la-kAH-pa-ny*
in the mountains	dans les montagnes (*f, pl*)	*dAH lay mOH-ta-ny*
knapsack	sac (*m*) à dos	*sak a doh*
lake	lac (*m*)	*lak*
mountain boots	chaussures (*f, pl*) de montagne	*sh-oh-sewr de mOH-ta-ny*
mountain climbing	alpinisme (*m*)	*al-pee-nees-me*
on vacation	en vacances (*f, pl*)	*AH vak-AH-ss*
river	fleuve (*m*)	*fluhv*
rope	corde (*f*)	*kord*
sea	mer (*f*)	*mehr*
skiing	ski (*m*)	*skee*
• ski resort	station (*f*) de ski	*stas-yOH de skee*
sleeping bag	sac (*m*) de couchage	*sak de koosh-azh*
tent	tente (*f*) de camping (*m*)	*tAHt de kAH-peen*
trip	voyage (*m*)	*vwa-ya-zh*
vacation	vacances (*f, pl*)	*vak-AH-s*

c. ASKING FOR DIRECTIONS

across	à travers (*prep*)	*a-tra-vehr*
ahead	avant (*adv*)	*a-vAH*
at the end of	au bout de	*oh boo de*
	à la fin de	*a la fEH de*
at the top of	au sommet de	*oh sum-eh de*
back	arrière (*adv*)	*ar-yehr*
behind	derrière (*adv*)	*dehr-yehr*
cross (over)	traverser (*v*)	*trav-ehr-say*

• **cross the street**	traverser (*v*) la rue	*trav-ehr-say la rew*
down	bas (*adv*)	*bah*
enter	entrer (*v*) (dans)	*AH-tray (dAH)*
everywhere	partout (*adv*)	*par-too*
exit, go out	sortir (*v*)	*sor-teer*
far (from)	loin (de) (*adv*)	*lwEH de*
follow	suivre (*v*)	*sweev-re*
go	aller (*v*)	*al-ay*
go down	descendre (*v*)	*day-sAH-dre*
go up	monter (*v*)	*mOH-tay*
here	ici (*adv*)	*ee-see*
in front of	devant (*prep, adv*)	*de-vAH*
inside	dedans (*prep, adv*)	*de-dAH*
near	près (*de*) (*adv*)	*preh de*
outside	dehors (*adv*)	*de-or*
straight ahead	tout droit (*adv*)	*too-drwa*
there	là (*adv*)	*lah*
through	par (*prep*)	*par*
to the east	à l'est	*al ehst*
to the left	à gauche	*a goh-sh*
to the north	au nord	*oh nor*
to the right	à droite	*a drwat*
to the south	au sud	*oh sewd*
to the west	à l'ouest	*al west*
toward	vers (*prep*)	*vehr*
turn	tourner (*v*)	*toor-nay*

Can you tell me where . . . ? Pouvez-vous me dire où . . . ? *poo-vay voom deer oo*
How do you get to . . . ? Comment va-t-on à . . . ? *kumAH va-tOH a*
Where is . . . ? Où est . . . ? *oo eh*
Turn left . . . Tournez à gauche . . . *toor-nay a goh-sh*
Turn right . . . Tournez à droite . . . *toor-nay a drwat*
I am looking for . . . Je cherche . . . *zhe sh-ehrsh*
How far away . . . ? A quelle distance . . . *?a kehl dee-stAH-s*

LA VOITURE (L'AUTOMOBILE)

The Car

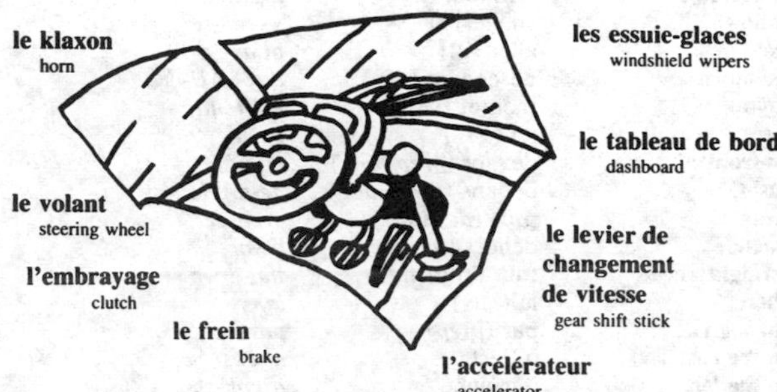

SCHOOL AND WORK

37. SCHOOL

a. TYPES OF SCHOOLS AND GRADES

coed school	école (*f*) mixte	*ay-kul meekst*
conservatory	conservatoire (*m*)	*kOH-sehr-va-twar*
day care	école (*f*) maternelle	*ay-kul ma-tehr-nehl*
elementary school	école (*f*) primaire élémentaire	*ay-kul pree-mehr ay-lay-mAH-tehr*
evening school	école (*f*) d'adultes	*ay-kul dad-ewlt*
	école du soir	*ay-kul dew swar*
grade	classe (*f*)	*klahss*
• **grade one**	première classe (*f*)	*prem-yehr klahss*
• **grade two**	deuxième classe (*f*)	*duhz-yehm klahss*
high school	école (*f*) d'enseignement secondaire	*ay-kul dAHseh-ny-mAH se-gOH-dehr*
	lycée (*m*)	*lee-say*
junior high school	école (*f*) d'enseignement de cours moyen	*ay-kul dAHseh-ny-mAH de koor mwa-y-EH*
kindergarten	jardin (*m*) d'enfants	*zh-ardEH dAH-fAH*
nursery school	école (*f*) maternelle	*ay-kul ma-tehr-nehl*
private school	école (*f*) privée	*ay-kul pree-vay*
technical/vocational school	institut (*m*) d'enseignement technique	*EHstee-tew dAHseh-ny-mAH tehk-neek*
university	université (*f*)	*ew-nee-vehr-see-tay*
year (*e.g., at university*)	année (*f*)	*a-nay*
• **first year**	première année (*f*)	*prem-yehr a-nay*
• **second year**	deuxième année (*f*)	*duhz-yehm a-nay*

b. THE CLASSROOM

assignment book	carnet (*m*)	*kar-neh*
	calepin (*m*)	*kalpEH*
atlas	atlas (*m*)	*at-lahs*
ballpoint pen	stylo (*m*) à bille	*stee-lo a bee-y*
blackboard	tableau (*m*)	*tab-loh*
blackboard eraser	éponge (*f*) mouillée	*aypOH-zh moo-yay*
	vieux chiffon (*m*)	*vy-uh sheef-OH*
book	livre (*m*)	*leev-r*

bookcase	étagère (*f*)	*ay-ta-zh-ehr*
	bibliothèque (*f*)	*beeb-lee-yut-ehk*
chalk	craie (*f*)	*kreh*
compass	compas (*m*)	*kOH-pa*
cupboard	clapard (*m*)	*klap-ar*
desk (*pupil's*)	pupitre (*m*)	*pew-peet-re*
• **(*teacher's*)**	bureau (*m*)	*bew-roh*
	chaire (*f*)	*sh-ehr*
dictionary	dictionnaire (*m*)	*deek-see-yun-ehr*
encyclopedia	encyclopédie (*f*)	*AH-see-klup-ay-dee*
eraser	gomme (*f*) à effacer	*gum-a-ay-fa-say*
eyeglasses	lunettes (*f, pl*)	*lew-neht*
film projector	projecteur (*m*) de film	*pruzh-ehk-tur de feelm*
ink	encre (*f*)	*AH-kre*
magazine	magazine (*m*)	*ma-ga-zeen*
	revue (*f*)	*re-vew*
map	carte (*f*) géographique	*kart zh-ay-u-gra-feek*
notebook	cahier (*m*)	*ka-yay*
overhead projector	rétroprojecteur (*m*)	*ray-troh-pruzh-ehk-tur*
paper	papier (*m*)	*pap-yay*
pen	stylo (*m*)	*stee-lo*
pencil	crayon (*m*)	*kreh-yOH*
record player	tourne-disque (*m*)	*toorn-deesk*
ruler	règle (*f*)	*reh-gle*
school bag	sac (*m*) d'écolier	*sak day-kul-yay*
slide projector	projecteur (*m*) pour diapositives (*f, pl*)	*pruzh-ehk-tur poor dee-ya-poh-zee-teev*
tack	punaise (*f*)	*pew-nehz*
tape recorder	magnétophone (*m*)	*man-yay-tu-fun*
textbook	livre (*m*) de classe	*leev-re de klahss*
	livre (*m*) de cours	*leev-re de koor*
wall map	carte (*f*) murale	*kart mew-ral*

c. AREAS OF A SCHOOL

campus	campus (*m*)	*kAH-pewss*
classroom	salle (*f*) de classe	*sal de klahss*
gymnasium	gymnase (*m*)	*zh-eem-nahz*
	salle (*f*) de gymnastique	*sal de zh-eem-nas-teek*
hallway	couloir (*m*)	*kool-war*
laboratory	laboratoire (*m*)	*la-bu-rat-war*
language laboratory	laboratoire (*m*) de langues (*f, pl*)	*la-bu-rat-war de lAHg*
library	bibliothèque (*f*)	*beeb-lee-yut-ehk*

main office	direction (*f*)	*deer-ehks-yOH*
professor's office	cabinet (*m*) du professeur	*ka-been-eh dew pruf-ehs-ur*
school yard	cour (*f*)	*koor*
toilets	toilettes (*f, pl*)	*twa-leht*
	W.C.	*dooble-vay-say*

d. SCHOOL: PEOPLE

assistant	assistant(e) (*m, f*)	*ass-eest-AH(t)*
class (*of students*)	classe (*f*) d'élèves (d'étudiants)	*klahss day-lehv (day-tewd-yAH)*
janitor	nettoyeur (*m*)	*neht-wa-yur*
	nettoyeuse (*f*)	*neht-wa-yuhz*
librarian	bibliothécaire (*m, f*)	*beeb-lee-yut-ay-kehr*
president of a university	recteur (*m*)	*rehk-tur*
	femme (*f*) recteur	*fahm rehk-tur*
principal	directeur (*m*)	*dee-rehk-tur*
	directrice (*f*)	*dee-rehk-treess*
professor	professeur (*m*)	*pruf-ehs-ur*
	femme (*f*) professeur	*fahm pruf-ehs-ur*
pupil	élève (*m, f*)	*ay-lehv*
schoolmate	camarade (*m, f*) d'école	*ka-ma-rad day-kul*
secretary	secrétaire (*m, f*)	*se-kray-tehr*
student	étudiant (*m*)	*ay-tewd-yAH*
	étudiante (*f*)	*ay-tewd-yAHt*
teacher	enseignant(e) (*m, f*)	*AH-sehn-yAH(t)*
• **elementary school teacher**	maître (*m*)	*meht-re*
	maîtresse (*f*)	*meht-rehss*
• **high-school teacher/professor**	professeur (*m*)	*pruf-ehs-ur*
	femme (*f*) professeur	*fahm pruf-ehs-ur*
technician	technicien (*m*)	*tehk-nees-yEH*
	technicienne (*f*)	*tehk-nees-yehn*

e. SCHOOL: SUBJECTS

accounting	comptabilité (*f*)	*kOH-ta-bee-lee-tay*
anatomy	anatomie (*f*)	*a-na-tum-ee*
anthropology	anthropologie (*f*)	*AH-trup-ul-u-zh-ee*
archeology	archéologie (*f*)	*ar-kay-ul-u-zh-ee*
architecture	architecture (*f*)	*ar-shee-tehk-tewr*
art	art (*m*)	*ar*
arts, humanities	lettres (*f, pl*)	*leht-re*
astronomy	astronomie (*f*)	*as-trun-um-ee*

biology	biologie (*f*)	*bee-yul-u-zh-ee*
botany	botanique (*f*)	*but-an-eek*
calculus	calcul (*m*)	*kal-kewl*
chemistry	chimie (*f*)	*shee-mee*
commerce	commerce (*m*)	*kum-ehrs*
economics	économie (*f*)	*ay-kun-um-ee*
engineering	études (*f, pl*) polytechniques	*ay-tewd pul-ee-tehk-neek*
fine arts	beaux-arts (*m, pl*)	*boh-zar*
geography	géographie (*f*)	*zh-ay-ug-rafee*
geometry	géométrie (*f*)	*zh-ay-um-ay-tree*
history	histoire (*f*)	*eess-twar*
languages (foreign)	langues (*f, pl*) étrangères	*lAHg ay-trAH-zh-ehr*
law	études (*f, pl*) de droit	*ay-tewd de drwa*
literature	littérature (*f*)	*lee-tay-ra-tewr*
mathematics	mathématiques (*f, pl*)	*ma-tay-ma-teek*
medicine	médecine (*f*)	*mayd-seen*
music	musique (*f*)	*mew-zeek*
natural sciences	sciences (*f, pl*) naturelles	*syAHs na-tewr-ehl*
philosophy	philosophie (*f*)	*feel-uz-uf-ee*
physics	physique (*f*)	*fee-zeek*
physiology	physiologie (*f*)	*fee-zee-ul-uzh-ee*
political science	science (*f*) politique	*syAHs pul-ee-teek*
	science po	*syAHS-poh*
psychology	psychologie (*f*)	*psee-kul-uzh-ee*
sciences	sciences (*f, pl*)	*syAHs*
sociology	sociologie (*f*)	*suss-yul-uzh-ee*
statistics	statistique (*f*)	*sta-teess-teek*
subject	matière (*f*)	*mat-yehr*
trigonometry	trigonométrie (*f*)	*tree-gun-um-ay-tree*
zoology	zoologie (*f*)	*zu-ul-uzh-ee*

f. ADDITIONAL SCHOOL VOCABULARY

For concepts of thought, see section 22.

answer	réponse (*f*)	*rayp-OH-s*
• **answer**	répondre (*v*) (à)	*rayp-OH-dr (a)*
• **brief**	bref (*adj, m*)	*brehf*
	brève (*f*)	*brehv*

• **long**	long (*adj, m*)	*lOH*
	longue (*f*)	*lOHg*
• **right**	correct (*adj, m*)	*kor-ehkt*
	correcte (*f*)	*kor-ehkt*
• **short**	court (*adj, m*)	*koor*
	courte (*f*)	*koort*
• **wrong**	incorrect (*adj, m*)	*EHkor-ehkt*
	incorrecte (*f*)	*EHkor-ehkt*
assignments, homework	devoirs (*m, pl*)	*de-vwar*
attend school	assister (*v*) à l'école	*ass-ees-tay al ay-kul*
be absent	être (*v*) absent(e) (*adj, m, f*)	*eh-tre apsAH(t)*
be present	être (*v*) présent(e) (*adj, m, f*)	*eh-tre prayz-AH(t)*
be promoted	être (*v*) reçu(e) (*adj, m, f*)	*eh-tre res-ew*
class (*students*)	classe (*f*)	*klahss*
• **(*process itself*)**	leçon (*f*)	*le-sOH*
• **have a class**	avoir (*v*) une leçon	*avwar ewn le-sOH*
• **skip a class**	sauter (*v*) une classe	*soh-tay ewn klahss*
• **skip school, play hooky**	faire (*v*) l'école buissonnière	*fehr lay-kul bew-ee-sun-yehr*
• **There is no class today.**	Il n'y a pas de classe aujourd'hui.	*eeln-ya-pahd klahss oh-zh-oord-wee*
composition	thème (*m*)	*tehm*
copy	copie (*f*)	*kup-ee*
• **good, final copy**	bonne copie (*f*)	*bun kup-ee*
• **rough copy, draft**	copie (*f*) brute	*kup-ee brewt*
	copie (*f*) en état brut	*kup-ee AH-nay-ta brewt*
course	cours (*m*)	*koor*
• **take a course/subject**	suivre (*v*) un cours	*sweev-re UH koor*
degree (*university*)	diplôme (*m*) universitaire	*deep-lohm ew-nee-vehr-see-tehr*
• **Master**	licence (*f*)	*lee-sAHss*
• **Doctorate**	doctorat (*m*)	*duk-tor-a*
• **get a degree**	obtenir (*v*) un diplôme universitaire	*up-te-neer UH deep-lohm ew-nee-vehr-see-tehr*
dictation	dictée (*f*)	*deek-tay*
diploma	diplôme (*m*)	*deep-lohm*
• **high school**	baccalauréat (*m*)	*ba-ka-lor-ay-a*
• **get a diploma**	obtenir (*v*) un diplôme	*up-te-neer UH deep-lohm*
draw	dessiner (*v*)	*day-seen-ay*
• **drawing**	dessin (*m*)	*day-sEH*

education	éducation (*f*)	*ay-dew-kas-yOH*
• **get an education**	recevoir (*v*) une éducation	*res-vwar ewn ay-dew-kas-yOH*
	recevoir (*v*) une solide formation	*res-vwar ewn sul-eed formas-yOH*
error	erreur (*f*)	*ehr-ur*
	faute (*f*)	*foht*
essay	essai (*m*)	*ay-seh*
exam	examen (*m*)	*ehg-zam-EH*
• **entrance exam**	examen (*m*) d'entrée	*ehg-zam-EH dAH-tray*
• **oral exam**	examen (*m*) oral	*ehg-zam-EH or-al*
• **pass an**	être (*v*) reçu(e) à un examen	*eh-tre res-ew a UH nehg-zam-EH*
• **take an**	passer (*v*) un examen	*pah-say UH nehg-zam-EH*
• **written exam**	examen (*m*) écrit	*ehg-zam-EH ay-kree*
exercise	exercice (*m*)	*ehg-zehr-seess*
explanation	explication (*f*)	*ehks-plee-kas-yOH*
• **explain**	expliquer (*v*)	*ehks-plee-kay*
fail an exam	échouer à un examen	*ay-shway a UH nehg-zam-EH*
	être (*v*) collé(e) à un examen	*eh-tre kul-ay a UH nehg-zam-EH*
field (of study)	matière (*f*) d'études	*mat-yehr day-tewd*
give/hand back	rendre (*v*)	*rAH-dr*
grade/mark	note (*f*)	*nut*
grammar	grammaire (*f*)	*gram-ehr*
learn	apprendre (*v*)	*aprAH-dr*
• **learn by memory**	apprendre (*v*) par cœur	*aprAH-dr par kur*
lecture	conférence (*f*)	*kOHfay-rAHs*
• **lecture**	faire (*v*) une conférence	*fehr ewn kOHfay-rAHs*
	donner (*v*) une conférence	*dun-ay ewn kOHfay-rAHs*
listen to	écouter (*v*)	*ay-koo-tay*
mistake	faute (*f*)	*foht*
• **make mistakes**	faire (*v*) des fautes	*fehr day foht*
note	note (*f*)	*nut*
• **take notes**	prendre (*v*) des notes	*prAH-dr day nut*
problem	problème (*m*)	*prub-lehm*
• **solve a problem**	résoudre (*v*) un problème	*ray-zood-r UH prub-lehm*
question	question (*f*)	*kehst-yOH*
• **ask a question**	poser (*v*) une question	*poh-zay ewn kehst-yOH*

read	lire (*v*)	*leer*
• **reading (passage)**	lecture (*f*)	*lehk-tewr*
registration	inscription (*f*)	*EH-skreeps-yOH*
• **registration fee**	droits (*m, pl*) d'inscription	*drwa dEH-skreeps-yOH*
repeat	répéter (*v*)	*ray-pay-tay*
review	révision (*f*)	*ray-veez-yOH*
• **review**	faire (*v*) une révision	*fehr ewn ray-veez-yOH*
school	école (*f*)	*ay-kul*
• **finish school**	finir (*v*) la dernière année d'école	*fee-neer la dehrn-yehr a-nay day-kul*
• **go to school**	assister (*v*) à l'école	*a-seess-tay al ay-kul*
study	étudier (*v*)	*ay-tewd-yay*
take attendance	faire (*v*) l'appel	*fehr lap-ehl*
teach	enseigner (*v*)	*AH-sehn-yay*
test	épreuve (*f*)	*ay-pruhv*
thesis	thèse (*f*)	*tehz*
type	taper (*v*) à la machine	*tap-ay a la mash-een*
typewriter	machine (*f*) à écrire	*mash-een a ay-kreer*
understand	comprendre (*v*)	*kOH-prAH-dre*
write	écrire (*v*)	*ay-kreer*

38. WORK

a. JOBS AND PROFESSIONS

accountant	comptable (*m, f*)	*kOH-tabl*
actor	acteur (*m*)	*ak-tur*
actress	actrice (*f*)	*ak-treess*
architect	architecte (*m, f*)	*arsh-ee-tehkt*
baker	boulanger (*m*)	*bool-AH-zhay*
	boulangère (*f*)	*bool-AH-zh-ehr*
barber	coiffeur (*m*)	*kwaf-ur*
bricklayer	maçon (*m*)	*mass-OH*
bus driver	chauffeur (*m*)	*sh-oh-fur*
	femme (*f*) chauffeur	*fahm sh-oh-fur*
businessman	homme (*m*) d'affaires	*um daf-ehr*
businesswoman	femme (*f*) d'affaires	*fahm daf-ehr*
butcher	boucher (*m*)	*boosh-ay*
	bouchère (*f*)	*boosh-ehr*
carpenter	menuisier (*m*)	*me-new-eez-yay*
cook	cuisinier (*m*)	*kew-eez-een-yay*
	cuisinière (*f*)	*kew-eez-een-yehr*

dentist	dentiste (*m, f*)	*dAH-teest*
doctor	médecin (*m*)	*mayd-sEH*
	femme (*f*) médecin	*fahm mayd-sEH*
	docteur (*m*)	*duk-tur*
	femme (*f*) docteur	*fahm duk-tur*
• eye doctor	ophtalmologiste (*m, f*)	*uf-tal-mul-uzh-eest*
	oculiste (*m, f*)	*uk-ew-leest*
editor	rédacteur (*m*)	*rayd-akt-ur*
	rédactrice (*f*)	*rayd-ak-treess*
electrician	électricien (*m*)	*ay-lehk-tree-syEH*
engineer	ingénieur (*m*)	*EH-zhayn-yur*
	femme (*f*) ingénieur	*fahm EH-zhayn-yur*
factory worker	ouvrier (*m*)	*oovr-yay*
	ouvrière (*f*)	*oovr-yehr*
farmer	fermier (*m*)	*fehrm-yay*
	fermière (*f*)	*fehrm-yehr*
fireman	pompier (*m*)	*pOHp-yay*
hairdresser	coiffeur (*m*)	*kwaf-ur*
	coiffeuse (*f*)	*kwaf-uhz*
job	métier (*m*)	*mayt-yay*
	occupation (*f*)	*uk-ewp-ass-yOH*
journalist	journaliste (*m, f*)	*zh-oor-nal-eest*
lawyer	avocat(e) (*m, f*)	*a-vu-ka(t)*
mechanic	mécanicien (*m*)	*may-ka-neess-yEH*
	mécanicienne (*f*)	*may-ka-neess-yehn*
movie director	réalisateur (*m*)	*ray-al-eez-at-ur*
	réalisatrice (*f*)	*ray-al-eez-at-reess*
	metteur (*m*) en scène	*met-ur AH sehn*
	femme (*f*) metteur en scène	*fahm met-ur AH sehn*
musician	musicien (*m*)	*mew-zee-syEH*
	musicienne (*f*)	*mew-zees-yehn*
nurse	infirmier (*m*)	*EH-feerm-yay*
	infirmière (*f*)	*EH-feerm-yehr*
occupation	occupation (*f*)	*uk-ewp-ass-yOH*
painter (*of buildings, rooms*)	peintre (*m*)	*pEH-tre*
	femme (*f*) peintre	*fahm pEH-tre*
• (artist)	artiste peintre (*m, f*)	*ar-teest pEH-tre*
pharmacist	pharmacien (*m*)	*farm-ass-yEH*
	pharmacienne (*f*)	*farm-ass-yehn*
pilot	pilote (*m, f*)	*pee-lut*
plumber	plombier (*m*)	*plOHb-yay*
policeman	agent (*m*) de police (*f*)	*azh-AHd pul-eess*

policewoman	auxiliaire féminine de police	*uks-eel-yehr fay-meen-een de pul-eess*
professor	professeur (*m*)	*pruf-ehs-ur*
	femme (*f*) professeur	*fahm pruf-ehs-ur*
profession	profession (*f*)	*pruf-ehs-yOH*
professional	professionnel (*m*)	*pruf-ehs-yun-ehl*
	professionnelle (*f*)	*pruf-ehs-yun-ehl*
psychiatrist	psychiatre (*m, f*)	*psee-kee-atr*
psychologist	psychologue (*m, f*)	*psee-kul-ug*
scientist	scientifique (*m, f*)	*sy-AH-tee-feek*
secretary	secrétaire (*m, f*)	*se-kray-tehr*
surgeon	chirurgien (*m*)	*sheer-ewr-zh-y-EH*
	femme (*f*) chirurgien	*fahm sheer-ewr-zh-y-EH*
tailor	tailleur (*m*)	*tah-y-ur*
	couturière (*f*)	*koo-tewr-yehr*
teacher	professeur (*m*)	*pruf-ehs-ur*
	femme (*f*) professeur	*fahm pruf-ehs-ur*
typist	dactylographe (*f*)	*dak-teel-ug-raf*
	homme (*m*) dactylographe	*um dak-teel-ug-raf*
writer	écrivain (*m*)	*ay-kreev-EH*
	femme (*f*) écrivain	*fahm ay-kreev-EH*

b. INTERVIEWING FOR A JOB

See also section 11f—Basic Personal Information.

Name	Nom (*m*)	*nOH*
first name	prénom (*m*)	*prayn-OH*
surname, family name	nom (*m*) de famille	*nOHd fam-ee*
signature	signature (*f*)	*seen-ya-tewr*
Address	Adresse (*f*)	*ad-rehss*
street	rue (*f*)	*rew*
number	numéro (*m*)	*new-may-roh*
city	ville (*f*)	*veel*
postal code	code postal (*m*)	*kud pus-tal*
Telephone number	Numéro de téléphone (*m*)	*new-may-rohd tay-lay-fun*
area code	code régional (*m*)	*kud ray-zh-yun-al*
Date & place of birth	Date et lieu de naissance	*dat ay ly-uhd nehs-AH-ss*

date	date (*f*)	*dat*
place	lieu (*m*)	*ly-uh*
Age	Age (*m*)	*ah-zh*
Sex	Sexe (*m*)	*sehks*
male	mâle (*m*)	*mahl*
female	femelle (*f*)	*fem-ehl*
Marital Status	Etat (*m*) civil	*ay-ta see-veel*
divorced	divorcé(e) (*adj, m, f*)	*dee-vor-say*
married	marié(e) (*adj, m, f*)	*mar-yay*
single	célibataire (*m, f*)	*say-lee-ba-tehr*
widow	veuve (*f*)	*vuv*
widower	veuf (*m*)	*vuhf*
Nationality	Nationalité (*f*)	*nas-yun-al-ee-tay*

See also section 30d—Nationalities and Languages.

Education	Education (*f*)	*ay-dew-kas-yOH*
elementary school	école (*f*) primaire élémentaire	*ay-kul pree-mehr ay-laymAH-tehr*
junior high school	école (*f*) d'enseignement de cours moyen	*ay-kul dAHseh-ny-mAh de koor mwa-y-EH*
high school	lycée (*m*)	*lee-say*
university	université (*f*)	*ew-nee-vehr-see-tay*
Profession	Profession (*f*)	*pruf-ehss-yOH*
Résumé	Résumé (*m*)	*ray-zewm-ay*

c. THE OFFICE

adhesive tape	ruban (*m*) adhésif	*rewbAH ad-ay-zeef*
appointment book	agenda (*m*) de bureau	*azh-EH-da de bew-roh*
briefcase	serviette (*f*)	*sehrv-yeht*
calendar	calendrier (*m*)	*kal-AH-dr-yay*
chair	siège (*m*) de bureau	*sy-eh-zh de bew-roh*
	chaise (*f*) tournante	*sh-ehz toorn-AHt*
file	classeur (*m*)	*klahs-ur*
	dossier-classeur (*m*)	*duss-yay-klahs-ur*
filing card	fiche (*f*)	*feesh*
intercom	interphone (*m*)	*EH-tehr-fun*
pen	stylo (*m*)	*stee-lo*
pencil	crayon (*m*)	*kreh-yOH*
photocopier	photocopieur (*m*)	*fu-tu-cup-y-ur*
ruler	règle (*f*)	*reh-gle*

scissors	ciseaux (*m, pl*)	*see-zo*
staple	agrafe (*f*)	*ag-raf*
stapler	agrafeuse (*f*)	*ag-ra-fuhz*
tack	punaise (*f*)	*pew-nehz*
telephone	téléphone (*m*)	*tay-lay-fun*
typewriter	machine (*f*) à écrire	*mash-een a ay-kreer*
wastebasket	corbeille (*f*) à papier (*m*)	*kor-beh-y a pap-yay*
word processor	ordinateur (*m*) à traitement de texte	*or-dee-nat-ur a treht-mAH de tehk-st*
	machine (*f*) de traitement de texte	*mash-een de treht-mAH de tehk-st*

d. ADDITIONAL WORK VOCABULARY

advertising	publicité (*f*)	*pewb-lee-see-tay*
boss (*in an office*)	chef (*m*) de bureau	*sh-ehf de bew-roh*
career	carrière (*f*)	*kar-yehr*
classified ad	petite annonce (*f*)	*pteet anOHs*
commerce	commerce (*m*)	*kum-ehrs*
company	société (*f*) commerciale	*suss-yay-tay kum-ehrs-yal*
contract	contrat (*m*)	*kOH-tra*
earn	gagner (*v*)	*gan-yay*
employ	employer (*v*)	*AH-plwa-yay*
employee	employé(e) (*m, f*)	*AH-plwa-yay*
employer	employeur (*m*)	*AH-plwa-yur*
	employeuse (*f*)	*AH-plwa-yuhz*
employment agency	agence (*f*) d'emploi	*a-zh-AHs dAH-plwa*
factory	usine (*f*)	*ew-zeen*
fire *(dismiss)*	renvoyer (*v*)	*rAH-vwa-yay*
hire	employer (*v*)	*AH-plwa-yay*
manager	directeur (*m*)	*dee-rehk-tur*
	directrice (*f*)	*dee-rehk-treess*
market	marché (*m*)	*marsh-ay*
office	bureau (*m*)	*bew-roh*
plant	établissement (*m*)	*ay-tab-leess-mAH*
retirement, pension	retraite (*f*)	*re-treht*
	pension (*f*)	*pAH-syOH*
• **retire**	se retirer (*v*)	*se-re-tee-ray*
	être (*v*) en retraite	*eh-tre AH re-treht*
unemployment	chômage (*m*)	*sh-oh-mazh*
wage, salary	gages (*m, pl*)	*ga-zh*
	salaire (*m*)	*sal-ehr*
work	travail (*m*)	*tra-va-y*
• **work**	travailler (*v*)	*tra-va-yay*
• **work associate**	collègue (*m, f*)	*kul-ehg*

EMERGENCIES

39. REPORTING AN EMERGENCY

a. FIRE

alarm	alarme (*f*)	*al-arm*
ambulance	ambulance (*f*)	*AH-bewlAHs*
building	bâtiment (*m*)	*bah-teemAH*
	édifice (*m*)	*ay-dee-feess*
burn	brûlure (*f*)	*brew-lewr*
• **burn**	brûler (*v*)	*brew-lay*
call the fire department	appeler (*v*) les pompiers	*ap-lay lay pOHp-yay*
	appeler (*v*) les sapeurs-pompiers	*ap-lay lay sap-ur pOHp-yay*
catch fire	prendre (*v*) feu	*prAH-dre fuh*
	s'enflammer (*v*)	*sAH-flam-ay*
danger	danger (*m*)	*dAH-zh-ay*
destroy	détruire (*v*)	*day-trew-eer*
emergency exit	sortie (*f*) d'urgence	*sor-tee dewr-zh-AHs*
escape, get out	fuir (*v*)	*few-eer*
	se précipiter (*v*)	*se pray-see-pee-tay*
extinguish, put out	éteindre (*v*)	*aytEH-dre*
fire	feu (*m*)	*fuh*
	incendie (*m*)	*EH-sAH-dee*
• **be on fire**	être (*v*) en feu	*eh-tre AH fuh*
• **Fire!**	Feu!	*fuh*
• **fire alarm**	sirène (*f*) d'alerte au feu	*seer-ehn dal-ehrt oh fuh*
• **fire extinguisher**	extincteur (*m*)	*ehks-tEHkt-ur*
• **firefighter**	pompier (*m*)	*pOHp-yay*
	sapeur-pompier (*m*)	*sap-ur pOHp-yay*
• **fire hose**	tuyau (*m*) de pompe	*tew-ee-yo de pOHp*
• **fire hydrant**	borne (*f*) d'incendie	*born dEH-sAH-dee*
• **fire truck**	fourgon-pompe (*m*)	*foor-gOH-pOHp*
fireproof	incombustible (*adj*)	*EH-kOH-bews-teebl*
	ignifuge (*adj*)	*eeg-nee-few-zh*
first aid	soins (*m, pl*) d'urgence	*swEH dewr-zh-AH-s*
flame	flamme (*f*)	*flahm*
help	aider (*v*)	*ay-day*
• **Help!**	À l'aide! (*f*)	*al-ehd*
• **give help**	donner (*v*) de l'aide	*dun-ay de l-ehd*
ladder	échelle (*f*)	*ay-sh-ehl*

out	dehors (*adv*)	*de-or*
• **Everybody out!**	Dehors! Tous!	*de-or toos*
protect	protéger (*v*)	*prut-ay-zh-ay*
rescue	sauver (*v*)	*soh-vay*
shout	cri (*m*)	*kree*
• **shout**	crier (*v*)	*kree-ay*
siren	sirène (*f*)	*seer-ehn*
smoke	fumée (*f*)	*few-may*
spark	étincelle (*f*)	*ayt-EH-sehl*
victim	victime (*f*)	*veek-teem*

b. ROBBERY AND ASSAULT

argue	se disputer (*v*)	*se-dees-pew-tay*
	se quereller (*v*)	*se ke-ray-lay*
arrest	arrêter (*v*)	*ar-ay-tay*
assault	assaut (*m*)	*a-so*
Come quickly!	Venez vite!	*vnay veet*
crime	crime (*m*)	*kreem*
• **crime wave**	masse (*f*) de crimes	*mas de kreem*
• **criminal**	criminel(le) (*m, f*)	*kree-meen-ehl*
description	description (*f*)	*dehs-kreeps-yOH*
fight	se battre (*v*)	*se-bat-re*
firearm	arme (*f*) à feu	*arm-a-fuh*
gun	revolver (*m*)	*re-vul-vehr*
	pistolet (*m*)	*pees-tul-eh*
handcuffs	menottes (*f, pl*)	*me-nut*
hurry	se dépêcher (*v*)	*se-day-pay-shay*
injure, wound	blesser (*v*)	*bleh-say*
• **injury, wound**	blessure (*f*)	*blay-sewr*
	plaie (*f*)	*pleh*
kill	tuer (*v*)	*tew-ay*
	assassiner (*v*)	*a-sa-see-nay*
• **killer**	tueur (*m*)	*tew-ur*
	assassin (*m*)	*a-sas-EH*
knife	couteau (*m*)	*koo-toh*
• **switchblade**	couteau (*m*) pliant	*koo-toh plee-yAH*
	couteau (*m*) de poche	*koo-toh de pu-sh*
murder	meurtre (*m*)	*mur-tre*
	homicide (*m*)	*um-ee-seed*
• **to murder**	assassiner (*v*)	*a-sa-see-nay*
pickpocket	pickpocket (*m*)	*peek-puk-eht*
	voleur (*m*) à la tire	*vul-ur a la teer*
	voleuse (*f*) à la tire	*vul-uhz a la teer*

police	police (*f*)	*pul-eess*
• **policeman**	agent (*m*) de police	*azh-AHd pul-eess*
• **policewoman**	auxiliaire féminine de police	*uks-eel-yehr fay-meen-een de pul-eess*
• **call the police**	appeler (*v*) la police	*ap-lay la pul-eess*
rape	viol (*m*)	*vee-yul*
	violer (*v*)	*vee-yul-ay*
rifle	fusil (*m*)	*few-zee*
rob	voler (*v*)	*vul-ay*
• **robber, thief**	voleur (*m*)	*vul-ur*
	voleuse (*f*)	*vul-uhz*
• **armed robbery**	vol (*m*) à main armée	*vul-a-mEH arm-ay*
• **robbery**	vol (*m*)	*vul*
• **Stop thief!**	Au voleur!	*oh vul-ur*
steal	dérober (*v*)	*day-rub-ay*
	voler (*v*)	*vul-ay*
victim	victime (*f*)	*veek-teem*
violence	violence (*f*)	*vee-yul-AHs*
weapon	arme (*f*)	*arm*
• **shoot**	tirer (*v*)	*tee-ray*

Run for your life! Sauve qui peut! *soh-v kee puh*
Someone assaulted me! On m'a assailli(e)! *OH ma a-sa-yee*
Someone robbed me! On m'a volé(e)! *OH ma vul-ay*

c. TRAFFIC ACCIDENTS

accident	accident (*m*)	*aks-eed-AH*
• **serious accident**	accident (*m*) grave	*aks-eed-AH grav*
• **traffic accident**	accident (*m*) de voiture	*aks-eed-AH de vwa-tewr*
ambulance		
• **call an ambulance**	appeler (*v*) une ambulance	*ap-lay ewn AH-bewlAHs*
be run over	être (*v*) renversé(e)	*eh-tre rAH-vehr-say*
bleed	saigner (*v*)	*sayn-yay*
• **blood**	sang (*m*)	*sAH*
broken bone	os (*m*) cassé	*us kah-say*
	os (*m*) fracturé	*us frak-tew-ray*
bump	heurter (*v*)	*ur-tay*
collision, smash	collision (*f*)	*kul-eez-yOH*
• **collide**	entrer (*v*) en collision	*AH-tray AH kul-eez-yOH*
	se heurter (*v*)	*se-ur-tay*

crash	choc (*m*) percussion (*f*)	*shuk; pehr-kewss-yOH*
	percuter (*v*)	*pehr-kew-tay*
doctor	médecin (*m*)	*mayd-sEH*
	femme (*f*) médecin	*fahm mayd-sEH*
• **get a doctor**	chercher (*v*) un médecin	*sh-ehr-shay UH mayd-sEH*
first aid	soins (*m, pl*) d'urgence	*swEH dewr-zh-AH-s*
• **antiseptic**	antiseptique (*m*)	*AH-tee-sehp-teek*
• **bandage**	pansement (*m*)	*pAHs-mAH*
• **gauze**	gaze (*f*)	*gahz*
• **scissors**	ciseaux (*m, pl*)	*see-zo*
• **splint**	éclisse (*f*)	*ay-kleess*
• **tincture of iodine**	teinture (*f*) d'iode	*tEH-tewr dee-yud*
Help!	Au secours!	*oh-skoor*
hospital	hôpital (*m*)	*oh-pee-tal*
• **emergency (ward)**	service (*m*) des urgences	*sehr-veess day-zewr-zh-AHs*
• **X-rays**	rayons (*m, pl*) X	*reh-yOH eeks*
police	police (*f*)	*pul-eess*
• **call the police**	appeler (*v*) la police	*ap-lay la pul-eess*
shock	choc (*m*)	*shuk*
wound, injury	plaie (*f*)	*pleh*
	blessure (*f*)	*blay-sewr*

40. MEDICAL CARE

a. THE DOCTOR

See also Section 12—The Body.

acne	acné (*f*)	*ak-nay*
allergy	allergie (*f*)	*al-ehrzh-ee*
appendicitis	appendicite (*f*)	*ap-AH-dee-seet*
• **appendix**	appendice (*m*)	*ap-AH-deess*
appointment	rendez-vous (*m*)	*rAH-day-voo*
artery	artère (*f*)	*ar-tehr*
arthritis	arthrite (*f*)	*ar-treet*
aspirin	aspirine (*f*)	*as-pee-reen*
bandage	pansement (*m*)	*pAHs-mAH*
• **bandage**	panser (*v*)	*pAH-say*

blood	sang (*m*)	*sAH*
• **blood pressure**	tension (*f*) artérielle (veineuse)	*tAHs-yOH ar-tayr-yehl (vehn-uhz)*
• **blood test**	examen (*m*) hématologique	*ehg-zam-EH ay-ma-tu-luzh-eek*
	examen du sang	*ehg-zam-EH dew sAH*
	examen sérologique	*ehg-zam-EH say-ru-luzh-eek*
bone	os (*m, sing*)	*us*
	(*pl*) les os	*lay-zo*
brain	cervelle (*f*)	*sehr-vehl*
bronchitis	bronchite (*f*)	*brOH-sheet*
cold	rhume (*f*)	*rewm*
convalescence	convalescence (*f*)	*kOH-val-ay-sAHs*
cough	toux (*f*)	*too*
• **cough**	tousser (*v*)	*too-say*
cure	guérison (*f*)	*gay-reez-OH*
• **cure, look after**	guérir (*v*)	*gay-reer*
	soigner (*v*)	*swEHn-ay*
• **get cured,**	se guérir (*v*)	*se-gay-reer*
convalesce	être (*v*) en convalescence	*eh-tre AH kOH-val-ay-sAHs*
dandruff	pellicules (*f, pl*)	*pay-leek-ewl*
digestive system	système (*m*) digestif	*see-stehm dee-zh-ehs-teef*
• **anus**	anus (*m*)	*an-ewss*
• **defecate**	déféquer (*v*)	*day-fay-kay*
• **rectum**	rectum (*m*)	*rehk-tum*
• **stomach**	estomac (*m*)	*ehs-tum-a*
• **have a stomach ache**	avoir (*v*) mal à l'estomac	*av-war mal al ehs-tum-a*
doctor	médecin (*m*)	*mayd-sEH*
	femme (*f*) médecin	*fahm mayd-sEH*
• **at the doctor's**	chez le médecin	*shal mayd-sEH*
doctor's instruments	instruments (*m, pl*) du médecin	*EH-strewmAH dew mayd-sEH*
• **electro-cardiograph**	électrocardiographe (*m*)	*ay-lehk-tru-kard-yu-graf*
• **stethoscope**	stéthoscope (*m*)	*stay-tus-kup*
• **syringe**	seringue (*f*)	*se-rEHg*
• **thermometer**	thermomètre (*m*)	*tehr-mum-eht-re*
doctor's visit	visite (*f*) du médecin	*vee-zeet dew mayd-sEH*
examine (*medically*)	examiner (*v*)	*ehg-zam-ee-nay*
• **to get examined**	se faire (*v*) examiner	*se-fehr-ehg-zam-ee-nay*
eye doctor	ophtalmologiste (*m, f*)	*uf-tal-mul-uzh-eest*
	oculiste (*m, f*)	*uk-ew-leest*

• contact lenses	lentilles (*f*, *pl*) de contact	*lAH-tee-y de kOH-takt*
	verres (*m*, *pl*) de contact	*vehr de kOH-takt*
• eyeglasses	lunettes (*f*, *pl*)	*lew-neht*
• sight	vision (*f*)	*veez-yOH*
feel	se sentir (*v*)	*se-sAH-teer*
• feel bad	se sentir (*v*) mal	*se-sAH-teer mal*
• feel well	se sentir (*v*) bien	*se-sAH-teer byEH*
• strong	fort (*adj*, *m*)	*for*
	forte (*f*)	*fort*
• weak	faible (*adj*, *m*, *f*)	*feh-bl*
• How do you feel?	Comment vous sentez-vous?	*kum-AH voo sAH-tay voo*
• I feel . . .	Je me sens . . .	*zhem-sAH*
fever	fièvre (*f*)	*fy-ehvre*
flu	influenza (*f*)	*EH-flew-ehn-za*
	grippe (*f*)	*greep*
headache	mal (*m*) de tête	*mal de teht*
• have a headache	avoir (*m*) mal de tête	*avwar mal de teht*
heal	guérir (*v*)	*gay-reer*
health	santé (*f*)	*sAH-tay*
• healthy	sain (*adj*, *m*)	*sEH*
	saine (*adj*, *f*)	*sehn*
• be healthy	être (*v*) en bonne santé	*eht-re AH bun sAH-tay*
heart	cœur (*m*)	*kur*
• heart attack	crise (*f*) cardiaque	*kreez kard-yak*
hurt	avoir (*m*) mal	*avwar mal*
	faire (*v*) mal à	*fehr mal a*
infection	infection (*f*)	*EH-fehks-yOH*
injection	piqûre (*f*)	*peek-ewr*
itch	démangeaison (*f*)	*daym-AH-zh-ehz-OH*
lymphatic system	système (*m*) lymphatique	*see-stehm lEH-fa-teek*
measles	rougeole (*f*)	*roozh-ul*
medicine (you take)	médicament (*m*)	*may-deek-am-AH*
muscle	muscle (*m*)	*mew-sk-le*
nerves	nerfs (*m*, *pl*)	*nehr*
• nervous system	réseau (*m*) de nerfs	*ray-zoh de nehr*
	système (*m*) nerveux	*see-stehm nehr-vuh*
nurse	infirmier (*m*)	*EH-feerm-yay*
	infirmière (*f*)	*EH-feerm-yehr*
operation	intervention (*f*) chirurgicale	*EH-tehrv-AHs-yOH sheer-ewr-zh-ee-kal*
• operating room	salle (*f*) de chirurgie	*sal de sheer-ewr-zh-ee*

optician	opticien (*m*)	*up-teess-yEH*
	opticienne (*f*)	*up-teess-yehn*
pain	douleur (*f*)	*dool-ur*
• **painful**	douleureux (*adj, m*)	*dool-ur-uh*
	douleureuse (*f*)	*dool-ur-uhz*
patient	patient (*m*)	*pas-yAH*
pill	pilule (*f*)	*peel-ewl*
pimple	bouton (*m*)	*boot-OH*
pneumonia	pneumonie (*f*)	*pnuh-mun-ee*
pregnant	enceinte (*adj, f*)	*AH-sEHt*
prescription	ordonnance (*f*)	*or-dun-AHs*
pulse	pouls (*m*)	*poo*
respiratory system	système (*m*) respiratoire	*see-stehm rehs-pee-rat-war*
• **breath**	haleine (*f*)	*al-ehn.*
• **breathe**	respirer (*v*)	*rehs-pee-ray*
• **bad breath**	mauvaise haleine (*f*)	*muv-ehz al-ehn*
• **be out of breath**	être hors d'haleine (*f*)	*eh-tre or dal-ehn*
• **lung**	poumon (*m*)	*poo-mOH*
• **nostril**	narine (*f*)	*na-reen*
rheumatism	rhumatisme (*m*)	*rew-ma-teesme*
secretary	secrétaire (*m, f*)	*se-kray-tehr*
sedative	sédatif (*m*)	*say-da-teef*
sick	malade (*adj*)	*mal-ad*
• **get sick**	tomber (*v*) malade	*tOH-bay mal-ad*
• **sickness, disease**	maladie (*f*)	*mal-ad-ee*
sneeze	éternuement (*m*)	*ay-tehr-new-mAH*
• **sneeze**	éternuer (*v*)	*ay-tehr-new-ay*
sore back	avoir (*v*) mal au dos	*avwar mal oh doh*
sore/twisted neck	avoir (*v*) mal au cou	*avwar mal oh koo*
	avoir (*v*) un torticolis	*avwar UH tor-tee-kul-ee*
specialist	spécialiste (*m, f*)	*spay-sy-al-eest*
suffer	souffrir (*v*)	*soof-reer*
suppository	suppositoire (*m*)	*sew-po-zeet-war*
surgeon	chirurgien (*m*)	*sheer-ewr-zh-y-EH*
	femme (*f*) chirurgien	*fahm sheer-ewr-zh-y-EH*
• **surgery**	chirurgie (*f*)	*sheer-ewr-zh-ee*
swollen	gonflé(e) (*m, f*)	*gOH-flay*
tablet	comprimé (*m*)	*kOH-pree-may*
temperature (fever)	fièvre (*f*)	*fee-yehvre*
• **take one's temperature**	mesurer (*v*) la fièvre	*me-zew-ray la fee-yehvre*
throat	gorge (*f*)	*gor-zh*
• **sore throat**	mal (*m*) de gorge	*mal-de-gor-zh*
• **have a sore throat**	avoir (*v*) mal de gorge	*avwar mal-de-gor-zh*

throw up	rendre (*v*)	*rAH-dr*
• vomit	vomir (*v*)	*vum-eer*
tonsils	amygdales (*f*, *pl*)	*a-meeg-dal*
urinary system	système urinaire	*see-stehm ew-ree-nehr*
• kidney	rein (*m*)	*rEH*
• urinate	uriner (*v*)	*ew-ree-nay*
vein	veine (*f*)	*vehn*
wheelchair	fauteuil (*m*) roulant	*fo-tu-y rool-AH*

b. THE DENTIST

anesthetic	anesthésique (*m*)	*a-nehs-tay-zeek*
appointment	rendez-vous (*m*)	*rAH-day-voo*
cavity, tooth decay	carie (*f*) dentaire	*ka-ree dAH-tehr*
clean, brush (teeth)	brosser (*v*) les dents	*bruss-ay lay dAH*
crown	couronne (*f*)	*koor-un*
dentist	dentiste (*m*, *f*)	*dAH-teest*
• at the dentist's	chez le (la) dentiste	*shayl (la) dAH-teest*
• dentist's chair	fauteuil (*m*)	*fo-tu-y*
• dentist's office	cabinet (*m*) du (de la) dentiste	*kab-ee-neh dew (de la) dAH-teest*
denture, false teeth	dentier (*m*)	*dAHt-yay*
drill	fraise (*f*)	*frehz*
examine	examiner (*v*)	*ehg-zam-ee-nay*
extract, pull (a tooth)	extraire (*v*) une dent	*ehks-trehr ewn dAH*
• extraction	extraction (*f*)	*ehks-traks-yOH*
filling	obturation (*f*)	*up-tew-rahss-yOH*
mouth	bouche (*f*)	*boosh*
• gums	gencive (*f*)	*zh-AH-seev*
• jaw	mâchoire (*f*)	*mah-sh-war*
• lip	lèvre (*f*)	*lehv-re*
• Open your mouth!	Ouvrez la bouche!	*oov-ray la boosh*
• palate	palais (*m*)	*pal-eh*
• tongue	langue (*f*)	*lAHg*
needle	aiguille (*f*)	*ehg-ew-ee-y*
office hours	heures de bureau (*m*)	*ur de bew-ro*
rinse	(se) rinser (*v*)	*(se) rEH-say*
tooth	dent (*f*)	*dAH*
• canine	la dent canine	*la dAH kan-een*
• incisor	la dent incisive	*la dAH EH-see-seev*
• molar	la dent molaire	*la dAH mul-ehr*
• root	racine (*f*)	*ra-seen*
• wisdom tooth	dent (*f*) de sagesse	*dAH de sazh-ehss*

toothache	mal (*m*) aux dents	*mal oh dAH*
• **have a toothache**	avoir (*v*) mal aux dents	*avwar mal oh dAH*
• **My tooth hurts!**	Une dent me fait mal!	*ewn dAH me feh mal*
toothbrush	brosse (*f*) à dents	*bruss a dAH*
toothpaste	dentifrice (*m*)	*dAH-tee-freess*
X-rays	rayons (*m, pl*) X	*reh-yOH eeks*

41. LEGAL MATTERS

accusation	accusation (*f*)	*ak-ew-zas-yOH*
• **accuse**	accuser (*v*)	*ak-ew-zay*
• **accused (person)**	accusé(e) (*m, f*)	*ak-ew-zay*
address oneself to	s'adresser (*v*) à	*sad-rehs-ay a*
admit	admettre (*v*)	*ad-meht-re*
agree	être (*v*) d'accord	*eh-tre dak-or*
capital punishment	peine (*f*) capitale	*pehn ka-pee-tal*
chief of police	préfet (*m*) de police	*pray-feh de pul-eess*
controversy	controverse (*f*)	*kOH-truv-ehrss*
convince	convaincre (*v*)	*kOH-vEH-kre*
court	tribunal (*m*)	*tree-bewn-al*
• **court of appeal**	cour (*f*) d'appel	*koor dap-ehl*
courtroom	salle (*f*) du tribunal	*sal dew tree-bewn-al*
debate	débat (*m*)	*day-ba*
• **debate**	débattre (*v*)	*day-ba-tre*
defend oneself	se défendre (*v*)	*se-dayf-AH-dre*
disagree	se disputer (*v*)	*se-deess-pew-tay*
discuss	discuter (*v*)	*deess-kew-tay*
guilt	culpabilité (*f*)	*kewl-pa-bee-lee-tay*
• **guilty**	coupable (*adj, m, f*)	*koop-abl*
innocence	innocence (*f*)	*een-us-AH-s*
• **innocent**	innocent(e) (*adj, m, f*)	*een-us-AH(t)*
judge	juge (*m*)	*zh-ew-zh*
• **judge**	juger (*v*)	*zh-ew-zhay*
jury	jury (*m*)	*zh-ew-ree*
justice	justice (*f*)	*zh-ew-steess*
law	loi (*f*)	*lwa*
• **lawful, legal**	légal(e) (*adj, m, f*)	*lay-gal*
• **unlawful, illegal**	illégal(e) (*adj, m, f*)	*ee-lay-gal*
• **civil law**	loi (*f*) civile	*lwa see-veel*
	droit (*m*) civil	*drwa see-veel*
• **criminal law**	loi (*f*) pénale	*lwa pay-nal*
	droit (*m*) pénal	*drwa pay-nal*
lawsuit, charge	cause (*f*) civile	*kohz see-veel*

lawyer	avocat (*m*)	*a-vuk-a*
	femme (*f*) avocat	*fahm a vuk-a*
• **trial lawyer**	avoué (*m*)	*av-way*
	femme (*f*) avoué	*fahm av-way*
litigation	litige (*m*)	*lee-tee-zh*
• **litigate**	faire (*v*) litige	*fehr lee-tee-zh*
	faire (*v*) cause	*fehr koh-z*
magistrate	magistrat (*m*)	*mazh-ees-tra*
persuade	persuader (*v*)	*pehr-sew-ad-ay*
plea	plaidoirie (*f*)	*plehd-war-ee*
• **plea for mercy**	supplication (*f*) pour clémence	*sewp-lee-kas-yOH poor klaym-AH-s*
• **(to) plead**	plaider (*v*)	*play-day*
police station	commissariat (*m*) de police	*kum-ee-sar-ya de pul-eess*
prison, jail	prison (*f*)	*preez-OH*
• **imprison**	emprisonner (*v*)	*AH-pree-zun-ay*
• **life imprisonment**	emprisonnement (*m*) à perpétuité	*AH-pree-zun-mAH a pehr-pay-tew-ee-tay*
public prosecutor	procureur (*m*) de la République	*pruk-ewr-ur de la ray-pew-bleek*
right, privilege	droit (*m*)	*drwa*
sentence	jugement (*m*)	*zh-ew-zh-mAH*
• **life sentence**	à la prison à vie (*f*)	*a la preez-OH a vee*
• **prison sentence**	à prison (*f*)	*a preez-OH*
• **pass a sentence**	prononcer (*v*) un jugement	*prun-OH-say UH zh-ew-zh-mAH*
• **serve a sentence**	subir (*v*) une condamnation	*sew-beer ewn kOH-dah-nahs-yOH*
sue	citer (*v*) dans un procès-verbal	*see-tay dAHz-UH pruss-eh vehr-bal*
summons	citation (*f*)	*see-tahs-yOH*
trial	procès (*m*)	*pruss-eh*
• **be on trial**	être (*v*) en procès	*eh-tre AH pruss-eh*
• **put someone on trial**	mettre (*v*) quelqu'un en procès	*meht-re kehlk-UH AH pruss-eh*
verdict	verdict (*m*)	*vehr-deekt*
• **guilty**	coupable (*adj*)	*koop-abl*
• **not guilty**	non coupable (*adj*)	*nOH koop-abl*
witness	témoin (*m*)	*taym-wEH*
• **eyewitness**	témoin (*m*) oculaire	*taym-wEH uk-ew-lehr*
• **for the defense**	témoin (*m*) à décharge	*taym-wEH a day-shar-zh*
• **for the prosecution**	témoin (*m*) à charge	*taym-wEH a shar-zh*

THE CONTEMPORARY WORLD

42. SCIENCE AND TECHNOLOGY

a. THE CHANGING WORLD

For more vocabulary on basic matter, see Section 13.

antenna	antenne (*f*)	*AH-tehn*
• **dish antenna**	antenne (*f*) parabolique	*AH-tehn pa-ra-bul-eek*
astronaut	astronaute (*m, f*)	*as-tru-noht*
	cosmonaute (*m, f*)	*kus-mu-noht*
atom	atome (*m*)	*at-ohm*
• **electron**	électron (*m*)	*ay-lehk-trOH*
• **molecule**	molécule (*f*)	*mul-ay-kewl*
• **neutron**	neutron (*m*)	*nuh-trOH*
• **proton**	proton (*m*)	*prut-OH*
compact disk	disque compact (*m*)	*deesk-kOH-pakt*
fax machine	télécopieur (*m*)	*tay-lay-kup-yur*
	émetteur-récepteur (*m*) de fac-similé	*ay-meht-ur-ray-sehp-tur-de-fak-see-mee-lay*
	fax (*m*)	*fahks*
laser	laser (*m*)	*la-zehr*
• **light beam**	rayon (*m*) de lumière	*reh-yOH de lewm-yehr*
microwave	micro-onde (*f*)	*meek-ru-OHd*
missile	missile (*m*)	*mee-seel*
• **launch pad**	rampe (*f*) de lancement	*rAHp de lAHs-mAH*
monorail vehicle	monorail (*m*)	*mu-nu-rah-y*
nuclear industry	industrie (*f*) nucléaire	*EH-dews-tree new-klay-ehr*
• **fission reactor**	réacteur (*m*) à fission	*ray-akt-ur a feess-yOH*
• **fusion reactor**	réacteur (*m*) à fusion	*ray-akt-ur a fewz-yOH*
• **nuclear energy**	énergie (*f*) nucléaire	*ay-nehr-zh-ee new-klay-ehr*
• **nuclear fuel**	combustible (*m*) nucléaire	*kOH-bews-teebl new-klay-ehr*
• **nuclear reactor**	réacteur (*m*) nucléaire	*ray-akt-ur new-klay-ehr*
robot	robot (*m*)	*rub-oh*

satellite	satellite (*m*)	*sa-tay-leet*
• **artificial satellite**	satellite (*m*) artificiel	*sa-tay-leet ar-tee-fee-syehl*
scientific research	recherche (*f*) scientifique	*re-sh-ehrsh sy-AH-tee-feek*
spacecraft	vaisseau (*m*) spatial	*veh-so spas-yal*
• **lunar module**	module (*m*) lunaire	*mud-ewl lew-nehr*
• **space shuttle**	navette (*f*) spatiale	*na-veht spas-yal*
technology	technologie (*f*)	*tehk-nu-lu-zhee*
telecommunications	télécommunications (*f, pl*)	*tay-lay-kum-ewn-ee-kahs-yOH*
• **teleconferencing**	télé-audio-conférence (*f*)	*tay-lay-ohd-yu-kOH-fay-rAHs*
• **telex machine**	télex (*m*)	*tay-lehks*
	ordinateur-télex (*m*)	*or-dee-na-tur tay-lehks*
theory of relativity	théorie (*f*) de la relativité	*tay-or-ee de la re-la-tee-vee-tay*
• **quantum theory**	théorie (*f*) des quanta	*tay-or-ee day kwAH-ta*

b. COMPUTERS

artificial intelligence	intelligence (*f*) artificielle	*EH-tehl-ee-zh-AHs ar-tee-fee-syehl*
byte	multiplet (*m*)	*mewl-teep-leh*
compatible	compatible (*adj*)	*kOH-pa-tee-bl*
computer	ordinateur (*m*)	*or-dee-na-tur*
• **computer assisted instruction**	instructions (*f, pl*) automatisées	*EH-strewk-syOH ut-um-a-teez-ay*
• **computer language**	langage-machine (*m*)	*lAHg-azh-ma-sheen*
	langage (*m*) de programmation	*lAhgazh de prug-ram-ahs-yOH*
• **computer science**	informatique (*f*)	*EH-form-at-eek*
data	données (*f, pl*)	*dun-ay*
	information (*f*)	*EH-form-ass-yOH*
• **data processing**	traitement (*m*) de l'information	*trehtmAH de lEH-form-ass-yOH*
disk	disque (*m*)	*deesk*
• **floppy disk**	disquette (*f*)	*deesk-eht*
	disque (*m*) souple	*deesk-soop-le*
file, menu	archives (*f, pl*)	*arsh-eev*
flow chart	schéma (*m*) fonctionnel	*shay-ma fOH-ks-yun-ehl*
function	fonction (*f*)	*fOH-ks-yOH*
hardware	matériel (*m*)	*ma-tayr-yehl*
	hardware (*m*)	*ard-wehr*

integrated circuit	circuit (*m*) intégré	*seer-kew-ee EH-tay-gray*
interface	interface (*f*)	*EH-tehr-fahss*
keyboard	clavier (*m*)	*klav-yay*
• **keyboard operator**	claviste (*m, f*)	*klav-eest*
memory	mémoire (*f*)	*may-mwar*
• **random access memory**	mémoire (*f*) à accès sélectif	*may-mwar a aks-eh say-lehk-teef*
microcomputer	micro-ordinateur (*m*)	*meek-ro-or-dee-na-tur*
modem	modem (*m*)	*mud-ehm*
office automation	automatisation (*f*) de bureau	*ut-um-a-teez-ah-syOH de bew-roh*
optical reader	lecteur optique (*m*)	*lehk-tur up-teek*
peripherals	périphériques (*m, pl*)	*pay-reef-ay-reek*
personal computer	ordinateur (*m*) personnel	*or-dee-na-tur pehr-sun-ehl*
printer	imprimante (*f*) d'ordinateur	*EHpreem-AHt dor-dee-na-tur*
program	programme (*m*) d'un ordinateur	*prug-ram dUH nor-dee-na-tur*
• **programmer (*person*)**	programmeur (*m*)	*prug-ram-ur*
	programmeuse (*f*)	*prug-ram-uhz*
• **programmer (*machine*)**	programmateur (*m*)	*prug-ram-at-ur*
• **programming**	programmation (*f*)	*prug-ram-ahs-yOH*
screen	écran (*m*) de visualisation	*ay-krAH de veez-ew-al-eez-as-yOH*
• **software**	logiciel (*m*)	*luzh-ee-syehl*
	software (*m*)	*suf-wehr*
terminal	terminal (*m*)	*tehr-mee-nal*
user-friendly	ordinateur (*m*) d'usage facile	*or-dee-na-tur dewz-azh fa-seel*
	ordinateur (*m*) "user friendly"	*or-dee-na-tur ew-zehr frehn-lee*
word processing	machine (*f*) de traitement de texte	*mash-een de treht-mAh de tehkst*
• **word processor**	processeur (*m*)	*pru-say-sur*
• **microprocessor**	microprocesseur (*m*)	*meek-ro-pru-say-sur*

43. POLITICS

See also Sections 16, 17, 21, and 22.

arms race	course (*f*) aux armements	*koors oh zar-me-mAH*

arms reduction	réduction (*f*) des armements	*ray-dewks-yOH day-zar-me-mAH*
assembly	assemblée (*f*)	*as-AH-blay*
association	association (*f*)	*as-us-yah-syOH*
communism	communisme (*m*)	*kum-ew-neesme*
• communist	communiste (*m, f*)	*kum-ew-neest*
conservative party	parti (*m*) conservateur	*par-tee kOH-sehr-va-tur*
council	conseil (*m*)	*kOH-seh-y*
democracy	démocratie (*f*)	*day-muk-ra-see*
• democrat	démocrate (*m, f*)	*day-muk-rat*
• democratic	démocratique (*adj*)	*day-muk-ra-teek*
demonstration	manifestation (*f*)	*ma-nee-fehs-tas-yOH*
	manif (*f*)	*man-eef*
disarmament	désarmement (*m*)	*day-zar-me-mAH*
economy	économie (*f*)	*ay-kun-um-ee*
elect	élire (*v*)	*ay-leer*
• elections	élections (*f, pl*)	*ay-lehk-syOH*
govern	gouverner (*v*)	*goo-vehr-nay*
• government	gouvernement (*m*)	*goo-vehrn-mAH*
ideology	idéologie (*f*)	*ee-day-ul-uzh-ee*
inflation	inflation (*f*)	*EH-flah-syOH*
labor/trade union	syndicat (*m*)	*sEH-dee-ka*
legislation	législation (*f*)	*lay-zhee-slah-syOH*
liberal party	parti (*m*) libéral	*par-tee lee-bay-ral*
minister	ministre (*m*)	*mee-nee-stre*
monarchy	monarchie (*f*)	*mun-ar-shee*
• king	roi (*m*)	*rwa*
• queen	reine (*f*)	*rehn*
• prince	prince (*m*)	*prEHs*
• princess	princesse (*f*)	*prEHs-ehs*
parliament	parlement (*m*)	*parl-emAH*
• elected politician, representative	député (*m*)	*day-pew-tay*
	femme (*f*) député	*fahm day-pew-tay*
	représentant(e) (*m, f*)	*re-prayz-AH-tAH(t)*
• house/chamber of representatives	la Chambre des Députés	*la sh-AH-bre day day-pew-tay*
	(Assemblée Nationale)	*assAH-blay nas-yun-al*
• President of the French Republic	Président(e) (*m, f*) de la République Française	*pray-zeedAH(t) de la ray-pew-bleek frAH-sehz*
• Senate	Sénat (*m*)	*say-na*
• senator	sénateur (*m*)	*say-na-tur*
	femme (*f*) sénateur	*fahm say-na-tur*

• **universal suffrage/right to vote**	suffrage (*m*) universel	*sewf-razh ew-nee-vehr-sehl*
peace	paix (*f*)	*peh*
policy	politique (*f*)	*pul-ee-teek*
politician	homme (*m*) politique	*um pul-ee-teek*
	femme (*f*) politique	*fahm pul-ee-teek*
• **left wing**	gauche (*f*)	*go-sh*
• **right wing**	droite (*f*)	*drwat*
politics	politique (*f,sing*)	*pul-ee-teek*
• **political party**	parti (*m*) politique	*par-tee pul-ee-teek*
• **political power**	pouvoir (*m*) politique	*poov-war pul-ee-teek*
protest	protestation (*f*)	*prut-ehs-tah-syOH*
reform	réforme (*f*)	*ray-form*
republic	république (*f*)	*ray-pew-bleek*
revolt	révolte (*f*)	*ray-vult*
• **revolution**	révolution (*f*)	*ray-vul-ew-syOH*
riot	émeute (*f*)	*ay-muht*
socialism	socialisme (*m*)	*suss-yal-eesme*
• **socialist**	socialiste (*m, f*)	*suss-yal-eest*
state	état (*m*)	*ay-ta*
• **head of state**	chef (*m*) d'état	*sh-ehf day-ta*
strike	grève (*f*)	*grehv*
• **go on strike**	être (*v*) en grève	*eh-tre AH grehv*
	faire (*v*) grève	*fehr grehv*
Third World	Tiers Monde (*m*)	*tyehr mOHd*
underdeveloped countries	pays (*m, pl*) sous-développés	*peh-ee soo-day-vlup-ay*
unilateral	unilatéral(e) (*adj*)	*ew-nee-la-tehr-al*
vote	vote (*m*)	*vut*
• **vote**	voter (*v*)	*vut-ay*
war	guerre (*f*)	*gehr*
welfare	Assistance (*f*) sociale	*a-seest-AHs sus-yal*

44. CONTROVERSIAL ISSUES

a. THE ENVIRONMENT

For more vocabulary, see Sections 13 and 42.

air pollution	pollution (*f*) atmosphérique	*pul-ew-syOH at-mus-fay-reek*

chain stores	chaîne de magasins (*m, pl*)	*sh-ehn de ma-ga-zEH*
conservation	conservation (*f*)	*kOH-sehr-va-syOH*
consumption	consomption (*f*)	*kOH-sOH-psyOH*
ecology	écologie (*f*)	*ay-kul-uzh-ee*
ecosystem	écosystème (*m*)	*ay-ku-see-stehm*
energy	énergie (*f*)	*ay-nehr-zhee*
• **energy crisis**	crise (*f*) d'énergie	*kreez day-nehr-zhee*
• **energy needs**	besoins (*m, pl*) d'énergie	*be-zwEH day-nehr-zhee*
• **energy source**	source (*f*) d'énergie	*soors day-nehr-zhee*
• **energy waste**	déchets (*m, pl*) d'énergie	*day-sh-eh day-nehr-zhee*
environment	environnement (*m*)	*AH-veer-un-mAH*
fossil fuels	combustibles (*m, pl*) fossiles	*kOH-bews-teebl fuss-eel*
geothermal energy	énergie (*f*) géothermique	*ay-nehr-zhee zh-ay-u-tehrm-eek*
natural resources	ressources (*f, pl*) naturelles	*re-soors na-tewr-ehl*
petroleum	pétrole (*m*)	*pay-trul*
pollution	pollution (*f*)	*pul-ew-syOH*
radiation	radiation (*f*)	*rad-yah-syOH*
• **radioactive waste**	déchets (*m, pl*) radioactifs	*day-sh-eh rad-yo-akteef*
solar cell	cellule (*f*) solaire	*sehl-ewl sul-ehr*
solar energy	énergie (*f*) solaire	*ay-nehr-zhee sul-ehr*
thermal energy	énergie (*f*) thermique	*ay-nehr-zhee tehr-meek*
water pollution	pollution (*f*) des eaux	*pul-ew-syOH day-zoh*
wind energy	énergie (*f*) éolienne	*ay-nehr-zhee ay-ul-yehn*

b. SOCIETY

abortion	avortement (*m*)	*av-ort-mAH*
• **fetus**	foetus (*m*)	*fay-tewss*
AIDS	SIDA (*m*)	*see-da*
capital punishment	peine (*f*) capitale	*pehn ka-pee-tal*
censorship	censure (*f*)	*sAH-sewr*
drugs	drogue (*f*)	*drug*
• **drug addiction**	toxicomanie (*f*)	*tuks-ee-kum-an-ee*
• **drug pusher**	trafiquant(e) (*m, f*) des stupéfiants	*tra-feek-AH(t) day stew-pay-fyAH*
• **take drugs**	prendre (*v*) de la drogue	*prAH-dre de la drug*
	se droguer (*v*)	*se-drug-ay*

• **drug trafficking**	trafic (*m*) des stupéfiants	*tra-feek day stew-pay-fyAH*
feminism	féminisme (*m*)	*fay-meen-eesme*
• **feminist**	féministe (*m, f*)	*fay-meen-eest*
homosexual	homosexuel(le) (*m, f*)	*um-u-sehks-ew-ehl*
• **homosexuality**	homosexualité (*f*)	*um-u-sehks-ew-al-ee-tay*
• **gay**	gai(e) (*adj, m, f*)	*gay*
• **lesbian**	lesbienne (*f*)	*lehs-by-ehn*
• **lesbianism**	lesb(ian)isme	*leh-b(y-an)ee-sme*
morality	moralité (*f*)	*mu-ra-lee-tay*
nuclear war	guerre (*f*) nucléaire	*gehr new-klay-ehr*
nuclear weapon	arme (*f*) nucléaire	*arm new-klay-ehr*
• **antinuclear protest**	protestation (*f*) anti-nucléaire	*prut-ehs-tah-syOH AH-tee-new-klay-ehr*
• **atomic bomb**	bombe (*f*) atomique	*bOHb a-tum-eek*
• **chemical weapon**	arme (*f*) chimique	*arm shee-meek*
pornography	pornographie (*f*)	*por-nug-ra-fee*
prostitution	prostitution (*f*)	*prus-tee-tew-syOH*
racism	racisme (*m*)	*ra-see-sme*

c. EXPRESSING YOUR OPINION

according to me	selon moi	*slOH mwa*
as a matter of fact	à vrai dire	*a vreh deer*
by the way	à propos	*a pro-po*
for example	par exemple	*par-ehg-zAH-ple*
from my point of view	de mon point de vue	*de mOH pwEH de vew*
I believe that . . .	Je crois que . . .	*zhe krwa ke*
I don't know if . . .	Je ne sais pas si . . .	*zhen seh pah see*
I doubt that . . .	Je doute que . . .	*zhe doot ke*
I think that . . .	Je pense que . . .	*zhe pAHs ke*
I'd like to say . . .	Je voudrais dire . . .	*zhe vood-reh deer*
I'm not sure that . . .	Je ne suis pas sûr(e) que . . .	*zhen swee pah sewr ke*
I'm sure that . . .	Je suis sûr(e) que . . .	*zhe swee sewr ke*
in conclusion	en conclusion	*AH kOH-klew-zyOH*
in my opinion	à mon avis (opinion)	*a-mun-avee(up-ee-nyOH)*
in my view	à mon point de vue	*a-mOH pwEHd vew*
It seems that . . .	Il semble que . . .	*eel sAHble ke*
It's clear that . . .	Il est clair que . . .	*eel eh klehr ke*
	Il est évident que . . .	*eel eh tay-veed-AH ke*
that is to say	c'est-à-dire	*seh-ta-deer*
There's no doubt that . . .	Il n'y a pas de doute que . . .	*eel ny-a-pah de doot ke*
therefore	donc (*conj*)	*dOHk*

ENGLISH-FRENCH WORDFINDER

This alphabetical listing of all of the English words in *French Vocabulary* will enable you to find the information you need quickly and efficiently. If all you want is the French equivalent of an entry word, you will find it here. If you also want pronunciation and usage aids, or closely associated words and phrases, use the reference number(s) and letter(s) to locate the section(s) in which the entry appears. This is especially important for words that have multiple meanings.

advertising la publicité 20a, 38d
advice le conseil 17a
advise conseiller *(v)* 17a
affection l'affection *(f)* 11e
affectionate affectueux, affectueuse *(adj, m, f)* 11e, 21a
affectionately affectueusement *(adv)* 19b
Africa l'Afrique *(f)* 30b
after après *(adv)* 4e
afternoon l'après-midi *(m)* 4a
again de nouveau *(adv)*, encore une fois 4e
age l'âge *(m)* 11b, 38b
aggressive aggressif, aggressive *(adj, m, f)* 11e
aggressiveness l'aggressivité *(f)* 11e
agnostic agnostique *(adj, m, f)* 11d
ago il y a *(adv)* 4e
agree être *(v)* d'accord *(m)* 21a, 22b, 41
agriculture l'agriculture *(f)* 14a
ahead avant *(adv)* 3d, 36c
AIDS le SIDA 44b
air l'air *(m)* 6a, 13c
air conditioner le climatiseur 23e, 33e
air conditioning la climatisation 23e
air pollution la pollution atmosphérique 44a
airline la ligne aérienne 32a
airmail par avion 19e
airplane l'avion *(m)* 32c
airport l'aéroport *(m)* 32a
aisle l'allée *(f)*, le passage 28a, 32c
aisle seat la place côté passage 32c
alarm l'alarme *(f)* 39a
alarm clock le réveille-matin 4d, 25i
albatross l'albatros *(m)* 15b
alcoholic beverage la boisson alcoolique 24k
algebra l'algèbre *(f)* 1f
algebraic algébrique *(adj)* 1f
all tout *(adj)*, toute chose 3c
All aboard! En voiture! 34
all day toute *(adj)* la journée 4a
allegory l'allégorie 17a
allergy l'allergie *(f)* 40a
allude faire *(v)* allusion 17a
almost presque *(adv)* 3c
almost never presque *(adv)* jamais *(adv)* 4e
alphabet l'alphabet *(m)* 8a
already déjà *(adv)* 4e
although bien que *(conj)*, quoique *(conj)* 8p
altruism l'altruisme *(m)* 11e
altruist l'altruiste *(m, f)* 11e
altruistic altruiste *(adj, m, f)* 11e
always toujours *(adv)* 4e
amateur l'amateur *(m)*, le (la) dilettante 27b
ambition l'ambition *(f)* 11e
ambitious ambitieux, ambitieuse *(adj, m, f)* 11e
ambulance l'ambulance *(f)* 33a, 39a, 39c
America l'Amérique *(f)* 30b
American *(nationality)* Américain *(m)*, Américaine *(f)* 30d; *(language)* américain *(m)*, anglais *(m)* 30d
ammonia l'ammoniaque *(f)* 13c
among parmi *(prep)* 3d, 8g
amphitheater l'amphithéâtre *(m)* 36a
an un *(m, s)*, une *(f, s)* 8c
analogy l'analogie *(f)* 17a
anatomy l'anatomie *(f)* 37e
anchovy l'anchois *(m)* 24d
and et *(conj)* 8p
anesthetic l'anesthésique *(m)* 40b

anger la colère 11e, 21a
angle l'angle *(m)* 2b
angry en colère 11e; fâché(e) *(adj, m, f)* 21a
animal l'animal *(m)* 15a
ankle la cheville 12a
anniversary l'anniversaire *(m)* 11c, 29a
announce annoncer *(v)* 17a
announcement l'annonce *(f)* 17a
annually annuel, annuelle *(adj)*, annuellement *(adv)* 4c
answer la réponse 9, 17a, 37f; répondre *(v)* 9, 17a, 18b, 37f
answering machine le répondeur téléphonique enregistreur, le téléphone-répondeur 18a
ant la fourmi 15d
Antarctic Antarctique *(adj, m, f)* 13b
Antarctic Circle le Cercle (Pôle) antarctique 13e
antenna l'antenne *(f)* 20b, 42a
anterior antérieur*(e)* *(adj)* 4e
anthropology l'anthropologie *(f)* 37e
antibiotic l'antibiotique *(m)* 25h
antinuclear protest la protestation antinucléaire 44b
antiseptic l'antiseptique *(m)* 39c
anus l'anus *(m)* 40a
anxiety l'anxiété *(f)* 21a
anxious anxieux, anxieuse *(adj, m, f)* 11e, 21a
anxiousness l'anxiété *(f)* 11e, 21a
any ***(partitive)*** *see* **Partitive** 8d
apartment l'appartement *(m)* 23g
apartment building l'immeuble *(m)* 23g
aperitif l'apéritif *(m)* 24g
apostrophe l'apostrophe *(f)* 19c
appeal court la cour d'appel 41
appendicitis l'appendicite *(f)* 40a
appendix l'appendice *(m)* 20a, 28d, 40a
appetizer les hors-d'oeuvre variés *(m, pl)* 24g
appetizing appétissant(e) *(adj, m, f)* 24p
applaud applaudir *(v)* 28e
applause l'applaudissement *(m)* 28e
apple la pomme 14d, 24f
apple pie la tarte aux pommes 24g
apple tree le pommier 14c
appointment le rendez vous 40a, 40b
appointment book l'agenda de bureau 38c
approval l'approbation *(f)* 21b
approve approuver *(v)* 21b
approximately à peu près *(adv)* 3c; environ *(adv)* 3c
apricot l'abricot *(m)* 14d, 24f
April l'avril *(m)* 5b
Aquarius le Verseau 5d
Arab *(nationality)* Arabe *(m/f)* 30d; *(language)* l'arabe *(m)* 30d
Arabic arabe *(adj, m, f)* 1d
archbishop l'archevêque *(m, f)* 11d
archeology l'archéologie *(f)* 37e
archipelago l'archipel *(m)* 13b
architect l'architecte *(m, f)* 38a
architecture l'architecture *(f)* 28b, 37e
Arctic Arctique *(adj, m, f)* 13b
Arctic Circle le Cercle (Pôle) arctique 13e
area la superficie 3a, 13e; la surface 3a, 13e
area code le code régional 18b, 38b

argue disputer *(v)*, arguer (de) 17a; se disputer *(v)*, se quereller *(v)* 39b
argument l'argument *(m)*, la dispute 17a
Aries le Bélier 5d
arithmetic l'arithmétique *(f)* 1f
arithmetical arithmétique *(adj)* 1f
arithmetical operations les opérations fondamentales le
arm le bras 12a
armchair le fauteuil 23c, 35c
armed robbery le vol à main armée 39b
arms race *(politics)* la course aux armements 43
arms reduction la réduction des armements 43
arrest arrêter *(v)* 39b
arrival l'arrivée *(f)* 32a
arrive arriver *(v)* 3e
arrogant arrogant(e) *(adj, m, f)* 11e
art l'art *(m)* 11e, 28b, 37e
art gallery la galerie d'art 36a
artery l'artère *(f)* 40a
arthritis l'arthrite *(f)* 40a
artichoke l'artichaut *(m)* 14e, 24e
article l'article *(m)* 8a, 8b, 8c, 20a
articulate articuler *(v)* 17a
artificial artificiel(le) *(adj, m, f)* 13d, 25i
artificial intelligence l'intelligence *(f)* artificielle 42b
artificial satellite le satellite artificiel 42a
artist l'artiste *(m, f)* 28b
artistic artistique *(adj)* 11e
arts *(humanities)* les lettres *(f, pl)* 37e
as *(since)* comme *(conj)* 8p
as a matter of fact au fait 17b; à vrai dire 44c
as if comme si *(conj)* 8p
as much as tant...que 3c; autant...que 3c
as soon as aussitôt que *(conj)*, dès que *(conj)* 4e, 8p
Asia l'Asie *(f)* 30b
ask *(for)* demander *(v)* 9, 17a
ask a question poser *(v)* une question, faire *(v)* une demande 9, 37f
ask for the bill demander *(v)* le compte 35b
asparagus l'asperge *(f)* 14e, 24e
aspic en gelée *(f)* 24h
aspirin l'aspirine *(f)* 25h, 40a
assassin assassin *(m)*
assault l'assaut *(m)* 39b
assembly l'assemblée *(f)* 43
assignment book le calepin, le carnet 37b
assignments les devoirs *(m, pl)* 37f
assistant l'assistant(e) *(m, f)* 37d
association l'association *(f)* 43
Assumption (August 15, National French Holiday) l'Assomption *(f)* 5f, 29a
assure assurer *(v)* 21a
asterisk l'astérisque *(m)* 19c
astronaut l'astronaute *(m, f)*, le (la) cosmonaute 42a
astronomy l'astronomie *(f)* 13a, 37e
astute astucieux, astucieuse *(adj, m, f)* 11e
astuteness l'astuce *(f)* 11e
at à *(prep)* 3d, 8g
at home à la maison, chez soi 23f
at midnight à minuit *(m)* 4a
at night dans la nuit 4a; de nuit 4a
at noon à midi *(m)* 4a
at one o'clock à une heure 4b
at someone's place chez quelqu'un 3d
at the beach à la plage 36b
at the bottom au fond 3d

at the dentist's chez le (la) dentiste 40b
at the doctor's chez le docteur 40a
at the end of au bout de, à la fin de 36c
at the present time à l'heure actuelle 4a
at the same time en même temps, à la fois 4e
at the tip of one's tongue au bout de la langue 12a
at the top of au sommet de 36c
at three o'clock à trois heures 4b
at two o'clock à deux heures 4b
At what time? A quelle heure? 4b
atheism l'athéisme *(m)* 11d
atheist l'athée *(m, f)* 11d
athlete l'athlète *(m, f)* 27b
Atlantic Atlantique *(adj, m, f)* 13b
atlas l'atlas *(m)* 20a, 37b
atmosphere l'atmosphère *(f)* 13b
atmospheric atmosphérique *(adj)* 13b
atmospheric conditions les conditions *(f, pl)* atmosphériques 6a
atom l'atome *(m)* 13c, 42a
atomic bomb la bombe atomique 44b
attend school assister *(v)* à l'école *(f)* 37f
attic le grenier 23a
attitude l'attitude *(f)* 21a
attractive attractif, attractive *(adj)* 11a; attrayant(e) *(adj)* 11e
attractiveness la fascination 11e
audience les spectateurs *(m, pl)* 28e
audio-visual equipment les appareils audio-visuels *(m, pl)* 20b
August l'août *(m)* 5b
aunt la tante 10a
Australia l'Australie *(f)* 30b
Australian *(nationality)* Australien *(m)*, Australienne *(f)* 30d
Austria l'Autriche *(f)* 30b
Austrian *(nationality)* Autrichien *(m)*, Autrichienne *(f)* 30d
authentic authentique *(adj)* 13d
author l'écrivain, une femme écrivain, l'auteur, la femme auteur 20a
autobiography l'autobiographie *(f)* 28d
automobile l'auto(mobile) *(f)* 33a
autumn l'automne *(m)* 5c
avarice l'avarice *(f)* 11e
avaricious avare *(adj)* 11e
avenue l'avenue *(f)* 11f, 36a
average moyen(ne) *(adj, m, f)* 1f
average height la taille moyenne 11a
away au loin *(adv)* 3d
awful mauvais(e) *(adj, m, f)* 6a
awful weather un temps mauvais 6a
axis l'axe *(m)* 2b

B
baby le bébé 11b
bachelor célibataire *(n/adj, m, f)* 11c
back *(backward)* en arrière *(adv)* 3d; arrière *(adv)* 36c
back up reculer *(v)* 33c
bacon le bacon 24c
bad *(mean, nasty)* méchant(e) *(adj, m, f)* 11e
bad *(quality)* mauvais(e) *(adj, m, f)* 24p
Bad(ly)! Mal! *(adv)* 16a
bad breath la mauvaise haleine 40a
bad mood la mauvaise humeur 21a
bag le sac 23d; **shopping**

bag le sac à provisions 25a
baggage les bagages *(m, pl)* 31
bagpipes la cornemuse 28c
baked au four 24p
baker le boulanger, la boulangère 38a
bakery la boulangerie 24n
balcony le balcon 35c
ball la balle 27b; *(in basketball, football, volleyball)* le ballon 27b
ballet le ballet 28c
ballpoint pen le stylo à bille 19d, 25c, 37b
banana la banane 14d, 24f
bandage le pansement 25h; 39c, 40a; panser *(v)* 40a
bank la banque 26
bank book le carnet de banque 26
bank rate le taux bancaire 26
banknote ***(bill, currency)*** le billet de banque 26
baptism le baptême 11d
barber le coiffeur 12d, 38a
barber shop le salon de coiffure *(f)* pour hommes 12d
Barcelona Barcelone 30c
bark ***(cry of a dog)*** aboyer *(v)* 15a
barley l'orge *(f)* 24i
barn la grange 15a
barometer le baromètre 6c
barometric pressure la pression barométrique 6c
barrel le tonneau 23d
bartender le barman 24m
base ***(sports)*** la base 27b
baseball le base-ball 27b
basement le sous-sol 23a
basil le basilic 14e, 24j
basilica la basilique 36a
basin le bassin 13b
basket la corbeille 23d; le panier 23d
basket ***(in basketball)*** le panier 27b
basketball le basket(ball) 27b
bass drum la grosse caisse 28c
bassoon le basson 28c
Bastille Day ***(July 14)*** La Prise de la Bastille 29a
bat ***(animal)*** la chauve-souris, la pipistrelle 15a
bat ***(sports)*** la batte 27b
bath oil l'huile *(f)* de bain 25f
bathing suit le maillot de bain *(m)* 25k
bathroom la salle de bains *(m, pl)* 23b, 35c
bathtub la baignoire 23a, 35c
batter ***(sports)*** le batteur 27b
battery la pile 25b; *(of car)* la batterie 33e
bay la baie 13b
be able pouvoir *(v)* 21a
be about to être *(v)* sur le point de 4e
be absent être *(v)* absent(e) *(adj, m, f)* 37f
be absent-minded être *(v)* dans la lune 13a
be afraid avoir *(v)* peur *(f)* 21a
be against être *(v)* contre *(prep)* 21a
be ashamed avoir *(v)* honte *(f)* 21a
be at the tip of one's tongue être *(v)* sur le bout de la langue 12a
be awful ***(weather)*** faire *(v)* un temps mauvais 6a
be beautiful ***(weather)*** faire *(v)* beau temps 6a
be born naître *(v)* 11c
be called s'appeler *(v)* 11f
Be careful! Attention! 21c
be cold ***(persons)*** avoir *(v)* froid *(m)* 6b, 12b
be cold ***(weather)*** faire *(v)* froid 6a
be cool ***(weather)*** faire *(v)* frais 6a
be damp ***(weather)*** faire *(v)* humide 6a
be down ***(depressed)*** être *(v)* à plat 21a
be early être *(v)* de bonne heure 4e; être *(v)* tôt 4e

be enough suffire *(v)*, être *(v)* assez 3c
be fond of avoir *(v)* une passion pour 21b
be from... être *(v)* de... 11f
be green with fear être *(v)* vert de peur 7a
be healthy être *(v)* en bonne santé 40a
be hot *(persons)* avoir *(v)* chaud *(m)* 6b, 12b
be humid *(weather)* faire *(v)* humide 6a
be hungry avoir *(v)* faim *(f)* 12b, 24o
be in a bad mood être *(v)* de mauvaise humeur 11e
be in a good mood être *(v)* de bonne humeur 11e
be in the clouds *(distracted)* être *(v)* dans les nuages *(m, pl)* 6a
be interested in s'intéresser *(v)* à 22b
be late être *(v)* tard (en retard) 4e
be located se trouver *(v)* 13e
be mild *(weather)* faire *(v)* doux 6a
be muggy *(weather)* faire *(v)* un temps lourd 6a
be on a familiar *(first-name)* basis tutoyer *(v)* 16b
be on a formal basis vouvoyer *(v)* 16b
be on fire être *(v)* en feu 39a
be on strike être *(v)* en grève 43
be on the point/verge of être *(v)* sur le point de 4e
be on time être *(v)* à l'heure *(f)* 4a, 4e
be on trial être *(v)* en procès 41
be out of breath être *(v)* hors d'haleine 40a
be pregnant être *(v)* enceinte *(adj, f)* 11c
be present être *(v)* présent(e) *(adj, m, f)* 37f
be promoted être *(v)* reçu(e) *(adj, m, f)* 37f
be right (persons) avoir *(v)* raison *(f)* 22b
be run over être *(v)* renversé(e) 39c
be seated s'asseoir *(v)* 16b
Be seated, please. Asseyez-vous, s'il vous plaît 16b; Assieds-toi, s'il te plaît 16b
be sleepy avoir *(v)* sommeil *(m)* 12b
be the fool in an affair être *(v)* le pigeon dans une affaire 15b
be thirsty avoir *(v)* soif *(f)* 12b, 24o
be tired être *(v)* fatigué(e) *(adj)* 12b
be up *(good mood)* être *(v)* remonté(e) *(adj, m, f)* 21a
be windy faire *(v)* du vent *(m)* 6a
be wrong (persons) avoir *(v)* tort *(m)* 22b
beach la plage 13b, 36b
beak le bec 15b
beam of light le rayon de lumière 42a
bean le haricot, les fèves *(f, pl)* de haricot 14e, 24e
bear l'ours *(m)* 15a
beard la barbe 12a
beast la bête 15a
beautician l'esthéticien, l'esthéticienne 12d
beautiful beau, bel, beaux, belle, belles *(adj)* 11a, 25l
beautiful weather beau temps 6a
beauty la beauté 11a
because parce que *(conj)* 8p
become devenir *(v)* 4e, 25a
become angry se fâcher *(v)* 11e
become big grandir *(v)* 3c, 11a; agrandir *(v)* 3c; grossir *(v)* 3c
become bored s'ennuyer *(v)* 21a
become engaged se fiancer *(v)* 11c
become fat grossir *(v)* 11a

become friends devenir *(v)* amis *(m, pl)*; faire *(v)* l'amitié *(f)* 10b
become old vieillir *(v)* 11b
become red with anger devenir *(v)* rouge de colère 7a
become sick tomber *(v)* malade *(adj)* 11a
become small rendre *(v)* plus petit 3c; rapetisser *(v)* 3c
become thin maigrir *(v)* 11a
become weak s'affaiblir *(v)* 11a
bed le lit 23c, 35c
bed sheet le drap 23d
bedbug la punaise 15d
bedroom la chambre à coucher *(v)* 23b
bedside table la table de nuit *(f)*, la table de chevet 23c, 35c
bedspread le couvre-lit 23d
bee l'abeille *(f)* 15d
beech tree le hêtre 14c
beef le boeuf 24c
beer la bière 24k
beet la betterave 14e, 24e
before avant *(adv)*, auparavant *(adv)* 4e
beg to do *(something)* prier *(v)* de faire quelque chose 17a
begin commencer *(v)* 4e
beginning le commencement 4e
behind derrière *(adv)* 36c
Beijing/Peking Béjing/Pékin 30c
Belgian *(nationality)* Belge *(m/f)* 30d
Belgium la Belgique 30b
belief la crédence, la croyance 11d
believe croire *(v)* 11d, 22b
believe in croire en 11d
believer le (la) croyant(e) 11d
bell tower le campanile, le clocher 36a
bellhop le porteur 35b
below zero dessous zéro 6c
belt la ceinture 25k
Berlin Berlin 30c
beside *(next to)* à côté (de) 3d
best-seller le best-seller 20a, 25o
Best wishes! Meilleurs voeux! 16c, 29c
Better late than never! Mieux vaut tard que jamais! 4e
between entre 3d, 8g
between friends entre amis 10b
beverage la boisson 24k
beyond au-delà (de) 3d
bicycle la bicyclette 33a
Bicycle Path Piste Cycliste 33d
bicycle racing les courses cyclistes 27b
big grand(e) *(adj)* 3c, 11a, 25l; gros *(adj, m)*, grosse *(f)* 3c
bigness la grandeur 11a
bill *(banknote, currency)* le billet de banque 26
bill *(cash register tape)* la fiche de caisse 25a; le compte 35b
bill *(invoice)* la facture 25a; **check *(to pay in a restaurant)*** l'addition *(f)* 24m
billiard ball la bille 27a
billiard table la table de billard *(m)* 27a
billiards, to play jouer *(v)* au billard *(m)* 27a
billionth milliardième 1b
bingo le bingo 27a
bingo card la fiche 27a
biography la biographie 28d
biology la biologie 37e
bird l'oiseau *(m)* 15b
birth la naissance 11c
birthday l'anniversaire *(m)* de naissance *(f)* 11c, 29a
bisector la bissectrice 2b
bishop l'évêque 11d; *(in chess)* le fou 27a
bitter amer *(adj, m)*, amère *(adj, f)* 24p
black le noir 7a; **black coffee** le café noir 24k
blackbird le merle 15b

blackboard le tableau 37b
blackboard eraser l'éponge *(f)* mouillée; le vieux chiffon 37b
blade la lame 23d, 25f
blank cassette la cassette vierge 20b
blanket la couverture 23d, 35c
bleat bêler *(v)* 15a
bleed saigner *(v)* 39c
Bless you! *(after a sneeze)* A vos (tes) souhaits! Dieu vous (te) bénisse! 16c
blind aveugle *(n/adj, m, f)* 12c
blindness la cécité 12c
blond blond(e) *(adj)* 11a
blonde blonde *(f)* 11a
blood le sang 12a, 39c, 40a
blood pressure la tension artérielle (veineuse) 40a
blood test l'examen *(m)* hématologique, l'examen du sang, l'examen sérologique 40a
bloom fleurir *(v)* 14a
blouse le chemisier 25k
blue le bleu 7a
blueberry la myrtille 24f
blueprint la copie cyanotype 28b
bluestocking *(learned, bookish woman)* bas-bleu *(m)* 7a
boarding *(travel)* l'embarquement *(m)* 32a
boarding house la pension 35a
boarding pass la carte d'embarquement *(m)* 32a
boat le bateau 36b
bodily physique le physique 11a
body le corps 11a, 12a; ***(of a letter)*** le contenu, le corps 19c
body building le culturisme 27b
boiling point le point d'ébullition *(f)* 6c
bold *(brash)* effronté(e) *(adj)* 11e
bologna le saucisson 24c
bolt of lightning un coup d'éclair 6a
bond *(banking, commerce)* l'obligation *(f)* 26
bone l'os *(m)* 12a, 40a
book le livre 20a, 25o, 37b
book of adventure le livre d'aventure *(f)* 25o
bookcase l'étagère *(f)* à livres *(m, pl),* la bibliothèque 23c, 37b
bookstore la librairie 25o
boot la botte 25n
border la frontière 13e, 31; borner *(v)* 13e; toucher *(v)* 13e
bore ennuyer *(v)* 21a
bored *see* **become bored, feel bored**
boredom l'ennui *(m)* 21a
boss in an office le chef de bureau 38d
botanical botanique *(adj)* 14a
botany la botanique 14a, 37e
both les deux, tous les deux, toutes les deux 3c
bottle la bouteille 23d, 24l
bottom le fond 3d; au fond 3d
bouquet of flowers la botte de fleurs *(f)* 14b
bow *(of a stringed instrument)* l'archet *(m)* de violon 28c
bowl le bol, l'assiette *(f)* creuse 24l; **to bowl** jouer *(v)* au bowling 27b
bowling le bowling 27b
bowling alley la piste 27b
bowling ball la boule 27b
bowling pin la quille 27b
box la boîte 23d
box office le guichet 28a
boxing la boxe 27b
boxing glove le gant de boxe 27b
boxing ring *(sport)* le ring 27b
boy le garçon 11a, 11b
boyfriend l'ami, le petit ami 10b
bra le soutien-gorge 25k
bracelet le bracelet 25i
bracket le crochet 19c
brain le cerveau 12a; la cervelle 40a

brake le frein 33a, 33e; freiner *(v)* 33c
branch la branche 14a
brash effronté(e) *(adj)* 11e
brass instruments les cuivres *(m, pl)* 28c
Brazil le Brésil 30b
Brazilian *(nationality)* Brésilien *(m)*, Brésilienne *(f)* 30d
bread le pain 24i
break off a friendship rompre *(v)* une amitié 10b
breakdown *(machine, vehicle)* en panne 33c
breakfast le petit déjeuner 24a, 35b
breakfast included le petit déjeuner compris 35b
breath l'haleine 40a
breathe respirer *(v)* 12b, 40a
bricklayer le maçon 38a
bridal suite la chambre matrimoniale 35b
bride la mariée 11c
bridegroom le marié 11c
bridge le pont 33c, 36a
brief bref, brève *(adj, m, f)* 4e, 37f
briefcase la serviette 25c, 38c
briefly brièvement *(adv)*, en bref 4e, 17b
bright éclatant(e) *(adj)* 7b
brilliant brillant(e) *(adj)* 11e
bring apporter *(v)* 25a
brioche la brioche 24i
broccoli le brocoli 14e, 24e
brochure la brochure, le dépliant 20a, 30a
broiled grillé(e) *(adj, m, f)* 24b
broken bone l'os cassé (fracturé) 39c
broken line la ligne brisée 2b
bronchitis la bronchite 40a
bronze le bronze 13c
brooch la broche 25i
brook le ruisseau 36b
broom le balai 23d
broth le bouillon 24g
brother le frère 10a
brother-in-law le beau-frère 10a
brown le brun 7a
brush la brosse 12d, 25f; ***(artist's)*** le pinceau 28b
brush oneself se brosser *(v)* 12d
brush teeth se brosser *(v)* les dents 40b
buckle *(fasten)* seat belt boucler *(v)* la ceinture 32c
bud bourgeonner *(v)* 14a; le bourgeon 14a
Buddhism le Bouddhisme 11d
Buddhist Bouddhiste *(m/f)* 11d
budget le budget 26
buffalo le buffle 15a
build construire *(v)* 23f
building l'édifice *(m)*; le bâtiment 23g, 39a
bulb *(plant)* le bulbe 14a
bull le taureau 15a
bump heurter *(v)* 39c
bumper *(car)* le pare-chocs 33e
burn brûler *(v)* 39a; la brûlure 39a
bus l'autobus *(m)* 33a; ***(long-distance travel)*** l'autocar *(m)*, le car de voyage 34
bus driver le chauffeur, la femme chauffeur 34, 38a
bus station la gare, la station 34
business letter la lettre commerciale *(adj)* 19e
businessman l'homme d'affaires 38a
businesswoman la femme d'affaires 38a
busy occupé(e) *(adj)* 18b
but mais *(conj)* 8p
butcher le boucher, la bouchère 38a
butcher shop la boucherie 24n
butter le beurre 24h
butterfly le papillon 15d
buttermilk le babeurre, le lait de beurre 24h
button le bouton 25g
buy acheter *(v)* 23f, 25a

buy a ticket acheter *(v)* un billet 30a, 34; procurer *(v)* un billet 34
by boat en bateau *(m)* 30a
by plane en avion *(m)* 30a
by the way à propos 17b, 44c
by train par le train 30a
byte le multiplet 42b

C
cabbage le chou 14e, 24e
cabin *(travel)* la cabine 32c
cable le câble (téléphonique) 18a; ***(hardware)*** le câble 25b
cafeteria le restaurant self-service 24m
cake le gâteau 24g
calculate calculer *(v)* 1f
calculation le calcul 1f
calculus le calcul 37e
calendar le calendrier 5b, 38c
call appeler *(v)* 17a
call a taxi appeler *(v)* un taxi 35b
call an ambulance appeler *(v)* une ambulance 39c
call the fire department appeler *(v)* les pompiers, appeler *(v)* les sapeurs-pompiers 39a
call the police appeler *(v)* la police 39b, 39c
calling/business card la carte de visite 16b
calm calme *(adj)* 11e
calmness le calme 11e
camel le chameau 15a
camera l'appareil *(m)* de photo (l'appareil photographique) 25d
camera shop le magasin de photo 25d
camomile la camomille 24k
camping area le camping 36b
campus le campus 37c
Can you tell me? Pourriez-vous me dire...*(pol)*; Peux-tu me dire...*(fam)* 9
Can you tell me where...? Pouvez-vous me dire où...? 36c
Canada le Canada 30b
Canadian *(nationality)* Canadien *(m)*, Canadienne *(f)* 30d
canceled flight le vol annulé 32b
Cancer *(sign of the zodiac)* le Cancer 5d
canine *(tooth)* la dent canine 40b
canoe le canoë 36b
cap la casquette 36b
capacity la capacité 3c
capital *(finance)* le capital
capital city la capitale 13e, 30a
capital letter la lettre majuscule 19c
capital punishment la peine capitale 41, 44b
Capricorn *(sign of the zodiac)* le Capricorne 5d
car l'auto *(f)*, la voiture 33a
car body la carrosserie 33e
car gas l'essence *(f)* 13c
car racing les courses *(f, pl)* de voitures 27b
car radio l'autoradio *(m)* 20b
car window la vitre 33e
caramel pudding la crème au caramel 24h
carat le carat 25i
carbon *(element)* le carbone 13c; le charbon 13c
carburetor le carburateur 33e
card la carte 25e
cardigan le chandail 25k
cardinal cardinal(e) *(adj, m, f)* 1a, 1d
career la carrière 11f, 38d
carnation l'oeillet *(m)* 14b
carpenter le menuisier 38a
carpet le tapis 23c; **wall-to-wall carpeting** la moquette 23c
carriage *(of a typewriter)* le chariot 19d
carrot la carotte 14e, 24e
carry porter *(v)* 31
carry on (luggage) le sac de voyage 31

case *(container)* le bac, la douille 23d
cash *(money in currency and coins)* **to pay in cash** payer *(v)* en espèces 25a, 26, 35b
cash a check toucher *(v)* un chèque 26
cash desk la caisse 26
cash register la caisse 25a
cash register tape receipt la fiche de caisse 25a
cashier le caissier, la caissière 25a, 26
cassette la cassette 20b, 25j; **cassette tape** la bande magnétique 20b
castle le château 36a
cat le chat, la chatte 15a
catch attraper *(v)* 27b; **catch** *(the train, etc.)* prendre *(v)* 34
catch fire prendre *(v)* feu, s'enflammer *(v)* 39a
catcher's mask le masque du receveur 27b
catechism le catéchisme 11d
caterpillar la chenille 15d
catfish le poisson-chat 15c
cathedral la cathédrale 36a
Catholic Catholique *(m, f)* 11d
Catholicism le Catholicisme 11d
cauliflower le chou-fleur, les choux-fleurs *(m, pl)* 14e, 24e
cavity la carie dentaire 40b
ceiling le plafond 23a
celebrate one's birthday fêter *(v)* l'anniversaire *(m)* de naissance *(f)* 11c
celery le céleri 14e, 24e
cell la cellule 14a
cello le violoncelle 28c
Celsius Celsius 6c
censorship la censure 44b
center le centre 2a
centigrade centigrade *(n/adj, m)* 6c
centimeter le centimètre 3a
century le siècle 4c
chain la chaîne 25i
chain guard *(bicycle)* le couvre-chaîne 33a
chain stores la chaîne de magasins 44a
chair la chaise 23c; la chaise tournante, le siège de bureau 38c
chalet le chalet 35a
chalk la craie 37b
Chamber of Representatives *(deputies)* la Chambre des Députés 43
change changer *(v)* 4e, 25a
change *(money return in a transaction)* la monnaie, le rendu 25a
change gears changer *(v)* de vitesse 33c
change subject changer *(v)* de sujet *(m)* 17a
channel *(television)* la chaîne, le canal 20b
channel *(water)* le canal 13b
chapter le chapitre 28d
character le caractère 11e; *(in literature)* le personnage 28d
characteristic caractéristique *(n/adj, f)* 11e
characterize caractériser *(v)* 11e
charge *(law)* la cause 41
charge *(atom)* la charge 13c
Charge it to my bill. Mettez-le sur mon compte. 35b
charter flight l'avion charter *(m)* 30a
chat causer *(v)* 17a
cheap (à) bon marché, économe *(adj, m, f)* 24p
check *(in a restaurant)* l'addition *(f)* 24m
check *(to pay with a)* payer *(v)* en chèque 25a, 26, 35b
check the oil vérifier *(v)* l'huile 33c
checkbook le carnet de chèques 26
checkerboard le damier 27a
checker piece le pion 27a
checkers, to play jouer *(v)* aux dames 27a
cheek la joue 12a

Cheers! A votre santé! A la vôtre! 16c, 24l
cheese le fromage 24h; **grated** au gratin; **melted** fondu; **puffed** soufflé 24h
cheesecake le gâteau au fromage 24i
chemical chimique *(adj)* 13c
chemical weapon l'arme *(f)* chimique 44b
chemistry la chimie 13c, 37e
cherry la cerise 14d, 24f
cherry pie la tarte aux cerises 24g
cherry tree le cerisier 14c
chess, to play jouer *(v)* aux échecs 27a
chessboard l'échiquier *(m)* 27a
chest la poitrine 12a
chest of drawers la commode 23c, 35c
chestnut la châtaigne, le marron 14d
chestnut tree le châtaignier 14c
chick le poussin 15b
chicken le poulet 15b, 24c
chief of police le préfet de police 41
child l'enfant *(m, f)* 11b
children les enfants 11b
chimney la cheminée 23a
chin le menton 12a
China la Chine 30b
Chinese *(nationality)* Chinois *(m)*, Chinoise *(f)* 30d; *(language)* le chinois 30d
chlorine le chlore 13c
chlorophyll la chlorophylle 14a
chocolate le chocolat 24g
chocolate ice cream la glace au chocolat 24h
chocolate pie la tarte au chocolat 24g
choke *(vehicle)* le volet de départ 33e
Christian Chrétien, Chrétienne *(m, f)* 11d
Christianity le Christianisme 11d
Christmas le Noël 5f, 29a
chum le copain, la copine 10b
church l'église *(f)* 11d, 36a
cigar le cigare 25e
cigarette la cigarette 25e
cinema le cinéma, le ciné 28a
circle le cercle 2a
circumference la circonférence 2a
citric citrique *(adj)* 14d
citrus les agrumes *(m, pl)* 14d
city la ville 11f, 13e, 30a, 36a, 38b
city map la carte de la ville 36a
civil law le droit civil, la loi civile 41
clam la palourde 24d
clamp *(hardware)* l'étau *(m)* 25b
clap of thunder le tonnerre 6a
clarinet la clarinette 28c
class la classe 30a, 37f
class of students la classe d'étudiants (d'élèves) 37d
classical music la musique classique 25j, 28c
classified ad la petite annonce 38d
classroom la salle de classe 37c
clause la proposition 8a
clean propre *(adj)* 11a, 12d, 25g; nettoyer *(v)* 23f
clean oneself se débarbouiller *(v)* 12d
clear clair(e) *(adj)* 6a; **clear picture** la photo nette 25d
clear sky le ciel clair 6a
clear the table desservir *(v)* la table 23f, 24o
clerk l'employé(e) *(m, f)*, le commis 19e
clerk's window le guichet 19e
clever ingénieux, ingénieuse *(adj, m, f)* 11e
cleverness l'ingénuité *(f)* 11e

climate le climat 6a
climb monter *(v)* 3e
clip *(paper)* le trombone 19d
clock l'horloge *(f)* 4d, 25i
close an account arrêter *(v)* un compte, clore *(v)* un compte 26
close friend l'ami(e) intime 10b
closed fermé(e) *(adj, m, f)* 25a
closed circuit le circuit fermé 20b
closet l'armoire *(f)*, le placard 23b, 35c
closing *(of a letter)* la formule (la salutation) finale 19c
closing hours *(store)* les heures de fermeture 25a
clothes les vêtements *(m, pl)* 25g
clothes basket le panier à linge 25g
clothes hanger le cintre 23d, 35c
clothespin la pince à linge 25g
clothing les vêtements *(m, pl)*, l'habillement *(m)* 25k
clothing store le magasin d'habillement 25k
cloud le nuage 6a, 13b; la nuée 13b
cloudy nuageux *(adj, m)*, nuageuse *(adj, f)* 6a
clown le clown 11e
clubs *(cards)* le trèfle 27a
clutch pedal *(car)* la pédale d'embrayage 33e
coach *(sports)* l'entraîneur *(m/f)* 27b; *(of a train)* la voiture, le wagon 34
coal le charbon 13c
coal mine la mine de houille 13c
coal mining la houille 13c
coast la côte 13b
coat le manteau 25k; **fur coat** le manteau de fourrure 25k
coat *(suit)* la veste, le veston 25k
cockroach la blatte, le cafard 15d
coconut macaroon le macaron 24i
codfish la morue 15c, 24d
coed school l'école *(f)* mixte 37a
coffee le café 24k; **black coffee** le café noir 24k; **coffee pudding** la crème au café 24h; **coffee with cream** un café-crème 24k; **light coffee** (half-and-half) le café au lait 24k
coffee machine la cafetière électrique, le percolateur 23d
coffee pot la cafetière 23d
coin la pièce de monnaie *(f)* 27a; **coin token** le jeton 18a
coin collecting la numismatique 27a
cold le froid, froid(e) *(adj, m, f)* 6a, 6b, 24p; *(illness)* le rhume 40a
cold cuts la charcuterie 24c
cold water l'eau *(f)* froide 35c
colleague le (la) collègue 10b
collect telephone call téléphoner en P.C.V. 18b
collide entrer *(v)* en collision, se heurter *(v)* 39c
collision la collision 39c
cologne l'eau *(f)* de cologne 25f
colon deux points *(m, pl)* 19c
color la couleur 7a—7c; colorer *(v)* 7c
color photo la photo en couleur 25d
colored coloré(e) *(adj, m, f)* 7c
coloring le colorant 7c
comb le peigne 12d, 25f
comb *(one's hair)* se peigner *(v)* 12d
come venir *(v)* 3e
Come here! Venez *(pol)* ici! Viens *(fam)* ici! 17b
come in entrer *(v)* (dans) 16b; **Come in!** Entrez! *(pol)*; Entre! *(fam)* 16b
Come on! Allons! Allons donc! 20b

Come quickly! Venez (Viens) vite! 39b
come to light mettre *(v)* en lumière *(f)* 13a
comedian l'acteur (l'actrice) comique 28e
comedy la comédie 20a, 28e
comet la comète 13a
comics la bande dessinée 20a, 25o
comma la virgule 19c
commerce le commerce 37e, 38d
commercial *(advertising)* la publicité 20b
communicate communiquer *(v)* 17a
communication la communication 17a
communism le communisme 43
communist le (la) communiste 43
compact car la voiture compacte 33a
compact disk le disque compact 20b, 25j, 42a
company *(business)* la société commerciale 38d
compare comparer *(v)* 17a
comparison la comparaison 8a, 17a
compartment *(of a train)* le compartiment 34
compass le compas 2b, 37b; la boussole 3d
compatible compatible *(adj, m, f)* 42b
competition le concours 27b
complain se plaindre *(v)* 21a, 35b
complaint la plainte 21a, 35b
complementary complémentaire *(adj, m, f)* 2b
complex complexe *(adj)* 1d
complicated compliqué(e) *(adj, m, f)* 22a
Compliments! Mes compliments! *(m, pl)* 29c
composer le compositeur, la femme compositeur, la compositrice 25j, 28c
composition la composition 28c; le thème 37f
compound le composé 13c
computer l'ordinateur *(m)* 42b
computer-assisted instruction les instructions *(f, pl)* automatisées 42b
computer language le langage-machine, le langage de programmation 42b
computer printer l'imprimante *(f)* d'ordinateur 42b
computer science l'informatique *(f)* 42b
concave concave *(adj)* 2b
concept le concept 22a
concert le concert 28c
conclude conclure *(v)* 17a
conclusion la conclusion 17a
conditional conditionnel(le) *(adj, m, f)* 8a
condominium l'immeuble *(m)* en copropriété *(f)* 23g
conductor *(of a public vehicle)* le conducteur, la conductrice 34
cone *(geometry)* le cône 2a; **ice cream cone** le cornet 24h
confirmation la confirmation 11d
conformist le (la) conformiste 11e
congratulate féliciter *(v)* 17a
Congratulations! Félicitations! *(f, pl)* 16c, 29c
conjugation la conjugaison 8a
conjunction la conjonction 8a
connection *(travel)* la correspondance 32a, 34
conscience la conscience 11e, 22a
conscientious consciencieux *(adj, m)*, consciencieuse *(f)* 11e, 22a
consecutive consécutif, consécutive *(adj)* 2b
consequently donc *(conj)* 8p

conservation la conservation 44a
conservative conservateur, conservatrice *(adj, m, f)* 11e
conservative party *(politics)* le parti conservateur 43
conservatory le conservatoire 37a
consonant la consonne 8a
constant constant(e) *(adj, m, f)* 1f
consumption la consomption 44a
contact lenses les lentilles *(f, pl)* de contact, les verres *(m, pl)* de contact 40a
contents le contenu 19c
continent le continent 13e, 30a
continental continental(e) *(adj, m, f)* 6a, 13e
continually continuellement *(adv)* 4e
continue continuer *(v)* 4e
contract le contrat 38d
controversy la controverse 41
convalesce être *(v)* en convalescence 40a
convalescence la convalescence 40a
conversation la conversation 17a
convex convexe *(adj, m, f)* 2b
convince convaincre *(v)* 22b, 41
cook le cuisinier, la cuisinière 38a; cuire *(v)*, faire *(v)* la cuisine 24o
cookie le sablé, le petit-beurre, le gâteau sec 24i
cooking la cuisine 24b
cool frais *(adj, m)*, fraîche *(adj, f)* 6a
cool weather faire *(v)* frais 6a
coordinate la coordonnée 2b
co-pilot le (la) copilote 32c
copper le cuivre 13c
copy la copie 37f
corn le maïs 14e, 24i
corner le coin 36a
corner *(street)* le coin de la rue 33c
correspondence la correspondance 19e
corridor le couloir 23a
cortisone la cortisone 25h
cosecant la cosécante 2b
cosine le cosinus 2b
cosmetics/perfume shop la parfumerie 25f
cosmos le cosmos 13a
cost coûter *(v)* 24o, 25a; **price** le prix, le coût 25a
cost of living le coût de la vie 26
cotangent la cotangente 2b
cotton le coton 13c, 25l
cough la toux; tousser *(v)* 40a
council le conseil 43
count compter *(v)* 1f
countable comptable *(adj)* 1f
counter le comptoir 25a
country le pays 11f, 13e, 30a
courage le courage 11e
courageous courageux, courageuse *(adj)* 11e
course le cours 37f
court *(of law)* le tribunal 41
court of appeal la cour d'appel 41
courtesy la courtoisie 11e
courteous courtois(e) *(adj)* 11e
courtroom la salle du tribunal 41
cousin le cousin, la cousine 10a
cover la couverture 20a
cover charge *(dining out)* le couvert 24m
cow la vache 15a
crash le choc, la percussion; percuter *(v)* 39c
crayon le crayon de couleur 7c
crazy fou, fol, folle *(adj)* 11e
cream la crème 24h, 25f
cream cake *(pie)* le gâteau à la crème 24i

cream puff le chou à la crème 24i
creamed horn le cornet feuilleté à la crème 24i
creative créatif *(adj, m)*, créative *(adj, f)* 11e
credit le crédit 26
credit card *(to pay with a credit card)* payer *(v)* en carte *(f)* de crédit 25a; la carte de crédit 26, 35b
crime le crime 39b
crime wave la masse de crimes 39b
criminal le criminel, la criminelle 39b
crew *(travel)* l'équipe *(f)* 32c
criminal law le droit pénal, la loi pénale 41
critical critique *(adj)* 11e
criticism la critique 20a, 28d
crocodile le crocodile 15c
cross over traverser *(v)* 36c
cross the street traverser *(v)* la rue 36c
crouton le croûton 24i
crown la couronne 40b
cruise la croisière 36b
crust la croûte 24i
cry *(weep)* pleurer *(v)* 11e, 21a
crying en larmes *(f, pl)* 11e
cube le cube 2a
cube root la racine cubique 1e
cubed au cube 1e
cubic centimeter le centimètre cubique 3a
cubic kilometer le kilomètre cubique 3a
cubic meter le mètre cubique 3a
cubic millimeter le millimètre cubique 3a
cucumber le concombre 14e, 24e
cue *(billiards)* la queue de billard *(m)* 27a
cultivate cultiver *(v)* 14a
cultivation la culture 14a
cultured cultivé(e) *(adj)* 11e
cup la tasse 23d, 24l
cupboard le placard 37b
cure la guérison; guérir *(v)* 40a
curiosity la curiosité 11e
curious curieux, curieuse *(adj)* 11e
curler le bigoudi 12d, 25f
curls les boucles *(f)* de cheveux 12d; les cheveux *(m, pl)* frisés 12d
curly-haired les cheveux *(m, pl)* bouclés 11a
currency *(bill, banknote)* le billet de banque 26
current le courant 35c
current account le compte courant 26
curtains les rideaux *(m, pl)* 23c, 28e, 35c
curve la courbe 2b, 33c
curved line la ligne courbe 2b
cushion *(billiard table)* le rebord élastique 27a
custard le flan 24h
customer le client, la cliente 25a, 26
customs la douane 31
customs officer le douanier 31
cut couper *(v)* 24o
Cut it out! Arrêtez! Arrêtez donc! 20b
cut one's hair se faire *(v)* couper *(v)* les cheveux *(m, pl)* 12d
cutlet la côtelette 24g
cyclamen le cyclamen 14b
cylinder le cylindre 2a
cymbals les cymbales *(f, pl)* 28c
cypress tree le cyprès 14c

D

dad le papa 10a
dahlia le dahlia 14b
daily quotidien, quotidienne *(adj)*, quotidiennement *(adv)* 4c, 20a
daily newspaper le journal quotidien 20a

dairy product le produit laitier 24h
dairy shop la laiterie 24n
daisy la marguerite 14b
Damn it! Zut! Zut alors! 20b
damp humide *(adj)* 6a
dance danser *(v)* 28c, 29b; le bal 28c, 29b
dance music la musique de danse 25j
dancer le danseur, la danseuse 28c
dandruff les pellicules *(f, pl)* 40a
danger le danger 39a
Danish *(nationality)* Danois *(m),* Danoise *(f)* 30d; ***(language)*** le danois 30d
dark *(color)* sombre *(adj)* 7b
dark *(weather)* faire *(v)* sombre *(adj)* 6a
dark blue le bleu foncé 7a
dark-haired les cheveux *(m, pl)* bruns 11a
dashboard le tableau de bord 33e
data les données *(f, pl),* l'information *(f)* 42b
data processing le traitement de l'information 42b
date la date 5e, 11f, 19c; *(fruit)* la datte 14d, 24f
date of birth la date de naissance *(f)* 11f, 38b
daughter la fille 10a
daughter-in-law la belle-fille 10a
dawn l'aube *(f)* 4a
day le jour 4a, 4c
day after tomorrow le lendemain 4a
day before yesterday avant-hier *(adv)* 4a
day care l'école maternelle 37a
day of the week le jour de la semaine 5a
deaf sourd, sourde *(adj, m, f)* 12c
deafness la surdité 12c
Dear... Cher, Chère, Chers, Chères . . . 19b
dear friend cher ami, chère amie 10b
Dear Madam. . . Madame, Chère Madame. . . 19a
Dear Sir. . . Monsieur, Cher Monsieur. . . 19a
death la mort 11c
debate le débat; débattre *(v)* 17a, 41
debit le débit 26
debt la dette 26
decade la décennie 4c
decagon le décagone 2a
December le décembre 5b
decimal décimal(e) *(adj, m, f)* 1f
declarative déclaratif *(adj, m),* déclarative *(adj, f)* 8a, 8n
declare déclarer *(v)* 17a, 31
decorating la décoration 23c
decrease diminuer *(v),* la diminution 3c
deer le cerf 15a
defecate déféquer *(v)* 40a
defend oneself se défendre *(v)* 41
definite défini(e) *(adj, m, f)* 8a, 8b
definition la définition 20a
degree le degré 2b, 6c
degree *(university)* la licence 11f, 37f; le doctorat 11f, 37f; le diplôme universitaire 37f
delicate délicat(e) *(adj)* 11e
delicatessen la charcuterie 24n
Delighted! Heureux! Heureuse! 16b
democracy la démocratie 43
democrat le (la) démocrate 43
democratic démocratique *(adj, m, f)* 43
demonstrate démontrer *(v)* 22b
demonstration *(politics)* la manifestation, la manif 43
demonstrative démonstratif *(adj, m),* démonstrative *(adj, f)* 8a, 8e, 8m
Denmark le Danemark 30b

dense dense *(adj)* 3b
density la densité 3b
dentist le (la) dentiste 38a, 40b
dentist's chair le fauteuil 40b
dentist's office le cabinet du (de la) dentiste 40b
denture le dentier 40b
deny nier *(v)* 17a
deodorant le déodorant 25f
depart partir *(v)* 3e, 34
department *(of a store)* le rayon 25a
department store le grand magasin 25a
departure le départ 32a
deposit le versement 26; verser *(v)* 26
deposit slip la fiche de versement 26
depot *(station)* la gare, la station 34
depressed déprimé(e) *(adj, m, f)* 21a
depression la dépression 21a
descend descendre *(v)* 3e
describe décrire *(v)* 17a
description la description 17a, 39b
descriptive descriptif *(adj, m)*, descriptive *(adj, f)* 8a
desert le désert 13b, 24g
desk *(pupil's)* le pupitre; *(teacher's)* le bureau, la chaire 37b; le bureau 38c
desperate désespéré(e) *(adj, m, f)* 21a
desperation le désespoir 21a
dessert le dessert 24g
destroy détruire *(v)* 39a
detest détester *(v)* 21b
dial *(of a timepiece)* le cadran 4d, 25i
dial a telephone number composer le numéro 18b
diameter le diamètre 2a
diamond le diamant 25i; *(cards)* le carreau 27a
diamond anniversary les noces *(f)* de diamant 11c
dice *(to play)* jouer *(v)* aux dés *(m, pl)* 27a
dictate dicter *(v)* 17a
dictation la dictée 37f
dictionary le dictionnaire 20a, 25o, 37b
die mourir *(v)* 11c
difference la différence 1f
difficult difficile *(adj, m, f)* 22a
dig creuser *(v)* 14a
digestive system le système digestif 40a
digit le chiffre 1d
digress faire *(v)* une digression 17a
diligence la diligence 11e
diligent diligent (e) *(adj)* 11e
dimension la dimension 3b
dining room la salle à manger *(v)* 23b
dinner le dîner 24a
diploma le diplôme 11f, 37f
diplomatic diplomatique *(adj)* 11e
direct direct(e) *(adj, m, f)* 8a, 8i
direct dialing téléphoner *(v)* en direct 18b
direct train le train direct 34
direction la direction 3d
dirty sale *(adj)* 11a, 12d, 25g
dirty word le mot grossier 20b
disagree être *(v)* en désaccord *(m)* 21a; se disputer *(v)* 41
disagreement le désaccord 21a
disappoint décevoir *(v)* 21a
disappointed déçu(e) *(adj, m, f)* 21a
disappointment la déception 21a
disarmament le désarmement 43
disco la discothèque 29b
discount le rabais, la remise 25a
discourse le discours 8a
discourteous discourtois(e) *(adj)* 11e

discuss discuter *(v)* 17a, 41
discussion la discussion 17a
disease la maladie 40a
disgust le dégoût 21b
disgusted dégoûté(e) *(adj, m, f)* 21b
dish antenna l'antenne *(f)* parabolique 42a
dishonest malhonnête *(adj)* 11e
dishonesty la malhonnêteté 11e
dishwasher le lave-vaisselle 23d
disk le disque 42b; **floppy disk** la disquette, le disque souple 42b
dislike (not to like) ne pas aimer *(v)* 21b
disorganized désorganisé(e) *(adj, m, f)* 11e
dissatisfaction l'insatisfaction *(f)* 21a
dissatisfied insatisfait(e) *(adj, m, f)* 21a
distance la distance 3d, 33c
divide diviser *(v)* 1e
divided by divisé par 1e
division la division 1e
divorce le divorce; divorcer *(v)* 11c
divorced divorcé(e) *(adj)* 11c, 38b
do faire *(v)* 18b; **do the dishes** faire *(v)* la vaisselle 23f
Do you have a vacant room? Avez-vous une chambre libre? 35b
doctor le médecin, la femme médecin, le docteur, la femme docteur 38a, 39c, 40a
doctorate degree le doctorat 37f
doctor's instruments les instruments *(m, pl)* du médecin 40a
doctor's visit la visite du médecin 40a
documentary documentaire *(adj, m, f)* 20b
documents les documents *(m, pl)* 31
does not equal n'est pas égal à 1f
dog le chien, la chienne 15a
dollar le dollar 26
dolphin le dauphin 15c
donkey l'âne *(m)* 15a
Don't mention it! Il n'y a pas de quoi! De rien! 16c
door la porte 23a; *(of car)* la portière 33e
doorbell le bouton de sonnette *(f)* 23a
doorman le portier 35b
double double *(n/adj, m, f)* 3c
double bass la contrebasse 28c
double bed le grand lit 35c
double roll *(of bread)* le petit pain double 24i
double room une chambre double 35b
doubt le doute 22a; douter *(v)* 22b
dove la colombe 15b
down bas *(adv)* 3d, 36c; en bas 3d
downtown en ville *(f)*, le centre de la ville 30a, 36a
Dr. *(M.D. degree)* Dr., le docteur, la femme docteur, le docteur femme, 11f, 16b; *(Ph.D. degree)* Dr., le docteur, la doctoresse 16b
draft *(promissory note)* le billet à ordre 26
draft *(rough copy)* la copie brute, la copie en état brut 37f
drama le drame 20a, 28e
draw dessiner *(v)* 2b, 37f
draw *(score in sports)* le match nul 27b; terminer *(v)* à match nul (à égalité) 27b
drawer le tiroir 23c
drawing le dessin 37f
drawing instruments les instruments *(m)* de dessin *(m)* 2b
dress la robe 25k
dresser la commode 23c, 35c
dressing room la cabine 25k

dried cod la merluche 24d
drill (*dentist's*) la fraise 40b
drill (*hardware*) la foreuse 25b
drink boire *(v)* 12b, 24o; la boisson 24k
drive conduire *(v)* 3e, 33b, 33c
driver (*of a car*) le chauffeur, l'automobiliste *(m/f)* 33b
driver's license le permis de conduire 33b
drop *(e.g.*, of rain) la goutte 6a
drug addiction la toxicomanie 44b
drug pusher le (la) trafiquant(e) des stupéfiants 44b
drug trafficking le trafic des stupéfiants 44b
drugs la drogue 44b
drugstore la pharmacie 25h
drum (*music*) la caisse 28c
dry sec *(adj, m)*, sèche *(adj, f)* 6a
dry cleaner le nettoyage à sec 25g
dry oneself se sécher *(v)* 12d
dryer (*clothes*) le sèche-linge 23d
duck le canard 15b, 24c
dull (*color*) terne *(adj)* 7b
dumpling la boulette 24g
dump truck le camion à triple mouvement 33a
during pendant *(prep)* 4e
Dutch (*nationality*) Hollandais *(m)*, Hollandaise *(f)* 30d; ***(language)*** le hollandais 30d
duty tax le tarif douanier 31
dynamic dynamique *(adj)* 11e

E

each chaque *(adj)* 3c
eagle l'aigle *(m)* 15b
ear l'oreille *(f)* 12a
early de bonne heure *(adv)*, tôt *(adv)* 4e, 32b, 34; ***(arrival/departure time)*** en avance 32b, 34
earn gagner *(v)* 38d
earphone l'écouteur *(m)* 18a
earring la boucle d'oreille 25i
Earth la Terre 13a
earthquake le tremblement de terre 13b
easel le chevalet 28b
east l'est *(m)* 3d; **to the east** à l'est 3d
Easter les Pâques *(f)* 5f, 29a
eastern oriental(e) *(adj)* 3d
easy facile *(adj, m, f)* 22a
eat manger *(v)* 12b, 24o
eccentric excentrique *(adj)* 11e
eclair l'éclair *(m)* 24i
eclipse l'éclipse *(f)* 13a
ecology l'écologie *(f)* 44a
economics l'économie *(f)* 37e
economy l'économie *(f)* 43
economy class (*travel*) en touriste 30a; la classe touriste 32a, 34
ecosystem l'écosystème *(m)* 44a
edge le bord 3d
editor le rédacteur, la rédactrice 20a, 38a
editorial éditorial(e) *(adj, m, f)* 20a
education l'éducation *(f)* 11f, 37f, 38b
eel l'anguille *(f)* 15c, 24d
egg l'oeuf *(m)* 24h
eggplant l'aubergine *(f)* 14e, 24e
egoism l'égoïsme *(m)* 11e
egoist l'égoïste *(m, f)* 11e
egoistic égoïste *(adj)* 11e
Egypt l'Egypte *(f)* 30b
eight huit 1a
eighteen dix-huit 1a
eighth huitième 1b
eighty quatre-vingts 1a
eighty-one quatre-vingt-un 1a
elastic élastique *(n, m/adj)* 13d
elbow le coude 12a

elderly person une personne âgée 11b
elect élire *(v)* 43
elected politician le député, la femme député 43
elections les élections *(f, pl)* 43
electric razor le rasoir électrique 12d, 25f
electrical électrique *(adj, m, f)* 13c, 25b
electrician l'électricien *(m)* 38a
electricity l'électricité *(f)* 13c, 23e
electrocardiograph l'électrocardiographe *(m)* 40a
electron l'électron *(m)* 13c, 42a
elegance l'élégance *(f)* 11a
elegant élégant(e) *(adj)* 11a, 25l
elegantly élégamment *(adv)* 11a
element l'élément *(m)* 13c
elementary school l'école *(f)* primaire élémentaire 37a, 38b
elementary school teacher le maître, la maîtresse 37d
elephant l'éléphant *(m)* 15a
elevator l'ascenseur *(m)* 23g, 35b
eleven onze 1a
eleventh onzième 1b
eloquence l'éloquence *(f)* 11e
eloquent éloquent(e) *(adj)* 11e
emerald l'émeraude *(f)* 25i
emergency exit la sortie d'urgence *(f)* 39a
emergency lane la piste d'urgence *(f)* 33d
emergency ward le service des urgences 39c
emphasis l'emphase *(f)* 17a
emphasize accentuer *(v)* 17a
employ employer *(v)* 38d
employee l'employé(e) *(m, f)* 11f, 26, 38d
employer l'employeur, l'employeuse 11f, 38d
employment l'emploi *(m)* 11f
employment agency l'agence *(f)* d'emploi *(m)* 38d
empty vide *(adj)*, vider *(v)* 3c
encourage encourager *(v)* 21a
encouragement l'encouragement *(m)* 21a
encyclopedia l'encyclopédie *(f)* 20a, 25o, 37b
end la fin 4e; finir *(v)* 4e
endorse endosser *(v)* 26
endorsement l'endossement *(m)*, l'endos *(m)* 26
enemy l'ennemi(e) 10b
energetic énergique *(adj)* 11e
energy l'énergie *(f)* 11e, 13c, 44a
energy crisis la crise d'énergie *(f)* 44a
energy needs les besoins *(m)* d'énergie *(f)* 44a
energy source la source d'énergie *(f)* 44a
energy waste les déchets *(m)* d'énergie *(f)* 44a
engaged fiancé(e) *(adj)* 11c
engagement les fiancailles *(f, pl)* 11c, 29a
engineer l'ingénieur, la femme ingénieur 38a
engineering les études *(f, pl)* polytechniques 37e
England l'Angleterre *(f)* 30b
English *(nationality)* Anglais *(m)*, Anglaise *(f)* 30d; ***(language)*** l'anglais *(m)* 30d
enjoy oneself s'amuser *(v)* 21a
Enjoy your meal! Bon appétit! 16c, 24l
enjoyment l'amusement *(m)* 21a
enlarge *(clothing)* faire *(v)* élargir 25m

enough assez *(adv)* 3c; suffisant(e) *(adj)* 3c
Enough! Assez! 21c
enter entrer *(v)* (dans) 3e, 16b, 36c
entire entier, entière *(adj)* 3c
entrance l'entrée *(f)* 23a, 25a, 35b
entrance exam l'examen *(m)* d'entrée 37f
envelope l'enveloppe *(f)* 19d, 19e, 25c
envious envieux, envieuse *(adj)* 11e
environment l'environnement *(m)* 13b, 44a
envy l'envie *(f)* 11e
equality l'égalité *(f)* 1f
equals est égal à 1f
equation l'équation *(f)* 1f
equator l'équateur 13e
equilateral équilatéral *(adj)* 2a
equinox l'équinoxe *(m)* 5c
eraser *(for pencil)* la gomme 2b, 19d; la gomme à effacer 37b
error l'erreur *(f)*, la faute 37f
eruption l'éruption *(f)* 13b
escape fuir *(v)*, se précipiter *(v)* 39a
essay l'essai *(m)* 20a, 37f
Europe l'Europe *(f)* 30b
even pair *(adj, m)* 1d
even though même si *(conj)* 8p
evening le soir 4a
evening school l'école *(f)* d'adultes, l'école du soir 37a
every tout, toute, tous, toutes *(adj)* 3c; chaque *(adj, m/f)* 3c
everbody, everyone tout le monde 3c, 8o
Everybody out! Dehors! Tous! 39a
everything tout, toute, toute chose, toutes les choses 3c, 8o
everywhere partout *(adv)* 36c
exam l'examen *(m)* 37f
examine examiner *(v)* 40a, 40b
exchange échanger *(v)* 25a; le change, changer *(v)* 26
exchange rates le cours du change 26
exclamation mark le point d'exclamation *(f)* 19c
excursion l'excursion *(f)* 30a
excuse l'excuse *(f)* 17a
Excuse me! Excusez-moi! *(pol)*, Excuse-moi! *(fam)*, Pardonnez-moi! *(pol)*, Pardonne-moi! *(fam)* 16c
excuse oneself s'excuser *(v)* 17a
exercise l'exercice *(m)* 37f
exhibition l'exposition *(f)* 28b
existence l'existence *(f)* 22a
exit sortir *(v)* 3e, 25a, 36c; la sortie 35b
expensive cher *(adj, m, s)*, chère *(adj, f, s)* chers *(adj, m, pl)* chères *(adj, f, pl)* 24p; coûteux *(adj, m)*, coûteuse *(adj, f)* 24p, 25a
expiration *(date)* l'échéance *(f)* 26
explain expliquer *(v)* 17a, 37f
explanation l'explication *(f)* 17a, 37f
express exprimer *(v)* 17a
express bus l'autocar express 34
express oneself s'exprimer *(v)* 17a
express train le train express 34
expression l'expression *(f)* 17a
extension l'extension *(f)* 3b
extinguish éteindre *(v)* 39a
extract extraire *(v)* 40b
extract a root *(numbers)* extraire *(v)* la racine 1e
extraction l'extraction *(f)* 40b
eye l'oeil *(m)* 12a; les yeux *(m, pl)* 12a

eye doctor l'ophtalmologiste *(m/f)*, l'oculiste *(m/f)* 38a, 40a
eyebrow le sourcil 12a
eyeglasses les lunettes *(f)* 37b, 40a
eyelash le cil 12a
eyelid la paupière 12a
eyewitness le témoin oculaire 41

F
fable la fable 28d
fabric le tissu 25l
face le visage, la figure 12a
face powder la poudre 25f
factor le facteur 1f; mettre *(v)* en facteurs *(m, pl)* 1f
factorization la factorielle 1f
factory l'usine *(f)* 38d
factory worker l'ouvrier, l'ouvrière 38a
Fahrenheit Fahrenheit 6c
fail an exam échouer *(v)* à un examen, être collé(e) à un examen 37f
fairy tale le conte de fées *(f)* 28d
faith la foi 11d; la confiance 21a
faithful fidèle *(adj)* 11d, 11e
fake faux, fausse *(adj)* 13d
fall tomber *(v)* 3e
fall *(season)* l'automne 5c
fall asleep s'endormir *(v)* 12b
fall in love tomber *(v)* amoureux 11c
false faux *(adj, m)*, fausse *(adj, f)* 25i
false teeth le dentier 40b
family la famille 10a
family friend l'ami(e) de famille *(f)* 10b
family name le nom de famille *(f)* 11f, 38b
family relationship la parenté 10a
fan *(of a vehicle)* le ventilateur d'aération 33e
far loin *(adv)* 3d; **far from** loin de 36c; lointain(e) *(adj)* 3d
Farewell! Adieu! 16a
farm la ferme 15a
farmer le fermier, la fermière 15a, 38a
farmland le terrain agricole 13b
fascinate fasciner *(v)* 11e
fascinating fascinant(e) *(adj)* 11e
fascination la fascination 11e
fashion la mode 25k, 25l
fast vite *(adj/adv)* 3d; rapide 3d
fasten *(buckle)* seat belt boucler *(v)* la ceinture 32c
fat gros, grosse *(adj)* 11a
father le père 10a
father-in-law le beau-père 10a
faucet le robinet 23a, 35c
fax le FAX 18a, 18b
fax machine le transmetteur FAX 18a; le télécopieur, l'émetteur-récepteur de fac-similé, le fax 42a
fear la peur; avoir *(v)* peur 21a
Feast of the Assumption *(National French Holiday)* l'Assomption *(f)* 5f, 29a
feather la plume 15b
February le février 5b
feel sentir *(v)* 12c, 21a; se sentir *(v)* 40a
feel bad avoir *(v)* mal *(m)* 12b; se sentir *(v)* mal *(m)* 12b, 40a
feel bored crever *(v)* d'ennui *(m)* 21a
feel like avoir *(v)* envie de 21a
feel well aller *(v)* bien *(adv)* 12b; se sentir *(v)* bien *(adv)* 12b, 40a
feeling *see* **mood**
felt pen le crayon feutre 7c
felt tip pen le stylo-feutre 19d
female la femelle 11a, 38b
feminine féminin(e) *(adj, m, f)* 8a, 11a

feminism le féminisme 44b
feminist le (la) féministe 44b
fence la barrière, la clôture 15a
fencing *(sport)* l'escrime *(f)* 27b; **to fence** faire *(v)* de l'escrime 27b
fender *(of vehicle)* le pare-chocs intégré 33e
fennel le fenouil 14e
fetus le foetus 44b
fever la fièvre 40a
fiance le fiancé 10b, 11c
fiancee la fiancée 10b, 11c
fiber la fibre 13c
fiction l'ouvrage *(m)* de fiction 20a; le livre de fiction *(f)* 28d
field le champ 13b, 27b
field of study la matière d'études 37f
fifteen quinze 1a; **about fifteen** une quinzaine 1c
fifth cinquième 1b
fifty cinquante 1a; **about fifty** une cinquantaine 1c
fifty-one cinquante et un 1a
fifty-two cinquante-deux 1a
fig la figue 14d, 24f
fig tree le figuier 14c
fight se battre *(v)* 39b
figure of speech la figure de rhétorique 17a
file, menu *(computers)* les archives *(f, pl)* 42b
file *(hardware)* la lime 25b
file *(office)* le classeur, le dossier-classeur 38c
filet le filet 24g
filing card la fiche 38c
fill remplir *(v)* 3c
fill up *(gasoline, petrol tank)* faire *(v)* le plein 33c
filling *(tooth)* l'obturation *(f)* 40b
film le film 25d, 28a
film projector le projecteur de film 37b
filter *(of vehicle)* le filtre 33e
fin la nageoire 15c
fine *(traffic ticket)* la contravention 33c
Fine! Bien! *(adv)* 16a
fine arts les beaux-arts *(m, pl)* 37e
finger le doigt 12a
fingernail l'ongle *(m)* 12a
finish finir *(v)* 4e
finish school finir *(v)* l'école *(f)* 11f; finir la dernière année d'école 37f
fir tree le sapin 14c
fire le feu, l'incendie *(m)* 13c, 39a
Fire! Feu! 39a
fire *(to discharge an employee)* renvoyer *(v)* 38d
fire alarm la sirène d'alerte 39a
fire extinguisher l'extincteur *(m)* 39a
fire hose le tuyau de pompe 39a
fire hydrant la borne d'incendie 39a
fire truck le fourgon-pompe 33a, 39a
firearm l'arme *(f)* à feu 39b
firefighter le pompier, le sapeur-pompier 39a
fireman le pompier 38a
fireplace l'âtre *(m)* 23a
fireproof ignifuge *(adj)*, incombustible *(adj)* 39a
first premier *(adj, m)*, première *(adj, f)* 1b, 8a
first aid les soins *(m, pl)* d'urgence 39a, 39c
first class *(travel)* en première classe *(f)* 30a, 32a, 34
first name le prénom 11f, 38b
first showing *(entertainment)* la première représentation 28a
fish le poisson 15c, 24d; pêcher *(v)*, aller *(v)* à la pêche 15c
fish stew la bouillabaisse 24g
fish store la poissonnerie 24n
fishbone l'arête *(f)* 15c
fisherman le pêcheur, la pêcheuse 15c
fishing la pêche 15c, 36b

fishing rod la canne à pêche 15c
fission reactor le réacteur à fission 42a
fit ***(size)*** la mesure, la taille 3b, 25k
five cinq 1a
fix ajuster *(v)*, réparer *(v)* 25i, 33c
fixed bank rate le taux fixe 26
fixed price le prix fixe 24m, 25a
flame la flamme 39a
flash le flash 25d
flash of lightning le coup d'éclair, faire *(v)* des éclairs 6a
flashlight la lampe de poche 25b
flatter flatter *(v)* 21a
flattery la flatterie 21a
flavor la saveur 12c
flea la puce 15d
Flemish ***(language)*** le flamand 30d
flight le vol 32a; **canceled flight** le vol annulé 32b
flight attendant le steward, l'hôtesse de l'air 32c
floor le plancher, le parquet 23a
floor ***(level, story of a building)*** l'étage *(m)* 23a, 35b
floppy disk la disquette, le disque souple 42b
Florence Florence 30c
flour la farine 24i
flow couler *(v)* 13b
flow chart le schéma fonctionnel 42b
flower fleurir *(v)* 14a; la fleur 14a
flower bed le parterre de fleurs 14b
flu l'influenza *(f)*, la grippe 40a
fluorescent fluorescent(e) *(adj, m, f)* 25b
flute la flûte 28c
fly ***(insect)*** la mouche 15d
focus mettre *(v)* en mise au point 25d
fog le brouillard 6a
foggy brumeux *(adj, m)*, brumeuse *(adj, f)* 6a
foil ***(fencing)*** le fleuret français 27b
foliage le feuillage 14a
folk music la musique folklorique 28c
follow suivre *(v)* 3e, 36c
food la nourriture 24a
food coloring le colorant alimentaire 7c
fool le bouffon 11e
foolish bête *(adj, m, f)* 11e
foot le pied 12a
football le football américain 27b
footnote la note en bas de page 20a
for pour 8g
for example par exemple 44c
for now pour maintenant 4e
for sale à vendre *(v)* 25a
for ***(since)*** **three days** depuis trois jours 4e
for the first time pour la première fois 16b
force an uneasy smile sourire *(v)* jaune 7a
forehead le front 12a
foreign currency la monnaie étrangère 31
foreign languages les langues *(f, pl)* étrangères 37e
foreigner l'étranger *(m)*, l'étrangère *(f)* 31
forest la forêt 13b
forget oublier *(v)* 22b
fork la fourchette 23d, 24l
form ***(to fill out)*** la formule 31
Fortunately! Heureusement! *(adv)* 21c
forty quarante 1a; **about forty** une quarantaine 1c
forty-one quarante et un 1a
forty-two quarante-deux 1a
forward avant *(adv)* 3d
fossil le fossile 13c
fossil fuels les combustibles *(m)* fossiles 13c, 44a
foul line ***(sports)*** la ligne de pénalité 27b

four quatre 1a
four-sided figures les figures *(f)* à quatre côtés 2a
four thousand quatre mille 1a
fourteen quatorze 1a
fourth quatrième 1b
fox le renard 15a
fraction la fraction 1d
fractional fractionnel(le) *(adj, m, f)* 1d
France la France 30b
Frankfurt Francfort 30c
free *(not occupied)* libre *(adj, m, f)* 18b
freeze geler *(v)* 6a
freezer le congélateur 23d
French *(nationality)* Français *(m)*, Française *(f)* 30d; *(language)* le français 30d
French foil *(fencing)* le fleuret français 27b
French Franc le franc français 26
French fries les frites *(f, pl)* 24g
frequent fréquent(e) *(adj, m, f)* 4e
frequently fréquemment *(adv)* 4e
fresco painting la fresque 28b
Friday le vendredi 5a
fried frit(e) *(adj, m, f)* 24p
fried egg l'oeuf *(m)* sur le plat 24h
friend l'ami(e) 10b
friendly amical(e) *(adj)* 11e
friendship l'amitié *(f)* 10b
frog la grenouille 15c
from de *(prep)* 3d, 8g
from my point of view de mon point de vue 44c
from now on dès maintenant 4e
From what country are you? De quel pays êtes-vous? 13e
front page *(of newspaper)* la une, la première page 20a
frozen gelé(e) *(adj, m, f)* 6a
fruit le fruit 14d, 24f
fruit flan le flan aux fruits 24i
fruit tartlet la tartelette aux fruits 24g
fruit tree le fruitier 14c
fuel le carburant 13c
full plein *(adj/m)*, pleine *(f)* 3c
full moon la pleine lune 13a
fun l'amusement *(m)*; **to have fun** s'amuser *(v)* 21a
function la fonction 1f, 42b
funny comique *(adj)* 11e; drôle *(adj)* 11e; marrant(e) *(adj, m, f)* 11e
fur coat le manteau de fourrure 25k
furnace la chaudière 23e
furniture le meuble 23c
fuse *(hardware)* le fusible, le plomb fusible 25b
fusion reactor le réacteur à fusion 42a
fussy méticuleux, méticuleuse *(adj, m, f)* 11e
future le futur, l'avenir *(m)* 4e, 8a

G

Gaelic *(language)* le gaélique 30d
gain weight prendre *(v)* du poids 11a
galaxy la galaxie 13a
game le jeu, le match, la partie 27a, 27b
garage le garage 23a, 35b
garbage bin la poubelle 36a
garbage truck le camion de collecte 33a
garden le jardin 14e, 23a
garlic l'ail *(m)* 14, 24g, 24j
gas le gaz 13c, 23e
gasoline l'essence *(f)* 33c
gasoline pedal la pédale d'accélérateur 33e
gasoline pump la pompe à essence 33e
gasoline service station la station-service 33c

gasoline tank le réservoir d'essence 33e
gate ***(travel)*** la porte 32a
gather récolter *(v)*, cueillir *(v)* 14a
gauze la gaze 39c
gay ***(homosexual)*** gai(e) *(adj, m, f)* 44b
gearshift le levier de changement 33e
Gemini les Gémeaux *(m, pl)* 5d
gender le genre 8a
general delivery ***(post office)*** la poste restante 19e
generator la dynamo 33e
generosity la générosité 11e
generous généreux, généreuse *(adj)* 11e
genre le genre 28d
gentle gentil(le) *(adj, m, f)* 11e
gentleman le monsieur 11a
geographical géographique *(adj)* 13e
geography la géographie 13e, 37e
geometrical géométrique *(adj)* 2b
geometry la géométrie 2b, 37e
geothermal energy l'énergie *(f)* géothermique 44a
geranium le géranium 14b
German ***(nationality)*** Allemand *(m)*, Allemande *(f)* 30d; *(language)* l'allemand *(m)* 30d
Germany l'Allemagne *(f)* 30b
gerund le gérondif 8a
get a degree obtenir *(v)* un diplôme universitaire 37f
get a diploma obtenir *(v)* un diplôme 37f
get a doctor chercher *(v)* un médecin 39c
get a loan obtenir *(v)* un prêt 26
get a suntan se bronzer *(v)* 36b
get an education recevoir *(v)* une éducation; recevoir *(v)* une solide formation 37f
get cured se guérir *(v)* 40a
get dressed s'habiller *(v)* 25m
get examined se faire *(v)* examiner 40a
Get lost! Allez-vous en! Va-t'en! 20b
get out ***(to escape a danger)*** fuir *(v)*, se précipiter *(v)* 39a
get sick tomber *(v)* malade 40a
get some sun prendre *(v)* un peu de soleil *(m)* 36b
get up se lever *(v)* 3e, 12b
get used to s'habituer *(v)* 11c
gift le cadeau 11c, 25a
gingerbread le pain d'épices 24i
giraffe la girafe 15a
girl la jeune fille 11a, 11b
girlfriend l'amie, la petite amie 10b
give a gift donner *(v)* un cadeau 11c
give a tip ***(gratuity)*** donner *(v)* un pourboire 24m
give back rendre *(v)* 37f
give back the key . . . rendre *(v)* la clef . . . 35b
give birth accoucher *(v)* 11c
give help donner *(v)* de l'aide 39a
Give my regards to . . . Un bon souvenir à . . . 19b
give the porter a tip donner *(v)* un pourboire au porteur 35b
gladiolus le glaïeul 14b
glass ***(drinking)*** le verre 23d, 24l
glazed, iced, icing glacé(e) *(adj, m, f)* 24i
globe le globe 13e
glove le gant 25k, 27b
glove compartment ***(of a car)*** la boîte à gants, le vide-poches 33e
glue la colle 19d
go aller *(v)* 3e, 36c
Go ahead! Allez-y! *(pol)*, Vas-y! *(fam)* 17b

go away s'en aller *(v)* 3e
go down descendre *(v)* 3e, 36c
go forward avancer *(v)* 33c
go on a trip *see* **take a trip**
go on board monter *(v)* à bord 32a
go on foot aller *(v)* à pied *(m)* 3e
go on strike faire *(v)* la grève, être *(v)* en grève 43
go out sortir *(v)* 3e, 29b, 36c
go to bed se coucher *(v)* 12b
go to school aller *(v)* à l'école *(f)* 11c, 11f; assister *(v)* à l'école 37f
go up monter *(v)* 3e, 36c
goal le but 27b
goalie le gardien (la gardienne) de but 27b
goat la chèvre 15a
God le Dieu 11d
gold l'or *(m)* 13c, 25i
gold *(color)* or *(m)* de couleur 7a
golden anniversary les noces *(f)* d'or 11c
goldfish le poisson rouge 15c
golf, to play jouer *(v)* au golf *(m)* 27b
good bon *(adj, m),* bonne *(adj, f)* 11e, 24p
good *(at something)* habile *(adj)* 11e
Good afternoon! Bonjour! 16a
Good evening! Bonsoir! 16a
good, final copy la bonne copie 37f
Good heavens! Oh! là! là! 21c
Good luck! Bonne chance! 16c
good mood la bonne humeur 21a
Good morning! Bonjour! 16a
Good night! Bonsoir! Bonne nuit! ***(when going to bed)*** 16a
Good-bye! Au revoir! 16a
goodness la bonté 11e
goose l'oie *(f)* 15b
gossip le potin, potiner 17a
govern gouverner *(v)* 43
government le gouvernement 43
graceful gracieux, gracieuse *(adj, m, f)* 11e
grade la classe 37a
grade *(mark)* la note 37f
grade one en première classe 37a
grade two en deuxième classe 37a
graduate obtenir *(v)* un diplôme 11f
graduate *(from a university)* recevoir *(v)* sa licence (son doctorat) 11f
grain le froment, le blé 14a
gram le gramme 3a
grammar la grammaire 8a, 37f
grand piano le piano à queue *(f)* 28c
grandchildren les petits-enfants *(m)* 10a
grandfather le grand-père 10a
grandfather clock l'horloge *(f)* à pendule *(f),* l'horloge *(f)* normande 4d
grandmother la grand-mère 10a
grapefruit le (la) pamplemousse 14d, 24f
grapes le raisin 14d, 24f
grass l'herbe *(f)* 13b, 14e
grated cheese le fromage au gratin 24h
gratuity *(tip)* le pourboire 24m
gravitation la gravitation 13a
gravity la gravité 13a
gravy au jus 24b
gray le gris 7a
Greece la Grèce 30b
greed l'avarice *(f)* 11e
greedy avare *(adj)* 11e

Greek ***(nationality)*** Grec *(m)*, Grecque *(f)* 30d; ***(language)*** le grec 30d
green le vert 7a; **to be green with fear** être *(v)* vert de peur 7a
green pepper le piment 14e
greenhouse la serre 14a
greet saluer *(v)* 16a
greeting la salut, la salutation 16a
Greetings! Sincères salutations! 19b
grilled grillé(e) *(adj, m, f)* 24b
grocery store l'épicerie *(f)* 24n
groom (bridegroom) le marié 11c
grooming la laque pour les cheveux 12d
ground floor (main floor) le rez-de-chaussée 23a, 23g
grow croître *(v)* 3c
grow up grandir *(v)* 11b
growth la croissance 3c
guide le (la) guide 36a
guidebook le guide 25o
guilt la culpabilité 41
guilty coupable *(adj, m, f)* 41
guitar la guitare 28c
guitarist le (la) guitariste 28c
gulf le golfe 13b
gums ***(mouth)*** la gencive 40b
gun le revolver, le pistolet 39b
gymnasium le gymnase 27b; la salle de gymnastique 37c

H

habit (custom) l'habitude *(f)* 11e
hail ***(weather)*** la grêle 6a; grêler *(v)* 6a
hair ***(on head)*** les cheveux *(m, pl)* 12a
hair dryer le séchoir à cheveux 25f
hairdresser le coiffeur, la coiffeuse 12d, 38a
hairspray le spray 12d
half demi *(m)*, demie *(f)* 1c, 3c
hallway le couloir 37c
ham le jambon 24c
hammer le marteau 25b
hand la main 12a
hand ***(of a timepiece)*** l'aiguille *(f)* 4d, 25i
hand back rendre *(v)* 37f
hand luggage les bagages *(m, pl)* à main 31
handcloth la serviette de toilette *(f)* 12d
handcuffs les menottes *(f, pl)* 39b
handkerchief le mouchoir 25k
handle le manche 23d; ***(car door)*** la poignée 33e
handlebar ***(bicycle)*** le guidon 33a
handshake la poignée de main 16a
handsome beau, bel, beaux 11a
hang up ***(telephone)*** accrocher *(v)* 18b
happen se produire *(v)* 4e
happiness le bonheur 11e, 21a; le contentement 11e; la félicité 11e
happy content(e) *(adj)* 11e, 21a; fortuné(e) *(adj)* 11e; heureux, heureuse *(adj)* 11e, 21a
Happy birthday! Bon anniversaire! *(m)* 11c, 29c
Happy Easter! Bonnes Pâques! *(f, pl)* 29c
Happy New Year! Bonne et heureuse année! *(f)* 16c, 29c
Happy to make your acquaintance! Heureux (Heureuse) de faire votre (ta) connaissance! 16b
hard dur(e) *(adj, m, f)* 13d
hard-boiled egg l'oeuf *(m)* dur 24h
hardware la quincaillerie 25b
hardware ***(computers)*** le matériel, le hardware 42b

hardware store la quincaillerie 25b
hard-working diligent(e) *(adj)* 11e
hare le lièvre 15a
harmony l'harmonie *(f)* 28c
harp la harpe 28c
harpsichord le clavecin 28c
hat le chapeau 25k
hate la haine 11e, 21b; haïr *(v)* 11e, 21b
hateful détestable *(adj)* 11e
hatred la haine 11e, 21b
have a baby avoir *(v)* un enfant 11c
have a class avoir *(v)* une leçon 37f
Have a good holiday! Bonnes vacances! *(f, pl)* 16c, 29c
Have a good time! Amusez-vous bien! *(pol),* Amuse-toi bien! *(fam)* 16c
Have a good trip! Bon voyage! *(m)* 16c
Have a happy birthday! Bon anniversaire! *(m)* 11c, 16c, 29c
have a headache avoir *(v)* mal de tête 40a
Have a nice day! Bonne journée *(f)* 29c
Have a nice trip! Bon voyage! *(m)* 30a
have a snack prendre *(v)* un goûter 24o
have a sore back avoir *(v)* mal au dos 40a
have a sore neck avoir *(v)* mal au cou 40a
have a sore throat avoir *(v)* mal de gorge 40a
have a stomach ache avoir *(v)* mal à l'estomac 40a
have a toothache avoir *(v)* mal aux dents 40b
have a twisted neck avoir *(v)* mal au cou (un torticolis) 40a
have baggage taken to one's room faire *(v)* porter les bagages dans la chambre 35b
have chills être *(v)* frileux *(adj, m),* frileuse *(adj, f)* 6b
have dinner dîner *(v)* 24o
have fun s'amuser *(v)* 29b; **Have fun!** Amusez-vous! *(pol)* Amuse-toi! *(fam)* 29c
have lunch déjeuner *(v)* 24o
have one's head in the clouds être *(v)* dans les nuages *(m, pl)* 6a
have patience avoir *(v)* de la patience 21a
have to (must) devoir *(v)* 21a
have white hair avoir *(v)* les cheveux blancs *(m, pl)* 11b
hazard flash *(of a vehicle)* les feux *(m, pl)* de détresse 33e
he il 8h; lui 8l
He/She is a pain in the neck! C'est un casse-pieds! 12a
head la tête 12a
head of state le chef d'état 43
head office le siège central 26
headache le mal de tête 40a
heading *(of a letter)* l'en-tête *(f)* 19c
headline la manchette 20a
headlights *(of a vehicle)* les phares *(m, pl),* les projecteurs *(m, pl)* 33e
headphones le casque à écouteurs 20b; l'écouteur *(m)* auriculaire 32c
heal guérir *(v)* 40a
health la santé 11a, 40a
healthy sain(e) *(adj)* 11a, 40a; en bonne santé *(f)* 11a, 40a
hear entendre *(v)* 12c
hearing l'ouïe *(f)* 12c
heart le coeur 12a, 27a, 40a
heart attack la crise cardiaque 40a
heat la chaleur 13c
heater *(of a vehicle)* le système de chauffage 33e
heating le chauffage central 23d
heavy lourd(e) *(adj, m, f)* 3b, 11a, 13d, 31
Hebrew *(language)* le hébreu 30d

hectare l'hectare *(m)* 3a
hectogram l'hectogramme *(m)* 3a
hedge la haie 14a
height la taille, la stature 11a
Hello! Bonjour! ***(during daytime);*** Bonsoir! ***(during evening hours)*** 16a, 17b ***(answering a telephone call)*** Allô! 18b
helmet le casque 27b
help aider *(v)* 39a
Help! Au secours! 39c; A l'aide! 39a
hemisphere l'hémisphère *(m)* 13e
hemispheric hémisphérique 13e
hen la poule 15b
heptagon l'heptagone *(m)* 2a
her *(possessive)* son *(m, s),* sa *(f, s),* ses *(m/f, pl)* 8f; la 8i; elle 8l
herb l'herbe *(f)* 24j
here ici *(adv)* 3d, 36c
heredity l'hérédité *(f)* 11c
hero le héros 28e
heroine l'héroïne *(f)* 28e
herring le hareng 24d
herself *(reflexive)* se 8k
hesitate hésiter *(v)* 17a
hesitation l'hésitation 17a
hexagon l'hexagone *(m)* 2a
Hi! Salut! 16a, 17b
high school l'école *(f)* d'enseignement secondaire, le lycée 37a, 38b
high school diploma le baccalauréat 37f
high school teacher/professor le professeur, la femme professeur 37d
high temperature la température élevée 6c
highway l'autoroute *(f)* 33c
highway police l'agent *(m)* de police routier 33b
hill la colline 13b
him le 8i; lui 8l
himself *(reflexive)* se 8k
Hindu Hindou(e) *(n/adj, m, f)* 11d
hip la hanche 12a
hippopotamus l'hippopotame *(m)* 15a
hire *(to employ)* employer *(v)* 38d
his son *(m, s),* sa *(f, s),* ses *(m/f, pl)* 8f
history l'histoire *(f)* 37e
hit *(ball)* battre *(v)* 27b
hobby le passe-temps 27a
hockey le hockey 27b; **ice hockey** le hockey sur glace 27b
hockey player le joueur (la joueuse) de hockey 27b
hockey stick la crosse, le stick 27b
hole le trou 25g
holiday *(official)* le jour férié 5a, 29a
holidays les jours *(m, pl)* de fête *(f)* 29a
Holland La Hollande 30b
home base *(sports)* la base du batteur 27b
homework les devoirs *(m, pl)* 37f
homosexual homosexuel(le) *(m, f)* 44b
homosexuality l'homosexualité *(f)* 44b
honest honnête *(adj)* 11e
honesty l'honnêteté *(f)* 11e
honey le miel 24j
honeymoon la lune de miel *(m)* 11c, 13a
hood *(of a vehicle)* le capot 33e
hook *(fishing)* l'hameçon *(m)* 15c
hope l'espoir 21a; espérer *(v)* 21a
horizontal horizontal(e) *(adj)* 3d
horn *(musical instrument)* le cor 28c
horn *(of a vehicle)* le klaxon, l'avertisseur *(m)* sonore 33e
horoscope l'horoscope *(m)* 5d
horse le cheval 15a

horsepower le cheval-vapeur 33e
horse racing les courses *(f)* de chevaux, la course au galop 27b
horticulture l'horticulture *(f)* 14a
hospital l'hôpital *(m)* 39c
hot chaud(e) *(adj, m, f)* 6a, 6b, 24p
hot water l'eau *(f)* chaude 35c
hotel l'hôtel *(m)* 35a; **luxury hotel** l'hôtel de luxe 35a
hotel clerk l'employé *(m),* l'employée *(f)* 35b
hour l'heure *(f)* 4c
hourly à l'heure 4c
house la maison 23a
House/Chamber of Representatives (Deputies) la Chambre des Députés 43
house number le numéro de la maison 11f
how comment *(adv)* 9
How are you? Comment allez-vous? *(pol)* 16a; Comment vas-tu? *(fam)* 16a
How come? Mais comment? 9
How do you feel? Comment vous sentez-vous? 40a
How do you get to. . . ? Comment va-t-on à. . . ? 36c
How do you say. . . in French? Comment dit-on. . . en français? 17b
How do you spell your name? Comment s'écrit votre (ton) nom? 11f
how much/many combien *(adv)* 3c, 9
How much do you weigh? Combien pesez-vous? 11a
How much does it come to? Ça fait combien? 25a
How much does it cost? Ça coûte combien? 25a
How much is it? C'est combien? 25a
How old are you? Quel âge avez-vous (as-tu)? 11b
How tall are you? Quelle taille avez-vous? 11a
How's it going? Comment ça va? Ça va? 16a
How's the weather? Quel temps fait-il? 6a
however pourtant *(conj)* 8p
howl hurler *(v)* 15a
hug l'embrassement 19b
human humain(e) *(adj, m, f)* 11d, 15a
human being l'être *(m),* l'être *(m)* humain 11d, 15a
humanitarian humanitaire *(adj)* 11e
humanities (arts) les lettres *(f, pl)* 37e
humanity l'humanité *(f)* 11d
humble humble *(adj)* 11e
humid humide *(adj)* 6a
humidity l'humidité *(f)* 6a
humility l'humilité *(f)* 11e
humor l'humour *(m)* 11e
hundredth centième 1b
hunger la faim 12b
hunter le chasseur, la chasseuse 15a
hunting la chasse 15a
hurricane l'ouragan *(m)* 6a
hurry se dépêcher *(v)* 39b
hurt avoir *(v)* mal, faire *(v)* mal à 40a
husband le mari 10a, 11c; l'époux 11c
hydrogen l'hydrogène *(m)* 13c
hyena l'hyène *(f)* 15a
hygiene l'hygiène *(f)* 12d
hygienic hygiénique *(adj, m, f)* 12d
hyphen le tiret, le trait d'union 19c
hypothesis l'hypothèse *(f)* 22a

I

I je 8g
I am. . . (+ *name*) Je suis. . . 16b
I am. . . old J'ai. . . ans 11b

I am. . . tall J'ai la taille. . . 11a
I believe that. . . Je crois que. . . 44c
I can't stand him (her)! Je ne peux pas le (la) supporter! 21b
I can't stand the cold! Je ne supporte pas le froid! 6b
I can't stand the heat! Je ne supporte pas la chaleur! 6b
I don't believe it! Je ne le crois pas! 21c
I don't feel like. . . Je n'ai pas envie de. . . 21c
I don't know if. . . Je ne sais pas si. . . 44c
I don't understand. Je ne comprends pas. 9, 17b
I doubt that. . . Je doute que. . . 44c
I feel. . . Je me sens. . . 40a
I have some of it (them). J'en ai. 3c
I live on. . . Street Je demeure rue. . . 11f
I love the cold! J'aime le froid! 6b
I love the heat! J'aime la chaleur! 6b
I think that. . . Je pense que. . . 44c
I was born in. . . (year) Je suis né(e) *(m, f)* en. . . 5e
I was born on. . . Je suis né(e) le. . . 11c
I weigh. . . Je pèse. . . 11a
I wish! (If only. . . !) Si seulement. . . ! 21c
I would like to say that. . . Je voudrais dire que. . . 44c
ice la glace 6a, 13b; **ice chips** les glaçons *(m, pl)* 24p
ice cream la glace, la crème glacée 24h; **cone** le cornet 24h
ice hockey le hockey sur glace 27b
ice skate patiner *(v)* sur glace *(f)* 27b
iced bun le gâteau américain 24i
icing, iced, glazed glacé(e) *(adj, m, f)* 24i
idea l'idée *(f)* 22a
idealism l'idéalisme *(m)* 11e
idealist, idealistic idéaliste *(m, f)* 11e
identification l'identification *(f)* 11f
identification card (papers) la carte d'identité 31, 35b
identify identifier *(v)* 17a
ideology l'idéologie *(f)* 43
if si *(conj)* 8p
ignorant ignorant(e) *(adj, m, f)* 22a
illegal illégal(e) *(adj, m, f)* 41
illustration l'illustration *(f)* 20a
I'm not sure that. . . Je ne suis pas sûr(e) que. . . 44c
I'm serious! Je suis sérieux *(adj, m)* sérieuse *(adj, f)*! 21c
I'm sorry! Je regrette! 21c
I'm sure that. . . Je suis sûr(e) que. . . 17b, 44c
imaginary imaginaire *(adj, m, f)* 1d
imagination l'imagination *(f)* 11e, 22a
imaginative imaginatif, imaginative *(adj, m, f)* 11e
imagine imaginer *(v)* 22b
impatient impatient(e) *(adj, m, f)* 11e
imperative impératif *(adj, m)*, impérative *(adj, f)* 8a, 8n
imperfect imparfait(e) *(adj, m, f)* 8a
import importer *(v)* 31
Impossible! Pas possible! 21c
imprison emprisonner *(v)* 41
impudence l'impudence *(f)* 11e
impudent impudent(e) *(adj, m, f)* 11e
impulse l'impulsion *(f)* 11e
impulsive impulsif, impulsive *(adj, m, f)* 11e

in dans *(prep)* 3d, 8g
in an hour's time dans une heure 4e
in black and white en noir et blanc 25d
in conclusion en conclusion 44c
in front of devant *(adv/prep)* 3d, 36c
in love amoureux *(adj)* 11c
in my opinion à mon opinion 22a, 44c; à mon avis 44c
in my view à mon point de vue 44c
in order that afin que *(conj)*, pour que *(conj)* 8p
in the afternoon dans *(de)* l'après-midi *(m)* 4a
in the country(side) à la campagne 36b
in the evening dans le soir, du soir 4a
in the latest style/fashion à la mode, au dernier cri 25l
in the meanwhile dans l'intervalle *(m)* 4e
in the middle au centre, au milieu 3d
in the morning dans le matin 4a; du matin 4a
in the mountains dans les montagnes 36b
in time à temps *(m)* 4e
in two minutes' time dans deux minutes 4e
incisor *(tooth)* la dent incisive 40b
income le revenu 26
increase l'augmentation *(f)* augmenter *(v)* 3c
indecisive indécis(e) *(adj, m, f)* 11e
indefinite indéfini(e) *(adj, m, f)* 8a, 8c
independent indépendant(e) *(adj, m, f)* 11e
index l'index *(m)* 20a
index finger l'index *(m)* 12a
indicate indiquer *(v)* 17a
indication l'indication *(f)* 17a
indicative indicatif *(adj, m)*, indicative *(adj, f)* 8a
indifference l'indifférence *(f)* 21a
indifferent indifférent(e) *(adj, m, f)* 21a
indirect indirect(e) *(adj, m, f)* 8a, 8j
individualist individualiste *(adj)* 11e
industrial industriel(le) *(adj, m, f)* 13c
industry l'industrie *(f)* 13c
inelegant inélégant(e) *(adj)* 11a
inexpensive à bon marché, économe *(adj, m, f)* 25a
infection l'infection *(f)* 40a
infinitive l'infinitif *(m)* 8a
inflation l'inflation *(f)* 43
inform informer *(v)*, faire savoir *(v)* 17a
informal restaurant le bistro (bistrot) 24m
information le renseignement 18b
information desk le bureau de renseignements 32a
infrared light la lumière infrarouge 13a
ingenious ingénieux, ingénieuse *(adj, m, f)* 11e
ingenuity l'ingénuité *(f)* 11e
ingenuous ingénu(e) *(adj, m, f)* 11e
inherit hériter *(v)* 11c
injection l'injection *(f)*, la piqûre 25h, 40a
injure blesser *(v)* 39b
injury la blessure, la plaie 39b, 39c
ink l'encre *(f)* 19d, 37b
innocence l'innocence *(f)* 11e, 41
innocent innocent(e) *(adj, m, f)* 11e, 41
inorganic inorganique *(adj, m, f)* 13c
insect l'insecte *(m)* 15d
inside dedans *(prep/adv)* 3d, 36c
insolence l'insolence *(f)* 11e

insolent insolent(e) *(adj, m, f)* 11e
instant l'instant *(m)* 4c
instrument l'instrument *(m)* 28c; **to play an instrument** jouer *(v)* de (du, de l', de la) 28c
insulation l'isolant *(m)* 25b
insulin l'insuline *(f)* 25h
insurance l'assurance *(f)* 26, 30a
insurance card la carte d'assurance 33b
integer le nombre entier 1d
integrated circuit le circuit intégré 42b
intelligence l'intelligence *(f)* 11e
intelligent intelligent(e) *(adj, m, f)* 11e
intercom l'interphone *(m)* 18a, 38c
interest l'intérêt *(m)* 26
interest rate le taux d'intérêt 26
interesting intéressant(e) *(adj, m, f)* 22a
interface *(computers)* l'interface *(f)* 42b
intermission l'entracte *(m)* 28e
interrogative interrogatif *(adj, m)*, interrogative *(f)* 8a
interrupt interrompre *(v)* 17a
interruption l'interruption *(f)* 17a
intersection le carrefour, le croisement 33c, 33d, 36a
interview l'interview *(f)* 20a, 20b
intransitive intransitif *(adj, m)*, intransitive *(adj, f)* 8a
introduce someone présenter *(v)* quelqu'un 16b
introduction la présentation 16b
invertebrate invertébré(e) *(adj, m, f)* 15a
invest investir *(v)* 26
investment l'investissement *(m)* 26
invitation l'invitation *(f)*, le faire-part 19e
invite inviter *(v)* 17a
iodine l'iode *(m)* 13c
irascible irascible *(adj)* 11e
Ireland l'Irlande *(f)* 30b
Irish *(nationality)* Irlandais *(m)*, Irlandaise *(f)* 30d
iron *(metal)* le fer 13c; *(for ironing, pressing)* le fer à repasser 25g; repasser *(v)* 25g
ironical ironique *(adj)* 11e
irony l'ironie *(f)* 11e
irrational irrationnel(le) *(adj, m, f)* 1d
irregular irrégulier *(adj, m)*, irrégulière *(adj, f)* 8a
irritable irritable *(adj)* 11e
Is. . . *(name of person)* in? Est-ce que. . . est là? 18b
is equivalent to est équivalent à 1f
is greater than est supérieur à 1f
is less than est inférieur à 1f
is similar to est pareil à 1f
Islamic Islamique *(adj)* 11d
island l'île *(f)* 13b
Isn't it so? N'est-ce pas? 17b
isosceles isocèle *(adj)* 2a
Israel l'Israël *(m)* 30b
Israeli *(nationality)* Israélite *(m, f)* 30d
it *(subject pro)* il *(m,s)*, elle *(f, s)* 8h; *(direct obj pro)* le *(m)*, la *(f)* 8i
It costs an arm and a leg! Cela coûte les yeux de la tête! (*lit.*, It costs both eyes of your head!) 25a
It doesn't matter! Peu importe! 21c
It seems that. . . Il semble que. . . 17b, 44c
It's. . . C'est. . . 7a
It's a bit cold *(weather)*. Il fait un peu froid. 6a
It's a bit hot *(weather)*. Il fait un peu chaud. 6a
It's a quarter to three. Il est trois heures moins un quart.

4b; Il est deux heures quarante-cinq. 4b
It's awful *(weather)!* Il fait un temps affreux! 6a
It's beautiful *(weather).* Il fait beau temps. 6a
It's clear that. . . Il est clair que. . . , Il est évident que. . . 44c
It's cloudy. Il fait un temps couvert. 6a
It's cold *(weather).* Il fait froid. 6a
It's cool *(weather).* Il fait frais. 6a
It's dark *(weather)* today. Il fait sombre aujourd'hui. 6a
It's exactly three o'clock. Il est trois heures précises. 4b
It's five o'clock (AM). Il est cinq heures. 4b
It's five o'clock (PM). Il est dix-sept heures. 4b
It's foul weather. Il fait un temps pourri. 6a
It's four twenty-five. Il est quatre heures vingt-cinq. 4b
It's hot *(weather).* Il fait chaud. 6a
It's humid *(weather).* Il fait humide. 6a
It's January second. C'est le deux janvier. 5e
It's mild *(weather).* Il fait doux. 6a
It's muggy *(weather).* Il fait un temps lourd. 6a
It's my pleasure! C'est mon plaisir! 16b
It's necessary that. . . Il est nécessaire que. . . ; Il faut que. . . 17b
It's 1991. C'est mille neuf cent quatre-vingt-onze. 5e
It's not true. Ce n'est pas vrai. 17b
It's obvious that. . . Il est évident que. . . 17b
It's October first. C'est le premier octobre. 5e
It's one o'clock. Il est une heure. 4b
It's one ten. Il est une heure dix. 4b
It's pleasant *(weather).* Il fait un temps agréable. 6a
It's raining. Il pleut. 6a
It's raining buckets. Il pleut à seaux. 6a
It's rainy. Il fait un temps pluvieux. 6a
It's snowing. Il neige. 6a
It's sunny Il fait (du) soleil. 6a
It's ten minutes to six. Il est six heures moins dix. 4b
It's ten o'clock (AM). Il est dix heures. 4b
It's ten o'clock (PM). Il est vingt-deux heures. 4b
It's three fifteen. Il est trois heures et quart. 4b
It's three o'clock. Il est trois heures. 4b
It's three o'clock on the dot. Il est trois heures juste (pile). 4b
It's three thirty. Il est trois heures et demie. 4b
It's thundering! Il tonne! 6a
It's true! C'est vrai! 17b
It's two o'clock. Il est deux heures. 4b
It's very cold *(weather).* Il fait très froid. 6a
It's very hot *(weather).* Il fait très chaud. 6a
It's windy! Il fait du vent! 6a
Italian *(nationality)* Italien *(m)*, Italienne *(f)* 30d; ***(language)*** l'italien *(m)* 30d
italics en italique *(m)* 19c
Italy l'Italie *(f)* 30b
itch la démangeaison 40a

J
jacket la veste, le veston 25k
jail la prison 41
jam (preserves) la confiture 24j
janitor le nettoyeur, la nettoyeuse 37d
January le janvier 5b
Japan le Japon 30b

Japanese *(nationality)* Japonais *(m)*, Japonaise *(f)* 30d; *(language)* le japonais 30d
jaw la mâchoire 12a, 40b
jazz le jazz 25j, 28c
jealous jaloux, jalouse *(adj, m, f)* 11e
jelly la gelée 24j
jelly roll le roulé 24i
jest plaisanter *(v)* 17a
jewel le bijou 25i
jewelry store la bijouterie, la joaillerie 25i
Jewish Juif, Juive 11d
job le travail 11f; le métier, l'occupation *(f)* 38a
jog faire *(v)* du jogging *(m)* 27a
jogging le jogging 27a
joke la plaisanterie 17a
joker *(cards)* le joker 27a
journalist le (la) journaliste 20a, 38a
journey le voyage 30a
joy la joie 21a
judge le juge; juger *(v)* 41
judgment le jugement 22a
juice le jus 24k
July le juillet 5b
June le juin 5b
junior high school l'école *(f)* d'enseignement de cours moyen 37a, 38b
Jupiter Jupiter *(m)* 13a
jury le jury 41
just now à l'instant *(m)* 4e
justice la justice 22a, 41

K

keep quiet se taire *(v)* 17a
kettle la bouilloire 23d
key la clef 23d, 35b
keyboard le clavier 19d, 42b
keyboard instruments les instruments *(m/pl)* à clavier *(m)* 28c
keyboard operator le (la) claviste 42b
kick donner *(v)* un coup de pied 27b
kidney le rein 40a
kill tuer *(v)*, assassiner *(v)* 39b
killer le tueur, l'assassin *(m)* 39b
kilogram le kilogramme 3a
kilometer le kilomètre 3a
kindergarten le jardin d'enfants 37a
kindness la bonté 11e
king le roi 27a, 43
kiosk le kiosque à journaux 36a
kiss le baiser 11c, 19b; embrasser *(v)* 11c, 21b
kitchen la cuisine 23b
knapsack le sac à dos *(m)* 27b, 31, 36b
knee le genou 12a
knife le couteau 23d, 24l, 39b; **blade** la lame 23d; **handle** le manche 23d
knight *(in chess)* le cavalier 27a
know *(a fact)* savoir *(v)* 22b
know *(be acquainted with)* connaître 22b
know someone connaître quelqu'un 16b, 22b
knowledge la connaissance 22a
knowledgeable connaisseur *(adj, m)*, connaisseuse *(f)* 22a
Knucklehead! Tête de noeud! 12a
knuckles les jointures *(f)* des doigts *(m, pl)* 12a

L

label l'étiquette *(f)* 25a
labor/trade union le syndicat 43
laboratory le laboratoire 13c, 37c
lack manquer (à) *(v)* 25a
ladder l'échelle *(f)* 39a
ladle la louche 23d
lady la dame 11a
laity la laïcité 11d
lake le lac 13b, 36b
lamb l'agneau *(m)* 15a, 24c
lamp la lampe 23c, 35c

land la terre 13b; le terrain 13b; ***(airplane)*** atterrir *(v)* 32c
landing *(airplane)* l'atterrissage *(m)* 32c
landing gear *(airplane)* le train d'atterrissage 32c
landlord le (la) propriétaire 23g
landscape le paysage 13b
lane *(traffic)* la piste 33c
language laboratory le laboratoire de langues 37c
languages *(foreign)* les langues *(f, pl)* étrangères 37e
large grand(e) *(adj)* 3c, 11a; gros *(adj, m)*, grosse *(f)* 3c
large bill *(banknote, currency)* le gros billet 26
laser le laser 42a
last *(previous)* dernier *(adj, m)*, dernière *(f)*, passé(e) *(adj)* 4e
last durer *(v)* 4e
last a long time durer *(v)* longtemps *(adv)* 4e
last a short time durer *(v)* peu de temps 4e
last month le mois dernier (passé) 4e
last night cette nuit (actual night), hier soir (actual evening) 4a
last year l'an *(m)* dernier *(m)*, l'année *(f)* dernière *(f)* 4e
late tard *(adv)*, en retard *(adv)* 4e, 34; ***(arrival/departure)*** en retard 32b, 34
Latin America l'Amérique *(f)* Latine 30b
latitude la latitude 13e
laugh rire *(v)* 11e, 21a
laughter le rire 11e, 21a
launch pad la rampe de lancement 42a
laundry la lessive, le linge 25g
lava la lave 13b
law les études *(f, pl)* de droit 37e; la loi 41
lawful légal(e) *(adj, m, f)* 41
lawsuit la cause civile 41
lawyer l'avocat *(m)*, l'avocate *(f)* 38a, 41; **trial lawyer** l'avoué *(m)*, la femme avoué 41
layer la couche 13b
layperson laïc, laïque *(adj, m, f)* 11d
laziness la paresse 11e
lazy paresseux, paresseuse *(adj, m, f)* 11e
lead le plomb 13c
leaded gasoline l'essence *(f)* plombée 33c
leaf la feuille 14a
leaf through *(a book, magazine, etc.)* feuilleter *(v)* 20a
leap year l'année *(f)* bissextile 5b
learn apprendre *(v)* 22b, 37f
learn by memory apprendre *(v)* par coeur 37f
leather le cuir 13c, 25l
leave partir *(v)* 3e, 34
lecture la conférence; donner *(v)* une conférence 17a; faire une conférence 37f
left *(location)* gauche *(adj)* 3d; **to the left** à gauche 3d, 33c
left wing *(politics)* la gauche 43
leg la jambe 12a
legal légal(e) *(adj, m, f)* 41
legislation la législation 43
lemon le citron 14d, 24f
lemon tree le citronnier 14c
length la longueur 3a
lengthen *(clothing)* faire *(v)* allonger *(v)* 25m
lens *(camera)* l'optique *(f)* de prise de vues 25d
lentil la lentille 14e
Leo *(sign of the zodiac)* le Lion 5d
leopard le léopard 15a
lesbian la lesbienne 44b
lesbianism le lesbianisme, le lesbisme 44b
less moins *(adv)* 3c
letter la lettre 8a, 19c, 19d
letter carrier le facteur (de lettres) 19e

letterhead le papier à en-tête 19d
lettuce la laitue 14e, 24e
level le niveau 3d; ***(story, floor of a building)*** l'étage *(m)* 35b
Level Crossing le Passage à niveau 33d
liar le menteur, la menteuse 17a
liberal libéral(e) *(adj)* 11e
liberal party *(politics)* le parti libéral 43
Libra la Balance 5d
librarian le (la) bibliothécaire 37d
library la bibliothèque 37c
license plate la plaque 33e
lid le couvercle 23d
lie *(falsehood)* le mensonge 17a; ***(to tell a lie)*** mentir *(v)* 17a
lie down se coucher *(v)* 3e
life la vie 11c
life imprisonment l'emprisonnement *(m)* à perpétuité 41
life sentence à la prison à vie 41
lifejacket le gilet de sauvetage 32c
lift lever *(v)* 3e
lift (elevator) l'ascenseur 23g
light *(color)* clair *(adj)* 7b
light *(weight)* léger, légère *(adj, m, f)* 3b, 11a, 13d, 31; la lumière 6a, 13a ***(power)*** l'éclairage *(m)* 23e
light beam le rayon de lumière 42a
light blue le bleu clair 7a
light bulb l'ampoule *(f)* 25b, 25d
light music la musique légère 28c
light saber *(fencing)* le sabre d'escrime *(f)* 27b
light year l'année *(f)* lumière 13a
lighter *(cigar, cigarette)* le briquet 25e
lightning l'éclair *(m)* 6a
lights *(electric)* les lumières 35c
lights *(headlights of a vehicle)* les phares *(m, pl)*, les projecteurs *(m, pl)* 33e
like aimer *(v)* bien 11e, 21b
likeable *(person)* aimable *(adj, m, f)*, sympathique *(adj, m, f)* 11e
liking *(taste for)* le penchant 21b
lily le lis (lys) 14b
lima bean la fève 14e
line la ligne 2b, 19c; la queue 26
line of work le genre de travail *(m)* 11f
line up faire *(v)* la queue 15a, 26
lion le lion 15a
lip la lèvre 12a, 40b
lipstick le rouge (le fard) à lèvres 25f
liqueur la liqueur 24k
liquid le liquide 13c
listen (to) écouter *(v)* 12c, 17a, 20b, 37f
Listen! Ecoutez! *(pol)*, Ecoute! *(fam)* 17b
liter le litre 3a
literal litéral(e) *(adj, m, f)* 17a
literary work l'ouvrage *(m)* 28d
literature la littérature 28d, 37e
litigate faire *(v)* litige, faire cause 41
litigation le litige 41
little *(size)* petit(e) *(adj)* 3c, 11a; ***(quantity)*** peu *(adv)* 3c
little finger le petit doigt 12a
live vivre *(v)* 11c
live somewhere demeurer *(v)* 11f; habiter *(v)* 23f
lively vif, vive *(adj, m, f)* 7b, 11e
liver le foie 24c
living room le salon, la salle de séjour *(m)* 23b
loan le prêt 26; **get a loan** obtenir *(v)* un prêt 26

lobby le foyer 28a, 35b
lobster le homard, la langouste 24d
local train le train omnibus 34
locate localiser *(v)* 13e; situer *(v)* 13e
located se trouver *(v)* 13e
location la localité 13e
logarithm le logarithme 1f
logarithmic logarithmique *(adj)* 1f
London Londres 30c
long long *(adj, m)*, longue *(f)* 3b, 37f
long-distance telephone call l'appel *(m)* à l'extérieur *(m)* 18b
long loaf of bread le pain long 24i
long stick of bread la baguette, la flûte 24i
long-term à long terme 4e
longitude la longitude 13e
look (at) regarder 12c, 20b
look for something (or someone) chercher *(v)* 25a
look forward to s'attendre à *(v)* 4e
loose *(clothing)* ample *(adj, m, f)*, non-ajusté(e) *(adj, m, f)*, vague *(adj, m, f)* 25l
loose change la monnaie 26
lose perdre *(v)* 27b
lose weight perdre *(v)* du poids 11a
loss la perte 27b
lost and found les objets *(m, pl)* perdus 32a
lotion la lotion 25
lots of beaucoup (de) *(adv)* 3c
loudspeaker le haut-parleur 20b
louse le pou, les poux 15d
lovable adorable *(adj, m, f)* 11e
love l'amour *(m)* 11c, 11e, 21b; aimer *(v)* 11c, 11e, 21b
love affair l'affaire *(f)* d'amour *(m)* 10b
lover l'amant(e) *(m, f)* 10b
low season *(tourism)* la basse saison 35b
low temperature la température basse 6c
luggage les bagages *(m, pl)* 31, 35b
lunar eclipse l'éclipse *(f)* lunaire 13a
lunar module le module lunaire 42a
lunch le déjeuner 24a
lung le poumon 12a, 40a
luxury hotel l'hôtel *(m)* de luxe 35a
lymphatic system le système lymphatique 40a

M

macaroon le macaron 24i
mackintosh (raincoat) l'imperméable *(m)* 25k
mad (crazy) fou, fol, folle *(adj)* 11e
madness la folie 11e
magazine le magazine, la revue 20a, 25o, 37b
maggot l'asticot *(m)* 15d
magistrate le magistrat 41
maid la bonne, la domestique 35b
mail le courrier, la poste 19e; mettre *(v)* une lettre à la poste 19e
mail delivery la distribution du courrier *(m)* 19e
mailbox la boîte à lettres *(f, pl)* 19e, 23a
mailman *see* **letter carrier**
main principal(e) *(adj, m, f)* 8a
main door la porte principale 35b
main floor le rez-de-chaussée 35b
main office la direction 37c
make faire *(v)* 18b, 23f
make a movie tourner *(v)* un film 28a
make a request faire *(v)* une demande 9
make a telephone call faire *(v)* un appel téléphonique 18b
make mistakes faire *(v)* des fautes 37b
make the bed faire *(v)* le lit 23f

make-up le fard 12d; le maquillage 12d, 25f
male le mâle 11a, 38b
malicious malicieux, malicieuse *(adj, m, f)* 11e
malign diffamer *(v)* 17a
malleable malléable *(adj, m, f)* 13d
mammal le mammifère 15a
man l'homme *(m)* 11a
manager le directeur, la directrice 26, 35b, 38d; le gérant, la gérante 35b
mandarin orange la mandarine 14d, 24f
mandolin la mandoline 28c
manicure les soins *(m, pl)* esthétiques des mains *(f, pl)* 12d
Many thanks! Merci mille fois! Merci infiniment! 16c
map la carte 13e; **map of France** la carte de France 13e; la carte géographique 37b
maple tree l'érable *(m)* 14c
March le mars 5b
margin la marge 19c
marinated mariné(e) *(adj, m, f)* 24b
marital status l'état *(m)* civil 11c, 38b
mark (grade) la note 37f
marker *(for writing)* le marqueur, le crayon-feutre 19d, 25c
market le marché 24n, 38d
marmalade la confiture d'oranges 24j
marriage le mariage 11c
married marié(e) *(n/adj, m, f)* 11c, 38b
marry *(someone)* épouser *(v)*, se marier *(v)* avec 11c
Mars Mars *(m)* 13a
Marseilles Marseille 30c
mascara le mascara 12d; le fard pour les yeux 25f
masculine masculin(e) *(adj, m, f)* 8a, 11a
mask le masque 27b
masking tape le papier cache 25b
Mass la Messe 11d
mass la masse 3b
massage le massage 12d
masterpiece *(art)* le chef d'oeuvre 28b
master's degree la licence 37f
match *(sports)* le jeu, le match, la partie 27b
matches les allumettes *(f)* 25e
material le matériel 13c
mathematics les mathématiques *(f, pl)* 37e
matter la matière 13c; **to matter (be of importance)** importer *(v)* 21a
matrimony le mariage 11c
maximum le maximum 3b, 31; **maximum temperature** la température maximum 6c
May *(month)* le mai 5b
May I. . . ? Puis-je. . . ? 16c
May I come in? Puis-je entrer? 16c
May I help you? Vous désirez? Puis-je vous aider? 16c
me me 8i; moi 8l
meal le repas 24a
mean (nasty) méchant(e) *(adj, m, f)* 11e
mean (signify, have in mind) signifier *(v)*, vouloir dire *(v)* 17a
meaning la signification, le sens 17a
meanness la méchanceté 11e
measles la rougeole 40a
measure mesurer *(v)* 3b
measuring tape le mètre à ruban 3b
meat la viande 24c
mechanic le mécanicien, la mécanicienne 33c, 38a
mechanical mécanique *(adj, m, f)* 25b
medicine *(field of study)* la médecine 37e
medicine (medication) le médicament 25h, 40a
mediocre médiocre *(adj, m, f)* 21b

Mediterranean méditerranéen *(adj, m)*, méditerranéenne *(f)* 6a
medium moyen *(adj)* 3b
medium (average) height la taille moyenne 11a
medium *(cooked food)* à point 24b
meet rencontrer *(v)* 16b
Melba toast la biscotte 24i
melon le melon 14d
melted cheese le fromage fondu 24h
melting point le point de fusion *(f)* 6c
membrane la membrane 14a
memory la mémoire 42b
mend raccommoder *(v)* 25g
men's shop/clothing le magasin d'habillement masculin 25k
mention mentionner *(v)* 17a
menu la carte, le menu 24g
meow miauler *(v)* 15a
mercury le mercure 6c, 13c
Mercury Mercure *(m)* 13a
Merge Confluence 33d
meridian le méridien 13e
meringue la meringue 24i
Merry Christmas! Joyeux Noël! *(m)* 16c, 29c
message le message 18b, 35b
metal le métal 13c
metamorphosis la métamorphose 15d
metaphor la métaphore 17a
meteor le météore 13a
meter le mètre 3a
meter postage la vignette 19e
methane le méthane 13c
Mexico le Mexique 30b
microcomputer le micro-ordinateur 42b
microphone le microphone 20b
microprocessor le microprocesseur 42b
microscope le microscope 13c
microwave la micro-onde 42a
microwave oven le four à micro-onde *(f)* 23d
middle finger le médius 12a
midnight le minuit 4a
Milan Milan 30c
mild *(weather)* doux *(adj, m)*, douce *(adj, f)* 6a
mild *(temperature of liquid)* tiède *(adj, m, f)* 24p
milk le lait 24h
millimeter le millimètre 3a
millionth millionième 1b
mime le (la) mime 28d
mind l'esprit *(m)* 22a
mineral le minéral 13c
mineral water l'eau *(f)* minérale 24k
minimum le minimum 3b; **minimum temperature** la température minimum 6c
minister le ministre, la femme ministre 11d, 43
mint la menthe 14e, 24j
minus moins *(adv)* 1e, 6c
minute la minute 4c
mirror le miroir 23c, 35c; la glace 35c
mischievous capricieux, capricieuse *(adj, m, f)* 11e
Miss Mademoiselle 11f, 16b
miss *(the train, etc.)* manquer *(v)*, rater *(v)* 34
missile le missile 42a
mistake la faute 37f; **to make mistakes** faire *(v)* des fautes 37f
modal modal(e) *(adj, m, f)* 8a
model *(molecule)* le modèle 13c
modem *(computers)* le modem 42b
molar *(tooth)* la dent molaire 40b
mole la taupe 15a
molecular formula la formule moléculaire 13c
molecule la molécule 13c, 42a
mom la maman 10a
moment le moment 4c
monarchy la monarchie 43

Monday le lundi 5a
money l'argent *(m)* 26
money order le mandat de paiement *(m)* 19e, 26
monk le moine 11d
monkey le singe 15a
monorail vehicle le monorail 42a
month le mois 4c
month of the year le mois de l'année 5b
monthly mensuel *(adj)*, mensuellement *(adv)* 4c, 5b
monument le monument 36a
mood *(grammar)* le mode 8a
mood *(feeling)* l'humeur *(f)* 11e, 21a
moon la lune 5c, 6a, 13a
moonray/moonbeam le rayon de lune *(f)* 13a
morality la moralité 44b
more plus *(adv)* 3c
morning le matin 4a
mortgage l'hypothèque *(f)* 26
Moscow Moscou 30c
mosque la mosquée 11d
mosquito la moustique 15d
motel le motel 35a
moth la phalène 15d
mother la mère 10a
mother-in-law la belle-mère 10a
motion la motion 3e
motor le moteur 33e
motorcycle la motocyclette, la moto 33a
motorcycle driver le (la) motocycliste 33a
mountain la montagne 13b
mountain boot la chaussure d'escalade *(f)* 27b; la chaussure de montagne 36b
mountain chain la chaîne de montagnes *(f, pl)* 13b
mountain climbing l'alpinisme *(m)* 27b, 36b
mountainous montagneux, montagneuse *(adj, m, f)* 13b
mouse la souris 15a
moustache la moustache 12a
mouth la bouche 12a, 40b
move bouger *(v)*, remuer *(v)* 3e
move oneself bouger *(v)*, se déplacer *(v)* 3e
move *(out of a house)* déménager *(v)* 23f
movement le mouvement 3e
movie *(film, motion picture)* le film 28a
movie camera la caméra, l'appareil *(m)* cinématographique 25d
movie director le réalisateur, la réalisatrice, le metteur en scène, la femme metteur en scène 28a, 38a
movies *(cinema)* le cinéma, le ciné 28a
Mr. M., Monsieur 11f, 16b
Mrs. Mme, Madame 11f, 16b
Ms. Mlle, Mademoiselle 11f, 16b
much beaucoup *(adv)* 3c
muffler *(of a vehicle)* le pot d'échappement 33e
mugginess *(weather)* la lourdeur 6a
muggy *(weather)* lourd *(adj, m)*, lourde *(adj, f)* 6a
mule le mulet 15a
multiple le multiple 1f
multiplication la multiplication 1e
multiplication table la table de multiplication *(f)* 1e
multiplied by multiplié par 1e
multiply multiplier *(v)* 1e
mumble grommeler *(v)* 17a
murder le meurtre, l'homicide 39b; assassiner *(v)* 39b
murmur murmurer *(v)* 17a
muscle le muscle 12a, 40a
museum le musée 36a
mushroom le champignon 14e, 24e
music la musique 25j, 28c, 37e
musician le musicien, la

musicienne 28c, 38a
Muslim Musulman(e) *(m, f)* 11d
mussels la moule 24d
must *see* **have to**
mute ***(person)*** muet, muette *(adj, m, f)* 12c
my mon *(m, s)*, ma *(f, s)*, mes *(m/f, pl)* 8f
My God! Mon Dieu! 21c
My name is. . . Mon nom est. . . 11f; Je m'appelle. . . 16b; **I am. . .** Je suis. . . 16b
My tooth hurts! Une dent me fait mal! 40b
myself ***(reflexive)*** me 8k
mystery novel le roman policier 20a, 25o
myth le mythe 11d, 28d
mythology la mythologie 28d

N
nag (torment, pester) grogner *(v)* 17a
nail ***(hardware)*** le clou 25b
nail polish le vernis à ongles *(m, pl)* 12d, 25f
naive naîf, naîve *(adj, m, f)* 11e
name le nom 11f, 38b
napkin la serviette 23d, 24l
Naples Naples 30c
napoleon ***(pastry)*** le millefeuille 24i
narrow étroit *(adj, m)*, étroite *(f)* 3b
nation la nation 13e, 30a
national national(e) *(adj, m, f)* 13e
National Assembly l'Assemblée *(f)* Nationale 43
nationality la nationalité 11f, 38b
natural naturel(le) *(adj, m, f)* 1d, 13b
natural gas le gaz naturel 13c
natural resources les ressources *(f)* naturelles 13c, 44a
natural sciences les sciences *(f, pl)* naturelles 37e
nature la nature 13b
near près (de) *(adv)* 3d, 36c
nearly presque *(adv)* 3c
neat ordonné(e) *(adj, m, f)* 11e
neck le cou 12a; **stiff** (twisted) **neck** le torticolis 40a; **sore neck** le mal au cou 40a
necklace le collier 25i
necktie la cravate 25k
need le besoin; avoir *(v)* besoin de 21a
needle l'aiguille *(f)* 40b
negative négatif, négative *(adj, m, f)* 1d, 8n
neigh hennir *(v)* 15a
neon au néon 25b
nephew le neveu 10a
Neptune Neptune *(m)* 13a
nerves les nerfs *(m, pl)* 40a
nervous system le réseau de nerfs, le système nerveux 40a
net ***(sports)*** le but 27b
network le réseau 20b
neutron le neutron 13c, 42a
never jamais *(adv)* 4e
new moon la nouvelle lune 13a
New Year le Nouvel An 5f
New Year's Day le Jour de l'An 5f, 29a
New Year's Eve la Veille du Nouvel An 5f; la Veille du Jour de l'An 29a
New Zealand la Nouvelle-Zélande 30b
newlyweds les nouveaux-mariés *(m, pl)* 11c
news les actualités 20a
news report les nouvelles *(pl)* du jour, les actualités 20b
newscast ***(on radio)*** le journal parlé 20b; ***(on television)*** le journal télévisé 20b
newspaper le journal 20a, 25o
newsstand le kiosque à journaux 34
next to à côté (de) *(prep)* 3d
nice ***(person)*** sympathique *(adj, m, f)* 11e

niece la nièce 10a
night la nuit 4a
nightingale le rossignol 15b
nine neuf 1a
nineteen dix-neuf 1a
ninety quatre-vingt-dix 1a
ninety-one quatre vingt-onze 1a
ninth neuvième 1b
nitrogen l'azote *(m)*, le nitrogène 13c
No! Non! 16c
No Entry Défense d'entrer 33d
No Left Turn Virage à gauche interdit 33d
no one personne 3c, 8o
No Parking Stationnement interdit 33d
No Passing Interdiction de dépasser 33d
No Problem! Pas de problème! 22a
No Right Turn Virage à droite interdit 33d
No Smoking Défense de fumer 32a
No Stopping Arrêt interdit 33d
No Thoroughfare Circulation interdite 33d
No U-Turn Virage U interdit 33d
No way! Pas de moyen! 17b, 20b
noise le bruit 12c
noisy bruyant(e) *(adj, m, f)* 12c
nonconformist le (la) non-conformiste 11e
nonfiction l'ouvrage *(m)* de réalité 20a
nonsmoking compartment non-fumeurs 34
noon le midi 4a
north le nord 3d; **to the north** au nord 3d
North America l'Amérique *(f)* du Nord 30b
North Pole le Pôle Nord 13e
northern septentrional(e) *(adj)* 3d
Norway la Norvège 30b
Norwegian *(nationality)* Norvégien *(m)*, Norvégienne *(f)* 30d; *(language)* le norvégien 30d
nose le nez 12a
nostril la narine 12a, 40a
Not bad! Pas mal! *(adv)* 16a
not guilty non coupable 41
not nice antipathique *(adj, m, f)* 11e
note la note 37f; **to take notes** prendre *(v)* des notes 37f
note *(communication)* le billet 19e, 20a; *(music)* la note 28c
note pad le bloc-notes 25c
notebook le cahier 37b
nothing rien *(adv/pro)*, nul *(adj/pro, m)*, nulle *(f)* 3c
nothing to declare rien à déclarer 31
noun le nom 8a
novel le roman 20a, 25o, 28d
November le novembre 5b
now maintenant *(adv)* 4e, 17b; à présent 4e
nowadays de nos jours 4e
nowhere nulle part *(adv)* 3d
n-sided figures les figures *(f)* à côtés n 2a
nth root à la racine n 1e
nuclear energy l'énergie *(f)* nucléaire 13c, 42a
nuclear fuel le combustible nucléaire 42a
nuclear industry l'industrie *(f)* nucléaire 42a
nuclear reactor le réacteur nucléaire 42a
nuclear war la guerre nucléaire 44b
nuclear weapon l'arme *(f)* nucléaire 44b
nucleus *(atom)* le noyau 13c; le nucléole 13c, 14a
number le nombre 1d, 8a; le numéro 1d, 38b; numéroter *(v)* 1d
numeral le numéral 1d
numerical numérique *(adj)* 1d

nun la religieuse 11d
nurse l'infirmier *(m)*, l'infirmière *(f)* 38a, 40a
nursery school l'école *(f)* maternelle 37a
nylon le nylon 25l

O
oak tree le chêne 14c
oat l'avoine *(f)* 24i
obesity l'obésité *(f)* 11a
obituary la notice nécrologique 20a
object *(grammar)* le complément d'objet *(m)* 8a, 8i, 8j, 8l
oboe le hautbois 28c
obstinate obstiné(e) *(adj, m, f)* 11e
obtuse obtus *(adj)* 2b
obtuse-angled obtusangle *(adj)* 2a
occasionally de temps en temps *(adv)* 4e
occupation l'occupation *(f)* 38a
occur se produire *(v)* 4e
ocean l'océan *(m)* 13b
octagon l'octogone *(m)* 2a
octahedron l'octaèdre *(m)* 2a
October l'octobre *(m)* 5b
octopus la pieuvre, le poulpe 15c
odd impair *(adj, m)* 1d
odious antipathique *(adj, m, f)* 11e
of de 8g
of it en *(pron)* 3c, 8o
of the day du jour 24g
of them en *(pron)* 8o
offend offenser *(v)* 17a
office le bureau 38d
office automation l'automatisation *(f)* de bureau 42b
office hours les heures *(f, pl)* de bureau 40b
often souvent *(adv)* 4e
Oh, my! Oh! là! là! 21c
oil l'huile *(f)* 13c, 24j, 33e
oil filter le filtre à huile 33e
ointment la pommade 25h
OK! D'accord! Entendu! 16c
old vieux *(m)*, vieille *(f)* 11b
old age la vieillesse 11b
older brother la frère aîné 11b
older sister la soeur aînée 11b
olive l'olive *(f)* 14d, 24e
olive tree l'olivier *(m)* 14c
omelette l'omelette *(f)* 24h; **with cheese** au fromage; **with ham** au jambon; **with whipped cream** mousseline 24h
on sur *(prep)* 3d, 8g
On guard! *(fencing)* En garde! *(f)* 27b
on Mondays le lundi 5a
on sale en vente *(f)* 25a
on Saturdays le samedi 5a
on Sundays le dimanche 5a
on the air *(radio and television)* en émission 20b
on the dot *(telling time)* juste *(pile)* 4b
on time à l'heure 32b, 34
on vacation en vacances *(f, pl)* 36b
once une fois 4e
once in a while de temps à autre 4e
once upon a time il était une fois 4a, 4e
one un *(m)*, une *(f)* la; on 8h, 8o
one billion un milliard 1a
one-fifth un cinquième 1c
one-fourth un quart 1c
one-half un demi 1c
one hundred cent la; **about one hundred** une centaine 1c
one hundred and one cent un 1a
one hundred million cent millions 1a
one hundred thousand cent mille 1a
one million un million 1a
one million and one un million un 1a

one-third un tiers 1c
one thousand mille 1a; **about a thousand** un millier 1c
one thousand and one mille un 1a
one turn (360°) le tour 2b
oneself (reflexive pron) se 8k; soi 8l
One-Way Street Sens Unique 33d
one-way ticket le billet d'aller 30a
onion l'oignon *(m)* 14e, 24e
onion soup la soupe à l'oignon 24g
only seulement *(adv)* 4e
opal l'opale *(f)* 25i
opaque opaque 7b, 13d
open ouvert(e) *(adj, m, f)* 25a
open an account ouvrir *(v)* un compte 26
Open your mouth! Ouvrez la bouche! 40b
opening hours *(store)* les heures d'ouverture 25a
opera l'opéra *(m)* 28c
operating room la salle de chirurgie 40a
operation *(surgery)* l'intervention *(f)* chirurgicale 40a
operator *(telephone)* le (la) téléphoniste 18b
opinion l'opinion *(f)* 22a; **in my opinion** à mon opinion 22a
opposite opposé(e) *(adj, m, f)* 2b
optical reader le lecteur optique 42b
optician l'opticien, l'opticienne 40a
optimism l'optimisme *(m)* 11e
optimist l'optimiste *(m, f)* 11e
optimistic optimiste *(adj, m, f)* 11e
or ou *(conj)* 8p
oral oral(e) *(adj, m, f)* 17a
oral exam l'examen *(m)* oral 37f
orally oralement *(adv)* 17a
orange l'orange *(f)* 14d, 24f
orange *(color)* l'orangé *(m)* 7a
orange tree l'oranger *(m)* 14c
orbit l'orbite *(f)* 13a; être *(v)* en orbite, mettre *(v)* en orbite, placer *(v)* sur orbite 13a
orchestra l'orchestre *(m)* 28c
orchestra conductor le chef d'orchestre *(m)* 28c
orchid l'orchidée *(f)* 14b
order l'ordre *(m)*, ordonner *(v)* 17a; *(food)* commander *(v)* 24o
ordinal ordinal(e) *(adj, m, f)* 1b, 1d
organ *(music)* l'orgue *(m)* 28c
organic organique *(adj, m, f)* 13c
organism l'organisme *(m)* 14a, 15d
oriental oriental(e) *(m, f)* 11d
original original(e) *(adj, m, f)* 11e
Orthodoxe Orthodoxe *(m, f)* 11d
ostrich l'autruche *(f)* 15b
others autrui *(indef pron)* 8o
our notre *(m/f, s)*, nos *(m/f, pl)* 8f
ourselves (reflexive pron) nous 8k
out dehors *(adv)* 39a
out of focus *(photo)* la photo floue 25d
outlet la prise 18a, 25b
outside dehors *(adv)* 3d, 36c
outskirts (suburbs) la banlieue, les environs *(m, pl)* 30a
outspokenly carrément *(adv)*, franchement *(adv)* 17a
oven le four; **microwave oven** le four à micro-onde *(f)* 23d
overhead projector le rétroprojecteur 37b

owl le hibou 15b
ownership papers les documents *(m)* de propriété 33b
ox le boeuf, les boeufs 15a
oxygen l'oxygène *(m)* 13c
oyster l'huître *(f)* 24d

P
Pacific Pacifique *(adj, m, f)* 13b
pack (one's bags/luggage) faire *(v)* les bagages 31
package le colis, le paquet 19e, 25a
pad le bloc-notes 19d
pagan païen, païenne *(n/adj, m, f)* 11d
page la page 19d, 20a
pail le seau 23d
pain la douleur 40a
painful douloureux *(adj, m)*, douloureuse *(adj, f)* 40a
paint peindre *(v)* 7c, 23f, 28b
painter le peintre, la femme peintre 7c, 38a; l'artiste-peintre *(m/f)* 28b, 38a
painting (picture) le tableau 23c; la peinture 28b
pair la paire 3c, 25n
pajamas le pyjama 25k
palate le palais 40b
pale pâle *(adj)* 7b
palette la palette 28b
palm tree le palmier 14c
pamphlet le dépliant, la brochure 20a
pan la casserole, la sauteuse 23d
pancake la crêpe 24g
pantomime la pantomime 28e
pants (slacks) le pantalon 25k
paper le papier 19d, 25c, 37b
paper clip le trombone 19d
paragraph le paragraphe 19c
parakeet la perruche 15b
parallel line la ligne parallèle 2b
parallelogram le parallélogramme 2a
parenthesis la parenthèse 19c
parents les parents *(m)* 10a
Paris Paris 30c
park *(a vehicle)* stationner *(v)* 33c
park le parc 36a; **park bench** le banc 36a
parking le stationnement 33c
parking meter le parcmètre 36a
Parliament le Parlement 43
parrot le perroquet 15b
parsley le persil 14e, 24j
part la part, la partie 3c
participle le participe 8a
particle la particule 13c
partitive le partitif 8a, 8d
party la fête 29b
pass passer *(v)* 27b
pass a sentence (judgment) prononcer *(v)* un jugement 41
pass a vehicle dépasser *(v)* 33c
pass an exam être *(v)* reçu(e) à un examen 37f
pass by passer *(v)* 3e
passenger le passager, la passagère 32c, 33b
passenger van le fourgon automobile 33a
Passing Lane Piste pour dépasser 33d
passive passif *(adj, m)*, passive *(adj, f)* 8a
passport le passeport 31, 35b
passport control le contrôle de passeports 31
past le passé 4e; passé(e) *(adj, m, f)* 8a
past *(grammar)* le passé composé 8a, 8n
past absolute *(grammar)* le passé simple 8a
past participle le participe passé 8a
pasta la pâte 24g
pastel le pastel 28b
pastries les pâtisseries *(f, pl)* 24i

pastry shop la pâtisserie 24n
patience la patience 11e, 21a; **to have patience** avoir *(v)* de la patience 21a
patient patient(e) *(adj, m f)* 11e
paw la patte 15a
pawn *(in chess)* le pion 27a
pay payer *(v)* 25a, 26, 35b
pay customs/duty payer *(v)* les droits de douane 31
pay off acquitter *(v)* 26
pay phone le téléphone public 18a
pay through the nose payer *(v)* un oeil 12a
payment le paiement 26
peace la paix 43
peach la pêche 14d, 24f
peach pie la tarte aux pêches 24g
peach tree le pêcher 14c
peak le sommet 13b
peak season *(tourism)* la haute saison 35b
peanut l'arachide *(f)*, la cacahouète 24f
pear la poire 14d
pear tree le poirier 14c
pearl la perle 25i
peas les (petits) pois *(m)* 14e, 24e
pedal la pédale 33a
pedestrian le piéton, la piétonne 33b
pedestrian crossing le passage pour piétons, le passage piétonnier 33c, 36a
peel éplucher *(v)* 24o
Peking/Beijing Pékin/Béjing 30c
pelican le pélican 15b
pen le stylo 2b, 7c, 19d, 25c, 37b, 38c
penalty *(sports)* la pénalité 27b
pencil le crayon 2b, 19d, 25c, 37b, 38c
penguin le pingouin 15b
penicillin la pénicilline 25h
peninsula la péninsule, la presqu'île 13b
penis le pénis 12a
pension (retirement) la retraite, la pension 38d
pentagon le pentagone 2a
people les gens *(m & f, pl)* 11d; *(of a nation)* le peuple 43
pepper le poivre 24j
per hour à l'heure *(f)* 3a
per minute à la minute 3a
per second à la seconde 3a
perceive percevoir *(v)*, apercevoir *(v)* 12c
percent pour cent 1f
percentage le pourcentage 1f
perception la perception 12c
percussion instruments les instruments *(m, pl)* à percussion *(f)* 28c
perfect parfait(e) *(adj, m, f)* 8a
perfection la perfection 11e
perfectionist perfectionniste *(m, f)* 11e
perfume le parfum 12d, 25f
perfume/cosmetics shop la parfumerie 25f
period *(punctuation)* le point 19c
periodical *(weekly)* hebdomadaire *(adj/n, m, f)* 20a
peripherals les périphériques *(m, pl)* 42b
permanent wave la permanente 12d
perpendicular line la ligne perpendiculaire 2b
person la personne 8a, 11d
personal personnel(le) *(adj, m, f)* 8a
personal computer l'ordinatuer *(m)* personnel 42b
personality la personnalité 11e
perspire transpirer *(v)* 6b
persuade persuader *(v)* 22b, 41
pessimism le pessimisme 11e
pessimist le (la) pessimiste 11e

pessimistic pessimiste *(adj, m, f)* 11e
pet l'animal *(m)* favori *(domestiqué)* 15a
petal le pétale 14b
petrol ***see*** **gasoline**
petroleum le pétrole 13c, 44a
petunia le pétunia 14b
pharmaceutical drug le remède, le médicament 25h
pharmacist le pharmacien, la pharmacienne 25h, 38a
pharmacy la pharmacie 25h
Ph.D. Dr., le docteur, la doctoresse 16b
philosophy la philosophie 37e
phone (to telephone) téléphoner *(v)* 18b
phone bill la facture 18b
phone book l'annuaire *(m)* du téléphone, le bottin 18a
phone booth la cabine téléphonique 18a
phone call l'appel *(m)* téléphonique 18b
phone line la ligne téléphonique 18b
phone number le numéro de téléphone 11f, 18b
phone ***see also*** **telephone**
phonetics la phonetique 8a
photo la photo(graphie) 20a, 25d
photocopier le photocopieur 38c
photosynthesis la photosynthèse 14a
phrase la phrase 19c
physical physique *(adj, m, f)* 13c
physics la physique 13c, 37e
physiology la physiologie 37e
physique ***(appearance)*** l'aspect *(m)* physique 11a
pianist le (la) pianiste 28c
piano le piano 28c
pick ***(hardware)*** le pic, la pioche 25b
pick flowers cueillir *(v)* des fleurs 14b
pick up the phone décrocher *(v)* 18b
pickpocket le pickpocket, le voleur (la voleuse) à la tire 39b
picky tatillon, tatillone *(adj, m, f)* 11e
picnic le pique-nique 29a
picture (photo) la photo(graphie) 20a; 25d
pie la tarte 24g
piece la pièce 3c
piece of furniture le meuble 23c
piece of luggage la valise 31
pig le cochon 15a
pigeon le pigeon 15b
pill la pilule 25h, 40a
pillow l'oreiller 23d, 35c
pillowcase la taie d'oreiller 23d
pilot le (la) pilote 38a
pimple le bouton 40a
pine tree le pin 14c
pineapple l'ananas *(m)* 14d, 24f
pink le rose 7a; **to see life "in the pink"** voir *(v)* la vie en rose 7a
pipe ***(smoking)*** la pipe 25e
Pisces les Poissons *(m)* 5d
piston le piston 33e
pitcher ***(sports)*** le lanceur 27b
pizza parlor la pizzeria 24m
place l'endroit *(m)* 3d; le lieu 3d, 19c
place of birth le lieu de naissance *(f)* 11f, 38b
place of employment le lieu d'emploi *(m)* 11f
plain ***(terrain)*** la plaine 13b
plane ***(hardware)*** le rabot 25b
plane figures les figures *(f)* planes 2a
planet la planète 13a
plant la plante, planter *(v)* 14a
plant ***(commercial)*** l'établissement *(m)* 38d
plastic le plastique *(adj, m, f)* 13c

plate (dish) l'assiette *(f)* 23d, 24l
platinum le platine 13c
play jouer *(v)* 27a; le jeu 27b
play *(theater)* la pièce de théâtre 20a, 28e
play a musical instrument jouer *(v)* de (du, de l', de la) 28c
play a record passer *(v)* un disque 20b
play cards jouer *(v)* aux cartes *(f, pl)* 27a
play hooky faire *(v)* l'école buissonnière 37f
player le joueur, la joueuse 27b, 28c
playwright le (la) dramaturge, l'auteur *(m)* dramatique, la femme auteur dramatique 28e
plea la plaidoirie 41
plea for mercy la supplication pour clémence 41
plead plaider *(v)* 41
pleasant *(person)* aimable *(adj, m, f)* 11e; sympathique *(adj, m, f)* 11e; agréable *(adj, m, f)* 21b
Please! S'il vous plaît! *(pol)*, S'il te plaît! *(fam)* 16c
Please accept . . . *(in a business letter)* Veuillez accepter, Veuillez agréer . . . 19a
Please give my regards/greetings to . . . Mon bon souvenir à . . . 16a
pleasure plaisir *(m)* 16b; **The pleasure is mine!** C'est mon plaisir! 16b
pliers les pinces *(f, pl)*, les tenailles *(f, pl)* 25b
plot *(of a novel)* l'intrigue *(f)* 20a, 28d, 28e
plug *(hardware)* la fiche de prise de courant 25b
plug *(telephone)* la fiche téléphonique 18a
plum la prune 14d, 24f
plumber le plombier 38a
plumbing la plomberie 25b
pluperfect *(grammar)* le plus-que-parfait 8a
plural le pluriel, pluriel(le) *(adj, m, f)* 8a
plus plus *(adv)* le, 6c; et *(conj)* 1e
Pluto Pluton *(m)* 13a
pneumonia la pneumonie 40a
poached egg l'oeuf *(m)* poché 24h
pocket la poche 25g; **billiard table pocket** le trou 27a
pocket book le livre de poche 20a
pocket radio le poste à transistors de poche 20b
poem le poème 20a
poet le poète, la femme poète 28d
poetry la poésie 20a, 25o, 28d
point le point 2b; *(sports)* la marque 27b
point out indiquer *(v)* 17a
Poland la Pologne 30b
pole le pôle 13e; **North Pole** le Pôle Nord; **South Pole** le Pôle Sud 13e
police la police 33b, 39b, 39c
police station le commissariat de police 41
policeman l'agent *(m)* de police 33b, 38a, 39b
policewoman l'auxiliaire féminine de police 33b, 38a, 39b
policy *(politics)* la politique 43
Polish *(nationality)* Polonais *(m)*, Polonaise *(f)* 30d; *(language)* le polonais 30d
political party le parti politique 43
political power le pouvoir politique 43
political science la science politique, la science po 37e
politician l'homme *(m)* politique, la femme politique 43
politics la politique 43
pollen le pollen 14a
pollution la pollution 13c, 44a

polyester le polyester 25l
polyhedron le polyèdre 2a
pony le poney 15a
pool *(swimming)* la piscine 27b, 35b
poor pauvre *(adj, m, f)* 11e
Poor man! Pauvre homme! 21c
Poor woman! Pauvre femme! 21c
poplar tree le peuplier 14c
poppy le pavot, le coquelicot 14b
porch le porche, la véranda 23a
pork le porc 24c
pornography la pornographie 44b
portable phone le téléphone portatif 18a
portable radio la radio portative 20b
porter le porteur 32a, 34, 35b
portion le morceau, la portion 3c
portrait le portrait 28b
Portugal le Portugal 30b
Portuguese *(nationality)* Portugais *(m)*, Portugaise *(f)* 30d; *(language)* le portugais 30d
position la position 3d
positive positif, positive *(adj, m, f)* 1d
possessive possessif, possessive *(adj, m, f)* 8a, 8f, 8n, 11e
post office le bureau de poste 19e
postage l'affranchissement *(m)* 19e; **meter postage** la vignette 19e
postage stamp le timbre-poste 19e
postal box la case postale, la boîte postale 19e
postal code le code postal 19e, 38b
postal rate le tarif 19e
postcard la carte postale 19e
postdate postdater *(v)* 26
posterior postérieur(e) *(adj)* 4e
postman *see* **letter carrier**
pot *(cooking)* le faitout 23d
potato la pomme de terre 14d, 24e
potato salad la salade de pommes de terre 24e
pour verser *(v)* 24o
powder la poudre 25f, 25h
power brake le servofrein 33e
power steering la servodirection 33e
power window la vitre à commande automatique 33e
practice a sport faire *(v)* du sport *(m)* 27b
praise louer *(v)* 17a
prawn la langoustine 24d
pray prier *(v)* 11d, 17a
prayer la prière 11d, 17a
preach prêcher *(v)* 17a
precious précieux *(adj, m)*, précieuse *(adj, f)* 25i
predicate l'attribut *(m)* 8a
preface la préface 28d
prefer préférer *(v)* 21b
pregnancy la grossesse 11c
pregnant enceinte *(adj, f)* 11c, 40a
premier showing la première représentation 28a
preposition la préposition 8a, 8g, 8l
prescription l'ordonnance *(f)* 25h, 40a
present le présent 4e; présent(e) *(adj, m, f)* 4e, 8a, 8n, 37f; actuel(le) *(adj, m, f)* 4e
present participle le participe présent 8a
presently actuellement *(adv)* 4e
president of a university le recteur, la femme recteur 37d
President of the French Republic le (la) Président(e) de la République Française 43
presumptuous présomptueux, présomptueuse *(adj, m, f)* 11e
pretentious prétentieux, prétentieuse *(adj, m, f)* 11e
pretzel le bretzel 24i

previous précédent(e) *(adj, m, f)* 4e
previously précédemment *(adv)* 4e
price le prix 24m, 25a; **rate** le tarif 35b
price tag l'étiquette *(f)* 25a
priest le prêtre 11d
primate le primate 15a
prime le nombre premier 1d
prime meridian le méridien origine 13e
prince le prince 43
princess la princesse 43
principal le directeur, la directrice 37d
print imprimer *(v)* 20a
print medium l'imprimerie *(f)* 20a
Print your name Ecrivez votre nom (Ecris ton nom) en lettres majuscules 11f
printed matter les imprimés *(m, pl)* 19e
printer ***(computer)*** l'imprimante *(f)* d'ordinateur 42b
printing la typographie 20a
prism le prisme 2a
prison la prison 41
prison sentence à prison 41
private school l'école *(f)* privée 37a
privilege le droit 41
problem le problème 1f, 22a, 37f
problem to solve le problème à résoudre *(v)* 1f, 37f
produce market le marché aux légumes et fruits 24n
product le produit 1f
Prof. le Prof., le professeur, la femme professeur 11f
profession la profession 11f, 27b, 38a, 38b
professional professionnel(le) *(adj, m, f)* 11f, 38a
professor le professeur, la femme professeur 11f, 37d, 38a
professor's office le cabinet du professeur 37c
program le programme 20b, 28e
program ***(computer)*** le programme d'un ordinateur 42b
programmer ***(person)*** le programmeur, la programmeuse 42b; *(machine)* le programmateur 42b
programming ***(computer)*** la programmation 42b
projector le projecteur 20b
promise la promesse, promettre *(v)* 17a
promissory note le billet à ordre 26
promoted reçu(e) *(adj, m, f)* 37f
pronoun le pronom 8a, 8h—8o
pronounce prononcer *(v)* 17a
pronunciation la prononciation 8a, 17a
propose proposer *(v)* 17a
prostitution la prostitution 44b
protect protéger *(v)* 39a
protest la protestation 43
Protestant Protestant(e) *(m, f)* 11d
Protestantism le Protestantisme 11d
proton le proton 13c, 42a
protractor le goniomètre 2b
proud fier, fière *(adj, m, f)* 11e
provided that pourvu que *(conj)* 8p
province la province 13e
prudent prudent(e) *(adj, m, f)* 11e
prune le pruneau 14d, 24f
P.S. P.-S., le post-scriptum 19c
psychiatrist le (la) psychiatre 38a
psychologist le (la) psychologue 38a
psychology la psychologie 37e
public garden le jardin public 36a
public notices les affiches *(f, pl)* publiques 36a
public parking le stationnement public 33c

public phone le téléphone public 36a
public prosecutor le procureur de la République 41
public washrooms les toilettes *(f, pl)* publiques 36a
publish publier *(v)* 20a
publisher l'éditeur *(m)* 20a
puck le palet, le puck 27b
pudding la crème 24h
puffed cheese le fromage soufflé 24h
pull tirer *(v)* 3e
pull out a tooth extraire *(v)* une dent 40b
pulse le pouls 40a
pumpernickel bread le pain noir 24i
pumpkin la citrouille, la courge 14e
punch *(hardware)* le poinçon 25b
punctuation la ponctuation 19c
pupil l'élève *(m/f)* 37d
purchase l'achat *(m)*, acheter *(v)* 25a
pure pur(e) *(adj)* 7b, 13d
purple le pourpre 7a
put mettre *(v)*, placer *(v)* 3e
put a room in order mettre *(v)* une pièce en ordre 23f
put down poser *(v)* 3e
put on (se) mettre *(v)* 25m
put on make-up se farder *(v)*, se maquiller *(v)* 12d
put on perfume se parfumer *(v)* 12d
put out (extinguish) éteindre *(v)* 39a
put someone on trial mettre *(v)* quelqu'un en procès 41
pyramid la pyramide 2a

Q

quantity la quantité 3c
quantum theory la théorie des quanta 42a
quart le quart de gallon *(m)* 3a
queen la reine 27a, 43; *(in chess)* la dame 27a
question la question 37f; **to ask a question** poser *(v)* une question 37f
question mark le point d'interrogation *(f)* 19c
queue up faire *(v)* la queue 15a
quiche la quiche 24g; **with cheese** au fromage; **with ham** au jambon 24g
quickly vite *(adv)* 3e
Quiet! Silence! 21c
Quite well! Très bien! *(adv)* 16a
quotation mark le guillemet 19c
quotient le quotient 1f

R

rabbi le rabbin 11d
rabbit le lapin 15a
race *(population)* la race 11d; *(sports)* la course 27b
racism le racisme 44b
radiation la radiation 44a
radiator le radiateur 33e
radio la radio, la T.S.F. 20b, 23d, 35c
radioactive waste les déchets *(m)* radioactifs 13c, 44a
radish le radis 14e
radius le rayon 2a
railroad le chemin de fer 34; **station** la gare 34
railway crossing le passage à niveau gardé 36a
rain la pluie; pleuvoir *(v)* 6a
raincoat l'imperméable *(m)* 25k
rainy weather un temps pluvieux 6a
raise *(someone)* élever *(v)* 11c
raise to a power élever *(v)* à une puissance 1e
raisin le raisin sec 14d, 24f
ramp la rampe 33c
random access memory *(computers)* la mémoire à accès sélectif 42b
rape le viol; violer 39b
rare rare *(adj)* 4e
rare *(cooked food)* saignant(e) *(adj, m, f)* 24b

rarely rarement *(adv)* 4e
raspberry la framboise 14d, 24f
rat le rat 15a
rate le tarif 35b
ratio la proportion 1e
rational rationnel(le) *(adj, m, f)* 1d
razor le rasoir 12d, 25f; le rasoir électrique 12d, 25f
razor blade la lame 12d
read lire *(v)* 20a, 37f
reader *(person)* le lecteur, la lectrice 20a
reading *(passage, selection)* la lecture 37f
real réel(le) *(adj, m, f)* 1d
Really? Vraiment? 21c
reap récolter *(v)*, cueillir *(v)* 14a
rear window *(vehicle)* la lunette arrière 33e
rear-view mirror *(vehicle)* le rétroviseur intérieur 33e
reason la raison 22a; raisonner *(v)* 22b
rebellious rebelle *(adj, m, f)* 11e
receipt l'acquit *(m)*, le récépissé, le reçu 26, 35b
receive recevoir *(v)* 19e
receiver (telephone handset) le combiné 18a
recent récent(e) *(adj)* 4e
recently récemment *(adv)* 4e
reception la réception 11c
reciprocal réciproque *(adj)* 1d
recommend recommander *(v)* 17a
record (recording) le disque 20b, 25j; **to record** enregistrer *(v)* 20b; **to play a record** passer *(v)* un disque 20b
record player le tourne-disque 20b, 37b
rectangle le rectangle 2a
rectum le rectum 40a
red le rouge 7a; **to become red with anger** devenir *(v)* rouge de colère 7a
red-haired roux, rousse *(adj, m, f)* 11a
reduced price le prix réduit 25a
referee l'arbitre *(m/f)* 27b
reference book l'ouvrage *(m)* de référence 20a, 25o
refined raffiné(e) *(adj, m, f)* 11e
reflect (think) réfléchir *(v)* 22b
reflexive pronoun le pronom personnel réfléchi 8a, 8k
reflexive verb le verbe pronominal 8a
reform la réforme 43
refrigerator le refrigérateur, le frigo 23d
region la région 13e
registered letter la lettre recommandée 19e
registration l'inscription *(f)* 37f; **fee** les droits *(m, pl)* d'inscription 37f
registration papers *(vehicle)* la carte grise 33b
regular régulier *(adj, m)*, régulière *(adj, f)* 4e, 8a
regularly régulièrement *(adv)* 4e
relate raconter *(v)* 17a
relative relatif *(adj,m)*, relative *(adj, f)* 8a
relatives les proches parents *(m)* 10a
relax se relaxer *(v)* 12b
relief le soulagement 21a; **sigh of relief** le soupir de soulagement 21a
religion la religion 11d
religious pieux, pieuse *(adj, m, f)* 11d
remain rester *(v)* 29b
remember se rappeler *(v)*, se souvenir *(v)* de 22b
remote control *(television)* la télécommande 20b
rent le loyer; louer *(v)* 23g
rented car l'auto *(f)* en location 33a
repair réparer *(v)* 25i
repeat répéter *(v)* 17a, 37f
repetition la répétition 17a
reply la réponse, répondre *(v)* 19e

report le compte rendu, faire *(v)* un compte rendu, faire *(v)* un rapport sur 17a
reporter le (la) journaliste (reporter) 20a
representative le (la) représentant(e) 43
reproach reprocher *(v)* 17a
reproduce reproduire *(v)* 14a
reproduction la reproduction 14a
reptile le reptile 15c
republic la république 43
request la demande, demander *(v)* 17a
rescue sauver *(v)* 39a
reservation la réservation 24m, 32a, 35b
reserve réserver *(v)* 35b
reserved réservé(e) *(adj, m, f)* 11e, 24m
residence le domicile 11f
resistant résistant(e) *(adj, m, f)* 13d
respiratory system le système respiratoire 40a
rest se reposer *(v)* 12b
restaurant le restaurant 24m; **informal restaurant** le bistro (bistrot) 24m
restless agité(e) *(adj, m, f)* 11e
restore restaurer *(v)* 23f
résumé le résumé 38b
retire se retirer *(v)*, être en retraite 38d
retirement (pension) la retraite, la pension 38d
return retourner *(v)* 3e, 29b; revenir *(v)* 29b
return an item rendre *(v)* 25a
return address l'adresse *(f)* de l'expéditeur 19e
review la révision; faire *(v)* une révision 37f
review *(on media)* la critique 20a
revolt la révolte 43
revolution la révolution 43
rhetoric la rhétorique 17a, 28d
rhetorical rhétorique *(adj, m, f)* 17a
rhetorical question la demande rhétorique 17a
rheumatism le rhumatisme 40a
rhinoceros le rhinocéros 15a
rhombus le rhombe 2a
rhythm le rythme 28c
ribbon le ruban 19d
rice le riz 24i
rice pudding la crème de riz 24h
rice with vegetables le riz aux légumes *(m, f, pl)* 24g
rich riche *(adj, m, f)* 11e
rifle le fusil 39b
right *(privilege)* le droit 41
right *(location)* droit(e) *(adj, m, f)* 3d; **to the right** à droite 3d, 33c
right *(angle)* droit(e) *(adj, m, f)* 2b
right *(accurate)* correct(e) *(adj, m, f)* 37f
right away tout de suite *(adv)* 4e
right prism le prisme droit 2a
right wing *(politics)* la droite 43
right-angled rectangle *(adj)* 2a
right to vote le suffrage universel 43
ring *(jewelry)* la bague, l'anneau *(m)* 25i
ring *(telephone)* sonner *(v)* 18b
ring finger l'annulaire *(m)* 12a
rinse (se) rinser *(v)* 40b
riot l'émeute *(f)* 43
ripe mûr(e) *(adj, m, f)* 14a
rise se lever *(v)* 3e
rite le rite 11d
river le fleuve 13b, 36b
road le chemin 33c
road map la carte routière 33b
roar rugir *(v)* 15a

roast rôti(e) *(adj, m, f)* 24b
roast beef le rosbif 24g
rob voler *(v)* 39b
robber le voleur, la voleuse 39b
robbery le vol 39b
robot le robot 42a
robust robuste *(adj)* 13d
rock la roche, le rocher 13b
rock music la musique rock 25j
roll *(of bread)* le petit pain chapelet 24i
roll *(of film)* le rouleau de film (pellicule), la pellicule 25d
roll *(sweet)* la brioche 24i
roller skate patiner *(v)* à roulettes *(f, pl)* 27b
Roman romain(e) *(adj, m, f)* 1d
romance novel le roman d'amour 20a, 25o
romantic romantique *(adj, m, f)* 11e
Rome Rome 30c
roof le toit 23a, 33e
rook *(chess)* la tour 27a
room la pièce 23b; la chambre 35b
room with bath la chambre avec bain 35b
room with two beds la chambre à deux lits 35b
rooster le coq 15b
root la racine 14a, 40b
rope la corde 27b, 36b; **ropes** (boxing) les cordes *(f, pl)* 27b
rose la rose 14b
rosemary le romarin 14e, 24j
rotten pourri(e) *(adj, m, f)* 14a
rough brut, brute *(adj, m, f)* 11e; rude *(adj)* 13d
rough copy, draft la copie brute, la copie en état brut 37f
round bread le pain rond 24i
round-trip ticket le billet d'aller et retour 30a
row le rang 28a
ruby le rubis 25i
rude rude *(adj, m, f)*, grossier, grossière *(adj, m, f)* 11e
rug le tapis 23c; **wall-to-wall carpeting** la moquette 23c
ruler la règle 2b, 19d, 37b, 38c
rumor le bruit 17a
run courir *(v)* 3e, 12b, 27b
Run for your life! Sauve qui peut! 39b
run into someone rencontrer *(v)* quelqu'un 16b
runway *(airplane)* la piste 32c
rush hours les heures *(f, pl)* d'affluence 33c
rusk *(Melba toast)* la biscotte 24i
Russia la Russie 30b
Russian *(nationality)* Russe *(m/f)* 30d; *(language)* le russe 30d
rye and wheat bread le pain de campagne 24i
rye bread le pain au seigle 24i

S

saber *(fencing)* le sabre d'escrime *(f)* 27b
sad triste *(adj, m, f)* 11e, 21a
sadness la tristesse 11e, 21a
safe *(for valuables)* le coffre-fort 26
safety deposit box le coffre de sécurité 26
Sagittarius le Sagittaire 5d
salad la salade 24g
salamander la salamandre 15c
salami le salami 24c
salary le salaire 26, 38d
sale la vente 25a; **for sale** à vendre *(v)* 25a; **on sale** en vente *(f)* 25a
salmon le saumon 24d
salt le sel 13c, 24j
salty salé(e) *(adj, m, f)* 24p

salutation ***(of a letter)*** la formule (la salutation) initiale 19c
sand le sable 13b
sandwich le sandwich 24g; **with cheese** au fromage; **with ham** au jambon 24g
sapphire le saphir 25i
sarcasm le sarcasme 11e
sarcastic sarcastique *(adj, m, f)* 11e
sardine la sardine 15c, 24d
satellite le satellite 13a, 42a
satisfaction la satisfaction 21a
satisfied satisfait(e) *(adj, m, f)* 21a
Saturday le samedi 5a
Saturn Saturne *(m)* 13a
saucer la soucoupe 23d, 24l
sausage la saucisse 24c
save économiser *(v)*, épargner *(v)* 26
savings l'épargne *(f)* 26
saw ***(hardware)*** la scie 25b
saxophone le saxophone 28c
say dire *(v)* 17a
scalene scalène *(adj)* 2a
scarf l'écharpe *(f)* 25k
scene la scène 28e
scenery ***(theater)*** la mise en scène 28e
schedule l'horaire *(m)* 4e, 34
school l'école *(f)* 37f
school yard la cour 37c
school year l'année *(f)* scolaire 5b
schoolbag le sac d'écolier 37b
schoolmate le (la) camarade d'école 37d
science fiction la science-fiction 20a, 25o
sciences les sciences *(f, pl)* 37e
scientific research la recherche scientifique 42a
scientist le (la) scientifique 38a
scissors les ciseaux *(m, pl)* 12d, 19d, 38c, 39c
scooter le scooter 33a
score ***(sports)*** la marque 27b
Scorpio le Scorpion 5d
scorpion le scorpion 15d
screen l'écran *(m)* 25d, 28a
screen ***(computer)*** l'écran de visualisation 42b
screw la vis 25b
screwdriver le tournevis 25b
sculpt sculpter *(v)* 28b
sculptor le sculpteur 28b
sculptress la femme sculpteur 28b
sculpture la sculpture 28b
sea la mer 6a, 13b, 36b
seafood les fruits de mer 24d
seagull la mouette 15b
seal ***(animal)*** le phoque 15c
season la saison 5c
seat la place 28a, 32c, 34; le siège 28a, 33e
seat ***(bicycle)*** la selle 33a
seat belt la ceinture 32c, 33e
secant la sécante 2b
second deuxième, second(e) *(adj, m, f)* 1b, 8a; *(time)* la seconde 3a, 4c
secretary le (la) secrétaire 37d, 38a, 40a
sedative le sédatif 40a
seduction la séduction 11e
seductive séduisant(e) *(adj, m, f)* 11e
see voir *(v)* 12c, 30a
see life in the pink voir la vie en rose 7a
See you! Salut! 16a
See you later! A tout à l'heure! 16a
See you soon! A bientôt! 16a
See you Sunday! A dimanche! 16a
seed la semence; semer *(v)* 14a
segment ***(line)*** la ligne segmentée 2b
self-service le self-service 33c
self-sufficient indépendant(e) *(adj, m, f)* 11e

sell vendre *(v)* 23f, 25a
semicolon le point virgule 19c
Senate le Sénat 43
senator le sénateur, la femme sénateur 43
send envoyer *(v)*, expédier *(v)* 3e, 19e
sender le destinateur, l'expéditeur 19c, 19e
sense le sens; sentir *(v)* 12c
sense of humor le sens de l'humour 11e
sensitive sensible *(adj, m, f)* 11e
sentence *(grammar)* la phrase 8a, 8n, 19c
sentence *(law)* le jugement 41
sentimental sentimental(e) *(adj, m, f)* 11e
separate (se) séparer *(v)* 11c
separated séparé(e) *(adj, m, f)* 11c
separation la séparation 11c
September le septembre 5b
series *(television)* la série d'émissions 20b
serious sérieux *(adj, m)*, sérieuse *(f)* 11e
serious accident l'accident *(m)* grave 39c
sermon le sermon 17a
serve servir *(v)* 24o
serve a prison sentence subir *(v)* une condamnation 41
service le service 24m; **services** les services 35b
set *(numbers)* l'ensemble *(m)* 1f
set of drums *(music)* la batterie 28c
set the table mettre *(v)* le couvert 23f; mettre la table 24o
seven sept 1a
seventeen dix-sept 1a
seventh septième 1b
seventy soixante-dix 1a
several plusieurs *(adj/adv)* 3c
sew coudre *(v)* 25g
sewing machine la machine à coudre 23d
sex le sexe 11a, 38b
shade l'ombre *(f)* 6a
shadow l'ombre *(f)* 6a
shaft *(of motor)* l'arbre-moteur *(m)*, l'arbre de couche 33e
shake hands serrer *(v)* la main à quelqu'un, donner *(v)* la main à quelqu'un 16a
shame la honte 21a
shampoo le shampooing 12d, 25f, 35c
shave *(oneself)* (se) raser *(v)* 12d
shaving cream la crème à raser 25f
she elle 8h
shed light on tirer *(v)* quelque chose au clair 13a
sheep le mouton 15a
sheet *(bed)* le drap 23d; les draps 35c
sheet *(of paper)* la feuille de papier 25c
shelf l'étagère *(f)* 23a
shellfish les crustacés *(m, pl)* 24d
sherbet le sorbet 24g
shirt la chemise 25k
shock le choc 39c
shoe la chaussure 25n
shoe repair store la cordonnerie 25n
shoe store le magazin de chaussures 25n
shoelace le lacet 25n
shoot tirer *(v)* 39b
shop la boutique 25a; **to shop** faire *(v)* des achats, faire des emplettes, faire du shopping 25a
shop for food acheter *(v)* des provisions 24o
shop window la vitrine 25a
shopping bag le sac à provisions 23d
short *(height)* petit(e) *(adj, m, f)* 3c, 11a, 25l
short *(thing)* court(e) *(adj, m, f)* 3b, 37f
short story le conte, la nouvelle 20a, 28d
shorten *(clothing)* faire *(v)*

accourcir 25m
short-term à court terme 4e
shoulder l'épaule *(f)* 12a
shout le cri; crier *(v)* 17a, 39a
shovel la pelle 25b
show *(entertainment)* le spectacle 20b, 28c
shower la douche 23a, 35c
shrewd rusé(e) *(adj, m, f)* 11e
shrewdness la ruse 11e
shrimp la crevette 24d
Shut up! Taisez-vous! *(pol);* Tais-toi! *(fam)* 17a, 21c; se taire *(v)* 17a
shy timide *(adj, m, f)* 11e
sick malade *(adj)* 11a, 40a
sickness la maladie 11a, 40a
side *(angle)* côté *(adj)* 2b
side-view mirror *(vehicle)* le rétroviseur extérieur 33e
sidewalk le trottoir 36a
sigh of relief le soupir de soulagement *(m)* 21a
sight la vision 12c, 40a; la vue 12c
sign *(one's name)* signer *(v)* 11f, 19c, 26
signal le signal 33c
signature la signature 11f, 19c, 26, 38b
signs of the zodiac les signes *(m)* du zodiaque 5d
silence le silence 17a
silent silencieux *(adj, m),* silencieuse *(adj, f)* 17a; **to be silent** se taire *(v)* 17a
silk la soie, en soie 13c, 25l
silkworm le ver à soie 15d
silly bête *(adj, m, f)* 11e
silver l'argent *(m)* 13c, 25i
silver *(color)* argenté *(m)* 7a
silver anniversary les noces *(f)* d'argent 11c
simple simple *(adj, m, f)* 11e, 22a
simultaneous simultané(e) *(adj)* 4e
simultaneously simultanément *(adv)* 4e
since depuis *(prep)* 4e; comme *(conj)* 8p; depuis que *(conj)* 8p
since Monday depuis lundi 4e
since yesterday depuis hier 4e
sincere sincère *(adj, m, f)* 11e
sincerity la sincérité 11e
sine la sinus 2b
sing chanter *(v)* 28c
singer le chanteur, la chanteuse 25j, 28c
single *(unmarried)* célibataire 38b
single room une chambre à un lit 35b
singular le singulier, singulier *(adj, m),* singulière *(adj, f)* 8a
sink *(kitchen)* l'évier *(m)* 23a; *(bathroom)* le lavabo 23a, 35c
siren la sirène 39a
sister la soeur 10a
sister-in-law la belle-soeur 10a
sit down s'asseoir *(v)* 3e, 32c
six six 1a
sixteen seize 1a
sixth sixième 1b
sixty soixante 1a; **about sixty** une soixantaine 1c
size la mesure, la taille 3b, 25k; (of shoe) la pointure 25n
skate patiner *(v)* 27b; **(ice skate)** le patin à glace 27b
ski faire *(v)* du ski, skier *(v)* 27b
ski resort la station de ski 36b
skier le skieur, la skieuse 27b
skiing le ski 27b, 36b
skimmed milk le lait écrémé 24h
skin la peau 12a
skinny maigre *(adj)* 11a
skip a class sauter *(v)* une classe 37f
skip school faire *(v)* l'école buissonnière 37f

skirt la jupe 25k
sky le ciel 6a, 13b
sleep dormir *(v)* 12b
sleeping bag le sac de couchage 36b
sleeve la manche 25g
slice la tranche 24i; trancher *(v)* 24o
slice of cream cake la tranche de gâteau à la crème 24i
slide la diapositive 20b, 25d
slide projector le projecteur pour diapositives *(f, pl)* 20b, 37b
sliding door la porte coulissante 35c
slim maigre *(adj)* 11a
slip *(undergarment)* la combinaison, le fond de robe, le jupon 25k
slipper le chausson, la pantoufle 25n
Slippery When Wet Chaussée glissante 33d
sloppy désorganisé(e) *(adj, m, f)* 11e
slot *(for tokens)* la fente 18a
slow lent(e) *(adj)* 3e, 4e
slow down ralentir *(v)* 33c
slowly lentement *(adv)* 3e, 4e
small *(size)* petit(e) *(adj, m, f)* 3c, 11a, 25l
small bill *(banknote, currency)* le petit billet 26
small letter *(lower case letter)* la lettre minuscule 19c
small round loaf of bread la petite boule 24i
smart intelligent(e) *(adj, m, f)* 11e
smash *(auto collision)* la collision 39c
smell l'odeur *(f)* 12c; la senteur 12c; sentir *(v)* 12c
smile le sourire; sourire *(v)* 11e, 21a; **to force an uneasy smile** sourire *(v)* jaune 7a
smock la blouse 25k
smoke la fumée 13c, 39a
smoke shop le bureau de tabac 25e
smoking compartment fumeurs 34
smooth lisse *(adj)* 13d
snack le casse-croûte, le goûter 24a
snack bar le buffet 24m
snails les escargots *(m, pl)* 24g
snake le serpent 15c
sneeze l'éternuement; éternuer *(v)* 40a
snob *(n/adj, m, f)* 11e
snobbish hautain(e) *(adj, m, f)* 11e
snow la neige; neiger *(v)* 6a
snow goggles les lunettes *(f, pl)* de glacier *(m)* 27b
So? Et alors? 9
So, so! Comme-ci, comme-ça! *(adv)* 16a
so that afin que *(conj),* pour que *(conj)* 8p
soap le savon 12d, 25f, 35c
soap opera *(radio and television)* le mélo 20b
soap powder le savon en poudre 25g
soccer le foot 27b; **to play soccer** jouer *(v)* au foot 27b
soccer ball le ballon 27b
Social Welfare l'Assistance *(f)* sociale 43
socialism le socialisme 43
socialist le (la) socialiste 43
sociology la sociologie 37e
sock (clothing) la chaussette 25n
sodium le sodium 13c
sodium bicarbonate le bicarbonate de soude 25h
sodium citrate le citrate de soude 25h
sofa le canapé 23c
soft mou *(adj, m),* doux *(adj, m)* 13d
soft-boiled egg l'oeuf *(m)* à la coque 24h
soft drink la gazeuse 24k
software *(computers)* le logiciel, le software 42b
solar cell la cellule solaire 44a
solar eclipse l'éclipse *(f)*

solaire 13a
solar energy l'énergie *(f)* solaire 13c, 44a
solar system le système solaire 13a
sole *(fish)* la sole 15c, 24d
solid le solide 13c
solid figures les figures *(f)* solides 2a
solstice le solstice 5c
soluble soluble *(adj)* 13d
solution la solution 1f
solve résoudre *(v)* 1f
solve a problem résoudre *(v)* un problème 1f, 37f
some quelque(s) *(adj)* 3c; *see also* **Partitive** 8d
some of it (them) en *(pron)* 3c, 8o
some (people) des gens 8o
someone quelqu'un *(m)*, quelqu'une *(f) (pron)* 8o
Someone assaulted me! On m'a assailli(e)! 39b
Someone robbed me! On m'a volé(e)! 39b
something quelque chose *(pron)* 8o
something to declare quelque chose à déclarer 31
somewhere quelque part *(adv)* 3d
son le fils 10a
son-in-law le gendre 10a
song la chanson 25j, 28c
soon bientôt *(adv)* 4e
sooner or later tôt ou tard 4e
sore back le mal au dos 40a
sore throat le mal de gorge 40a
sore/twisted neck le mal au cou, le torticolis 40a
sorrow le chagrin 21a
soul l'âme *(f)* 11d
sound le son 12c
soundtrack la piste sonore 28a
soup la soupe, le potage 24g; **of the day** du jour 24g
sour aigre *(adj, m, f)* 24p
south le sud 3d; **to the south** au sud 3d
South America l'Amérique *(f)* du Sud 30b
South Pole le Pôle Sud 13e
southern méridional(e) *(adj)* 3d
space l'espace *(m)* 2b, 13a
space bar *(of a typewriter)* la barre d'espacement 19d
space shuttle la navette spatiale 42a
spacecraft le vaisseau spatial 42a
spades *(cards)* la pique 27a
Spain l'Espagne *(f)* 30b
Spanish *(nationality)* Espagnol *(m)*, Espagnole *(f)* 30d; *(language)* l'espagnol *(m)* 30d
spark l'étincelle *(f)* 39a
spark plug *(vehicle)* la bougie 33e
sparrow le moineau 15b
speak parler *(v)* 17a
speak badly of someone diffamer *(v)* quelqu'un 17a
speaker *(audio apparatus)* la caisse acoustique 20b
special delivery l'expédition express 19e
specialist le (la) spécialiste 40a
species l'espèce *(f)* 14a
speech le discours 17a
speed la vélocité 3a; la vitesse 33c
Speed Limit Vitesse maximum 33d
speed up accélérer *(v)* 33c
speedometer le compteur de vitesse 33e
spelling l'orthographe *(f)* 19c
spend *(money)* dépenser *(v)* 4e, 25a
spend *(time)* passer *(v)* 4e
sphere la sphère 2a
spice l'épice *(f)* 24j
spicy épicé(e) *(adj, m, f)* 24p
spider l'araignée *(f)* 15d
spinach l'épinard *(m)* 14e, 24e
spirit l'esprit *(m)* 11d
spiritual spirituel(le) *(adj, m, f)* 11d

splint l'éclisse *(f)* 39c
spoke *(bicycle)* le rayon 33a
spoon la cuiller (la cuillère) 23d, 24l
sporadic sporadique *(adj)* 4e
sporadically sporadiquement *(adv)* 4e
sport le sport 27b
sports car la voiture de sport 33a
sports fan l'enthousiaste *(m/f)* du sport, le fan, le (la) fanatique du sport 27b
spot *(stain)* la tache 25g
spouse l'époux, l'épouse 11c
spring *(metal coil)* le ressort 25i
spring *(season)* le printemps 5c
square le square 2a, 11f; la place 11f, 36a; le carré 2a
square bracket le crochet 19c
square centimeter le centimètre carré 3a
square kilometer le kilomètre carré 3a
square meter le mètre carré 3a
square millimeter le millimètre carré 3a
square root la racine au carré 1e
squared au carré 1e
squid le calmar 24d
stable stable *(adj, m, f)* 13d
stadium le stade 27b
stage *(theater)* la scène 28e
stain la tache 25g
stainless steel l'acier *(m)* inoxydable 13c
stairs l'escalier 23a, 35b
stamp *(postage)* le timbre-poste 19e, 27a
stamp collecting la collection de timbres 27a
stand in line faire *(v)* la queue 15a
staple l'agrafe *(f)* 19d, 25c, 38c
stapler l'agrafeuse *(f)* 19d, 25c, 38c
star l'étoile *(f)* 6a, 13a
starch l'amidon *(m)* 25g
start *(car)* mettre *(v)* en marche 33c
state l'état *(m)* 13e, 43
state (to make a statement) affirmer *(v)* 17a
statement l'affirmation *(f)* 17a
station *(radio dial)* l'indicatif *(m)* d'appel 20b
station *(train, bus, subway)* la gare, la station 34
stationery store la papeterie 25c
statistical statistique *(adj)* 1f
statistics la statistique 1f, 37e
steak le bifteck 24g
steal dérober *(v)*, voler *(v)* 39b
steel l'acier *(m)* 13c
steering wheel le volant 33e
stem la tige 14a
stereo stéréo(phonique) *(adj)* 20b
stethoscope le stéthoscope 40a
stiff (twisted) neck le torticolis 40a
still (as yet) encore *(adv)*, toujours *(adv)* 4e
stingy avare *(adj, m, f)* 11e; pingre *(adj, m, f)* 11e
stitch le point 25g
stock (share) l'action*(f)* 26
stock market / exchange la Bourse 26
stocking le bas 25n
stomach l'estomac *(m)* 12a, 40a
stone la pierre 13b
stool *(furniture)* le tabouret 23c
stop arrêter *(v)* 3e
Stop Arrêt 33d, 34
stop oneself s'arrêter *(v)* 3e
Stop thief! Au voleur! 39b
store le magasin 25a
store clerk l'employé(e) *(m/f)* 25a

store hours les heures *(f, pl)* 25a
store window la vitrine 25a
stork la cigogne 15b
storm la tempête 6a
story *(literature)* le conte, l'histoire*(f)* 17a
stove la cuisinière électrique (à gaz) 23d
straight *(angle)* droit *(adj)* 2b
straight ahead tout droit *(adv)* 36c
straight line la ligne droite 2b
strawberry la fraise 14d, 24f
strawberry ice cream la glace aux fraises 24h
street la rue 11f, 36a, 38b
street corner le coin de la rue 33c
street sign la plaque de nom de rue 36a
streetcar le tram, le tramway 33a
strength la force 11a
strike *(labor)* la grève 43
string la ficelle 19d, 25c; *(of a musical instrument)* la corde 28c
string bean le haricot vert 14e, 24e
stringed instruments les instruments *(m, pl)* à cordes *(f)* 28c
striped rayé(e) *(adj, m, f)* 25l
strong fort(e) *(adj)* 11a, 11e, 13d, 40a
structure la structure 13c
stubborn têtu(e) *(adj, m, f)* 11e
student l'étudiant(e) *(m/f)* 37d
study étudier *(v)* 22b, 37f
stuff l'étoffe *(f)*, le tissu 13c
stuffed egg l'oeuf *(m)* dur farci 24h
stupid stupide *(adj, m, f)* 11e
style *(fashion)* la mode, à la mode, au dernier cri 25k, 25l; *(writing)* le style 28d
subject le sujet 8a, 8g
subject *(learning matter)* la matière 37e
subjunctive subjonctif *(adj, m)*, subjonctive *(adj, f)* 8a
subordinate subordonné(e) *(adj, m, f)* 8a
substance la substance 13c
subtract soustraire *(v)* 1e
subtraction la soustraction 1e
suburbs la banlieue, les environs *(m, pl)* 30a
subway le métro(politain) 34
subway station la station de métro 34
sue citer *(v)* dans un procès-verbal 41
suffer souffrir *(v)* 40a
suffice suffire *(v)* 3c
sufficient suffisant(e) *(adj)* 3c
sugar le sucre 24j
suggest suggérer *(v)* 17a
suit *(clothing)* le complet, le costume 25k
suitcase la valise 31
sulphur le soufre, le sulfure 13c
sulphuric acid l'acide *(m)* sulfurique 13c
sum la somme 1f
sum up sommer *(v)* 1f
summarize résumer *(v)*, faire un résumé 17a
summary le sommaire, le résumé 17a
summer l'été *(m)* 5c
summons la citation 41
sun le soleil 5c, 6a, 13a
Sunday le dimanche 5a
sunlight la lumière solaire 13a
sunray le rayon de soleil *(m)* 13a
sunrise le lever du soleil 4a
sunset le coucher du soleil 4a
superintendent *(of apartment building)* le (la) concierge 23g
supermarket le supermarché 24n

superstitious superstitieux, superstitieuse *(adj, m, f)* 11e
supplementary supplémentaire *(adj)* 2b
suppository le suppositoire 40a
surgeon le chirurgien, la femme chirurgien 38a, 40a
surgery la chirurgie 40a
surname le nom de famille *(f)* 11f, 38b
surprise la surprise; surprendre *(v)* 21a
surprised surpris(e) *(adj, m, f)* 21a
swallow (bird) l'hirondelle 15b
swan le cygne 15b
swear ***(e.g., in court)*** jurer *(v)* 17a; *(e.g., profanity)* dire *(v)* des jurons 17a
swear word le juron 17a
sweater le pull-over, le sweater, le tricot 25k
Sweden la Suède 30b
Swedish ***(nationality)*** Suédois *(m),* Suédoise *(f)* 30d; *(language)* le suédois 30d
sweet doux *(adj, m),* douce *(f)* 11e, 24p
swim nager *(v)* 27b
swimming la natation 27b
swimming pool la piscine 27b, 35b
Swiss ***(nationality)*** Suisse *(m/f)* 30d
switch ***(light)*** l'interrupteur *(m)* 23a, 35c
switchblade le couteau pliant, le couteau de poche 39b
switchboard telephone operator le (la) standardiste 18b
Switzerland la Suisse 30b
swollen gonflé(e) *(adj, m, f)* 40a
swordfish l'espadon *(m)* 15c
symbol le symbole 1f, 17a
sympathetic compatissant(e) *(adj, m, f)* 21a
sympathy la compassion 21a
symphony la symphonie 28c
synagogue la synagogue 11d
synthesizer le synthétiseur 28c
synthetic synthétique *(adj, m, f)* 13d
syringe la seringue 40a
syrup le sirop 25h

T

T-shirt le T-shirt 25k
tab ***(of a typewriter)*** le tabulateur 19d
table la table 23c, 24l, 35c
tablecloth la nappe 23d, 24l
tablet ***(medication)*** le comprimé 25h, 40a
tableware les ustensiles *(m, pl)* à (de) table 23d, 24l; le couvert 24l
tack la punaise 37b, 38c
tail la queue 15a
tailor le tailleur, la couturière 38a
tailored suit ***(woman's)*** le costume tailleur 25k
take prendre *(v)* 25a, 34
take a holiday avoir *(v)* congé *(m)* 36b
take a picture (photo) prendre *(v)* une photo 25d
take a subject/course suivre *(v)* un cours 37f
take a trip faire *(v)* un voyage 30a
take a walk faire *(v)* une promenade 3e
take an exam passer *(v)* un examen 37f
take an excursion faire *(v)* une excursion 36a
take attendance faire *(v)* l'appel 37f
take back ***(return an item)*** rendre (v) 25a
take drugs prendre *(v)* de la drogue, se droguer *(v)* 44b
take notes prendre *(v)* des notes 37f
take off ***(remove)*** enlever *(v)* 25m; *(airplane)* le décollage 32c; décoller (v) 32c
take one's temperature mesurer *(v)* la fièvre 40a

take-out ***(food)*** à emporter *(v)* 24m, 24o
take place avoir lieu 4e
talcum powder le talc 25f
talented artistique *(adj)* 11e
talk parler *(v)* 17a; le discours 17a
tall grand(e) *(adj)* 3b, 11a; haut(e) *(adj)* 3b
tangent la tangente 2a, 2b
tanker ***(truck)*** le camion-citerne 33a
tape ***(magnetic)*** la bande magnétique 20b, 25j
tape recorder le magnétophone 20b, 37b
tapioca pudding le tapioca au lait 24h
tariff le tarif 31
tarot le tarot 27a
tartlet la tartelette 24i
taste goûter *(v)* 12c
tasty savoureux *(adj, m)*, savoureuse *(f)* 24p
Taurus le Taureau 5d
taxi le taxi 33a
tea le thé 24k
teach enseigner *(v)* 37f
teacher l'enseignant(e) *(m/f)* 37d; le professeur, la femme professeur 38a
teacher's desk le bureau, la chaire 37b
team l'équipe *(f)* 27b
teapot la théière 23d
tears ***(weeping)*** les larmes *(f, pl)* 21a
teaspoon la cuiller à café 23d, 24l
technical book le livre de technologie 25o
technical school l'institut *(m)* d'enseignement technique 37a
technician le technicien, la technicienne 37d
technology la technologie 42a
teenager adolescent(e) *(n, adj)* 11b
telecommunication la télécommunication 18a, 42a
telecommunications satellite le satellite de télécommunications 18a
teleconferencing la télé-audio-conférence 42a
telephone le téléphone, téléphoner *(v)* 18a, 18b, 23e, 35c, 38c
telephone credit card la télécarte 18a
telephone number le numéro de téléphone *(m)* 11f, 18b, 38b
telephone operator le (la) téléphoniste 18b
telephone set l'appareil *(m)* téléphonique 18a
telephone switchboard operator le (la) standardiste 18b
telephone ***see also*** **phone**
television la télévision 20b
television set le téléviseur 20b, 23d, 35c
telex le TELEX 18a, 18b
telex machine le transmetteur TELEX 18a; le télex, l'ordinateur-télex *(m)* 42a
tell dire *(v)* 17a
tell a joke dire (raconter) *(v)* une plaisanterie 17a
tell a story raconter *(v)* une histoire, conter 17a
teller (cashier) le caissier, la caissière 26
teller's window le guichet 26
telly (TV) la télé 20b
temperature la température 6c; *(fever)* la fièvre 40a
template le gabarit 2b
temple le temple 11d, 36a
temporarily temporairement *(adv)* 4e
temporary temporaire *(adj)* 4e
ten dix la; **about ten** une dizaine 1c
tenant le (la) locataire 23g
tennis ***(to play)*** jouer *(v)* au tennis 27b; *(the sport)* le tennis 27b
tennis racket la raquette 27b
tense ***(verb)*** le temps 8a, 8n
tent la tente de camping 36b
tenth dixième 1b

terminal le terminal 32a, 42b
termite le termite 15d
terrace la terrasse 23a
territory le territoire 13e
tetrahedron le tétraèdre 2a
test l'épreuve *(f)* 37f
text le texte 19c, 20a
textbook le livre de classe *(f)*, le livre d'étude *(f)* 25o, le livre de cours 37b
textile le textile 13c
Thailand la Thaïlande 30b
thank remercier *(v)* 17a, 21a
Thank goodness! Grâce à Dieu! 21c
Thank you! Merci! 16c
thankful reconnaissant(e) *(adj, m, f)* 21a
thankfulness la gratitude, la reconnaissance 21a
that ce *(m, s)*, cet *(m, s)*, cette *(f, s)* 8e
that is to say . . . c'est-à-dire . . . 44c
the le *(m, s)*, la *(f, s)*, l' *(m/f, s)*, les *(m/f, pl)* 8b
the one celui *(m)*, celle *(f)* 8m
the ones ceux *(m)*, celles *(f)* 8m
theater le théâtre 28e
their leur *(m/f, s)*, leurs *(m/f, pl)* 8f
them les 8i; eux *(m)*, elles *(f)* 8l
theme le thème 28d
themselves se 8k
then alors *(adv)*, lors *(adv)* 4e
theory of relativity la théorie de la relativité 42a
there là *(adv)* 3d, 36c
There's lightning! Il fait des éclairs! 6a
therefore donc *(conj)* 8p, 44c
thermal energy l'énergie *(f)* thermique 44a
thermometer le thermomètre 6c, 25h, 40a
thermostat le thermostat 6c, 35c
these ces *(m/f, pl)* 8e
thesis la thèse 37f
they ils *(m)*, elles *(f)* 8h; eux *(m)*, elles *(f)* 8l
thick épais *(adj, m)*, épaisse *(f)* 3b
thick soup le potage 24g
thief le voleur, la voleuse 39b
thigh la cuisse 12a
thin maigre *(adj)* 3b, 11a
think penser *(v)* 22b
third troisième *(adj, m, f)* 1b, 8a
Third World le Tiers Monde 43
thirst la soif 12b
thirteen treize 1a
thirteenth treizième 1b
thirty trente la; **about thirty** une trentaine 1c
thirty-one trente et un 1a
thirty-two trente-deux 1a
this ce *(m, s)*, cet *(m, s)*, cette *(f, s)* 8e
this afternoon cet *(adj, m)* après-midi *(m)* 4a
this evening ce *(adj, m)* soir *(m)* 4a
This is . . . (+ *name in telephone call*) Ici . . . 18b
This looks bad on me. Ceci ne me va pas bien. 25l
This looks nice on me. Ceci me va bien. 25l
this morning ce *(adj, m)* matin *(m)* 4a
this night cette nuit 4a
thorn l'épine *(f)* 14b
those ces *(m/f, pl)* 8e
thought la pensée 22a
thousandth millième 1b
threat la menace 17a
threaten menacer *(v)* 17a
three trois 1a
three-dimensional space l'espace *(m)* tridimensionnel 13a
three hundred trois cents 1a
three million trois millions 1a
three thousand trois mille 1a

three-year-old de trois ans 11b
throat la gorge 12a, 40a
through à travers, par *(prep)* 3d, 36c
throw lancer *(v)* 27b
throw up (vomit) rendre *(v)* 40a
thumb le pouce 12a
thunder le tonnerre 6a; faire *(v)* un bruit de tonnerre 6a
Thursday le jeudi 5a
tick *(insect)* la tique 15d
ticket le billet, le ticket 27b, 30a, 32a, 34
ticket *(traffic fine)* la contravention 33c
ticket cancelling machine le composteur de billets 34
ticket counter la délivrance des billets 34
ticket window le guichet 32a
tide la marée 13b
tie *(necktie)* la cravate 25k
tie *(score in sports)* le match nul 27b
tiger le tigre 15a
tight serré(e) *(adj, m, f)* 25l
tighten faire *(v)* serrer *(v)* 25m
time *(hour)* l'heure *(f)*; **every time** la fois; *(in general)* le temps 4a
Time flies! Le temps fuit! 4a
timetable *(schedule)* l'horaire 4e, 34
timpani la timbale 28c
tincture of iodine la teinture d'iode 25h, 39c
tint teindre *(v)*, la teinte 7c
tip le pourboire 24m; donner *(v)* un pourboire 24m
tire *(of wheel)* le pneu(matique) 33a, 33e
tissue le mouchoir de papier 25h
title le titre 11f, 16b, 20a
to à *(prep)* 3d, 8g
to go + à + city; to go to Paris aller *(v)* à Paris 30c
to go + prep. + country; to go to France aller *(v)* en France 30c
to her lui 8j
to him lui 8j
to me me 8j
to someone's place chez quelqu'un 3d
to sum up en somme 17b
to the east à l'est 36c
to the fourth power à la quatrième puissance 1e
to the left à gauche 3d, 33c, 36c
to the north au nord 36c
to the nth power à la puissance n 1e
to the power of à la puissance de 1e
to the right à droite 3d, 33c, 36c
to the south au sud 36c
to the west à l'ouest 36c
to them leur 8j
to this day jusqu'à ce jour *(adv)* 4e
to us nous 8j
To whom it may concern . . . A qui de droit 19a
to you te *(s, fam)*, vous *(pl)* 8j
toad le crapaud 15c
toast *(in honor of someone)* porter *(v)* un toast 17a
toast griller *(v)* 24o; **Melba toast** la biscotte 24i
toaster le grille-pain 23d
tobacco le tabac 25e
tobacconist le buraliste 25e
today aujourd'hui *(adv)* 4a
toe l'orteil *(m)* 12a
toilet les toilettes *(f, pl)* 32c, 35c; W.C. 35c, 37c
toilet paper le papier hygiénique 35c
token *(coin)* le jeton 18a; **slot for tokens** la fente 18a
tolerance la tolérance 21a
tolerate tolérer *(v)* 21a
Toll Péage 33d
toll booth le poste de péage 33c

tomato la tomate 14e, 24e
tomorrow demain *(adv)* 4a
tomorrow afternoon demain après-midi *(m)* 4a
tomorrow evening demain soir *(m)* 4a
tomorrow morning demain matin *(m)* 4a
tomorrow night demain pendant la nuit 4a; demain soir *(m)* 4a
tongue la langue 12a, 40b
tonight ce soir *(evening),* cette nuit *(actual night)* 4a
tonsils les amygdales *(f, pl)* 40a
Too bad! Dommage! 21b
too much trop *(adv)* 3c
tool l'outil *(m)* 25b
tools les outils *(m, pl)* 23d, 33c
tooth la dent 12a, 40b
tooth decay la carie dentaire 40b
toothache le mal aux dents 40b
toothbrush la brosse à dents *(f, pl)* 12d, 25h, 40b
toothpaste la pâte dentifrice 12d, 25h; le dentifrice 40b
toothpick le cure-dent 24l
top le sommet 3d, **at** (to) **the top** au sommet 3d
topaz la topaze 25i
tornado la tornade 6a
touch le toucher 12c; toucher *(v)* 12c
tour ***(travel)*** le voyage organisé 30a
tour bus l'autocar *(m)* de tourisme (d'excursion) 30a
tour guide le (la) guide 30a
tourist le (la) touriste 30a, 36c
Tow-Away Zone Zone de remorquage 33d
tow truck la dépanneuse 33a
toward vers *(prep)* 3d
towel la serviette de toilette 12d; la serviette de bain 35c
tower la tour 36a
town la ville 11f
track la piste 27b; *(of a train)* la voie 34
tractor truck le camion-tracteur 33a
trade/labor union le syndicat 43
traditional traditionnel(le) *(adj, m, f)* 11e
traffic la circulation 33c
traffic accident l'accident *(m)* de voiture 39c
traffic jam l'embouteillage *(m),* l'encombrement *(m)* 33c
traffic lane la piste 33c
traffic lights les feux *(m, pl)* 33c, 36a
traffic police l'agent *(m)* de patrouille 33b
tragedy la tragédie 20a, 28e
trailer la remorque 33a
train le train 34; **direct train** le train direct 34; **express train** le train express 34
train station la gare 34
transformer ***(hardware)*** le transformateur 25b
transitive transitif *(adj, m),* transitive *(adj, f)* 8a
translate traduire *(v)* 17a
translation la traduction 17a
transmission ***(radio, television)*** l'émission 20b
transparent transparent(e) *(adj, m, f)* 7b, 13d
transplant la transplantation, transplanter *(v)* 14a
transport truck le camion des marchandises 33a
trapezium le trapèze 2a
travel voyager *(v)* 30a
travel agency l'agence *(f)* de voyages *(m, pl)* 30a
traveler's check le chèque de voyage *(m)* 26, 35b
tray le plateau à servir 23d, 24l, 32c
tree l'arbre *(m)* 14c
trial le procès 41; **trial lawyer** l'avoué *(m),* la femme avoué 41; **to be on trial** être *(v)* en procès 41

triangle le triangle 2a
trigonometric trigonométrique *(adj)* 2b
trigonometry la trigonométrie 2b, 37e
trip le voyage 30a, 36b
triple triple *(n/adj, m, f)* 3c
tripod ***(easel)*** le chevalet 28b
trolley le trolley 33a
trombone le trombone 28c
tropic le tropique 13e
Tropic of Cancer le Tropique du Cancer 13e
Tropic of Capricorn le Tropique du Capricorne 13e
tropical tropique *(adj)* 13e; tropical(e) *(adj, m, f)* 6a
troublemaker provocateur, provacatrice *(adj, m, f)* 11e
trout la truite 15c, 24d
truck le camion 33a
trumpet la trompette 28c
trunk ***(of tree)*** le tronc 14a; *(of a vehicle)* le coffre 33e
trust la confiance 21a; avoir *(v)* confiance en 21a
try on ***(clothing)*** essayer *(v)* 25m
tuba le tuba 28c
Tuesday le mardi 5a
tulip la tulipe 14b
tuna fish le thon 15c, 24d
tunnel le tunnel 33c
turbulence la turbulence 32c
turkey le dindon 15b, 24c
turn tourner *(v)* 3e, 36c; *(vehicle)* virer *(v)* 33c
turn left tournez à gauche 36c
turn off éteindre *(v)* 20b, 35c
turn on allumer *(v)* 20b, 35c
turn page tourner *(v)* la page, feuilleter *(v)* 20a
turn right tournez à droite 36c
turn signal ***(vehicle)*** le clignateur 33e
turned out badly ***(photo, picture)*** la photo mal réussie 25d
turned out well ***(photo, picture)*** la photo bien réussie 25d
turtle la tortue 15c
TV la télé 20b
TV movie le téléfilm 20b
twelfth douzième 1b
twelve douze 1a
twenty vingt 1a; **about twenty** une vingtaine 1c
twenty-one vingt et un 1a
twenty-two vingt-deux 1a
twin le jumeau, la jumelle 10a
twist bun ***(pastry)*** la tresse 24i
twisted neck le torticolis 40a
two deux 1a
two billion deux milliards 1a
two hundred deux cents 1a
two hundred and one deux cent un 1a
two hundred thousand deux cent mille 1a
two million deux millions 1a
two thousand deux mille 1a
two thousand and one deux mille un 1a
two-year-old de deux ans 11b
type taper *(v)* à la machine 19d, 37f
typewriter la machine à écrire *(v)* 19d, 37f, 38c
typist l'homme dactylographe, la dactylographe 38a
typography la typographie 20a

U

Ugh! Pouah! 21c
ugliness la laideur 11a
ugly laid(e) *(adj, m, f)* 11a, 25l
Uhm . . . good! C'est très bon! C'est si bon! 17b
ultraviolet light la lumière ultraviolette 13a
unacceptable inacceptable *(adj)* 21b

Unbelievable! Incroyable! 21c
uncle l'oncle 10a
under sous *(prep)* 3d
underdeveloped countries les pays *(m, pl)* sous-développés 43
underlining le soulignement 19c
understand comprendre *(v)* 22b, 37f
underwear les sous-vêtements *(m, pl)* 25k
undress se déshabiller *(v)* 25m
unemployment le chômage 38d
Unfortunately! Malheureusement! 21c
unilateral unilatéral(e) *(adj, m, f)* 43
United States of America les Etats-Unis *(m, pl)* d'Amérique 30b
universal suffrage le suffrage universel 43
universe l'univers *(m)* 13a
university l'université *(f)* 37a, 38b
university degree la licence 11f; le doctorat 11f
unlawful illégal(e) *(adj, m, f)* 41
unleaded gasoline l'essence *(f)* non-plombée 33c
unless à moins que *(conj)* 8p
unmarried célibataire *(adj)* 11c
unpleasant désagréable *(adj, m, f)* 21b
until jusque(s) *(prep)* 4e; jusqu'à ce que *(conj)* 8p
up haut *(adv)*, en haut 3d
upright piano le piano droit 28c
Uranus Uranus *(m)* 13a
urinary system le système urinaire 40a
urinate uriner *(v)* 40a
us nous 8i, 8l
user-friendly *(computers)* l'ordinateur *(m)* d'usage facile, l'ordinateur "user-friendly" 42b
usually usuellement *(adv)* 4e

V
vacation les vacances *(f, pl)* 29a, 36b
vacuum cleaner l'aspirateur 23d
vagina le vagin 12a
vain vaniteux, vaniteuse *(adj, m, f)* 11e
valley le val, la vallée 13b
valve *(a vehicle)* la soupape, le clapet 33e
van le fourgon 33a
vanilla la vanille 24h
vanilla ice cream la glace à la vanille 24h
vapor la vapeur 13c
variable *(numbers)* la variable 1f
variable bank rate le taux variable 26
VCR le VCR, le magnétoscope, le système d'enregistrement *(m)* à vidéocassettes 20b
veal le veau 24c
vector le vecteur 2b
vegetable le (la) légume 14e, 24e
vegetable garden le potager 14e
vegetation la végétation 13b
vehicle le véhicule 33a
vein la veine 40a
Venice Venise 30c
vent *(vehicle)* le trou d'aération *(f)* 33e
Venus Vénus *(f)* 13a
verb le verbe 8a, 8n
verdict le verdict 41
versatile versatile *(adj, m, f)* 11e
vertebrate vertébré(e) *(adj, m, f)* 15a
vertex (angle) le sommet 2b
vertical vertical(e) *(adj)* 3d
vest le gilet 25k
Very well! Très bien! *(adv)*; Ça tape! 16a
VHS/SECAM/TV le VHS/SECAM/TV, le système séquentiel à mémoire 20b

vibrant vibrant(e) *(adj)* 7b
victim la victime 39a, 39b
video camera la caméra vidéo 25d
video game le jeu-vidéo 20b
videocassette recorder la vidéocassette 20b
videorock le vidéorock 20b
videotape la bande magnétique 20b
view la vue 35b
village le village 11f
vinegar le vinaigre 24j
viola la viole 28c
violence la violence 39b
violet la violette 14b
violin le violon 28c
violinist le (la) violoniste 28c
Virgo la Vierge 5d
virile viril(e) *(adj)* 11a
visa le visa 31
visit *(a person)* faire *(v)* une visite à 29b
visit *(a place)* visiter *(v)* 30a
vitamin la vitamine 25h
vocabulary le vocabulaire 17a
vocational school l'institut *(m)* d'enseignement technique 37a
volcano le volcan 13b
volleyball le volley-ball 27b
volume le volume 3a
volume control le réglage de volume 20b
vomit vomir *(v)* 40a
vote le vote; voter *(v)* 43
vowel la voyelle 8a
vulnerable vulnérable *(adj, m, f)* 11e

W

wafer la gaufrette 24i
waffle la gaufre 24i
wages les gages *(m, pl)* 38d
waist la taille 12a
wait *(for)* attendre *(v)* 4e, 19e, 34
waiter le serveur 24m
waiting room la salle d'attente *(f)* 32a
waitress la serveuse 24m
wake up se réveiller *(v)* 12b
wake-up call le réveil par téléphone 35b
walk marcher *(v)* 3e, 12b; aller *(v)* à pied *(m)* 3e; la promenade 3e
walkie-talkie le talkie-walkie 20b
wall le mur 23a
wall map la carte murale 37b
wall-to-wall carpeting la moquette 23c
walnut la noix 14d, 24f
walnut tree le noyer 14c
want to désirer *(v)*, vouloir *(v)* 21a
war la guerre 43
warm up se chauffer *(v)* 6b
warn avertir *(v)*, prévenir *(v)* 17a
warning l'avis *(m)*, la prévenance 17a
wash laver *(v)* 23f, 25g
wash basin *(sink)* le lavabo 23a, 35c
wash one's hair se laver *(v)* les cheveux *(m, pl)* 12d
wash oneself se laver *(v)* 12d
wash the clothes laver *(v)* le linge 23f
wash the dishes faire *(v)* la vaisselle 23f
washable lavable *(adj, m, f)* 25g
washing machine le lave-linge, la machine à laver *(v)* 23d
wasp la guêpe 15d
wastebasket la corbeille à papier 38c
watch regarder *(v)* 20b
watch *(timepiece)* la montre 4d, 25i; **The watch is fast.** La montre avance. 4d; **The watch is slow.** La montre retarde. 4d
watchband le bracelet d'une montre 4d, 25i

watch battery la pile d'une montre 4d
water l'eau *(f)* 13c, 23e, 24k; arroser *(v)* 14a
water fountain la fontaine 36a
water pollution la pollution des eaux 44a
water polo le water-polo 27b
water skiing le ski nautique 27b
watercolor l'aquarelle *(f)* 28b
watermelon la pastèque 14d, 24f
wave l'onde *(f)*, le flot, la vague 13b
we nous 8h, 8l
weak faible *(adj, m, f)* 11a, 11e, 13d, 40a
weakness la faiblesse 11a
weapon l'arme *(f)* 39b
wear porter *(v)* 25m
weather le temps 6a; **The weather is beautiful.** Il fait beau temps. 6a **The weather is rotten.** Il fait un temps pourri. 6a
weather forecast la prévision scientifique du temps 6c
weather report le bulletin météorologique 6c
wedding le mariage 11c, 29a; la noce 11c; les noces *(f, pl)* 29a
wedding invitation le faire-part de mariage 11c
wedding ring l'anneau *(m)* d'alliance 11c
Wednesday le mercredi 5a
week la semaine 4c
weekend le weekend, la fin de semaine 5a
weekly hebdomadaire *(adj)*, hebdomadairement *(adv)* 4c; *(periodical)* hebdomadaire *(adj, n, m, f)* 20a
weigh peser *(v)* 3b, 24o
weigh oneself se peser *(v)* 11a
weight le poids 3a, 11a, 31
weight lifting l'haltérophilie *(f)* 27b
Welfare l'Assistance *(f)* sociale 43
well-done *(cooked food)* bien cuit(e) *(adj, m, f)* 24b
well-mannered bien élevé(e) *(adj, m, f)* 11e
west l'ouest *(m)* 3d; **to the west** à l'ouest 3d
western occidental(e) *(adj, m, f)* 3d, 11d
whale la baleine 15c
What? Comment? Pardon? 9
What a bore! *(person)* Quel raseur! *(m);* Quelle raseuse! *(f)* 21c
What color is it? De quelle couleur est-ce? 7a
What day is it? Quel jour est-ce? 5a
What do you call this (that) in French? Comment appelle-t-on ceci (cela) en français? 9
What do you think of it? Qu'en pensez-vous? *(pol),* Qu'en penses-tu? *(fam)* 22b
What does it mean? Que veut dire cela? Que signifie cela? 9
What month are we in? Quel mois sommes-nous? 5b
What month is it? Quel mois est-ce? 5b
What time is it? Quelle heure est-il? 4b
What was I saying? Qu'est-ce que je disais? 17b
What year is it? Quelle année est-ce? 5e
What's the weather like? (How's the weather?) Quel temps fait-il? 6a
What's today's date? Quelle est la date aujourd'hui? 5e
What's your name? Quel est votre nom (ton nom)? 11f; Comment vous appelez-vous? *(pol),* Comment t'appelles-tu? *(fam)* 16b
wheat le froment, le blé 14a, 24i
wheel la roue 33e
wheelchair le fauteuil roulant 40a
wheel, landing gear *(airplane)* le train d'atterrissage 32c
when quand *(adv)* 4e, 8p, 9

When were you born? Quand êtes-vous né(e)? *(m, f, pol)* 5e
where où *(adv)* 3d, 9
Where do you live? Où demeurez-vous (demeures-tu)? 11f
Where is. . .? Où est. . .? 36c
whereas tandis que *(conj)* 8p
which *(one)* lequel *(m)*, laquelle *(f)* 9
while pendant que *(conj)* 4e; tandis que *(conj)* 8p
whipped cream la crème Chantilly 24h; **omelette with whipped cream** l'omelette *(f)* mousseline 24h
whisper chuchoter *(v)* 17a
white le blanc 7a
who qui *(pron)* 9
Who knows? Qui sait? 17b
Who's speaking? Qui parle? 18b
whole wheat bread le pain complet 24i
why pourquoi *(adv, conj)* 9
wide large *(adj)* 3b
widow la veuve 11c, 38b
widower le veuf 11c, 38b
width la largeur 3b
wife la femme, l'épouse 10a, 11c
wild animal l'animal *(m)* sauvage 15a
wildflower la fleur sauvage 14b
willingly volontiers *(adv)* 11e
wilted flower la fleur fanée 14b
win gagner *(v)*, le gain 27b
wind *(a timepiece)* remonter *(v)* 4d, 25i
wind *(weather)* le vent 6a; **It's windy.** Il fait du vent. 6a
wind energy l'énergie *(f)* éolienne 44a
wind instruments les instruments *(m, pl)* à vent 28c
windbreaker *(clothing)* le blouson 25k
window la fenêtre 23a; **store/shop window** la vitrine 25a
window seat la place côté fenêtre 32c
window sill le rebord de la fenêtre 23a
windshield *(vehicle)* le pare-brise 33e
windshield wiper l'essuie-glace *(m)*, l'essuie-vitre *(m)* 33e
windy weather faire *(v)* du vent 6a
wine le vin 24k
wine cellar la cave à vin *(m)* 23b
wineglass le verre à vin 24l
wing l'aile *(f)* 15b, 32c
winter l'hiver *(m)* 5c
wire le fil métallique 25b
wisdom la sagesse 11e, 22a
wisdom tooth la dent de sagesse 40b
wise sage *(adj, m, f)* 11e
with avec 8g
With cordial greetings. . . *(in a letter)* Sentiments cordiaux 19a
with ice chips avec glaçons *(m, pl)* 24p
with sauce (gravy) au jus 24b
withdraw *(banking)* prélever *(v)* 26
withdrawal *(banking)* le prélèvement 26
withdrawal slip la fiche de prélèvement *(m)* 26
within *(a certain time)* en *(prep)* 4e
witness le témoin 41; **for the defense** à décharge; **for the prosecution** à charge 41
wolf le loup 15a
woman la femme 11a
women's shop/clothing le magasin d'habillement féminin 25k
woods le (les) bois *(m)* 13b
wool la laine 13c; en laine 25l

word le mot *(written)*, la parole *(spoken)* 17a, 19c
word processor l'ordinateur *(m)* à traitement de texte, la machine de traitement 38c; le processeur 42b
work travailler *(v)* 11f, 38d; le travail 11f, 38d; (literary) l'ouvrage *(m)* 28d
workday le jour de travail 5a
Work in Progress Travaux 33d
work out *(body exercises)* pratiquer *(v)* les exercices du corps 27b
world le monde 13a, 30a
worm le ver 15d
wound la blessure, la plaie 39b, 39c; blesser *(v)* 39b
wrench *(hardware)* la pince universelle 25b
wrestling la lutte 27b
wrist le poignet 12a
wristwatch le bracelet-montre 4d, 25i; la montre-bracelet 25i
write écrire *(v)* 19e, 20a, 37f
writer l'écrivain *(m)*, la femme écrivain 28d, 38a
wrong incorrect(e) *(adj, m, f)* 37f
Wrong number! *(telephone)*
wrong incorrect(e) *(adj, m, f)* 37f
Wrong number! *(telephone)*
Mauvais numéro! 18b

X, Y, Z

X-rays les rayons X 39c, 40b
yawn le bâillement, bâiller *(v)* 17a
year l'an *(m)*, l'année *(f)* 4c
yell le cri; crier *(v)* 17a
yellow le jaune 7a;
yellow pages les pages jaunes *(f, pl)* 18a
Yes! Oui! 16c
yesterday hier *(adv)* 4a
yesterday afternoon hier après-midi 4a
yesterday morning hier matin 4a
yet encore *(adv)* 4e
Yield Cédez 33d
yogurt le yaourt 24h
you tu *(s, fam)*, vous *(s, pl, pol)*, te *(s, fam)* 8h, 8i; toi 8l; vous 8l
young jeune *(adj)* 11b
young lady la demoiselle 11a
young man le jeune homme 11a
younger plus jeune 11b
younger brother le frère cadet 11b
younger sister la soeur cadette 11b
your *(pol)* votre *(m/f, s)*, vos *(m/f, pl)* 8f; *(fam)* ton *(m, s)*, ta *(f, s)*, tes *(m/f, pl)* 8f
You're welcome! Je vous en prie! *(pol)*, Je t'en prie! *(fam)* 16c
Yours. . . *(closing of a letter)* Bien à toi *(fam)* 19b
Yours truly. . . *(in a business letter)* Salutations distinguées 19a
yourself *(reflexive)* te *(s, fam)*, vous *(s, pol)* 8k
yourselves *(reflexive)* vous 8k
youth la jeunesse 11b
youth hostel l'auberge *(f)* de la jeunesse 35a
youthful juvénile *(adj)* 11b
Yuch! Quel dégoût! 20b
zebra le zèbre 15a
zenith le zénith 13e
zero zéro 1a, 6c
zipper la fermeture à glissière, la fermeture éclair 25g
zodiac la zodiaque 5d
zone la zone 13e
zoo le zoo, le jardin zoologique 15a
zoology la zoologie 15a, 37e
zoom le zoom 25d
zucchini la courgette 14e